Forts and Roman Strategy

With gratitude to my parents,
the late Derrick and Joyce Coby,
and to my wife,
Sally Blandford

Forts and Roman Strategy

A New Approach and Interpretation

featuring five case studies
from Roman campaigns in Britain

Paul Coby

Pen & Sword
MILITARY

First published in Great Britain in 2022 by
Pen & Sword Military
An imprint of
Pen & Sword Books Ltd
Yorkshire – Philadelphia

ISBN 978 1 52677 210 7

Typeset by Mac Style
Printed and bound in India by Replika Press Pvt. Ltd.

Pen & Sword Books Limited incorporates the imprints of Atlas, Archaeology,
Aviation, Discovery, Family History, Fiction, History, Maritime, Military, Military
Classics, Politics, Select, Transport, True Crime, Air World, Frontline Publishing,
Leo Cooper, Remember When, Seaforth Publishing, The Praetorian Press,
Wharncliffe Local History, Wharncliffe Transport, Wharncliffe True Crime
and White Owl.

For a complete list of Pen & Sword titles please contact

PEN & SWORD BOOKS LIMITED
47 Church Street, Barnsley, South Yorkshire, S70 2AS, England
E-mail: enquiries@pen-and-sword.co.uk
Website: www.pen-and-sword.co.uk

Or

PEN AND SWORD BOOKS
1950 Lawrence Rd, Havertown, PA 19083, USA
E-mail: Uspen-and-sword@casematepublishers.com
Website: www.penandswordbooks.com

Contents

Foreword by M.C. Bishop   vi

Introduction: The Nature of the Roman Army in the First and Second Centuries AD   vii

Chapter 1   The Roman Army – Neither the Pentagon nor Predator   1

Part 1: The Case Studies   5

Chapter 2   Scapula's Failed Conquest of the Tribes of Wales   7

Chapter 3   Failed Conquest in Wales Becomes Containment under Gallus   37

Chapter 4   Governor Julius Frontinus' Masterclass in Wales   54

Chapter 5   Agricola in Scotland – Rome's First Frontier followed by
Rome's Failure? The Flavian Conquest and Retreat from
Scotland   92

Chapter 6   The Antonine Wall – Military Overstretch and Policy
U-Turns on Rome's North-West Frontier   137

Part 2: The Method   179

Chapter 7   A New Digital and Cartographical Approach   181

Chapter 8   The New Data-led Analytical Method (D-LAM)   198

Chapter 9   A New Graphical and Cartographic Tool-set   204

Chapter 10   Conclusions   220

Appendix 1: Visiting the Sites of the Campaigns   233
Appendix 2: Forts and Roman Strategy (FRoSt)   238
Bibliography   240
Index   244

Foreword

When Tacitus (*Annals* 4.5) wrote that there were a roughly equal number of auxiliaries and legionaries in the Roman Empire at the time of the death of the emperor Augustus, he left us a useful way of gauging the strength of provincial armies. That the province of Britannia was garrisoned with four (later three) legions says something significant about how militarily sensitive it was thought to be (there were four legions in much larger provinces like Syria, which faced the ever-present threat of Parthian invasion). The fact that the number of auxiliaries in Britain exceeded even that of legionaries only serves to underline its importance in Roman strategic (and, arguably, tactical) thinking.

It is often (perhaps rashly) assumed that everything possible is known about the Roman Army and its role in the invasion of Britain in AD 43 and the subsequent process of conquest. The evidence, some might claim, has been stretched as far as it can go and there are no new avenues to pursue. However, such assumptions have repeatedly been proved wrong over the years and new methodologies can provide important new insights into the past, and the Roman Army in particular.

Many years ago, Edward Luttwak's book *The Grand Strategy of the Roman Empire* both excited and challenged scholars to look at Roman frontier studies in new ways. Some were instantly attracted by his thesis, others more wary, but it nevertheless served to put the lie to the notion that 'everything is known'. Paul Coby's application of the Data-led Analytical Method (D-LAM) to Roman military enterprises in Britain will doubtless similarly find its adherents and detractors, but there can be no doubt that it will prompt new discussion of old issues and that is never a bad thing. Moreover, his proposal for a more nuanced approach to the mapping of Roman fortifications will, I suspect, enjoy widespread support.

Was there ever a Roman grand strategy? I for one do not know for certain, although I have my suspicions. However, what matters is not what I believe, but what you think, and there can be no better way of considering this question afresh than by reading this quietly revolutionary book.

M.C. Bishop
Pewsey, 21.1.22

Introduction

The Nature of the Roman Army in the First and Second Centuries AD

The first part of this book is built around five in-depth case studies of Roman campaigns in Britain over a period of just over 100 years in the first and second centuries AD.

In reality, the Roman Army in Britain was not the perfectly polished machine of some academic books and many popular histories. Neither was the Roman Army, in the experience of many of the peoples it encountered, the civilizing missionary of popular myth. The Roman Army was impressive in many respects – its uniformity across vast distances, its organization and its structure are remarkable for the pre-industrial age, but its brutality and ruthlessness were of its time.

As one of the five case studies shows, however, the Roman Army could make a terrible mess of what would have looked, at least in the planning stage, to be certain walkover victories. Governor Scapula had under his direct command the larger part of three of his four legions, together with supporting auxiliaries, artillery and supply chain, amounting to probably 30,000 or more men of the most effective fighting force of its time. Yet he could not conquer the Silures of South Wales – with a population, at an educated guess, of 60,000 at most – who could muster a fighting force of no more than 15,000. This was tactical military failure in the field, pure and simple. Comparisons with the recent Afghan and Iraq wars and invasions by British and United States forces do not seem farfetched.

A second case study shows strategic failure. Agricola had almost completed the full conquest of *Britannia*, only for his conquests to be given up due to the Emperor Domitian's withdrawal of the province's fourth legion, leading over the following years to the loss of all the lands north of the Tyne/Solway line.

A third case study, whilst not a direct military failure, is a study in strategic indecision at the grandest scale. Hadrian's signature policy and physical memorial – his Wall – was given up and slighted when Antonine Pius, his adopted successor, ordered a new wall built further north. This itself, the Antonine Wall, was occupied for a mere fifteen years, then partially given up, then reoccupied and finally given up by his successor Marcus Aurelius; as striking a piece of military indecision – and arguably incompetence – as you could conceive.

The other two case studies cover more successful Roman campaigns. Gallus, after Scapula's failure to conquer the Silures, stabilized the frontier in the West with an effective border built along the road from Wroxeter to Usk, leaving the majority of the Silures outside Roman control in the 50s AD. It was not until the 70s that Frontinus completed the conquest of Wales, with an iron framework of control created by a grid of forts and military roads locking the whole country down.

We see here not the technologically superior, all-conquering Roman Army often depicted, but an organization operating at full stretch and sometimes beyond. We see in the case studies the Roman Army in Britain facing new challenges that demanded new solutions. The army was an organization that had to adapt to challenges and find answers. It often took time, but the army usually did find solutions.

This book aims to understand how the Roman Army operated and fought in the first and second centuries. It is concerned with unpacking how it did that, using newly developed data analytic and visualization techniques: how this has been done is described in the second part of the book.

A different point of view

My professional background is as a Chief Information Officer (CIO) accountable for IT and digital technology in large global companies: British Airways, the John Lewis Partnership and, latterly, Johnson Matthey. I have deployed three aspects of my technical and professional experience to the question in hand:

- database analytic methods;
- visualization;
- organizational theory and practice.

For analysis I have used a simple and technically basic database and standard data definitions to analyze the known data about the Roman forts and other military installations under scrutiny. This data has been assembled from the many excellent published excavation reports, consolidated histories and syntheses about the campaigns featured in the case studies. Relevant extracts from the database are published in each of the chapters. My hope is that, seeing their usefulness, others will be led to adopt the data structures and definitions described, and to use them as a foundation to build on and develop – or indeed to disagree with – my hypotheses and conclusions. Further technical details for those interested in 'having a go' are set out in Appendix 2.

The second technique I have imported from the modern business world is data visualization. I have developed a portfolio of visualizations to analyze the Roman

Freepost Plus RTKE-RGRJ-KTTX
Pen & Sword Books Ltd
47 Church Street
BARNSLEY
S70 2AS

DISCOVER MORE ABOUT PEN & SWORD BOOKS

Pen & Sword Books have over 4000 books currently available, our imprints include; Aviation, Naval, Military, Archaeology, Transport, Frontline, Seaforth and the Battleground series, and we cover all periods of history on land, sea and air.

Can we stay in touch? From time to time we'd like to send you our latest catalogues, promotions and special offers by post. If you would prefer not to receive these, please tick this box. ☐

We also think you'd enjoy some of the latest products and offers by post from our trusted partners: companies operating in the clothing, collectables, food & wine, gardening, gadgets & entertainment, health & beauty, household goods, and home interiors categories. If you would like to receive these by post, please tick this box. ☐

We respect your privacy. We use personal information you provide us with to send you information about our products, maintain records and for marketing purposes. For more information explaining how we use your information please see our privacy policy at www.pen-and-sword.co.uk/privacy. You can opt out of our mailing list at any time via our website or by calling 01226 734222.

Mr/Mrs/Ms ....

Address...

Postcode.................................. Email address..

**Website: www.pen-and-sword.co.uk Email: enquiries@pen-and-sword.co.uk
Telephone: 01226 734555   Fax: 01226 734438**

Stay in touch: facebook.com/penandswordbooks or follow us on Twitter @penswordbooks

Army's approach to campaigning and control of conquered territories and their peoples. These range from the familiar, in the form of simple maps, to abstractions of how roads and forts interlock, and graphical analyses of the data.

The techniques and methodologies described here are designed to be reusable for the Roman Army in other contexts, and my hope is that these can be tested on other Roman frontiers: the Upper German and Raetian *Limes*, with their wealth of accessible and published data, would be an excellent challenge to test further the techniques described here. Other potential case studies could include the Dacian campaigns and frontier installations, and a good test would be the areas of the Eastern desert frontiers where there have been in-depth study and publication.

The third area of personal experience I have deployed is organizational theory. The Roman Army of this period is instantly recognizable to anyone who has been a director of a complex global organization. This came as something of a surprise to me, given the two millennia between then and now; the different economic systems; the cultural chasm; and the challenges of communication and primitive technology in the pre-industrial Roman world. There is a great deal, on the one hand, that is very familiar in the problems we can see Scapula, Frontinus and Agricola facing, such as resource overstretch, simultaneous challenges, conflicting priorities, changes in leadership and policy U-turns at HQ. It is the reaction of the Roman Army's leadership to these challenges that is noteworthy: the organization survives by finding solutions. Repeatedly, it achieves this, I believe, through its institutional capability – its 'organizational DNA'. The Roman Army had excellent career development, was able to learn from its mistakes, tested and learnt new solutions, kept good records and renewed its operating model. It had a strong culture and was thus able to operate in the most extreme circumstances and challenges and to renew itself.

It would be unwise to overstate modern comparisons, but the characteristics of the professional Roman Army created by Augustus and developed not just by emperors but by countless governors, legates, tribunes and centurions who served up to the end of the second century, are remarkably close to those highlighted by modern organizational consultants as hallmarks of how effective global corporations should operate.

Perhaps the key insight for the Roman Empire here is that effective – and even great – organizations can make bad mistakes, have periods of poor leadership and encounter problems they cannot immediately solve; but it is the strength of their core operating model and the operational processes and discipline embodied in their cultural DNA that pull them through.

There is a trap here: it is important not to conflate objective assessment – even admiration – of the organization and effectiveness of the Roman Empire and its army with a subjective assessment of the impact of 'Roman Civilization', good or bad, in material or ethical terms. The study of the Romans in Britain is a very topical and relevant subject, given current debates about the legacy of the British Empire, since it allows us to see Roman colonialism and British colonialism through different ends of the telescope. There has been a polarization of views about the Roman Empire in recent years. The view of Roman imperialism as a mission to civilize the world (the 'what did the Romans ever do for us, apart from baths, roads, central heating, literacy…' point of view) has rightly been challenged by a post-colonial recognition of Roman imperial violence, slavery and exploitation of native populations. While the former view was much beloved of classically educated British imperial administrators, the latter springs from modern re-evaluations of Britain's own imperial heritage and economy, built on foundations of slavery and colonial exploitation.

The experience of Rome and reactions to it by the colonized were radically different and divergent (Mattingly, 2011, 2016–17). You could join the empire by becoming a well-respected ally and client, transitioning to full citizenship, enjoying the benefits of empire-wide trade and exchange, developing an effective administration and preserving your local government independence, as did Cogidubnus of the Atrebates (Hennig, 2004, pp.37–62). Alternatively, you could live through decades of bloody warfare, followed by enslavement and exploitation, devoid of rights, subject to violently extracted taxes and expropriation of any mineral and agricultural wealth, as Caractacus described to Claudius at the 'British Triumph' (Tacitus, *Annals*, xii.37).

These debates about Roman Britain have got some way to run yet, as has a fully balanced perspective of British Imperialism and what it means for modern Britain, but there is no doubt that for every Romanized, toga-wearing, Latin-speaking and wine-drinking aristocrat in the *civitas* forum, there were tribal leaders outside (and probably inside) Hadrian's Wall who were determined to resist the invaders to the last. For every villa with fine mosaics, bathhouse and aisled barns, they were scores of native enclosures where life continued very much as it had before the conquest (Russell and Laycock, 2010). Behind the idealized depiction of Roman life on the information boards at *civitas* sites, we should see a conflict-riven exploitative colonial society, arguably like British Kenya from the 1920s to the 1960s, with big winners and big losers (Maxon, 2009, p.161).

Chapter 1

The Roman Army – Neither the Pentagon nor Predator

Did the Romans analyze military challenges, did they plan systematically and did they have a grand strategy?

There has been a prolonged and vexed but fundamentally elucidating debate between academics, historians and archaeologists as to whether the Roman state (which is in itself a controversial term) and the Roman Army had a conception of strategy and its relatively recent offspring, grand strategy. The classic articulation of the opposing positions comes, on the one hand, from the strategic theoretician and security consultant to the US government Edward Luttwak's *Grand Strategy of the Roman Empire* (1974, revised 2016) and, on the other, from the eastern frontier specialist Benjamin Isaac's *The Limits of Empire* (1992).

Luttwak envisages the Roman Army thinking, anachronistically, like the modern Pentagon. He proposes three centrally determined paradigms for Roman strategy:

- the Julio-Claudian system of client states and mobile armies;
- scientific frontiers and preclusive defence from the Fla renewed Empire of the fourth century vians to the *Severi*;
- defence-in-depth, from the crisis of the third century and the renewed Empire of the fourth century.

The use of the term 'grand strategy' presupposes a centrally determined and 'scientific' approach to managing the Roman Empire and its frontiers. Luttwak argues that the Romans combined military force, diplomacy and fortifications in response to changing threats, together with comprehensive strategies that systematically analyzed the threats:

> The empire was an immeasurably larger reality than any of them [emperors]. It encompassed countless nameless administrators and officers efficient and honest enough to recruit, train, equip, and supply hundreds of thousands of troops, including the shivering sentries who tenaciously guarded Hadrian's Wall and the auxiliary cavalry that daily patrolled desert frontiers in the extremes of heat, all of them doing their duty day after day... year after year. That was the empire. (Luttwak, 2016, p.x)

Isaac takes a directly contrary view: he believes that the Romans had no conception of political boundaries, that their militarized frontiers were never defence lines and that the army was an occupation force to keep conquests under Roman authority. Isaac argues that the Roman Empire had no such thing as grand strategy and that it was incapable of strategic thinking; rather, warfare was carried out at the whim of emperors and in pursuit of glory and booty. In his view, the Romans did not think strategically or scientifically; there was no Roman 'General Staff' capable of analysis; no military frontier nor effective mapping; and the Roman Army moved forward in a predatory fashion in pursuit of glory for the emperor and booty for the soldiers:

> Decisions regarding war and peace were under the principate made by the emperor whose power rested on the support of the standing army, precisely the body which was directly affected when a decision was taken to fight... . It is clear that a successful war of expansion was profitable to all participating soldiers... . Following the capture of Jerusalem by Titus' troops they were so loaded with plunder that in Syria the price of gold was depreciated to half its previous standard. (Isaac, 1990, pp.379–81)

Since the publication of these works, both positions have been much developed, debated and modified, by the writers themselves and by others.

The present study is firmly grounded in the belief that the Roman Army was 'a thinking and learning organization'. I believe that it did have systems and designs: you only have to consider their use of the same design plan for forts built in northern Scotland or deep in the Arabian desert; the first carefully placed to maximize fields of view into hostile territory and between forts, the second running along the 200mm rainfall contour (isohyet). The Roman Army and state was highly capable in surveying territory for the creation of military roads, centuriation (the Roman grid system) and general taxation purposes (Jones and Mattingly, 2002; Entwhistle, 2019). Or consider the way that promising officers' careers were centrally planned, with postings across the empire in military and civil roles, as was that of Publius Pertinax – briefly emperor in AD 193 – who was the son of a freed slave, started out as a schoolteacher, first commanded auxiliaries in Syria, was a tribune with the *VI Victrix* legion in Britain, then commanded a unit on Hadrian's Wall and later a unit in Moesia. Following that, Pertinax became a procurator in Italy distributing welfare. Back in the Army, he commanded the fleet on the Rhine, was then procurator in Dacia and defended the Alps against the Germans. Marcus Aurelius then made him legate of the *I Adiutrix* and consul in 175. Three governorships – of *Moesia Inferior, Moesia Superior* and *Dacia* – were followed by command of the East as Governor of Syria. The Roman Army had quite an impressive HR function.

Career development and planning does not mean, however, that the Roman Army thought like a modern army or that the Roman state and the Senate behaved like a modern state; nor was it the direct predecessor of the Prussian General Staff, let alone of the US Department of Defense. The Roman Army thought like the Roman Army: its approach to warfare was specific to itself, and unique to the Roman Army of the first and second centuries AD. As Luttwak explains, grand strategy is inferred from what is done and what is not done. In execution it was not a perfectly logical and analytical activity carried out in a laboratory. It existed in the real and messy world, where decisions have to be taken in the heat of the moment, are influenced by political imperatives and are often made on imperfect information by flawed leaders (Luttwak, 2016, p.xii). Plans can go horribly wrong and the grand strategy itself may be misconceived: the wars in Iraq and Afghanistan provide modern examples. Trajan's Parthian War in that same region is another example of a failed grand strategy. Nevertheless, this does not prove that grand strategy does not exist or that it was not the product of the operating model and culture of the Roman (or American) Empire.

In my view, when we see what Isaac regards as predatory opportunism, we are seeing only part of what the Roman Empire and Army were about. The grand strategy of the Roman Army existed in the complex and untidy world of its own time. No doubt glory and plunder were important motivations, but they existed inside the framework of a strategic approach to warfare and conquest, one that was continuously challenged and improved. As Luttwak has argued, the Romans developed and improved their operating model, not just at the grand strategic level, but also at the strategic and tactical levels, as time and space pitched new challenges at the Roman Army and state.

To nail my colours to the mast, I believe that in the Roman Army we are dealing with a very structured and systematic organization. There were blueprints for unit structures and these evolved over time with experience of campaigning. There were blueprints for forts for different types of unit, and through the *cursus honorum* there was structured career progression and thoughtful development for men of talent. As the Vindolanda tablets and Egyptian military papyri show, the Roman Army was an inveterate keeper of records and sent returns to HQ on all kinds of matters. The Roman Army and administration kept lists and itineraries setting out road systems and forts (the Antonine Itinerary and Notitia Dignitatum). They were able to organize pay deductions and savings for soldiers on a systematic basis; they could raise soldiers' and sailors' pay-rates across the empire with a central decree; and they systematically issued diplomas awarding Roman citizenship to auxiliaries after twenty-five years' service (twenty-six years for the navy).

Since there were blueprints for planning and constructing fortresses and forts, and for managing military and civilian careers, why would there not have been blueprints for how to occupy a relatively civilized tribe like the Catuvellauni and a different blueprint for conquering and subduing a 'barbaric' tribe that resisted such as the Silures? There was clearly a blueprint for building strategic roads deep into hostile territory, with standard-sized forts spaced a day's march apart, which was one element of the plan for occupation.

We believe that Nero and his advisers thought about giving up Britain (Suetonius, *Nero*, xviii) after Boudicca's revolt had devasted the province. Similarly, when the Danube frontier was shattered by the Dacians there was no hesitation in pulling a legion out of Britain and giving up Agricola's hard-won gains. It therefore seems reasonable to propose that Vespasian and Cerialis – a close confidant of the new emperor – planned the surge in manpower in *Britannia* and planned the campaigns at a high level; and furthermore, that the emperor and his advisers in Rome stayed in close touch with the progress of the campaigns. Cerialis' successor as governor, Frontinus, was a military theorist as well as a senior senator, and very proud of his work in charge of the aqueducts of Rome. Agricola was next as governor, and had had a career that had taken him to Britain twice already, first during the revolt and then as legate under Cerialis of the *Legio XX* (of dubious loyalty to the Flavian regime). Cerialis and Agricola were both British specialists, deployed there by Vespasian.

None of this is to deny that a powerful motive for the Roman Army – from the governor and legionary legates down to the 'squaddie' in the front line of the auxiliaries facing up to Calgacus' chariots at Mons Graupius in AD 83 – was the opportunity for plunder and rich pickings from the possessions and enslavement of conquered peoples. Furthermore, throughout the lifetime of the Roman Empire, emperors were driven by the desire for military glory. This could be because they had an ideological belief in the mission and expansion of Rome, which was clearly a motivation for Augustus and Trajan, or because they needed to impress and reward the army to reinforce their shaky hold on power, as was the case with Claudius and Antoninus Pius. It may also have been because they were becoming unhinged, like Caligula and his seashells or Nero and his abortive Eastern expedition; or combinations of all of the above. This was the world and the eco-system in which the Roman Army lived.

The case studies of the Roman Army on campaign in Britain that follow in this book test this thesis. They endeavour to answer various questions. How did the Roman Army and its leadership deploy its forces? How did it approach warfare and its enemies? What succeeded, what failed and what did the army do next? How did it link military roads with fortresses and forts? Finally, how did it interact with native populations – friendly and hostile – before and after conquest and occupation?

In answering these questions, we can see whether the Roman Army behaved like a logical thinking and learning organization, albeit one that was far from infallible and more often prone to failure than is usually recognized. Did it show evidence of planning, staff work and surveying, or did it act purely as a predator in pursuit of imperial glory, triumphs and riches?

Part 1

The Case Studies

Chapter 2

Scapula's Failed Conquest of the Tribes of Wales

A quarter-century of failure for the Roman Army in Britain begins

I possessed horses, men, arms and wealth. Is it surprising if I have been unwilling to give these up? For if it is your desire to rule over the whole world, does it follow that all men should readily accept servitude? (Tacitus, *Annals* xii.37)

This is what Caractacus is reported to have said to the Emperor Claudius and Empress Agrippina on the Praetorian parade ground when he featured as the prize exhibit in the Imperial triumph of AD 52. There is well-founded scepticism about such speeches put into the mouths of enemy leaders by Tacitus, shaped to fit his own ideological agenda. Had Caractacus learnt fluent Latin on the way to Rome? Many senators would have heard Caractacus speak, however, and some would still have been alive when Tacitus was writing. His speech would have been scripted and the triumph choreographed to allow Claudius to show imperial magnanimity towards his captives. But maybe, just maybe, Caractacus did say something like this, and perhaps he meant it?

The Roman conquest of Wales – the term is used geographically – took thirty years to complete, from AD 47–77. Whilst the campaign was ultimately successfully completed in just three or four campaigning seasons by Frontinus (see Chapter 4), it had been a long hard slog for the mighty, but far from invincible, Roman Army, punctuated by failures and withdrawals. This chapter and the next analyze the failed campaigns and tactics of the first twenty-five years of this three-decade aggression against the tribes of the West, and ask why it took the mighty Roman war machine so long.

The explanation, I believe, lies in the combination of fierce tribal resistance and difficult terrain. The Roman Army had real trouble, not in defeating the tribes of Wales – although, as we will see, this was by no means guaranteed – but in then holding down what they regarded as primitive people who had no large settlements or *oppida* to destroy or threaten and a less settled way of life. When warriors, their families and animals could melt away into trackless mountain wastes, deserts, forests or marshes, the Roman Army had nothing to destroy, enslave or terrorize. They had lost their leverage. This was true on all frontiers, from Scotland to beyond the Rhine and the Danube and into the North African deserts.

Furthermore, the proven Roman method of converting the local aristocracy to the ways of Rome, deployed with such success in much of Gaul and Spain, was simply not going to work in upland Wales. Tacitus helpfully explains the *modus operandi*:

> In order, by a taste of pleasures, to reclaim the natives from that rude and unsettled state which prompted them to war and reconcile them to quiet and tranquillity, he incited them … to erect temples, courts of justice, and dwelling houses … he provided a liberal education for the sons of their chieftains … the toga was frequently seen …. those luxuries … in reality constituted a part of their slavery. (Tacitus, *Agricola* 21)

Whilst this approach could, and would, work well with the Continent-focused elites of Chichester, Silchester and Cirencester, and even those of *Venta Icenorum* after Boudicca was defeated, it was never going to work in central Wales or Snowdonia. To be fair, the civilian Roman way of life did later take partial hold in the lowlands of South Wales at Caerleon and Carmarthen. However, in the mid-first century there simply was not the fertile ground of tribal leaders keen to become Roman (Russell and Laycock, 2010, pp.98–100).

Furthermore, the mid-first-century Roman Army was not well calibrated to deal with the kind of low intensity hit-and-run guerrilla warfare it encountered in the Welsh mountains and hills. The army, although supplemented with infantry and cavalry auxiliaries – as it had been since Caesar's Gallic campaigns in the mid-first century BC – was still primarily built around legionary heavy shock infantry. Try running up a Welsh mountainside wearing full *lorica segmentata* or *lorica hamata*, with helmet, shield and *gladius*, while at the same time maintaining formation with your century; then add hostile slingshots, tumbling rocks and thrown spears from an enemy forever just out of your reach.

The Roman Army of the mid-first century AD – of Plautius, Scapula and Gallus – was still based on legionaries, with less use of auxiliary troops than we see later with Cerialis, Frontinus and Agricola. Large campaign bases, many of which included legionary cohorts at their core, were the order of the day.

The peoples and terrain of first-century Wales and the Marches

There is a reasonable consensus about the political geography of first-century AD Wales and the Marches, although this reflects an uneasy combination of the well-thumbed Roman geographers and historians and emerging modern archaeological discoveries and analysis. This produces a collision of history with precise dates, written by the victors, with broadly dated archaeological evidence of native settlements that fundamentally look the same before and after the Roman Army has passed through.

That being said, the Roman Army excelled at scientific surveying and knowing their enemy, so I believe we should not be overly sceptical of what was written down. With that proviso, and putting the evidence from Tacitus' *Annals*, *Histories* and *Agricola* together with Dio's *Roman History*, Ptolemy's *Geography*, the *Antonine Itinerary* and the *Ravenna Cosmography*, the following is what the Romans encountered in the mid-to-late 40s AD (Figure 2.1).

There were three tribes, which are specifically recorded as resisting Rome:

- the Ordovices of central and north Wales;
- the Silures of the south-west and Brecon Beacons;
- the Decangi or Deceangli of the silver-rich north-east of Wales.

Chronology of the eleven campaigns to conquer Wales and the Marches

There were at least eleven distinct campaigns in the Roman subjugation of Wales over the course of eleven governorships.

Governor	Campaign	Dates	Key Events
Aulus Plautius AD 43–47	I	45–46	• Possible 'first contact' with the tribes of Wales
Ostorius Scapula 47–52			• Arrives and defeats Britons who had invaded allied territory – no record of location • Decides to disarm all Britons south of the Trent and Severn, provokes rebellion by the hitherto allied Iceni
	II	48	• Campaign against the Deceangli to acquire silver and lead mining area • Roman Army reaches coast facing Ireland • Retreat forced by rising of Brigantes in the rear
	III	50	• Campaign against the Silures, led by exiled Caractacus • *Leg. XX* moved from Colchester to Gloucester Kingsholm
	IV	51	• Defeat and capture of Caractacus after he moves to Ordovices • Triumph in Rome, with Caractacus as star captive
	V	52	• War goes badly for the Romans • Silures adopt guerrilla tactics and Scapula dies in office
Didius Gallus 52–57	VI	52–57	• Gallus restores situation but Silures defeat a legion • Some territorial gains for the Romans, foundation of Usk Legionary Fortress
Quintus Veranius 57–58	VII	57	• Veranius promises to 'lay whole province at Nero's feet' • Minor operations against Silures
Suetonius Paulinus 58–62	VIII IX	58–59 60	• Campaigns in 58 and 59 successful – probably in Wales • Amphibious assault on Druids in Anglesey, aborted due to Boudicca's revolt
Petronius Turpilianus 62–63			• Pacifying and stabilizing the province after Boudicca • Army deployed back into eastern and central England?

Governor	Campaign	Dates	Key Events
Trebellius Maximus 63–69			• Policy of peace on the western border of the province • Transfer of *Leg. XIV Gemina* to join Nero's projected Eastern campaign, which then briefly returns to *Britannia*
Vettius Bolanus 69–71			• Civil War and the 'Year of the Four Emperors' • *Leg. XIV Gemina* leaves to fight in Italy in the Civil War
Petillius Cerialis 71–74			• Cerialis arrives with *II Adiutrix*, with orders from Vespasian to complete conquest of *Britannia* • Campaigns in northern England, defeats the Brigantes
Julius Frontinus 74–77	X	74-77	• Frontinus founds two new legionary fortresses – Caerleon for *II Augusta* in south and Chester for *II Adiutrix* in north • Conquers most of Wales and builds forts and roads to hold it
Julius Agricola 77–84	XI	77	• Arrives late in campaigning season and suppresses Ordovices who have attacked forts under construction • Launches successful amphibious attack on Druids in Anglesey

Sources: Tacitus, *Annals* xii.31–40; Burnham and Davies, 2010, pp.37–38, with modifications and additions.

In addition, further to the west we find:

- the Demetae of Carmarthen;
- the Octapitae around St David's Head;
- the Gangani of the western Llyn Peninsula.

The two latter were probably septs or sections of the larger tribes.

Bordering the uplands in the Marches there were:

- the Dobunni in the Lower Severn Valley;
- the Ordovices in the Upper Severn Valley and the Cheshire Plain.

So much seems clear from the various histories and geographies (Figure 2.1 for approximate tribal boundaries). The archaeological evidence is, however, much less clear-cut. The only tribe of these eight which had used coinage from as far back as *c.* 35 BC was the Dobunni, who had their tribal centre at distant Cirencester. One interpretation is that the Severn was the western boundary of the Dobunni, with western Gloucestershire and southern Herefordshire being a border zone, including the iron working areas in the Forest of Dean. Pottery types, unsurprisingly, seem to have spanned tribal territories and do not align with tribal boundaries. Dio reports that the Dobunni had been subservient to the Catuvellauni of eastern Britain, and the presence of Gallo–Belgic imports in the early first century is evidence for trade and potentially for a politically subservient relationship (Cunliffe, 2005, p.193).

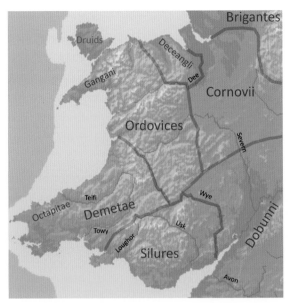

The Tribes of Wales and the Borders in the 1st Century AD

Approximate tribal boundaries (Jones and Mattingley 1990, 91)

Fig 2.1. The tribes of Wales were not the polities of the south and east of Britain with *oppida*, coinage and rulers/elites with a taste for imported luxuries. They appear to be fragmented groups clustered around hillforts, with largely pastoral economies.

Understanding Wales before the Roman wars is fraught with difficulties because of the lack of large-scale excavations and the difficulty of closely dating cultural material (Cunliffe, 2005, p.206). So, what follows must be tentative. A characteristic of most of Wales in the pre-Roman Iron Age is hillforts, with medium and large forts found in the Marches, and smaller forts in the west and south-west. This appears to be a society of multiple sub-tribal groupings, reflecting the politically fragmented structure of the tribes. The social and economic functions of hillforts are not well understood, however, and this may be too easy a conclusion. There are also a wide variety of other settlement types across the area that do not appear to correlate with tribal boundaries, so for precision using the old Welsh counties:

- stone-built farmsteads in north-west Wales;
- clustered ditched rectangular farmsteads in Montgomeryshire and western Shropshire;
- rectangular farmsteads in southern Cardiganshire and north Pembrokeshire.

The overall picture of Wales and the Marches on the eve of the Roman invasion is that the Dobunni were a quite populous and nucleated tribe with good mixed farmland, resembling in many ways the other tribes of southern Britain, generating good surpluses and supporting a tribal elite that minted coins and enjoyed luxury goods traded with the Roman Continent. They had an *oppidum* at Bagendon, near the later tribal capital at Cirencester (*Corinium*).

To the north were the Cornovii, who appear less developed and did not issue coins. The upland tribes of England and what is modern Wales appear to have been socially and economically fragmented, largely pastoral, societies. There is little evidence of the differentiated upper classes importing wine and Gallo–Roman ceramics which we find across southern Britain. There is nevertheless ample evidence of metal and bronze metalworking in what looks to be a military ranked society. It is therefore probable, when this is considered alongside the ubiquity of hillforts, that low-level raiding was endemic.

In what is now Wales, the Silures of the south-east were predominantly pastoralists. The limited evidence from excavated hillforts suggests they had little contact and interchange with the Romans until well into the Roman period, with fortifications remaining occupied and being modified and extended, for example at Sudbrook (Cunliffe, 2006, p.207). The Demetae of the south-west also show little Roman influence and, in contrast to the Silures, their settlements show continuity of occupation into the Roman era. For the Ordovices of the centre and north-west, there is even less evidence of Roman material impact before – and indeed after – the Roman occupation was completed. Hillforts like Dinorben were perhaps strengthened in the invasion period but, like Tre'r Ceiri, they continued in occupation throughout, as did enclosed farmsteads (Cunliffe, 2006, p.209).

With this low level of material culture, and with resistance to Roman imports, Wales unsurprisingly resembles the north of England and the Scottish Lowlands in the early first century (Burnham and Davies, 2010, pp.22–23). It is impossible to

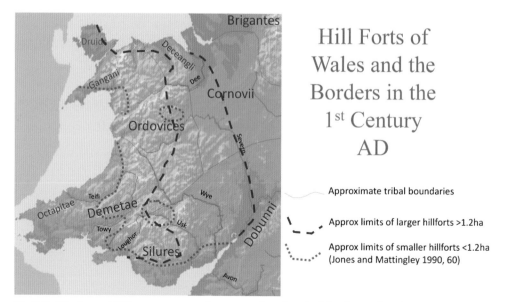

Fig 2.2. The larger hillforts – some very large – are found in the Marches and in the eastern uplands of Wales, whereas smaller forts (<1.2 hectare in size) are found in the west and south.

quantify with any precision the first-century population of this area, but estimates suggest a native population for Wales totalling between 330,000 and 500,000, which would equate to a fighting force of 66,000–100,000 able-bodied men across the entire region, assuming that fighting age men accounted for about 20 per cent of the total (Burnham and Davies, 2010, pp.135–36).

We therefore have a very challenging situation for the Roman Army of the first century, which had honed its way of warfare against the Eastern Mediterranean Hellenistic states, followed by defeating tribal confederations in Gaul and Spain, and finally fighting each other in the civil wars of the previous century. In Wales they faced a decentralized but militarized society with a primarily pastoral economy and many defensible hillforts in difficult terrain, and one very well able to manufacture basic but effective weaponry (Figure 2.2).

Why did the Romans want to conquer Wales and the Marches?

Given the time it took to conquer Wales and the commitment of vast resources it required, why did Roman governors bother with this challenge? Any answers are reasoned speculations, and we should not look for a single explanation. All states are complex organisms, and there were multiple motivations articulated by the Roman Senate and People (and the Army). We should look for answers in a combination of the following factors that drove the Roman Army forward:

- **Imperial** – prestige can never be discounted. The conquest of *Britannia* was Claudius' great Imperial project: he had succeeded where the great Julius Caesar had failed.
- **Tactical** – the necessity of defeating the resisters under Caractacus (and maybe others) from the tribes of the conquered zones, who would continue to raid the province and to ferment resistance if not defeated.
- **Exploitation** – Wales and the Marches contained gold, silver, lead and iron: mining and refining was swiftly got under way in Britain after conquest (Figure 2.3).
- **Conquest** – the Roman Army very much liked the dividends of war in the shape of loot, slaves and livestock that could be sold.
- **Strategic** – if the tribes of Wales were conquered, then the army could in time be released for other fronts, either in the north of Britain or on the Rhine and Danube.

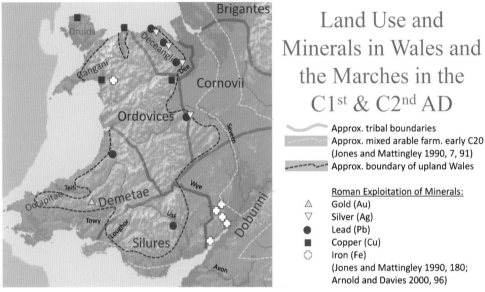

Land Use and Minerals in Wales and the Marches in the C1st & C2nd AD

Approx. tribal boundaries
Approx. mixed arable farm. early C20 (Jones and Mattingley 1990, 7, 91)
Approx. boundary of upland Wales

Roman Exploitation of Minerals:
△   Gold (Au)
▽   Silver (Ag)
●   Lead (Pb)
■   Copper (Cu)
✣   Iron (Fe)
(Jones and Mattingley 1990, 180; Arnold and Davies 2000, 96)

Fig 2.3. Before the invasion of AD 43, the Romans had a clear idea of the mineral wealth of *Britannia*, and this was probably a major factor in the decision to invade. The early targeting of the Deceangli by Scapula appears to confirm this.

State of the Province in AD47

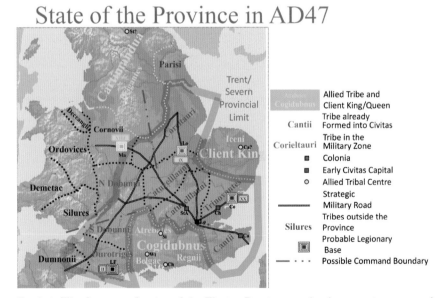

Trent/ Severn Provincial Limit

Allied Tribe and Client King/Queen
Tribe already Formed into Civitas
Tribe in the Military Zone
■   Colonia
■   Early Civitas Capital
○   Allied Tribal Centre
Strategic Military Road
Tribes outside the Province
Probable Legionary Base
Possible Command Boundary

Cantii
Corieltauri
Silures

Fig 2.4. The future uniformity of the Flavian Province masks the precariousness and complexity of *Britannia* under the Claudian and Neronian governors. The zone directly controlled by the Romans was a relatively small area, with allies and hostile tribes still holding large areas.

The campaign in Wales: a failed conquest

Ostorius Scapula and the assault on the Deceangli, Silures and Ordovices

As a result of Tacitus' account in the *Annals*, we know as much about Scapula's time in office as any governor of Britain, save only Agricola. Caractacus, son of the supreme king of the south and east, Cunobelinus, had been defeated by Aulus Plautius in AD 43. We have no knowledge of what further resistance he had offered, but he had won victories, as Tacitus reports. By the time of Scapula's arrival as governor in 47, he and other British resisters had holed up with the Silures in South Wales:

> The Romans now moved against the Silures whose natural spirit was reinforced by their faith in the prowess of Caractacus whose many battles against the Romans – some of uncertain outcome and some clear victories – had raised him to a position of pre-eminence amongst the other British chieftains. (Tacitus, *Annals* xii.33)

It is noteworthy that Caractacus, a tribal leader from the south-east of Britain, could become the natural leader of the Silures and also the Ordovices in the west. Although Cunobelinus was clearly the supreme king of the southern and eastern tribes, there is no evidence that he held sway this far to the west. As with Caesar in Gaul, the existential threat posed by the Romans to the tribal *status quo* seems to have driven some tribes and their leaders together in all-out resistance, whilst others saw the way the wind was blowing and became allies and collaborators. We can also see this reaction in how the states and tribes of Nigeria and Uganda were incorporated into the British Empire using indirect rule. In the Sokoto Caliphate, which was conquered by the British around 1900, military control and tax collection were operated by the British colonial authorities, whereas the direction of everything else was left in the hands of the indigenous aristocracies who had sided with the British during or after the conquest (Lugard, 1922).

Caractacus would have brought with him what Tacitus termed his *comitatus*, his personal following of warriors, no doubt augmented by refugees from the conquered areas of Britain (Tacitus, *Germania* 13–14). It appears that Caractacus and the tribes of Wales, together with the refugees from the subjugated tribes and allies of the province, were the explicit primary target from the start of Scapula's governorship, possibly on the express orders of Claudius on advice from Plautius. Scapula's first act was to show he was not to be trifled with:

The enemy had invaded allied territory with particular violence, since they thought that a new general, hampered by an unfamiliar army and the approach of winter, would not be able to confront them… [He] killed those Britons that resisted, pursued those that were scattered. (Tacitus, *Annals* xii.31)

We do not have a record of which of the Romans' British allies were invaded, but there are three candidates: the Iceni; Cartimandua and the Brigantes; and Cogidubnus and the Belgae/Atrebates/Regni. The first two can probably be discounted because of the reference to the Iceni quoted below and the fact the Brigantes were outside the province. It seems likely, therefore, that Cogidubnus – the arch-collaborator with Rome – may have been the target of the attacks and the beneficiary of Scapula's swift action.

Preparations for war in the west

To prepare for war in the west, Scapula needed to protect his rear areas: he could not afford a rising there, as Paulinus was to suffer in AD 60. He decided to disarm the tribes of what was clearly now seen as the Roman province of *Britannia* – whether they were allies of Rome or not. Tacitus explicitly states that the province at this time was recognized as being the tribes south of the Rivers Trent and Severn, which were seen as the effective boundary of the province. This therefore included the Iceni and also Cogidubnus' territories. The disarming provoked a rebellion from the Iceni:

> The first rebellion came from the Iceni, a tough people who had never been crushed in war because they had entered alliance with us willingly. The surrounding tribes followed their lead. (Tacitus, *Annals* xii.31)

Scapula defeated the rebels using just his auxiliaries in a battle at an unnamed camp, sometimes identified as Stonea Camp in the Fens or Holkham Camp in Norfolk. It was probably at this time that a compliant Prasutagus, with his consort Boudicca, was installed as 'King' of the Iceni. Tacitus reports that Scapula's vigorous strategy had worked, in that those who were hesitating between war and peace were reduced to docility.

Campaign II: the Deceangli

Scapula, having secured the province to his rear, was therefore free to pursue his aggressive policy in the west (Figure 2.5). Interestingly, of the three potential target tribes in Wales, he chose first to attack in AD 48 the so-called Decangi (clearly the Deceangli) of the north-east. Their territory, bounded by the sea to the north and

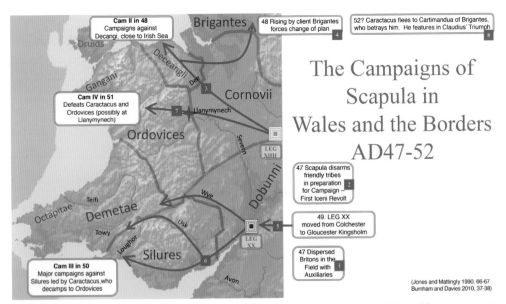

The Campaigns of Scapula in Wales and the Borders AD47-52

Cam II in 48
Campaigns against Decangi, close to Irish Sea

Cam IV in 51
Defeats Caractacus and Ordovices (possibly at Llanymynech)

48 Rising by client Brigantes forces change of plan

52? Caractacus flees to Cartimandua of Brigantes, who betrays him. He features in Claudius' Triumph

47 Scapula disarms friendly tribes in preparation for Campaign – First Iceni Revolt

49. LEG XX moved from Colchester to Gloucester Kingsholm

47 Dispersed Britons in the Field with Auxiliaries

Cam III in 50
Major campaigns against Silures led by Caractacus, who decamps to Ordovices

(Jones and Mattingly 1990, 66-67
Burnham and Davies 2010, 37-38)

Fig 2.5. Thanks to Tacitus we have knowledge of the targets and sequencing of Scapula's campaigns in the West against the tribes of Wales.

the River Dee and its estuary to the east and south, occupied both sides of the Clywdian Range (in Flintshire and Eastern Denbighshire) on which their hillforts are to be found. Halkyn Mountain in that range was rich in silver and in lead, its by-product when smelted, which was a strong motivation for this campaign (Arnold and Davies, 2000, p.101):

> Their territory was ravaged, and booty was seized far and wide. The enemy did not dare to engage in open warfare… The Romans were now not far from the coast facing Ireland. (Tacitus, *Annals* xii.32)

At this point Scapula was diverted by a rebellion of the allied but ever-restive Brigantes, who are probably best regarded as a relatively loose grouping of the peoples of northern England dominated by a ruling group based at Stanwick. Not for the last time, the Romans intervened in support of their client, Queen Cartimandua.

Campaign III: the Silures

Scapula's next target was the Silures in South Wales:

> Since neither violence nor clemency moved the Silures to abandon hostilities, they had to be kept down by legionary camps. In order to implement this strategy more speedily, a colony was established on captured territory at *Camulodunum* [Colchester]. (Tacitus, *Annals* xii.32)

Legionary Deployments on the Welsh Front

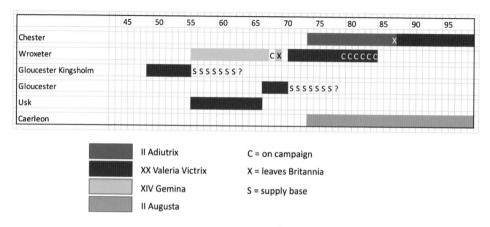

Fig 2.6. This is the most probable deployment of the four legions which were based in Wales and the Marches up to the end of the first century. In addition, vexillations (detached cohorts) would also be present when the army was not actively campaigning.

The colony was established in the former legionary fortress of *Legio XX* at Colchester. This legion then moved forward to a new campaign base at Gloucester Kingsholm (Figure 2.6), a site chosen because it was at the lowest fordable crossing of the River Severn. The base pointedly faced across the river towards the hills to the west and down the estuary to the south-west. The move was executed in AD 49 or 50, preparing for an attack in the following year:

> The Romans now moved against the Silures; whose natural spirit was reinforced by their faith in the prowess of Caractacus. (Tacitus, *Annals* xii.33)

Campaign IV: the Ordovices

Tacitus' account spends no more time on the Silures, since the engine of the resistance was Caractacus, who now moved north:

> He transferred the scene of his conflict to the territory of the Ordovices. He recruited from those who dreaded the establishment of the Roman peace and staked his fate on one last confrontation. (Tacitus, *Annals* xii.33)

Caractacus then decided to turn and fight. Why he did this, given his eight-year-long resistance and evasion of capture against the Romans, is a mystery. Caractacus must have by now acquired a very clear understanding of how the Roman military machine operated and of what he was facing, and indeed of the likelihood of defeat. His abandonment of guerrilla hit-and-run tactics for a full-on confrontational, all-or-nothing battle with the Roman Army is therefore more than puzzling. However, he was not the first or the last to do so: consider Vercingetorix in Gaul and Calgacus in Caledonia. Pressure and expectations from his followers from the defeated or allied tribes, and the effectiveness of the Roman Army in closing down his options in Wales, may have driven him to risk a pitched battle. It is possible that Roman scorched-earth policies meant that this was his last best chance, however long the odds. We can never know his thinking, but given that – arguably after Boudicca's revolt had been defeated – Nero contemplated abandoning the whole British enterprise (Suetonius, *Nero* xviii), Caractacus' decision to try to defeat a Roman army in a decisive battle in a position of his choosing was arguably not such an irrational decision.

Much effort has been devoted to trying to identify the site of Caractacus' great gamble. Sites proposed include Caer Caradoc near Church Stretton or British Camp in the Malvern Hills. A reasonable contender is Llanymynech hillfort on the border between Montgomeryshire and Shropshire. This is 57 hectares in size and could therefore accommodate Caractacus' force, with the River Vrynwy to its front (Jones, 1991, pp.57–63):

> The tribal leaders went round giving encouragement and stiffening the spirit of their troops, calming their fears, raising their hopes and offering other incitements to battle. Caractacus in particular was rushing from place to place, invoking that very day and that very battle as either the rebirth of liberty or the beginning of eternal servitude. He called upon his ancestors by name, those who had driven out Julius Caesar, the dictator. (Tacitus, *Annals* xii.34)

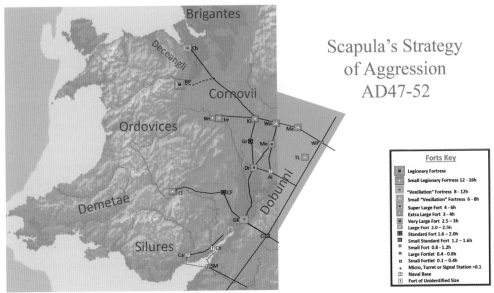

Fig 2.7. This map shows the forts and fortresses probably of the Scapulan period, together with likely early military roads, and plots them onto a map of the campaigning area.

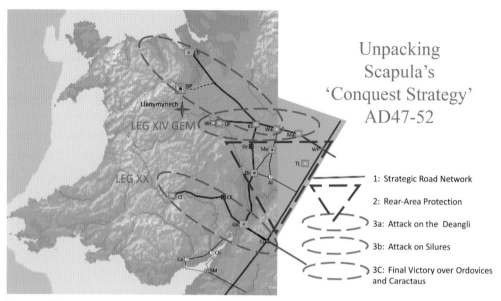

Unpacking
Scapula's
'Conquest Strategy'
AD47-52

1: Strategic Road Network

2: Rear-Area Protection

3a: Attack on the Deangli

3b: Attack on Silures

3C: Final Victory over Ordovices
and Caractaus

Fig 2.8. This map breaks down Scapula's several campaigns in Wales into their component parts for analysis.

The pitched battle itself seems to have gone very much according to the Roman script. Although Caractacus' wife and daughter were captured, and his brothers surrendered, he himself succeeded in escaping and fleeing to Queen Cartimandua of the Brigantes. Presumably, other elements of the Britons also escaped and would

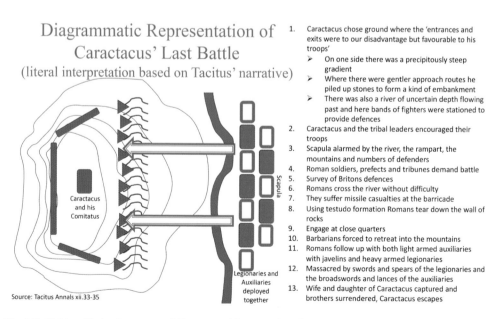

Diagrammatic Representation of
Caractacus' Last Battle
(literal interpretation based on Tacitus' narrative)

Caractacus
and his
Comitatus

Scapula

Legionaries and
Auxiliaries
deployed
together

Source: Tacitus Annals xii.33-35

1. Caractacus chose ground where the 'entrances and exits were to our disadvantage but favourable to his troops'
    ➤ On one side there was a precipitously steep gradient
    ➤ Where there were gentler approach routes he piled up stones to form a kind of embankment
    ➤ There was also a river of uncertain depth flowing past and here bands of fighters were stationed to provide defences
2. Caractacus and the tribal leaders encouraged their troops
3. Scapula alarmed by the river, the rampart, the mountains and numbers of defenders
4. Roman soldiers, prefects and tribunes demand battle
5. Survey of Britons defences
6. Romans cross the river without difficulty
7. They suffer missile casualties at the barricade
8. Using testudo formation Romans tear down the wall of rocks
9. Engage at close quarters
10. Barbarians forced to retreat into the mountains
11. Romans follow up with both light armed auxiliaries with javelins and heavy armed legionaries
12. Massacred by swords and spears of the legionaries and the broadswords and lances of the auxiliaries
13. Wife and daughter of Caractacus captured and brothers surrendered, Caractacus escapes

Fig 2.9. Taking Tacitus' account of Caractacus' last stand at face value produces this narrative of the battle. This is a highly diagrammatic representation since we do not know the site or the exact forces engaged.

have been able to survive to fight another day (see Figure 2.9 for a diagrammatic reconstruction of the battle). Cartimandua promptly handed Caractacus over to the Romans, and he starred in Claudius' triumph in Rome. Claudius graciously pardoned Caractacus and his family, but we do not know, alas, whether they 'lived happily ever after' in Roman comfort.

A key conclusion is that in these campaigns, Scapula defeated Caractacus and his *comitatus* – followers from many tribes attracted by his military prestige and anti-Roman leadership – together with refugees from defeated and anti-Roman factions from allied tribes. Undoubtedly, the Silures and then the Ordovices would have been present in force as the tribes who had been sheltering Caractacus and his followers. It is possible that substantial numbers escaped to fight another day – as Caractacus himself did – and so could regroup after the defeat. This would help to explain why the two Welsh tribes were very far from down and completely out after Caractacus' defeat and capture.

Campaign V: Things fall apart for Scapula

Scapula was awarded the insignia of a triumph but the Silures were indeed far from beaten. Tacitus reports three separate Roman defeats (Tacitus, *Annals* xii.38):

- The *Silures* surrounded legionary detachments that were building forts in their territory. The Romans were rescued by neighbouring garrisons but nevertheless lost the tribune in command, eight centurions and the bravest legionaries, implying the loss of 300–600 men in total – by any standards a substantial reverse in pitched battle for a legion.
- Shortly afterwards, the Silures put to flight a Roman foraging party, then saw off the cavalry squadrons sent to rescue them, followed by driving off the auxiliaries that Scapula sent. It was not until legionaries were deployed and engaged that the Silures fled at dusk.
- Finally, the Silures attacked two auxiliary cohorts which were plundering without caution because, according to Tacitus, of the greed of the commanding officers.

Tacitus reports that the Silures

were tempting other tribes to revolt as well, by generous distributions of spoils and captives, when worn out by the burden of his responsibilities Ostorius [Scapula] died. This was much to the enemy's delight as they felt that a general of considerable stature had been carried off. (Tacitus, *Annals* xii.39)

Well might the Silures rejoice, since it appears that Scapula must have thought he had defeated and cowed the Silures and Ordovices, only to find that they rose up again. He seems to have died exhausted by his efforts in office.

Analyzing the strategy adopted by Scapula

There are many Roman marching camps and practice camps to be found across Wales and the Marches, as there are in the Scottish Borders, Lowlands and along the East Coast. However, those in Wales span only three or four decades, and major typological differences and 'runs' of camps of almost the same size and design have not yet been detected. Therefore, it is unfortunately not possible to 'fit the camps to the campaign', as we can do in the north and Scotland. Nevertheless, we can see one set of 16-hectare marching camps which appear to trace a force moving west from the campaign assembly grounds at the end of Watling Street around Wroxeter, Burlington and Uffington, through Whittington to Penrhos (Jones and Mattingly, 2002, pp.79–80).

The best we can postulate, given the lack of pattern from marching camps, is that – exactly as we would expect – the Roman Army used the river valleys as lines of penetration (LOPs) into the interior of the Welsh uplands and mountains.

The dating of more permanent military installations to this phase is similarly problematic, given the short period in question and the variable quality of site analysis over the years. The Roman conquest and occupation of Wales and the Marches has, however, been the subject of meticulous analysis, undertaken first by Nash-Williams (1954), revised by Jarrett (1969) and most recently by Davies and Burnham (2010). Using the Toolbox methods set out in Chapters 8 and 9, the remains of forts and roads have been entered into the database and plotted on the human and physical geography of Wales and the Marches. When forts that are definite or probable candidates for foundation during Scapula's governorship are identified, some interesting hypotheses can be formulated which shed new light on why the first Roman invasion of Wales failed.

Scapula had inherited from Plautius and his legionary surveyors a fine network of strategic roads in the province (Figure 2.4). It is highly probable that much of the island of Britain was surveyed in the first years of the conquest, with alignments on visible features connecting the key sites (Entwhistle, 2019). Fundamental to Scapula's western campaigns were three strategic roads (their names being of course anachronistic):

- Watling Street running from the Channel ports in Kent through London and St Albans (*Verulamium*) and on to the north-west, reaching the Irish Sea at the mouth of the River Dee at what became Chester (*Dera*);
- Akeman Street connecting Colchester and London with the new legionary fortress at Gloucester founded by Scapula in AD 50 on the River Severn;
- the Fosse Way running laterally from Exeter to Lincoln, passing just behind Gloucester Kingsholm and crossing Watling Street in the Midlands at High Cross.

A great deal of ink has been spilt over whether there was something called the 'Fosse Way Frontier'. It is now generally recognized that this is an anachronistic concept (Jones and Mattingly, 2003). There are few forts along this road to form a frontier, and the idea that the limits of the Roman Empire or of the new province of *Britannia* should 'stop' along such a line would surely have seemed ludicrous to the Roman Army of the mid-first century. Having an effective lateral communications route behind the active fronts on which the legions were operating would, however, have made excellent strategic and logistical sense.

Legionary 'fronts'

The four legions of the province under Scapula had four theatres of operation:

- *II Augusta* in the south-west peninsula against the Durotriges and Dumnonii;
- *XX* in South Wales against the southern Dobunni and the Silures;
- *XIV Gemina* in the West Midlands against the northern Dobunni, Cornovii and Ordovices;
- *IX Hispana* in the East Midlands against the Corieltauvi and watching the Brigantes confederation.

This concept of 'legionary fronts' has been adopted for some time in the study of the conquest of Roman Britain (Webster, 1981, pp.42–53), but it is worth explicitly unpacking how this would have worked. The governor of the province was a senator who had both military and civil command of the province. On the military side, the next-highest-ranking officers were the commanders (*legati*) of the legions allocated to the province. These men were also senators and, given that there were generally only thirty legions in the whole Roman Empire, these were key appointments and elements of patronage: a prudent emperor would ensure loyal senators as governors of the key military provinces and as commanders of the legions. Within the legion there was then a balanced command structure with a mixture of senatorial leadership for the second-in-command *tribunus laticlavius* (broad-stripe tribune) and the *praefectus castrorum*, who was the third in command and would take over in battle from the legate if needed. The *praefectus castrorum* was always a long-serving centurion and had probably been the most senior of them as *primus pilus*. Below these three were the *tribuni angusticlavii* (narrow-stripe tribunes), who were usually from the Equestrian Order and had military experience commanding auxiliary units and carrying out other imperial functions. Finally, each legion had sixty centurions commanding the sixty centuries, who were promoted from the best leaders in the ranks of the legion.

Each legion had a number of auxiliary units attached to it; these were commanded by *praefecti* if they were 500-man (*quingenaria*) units, or by *tribuni* if they were the larger 1,000-man (*milliaria*) units. We frequently find legionary centurions seconded to command auxiliary cohorts.

The point of this excursion is that the legion provided a ready-made command structure to which a mission such as the conquest of a tribe or region could be assigned. The accompanying auxiliaries would readily 'lock on' to form an effective multi-role task force. This was how the US Command in Vietnam approached the war, with Corps Commands taking responsibility for geographical groups of provinces.

Nature of installations

In the ten chapters of the *Annals* that Tacitus devotes to Scapula's governorship of Britain, there is a constant and recurring theme about the complementary roles of the Roman legions and auxiliaries in the campaign:

> [Scapula] set himself to break through these defences even though he was commanding allied troops without legionary strength. (*xi.32*, with reference to the Iceni and surrounding tribes' revolt)

> [The Silures] had to be kept down by legionary camps. (*xii.32*, referring to the move of *Legio XX* from Colchester to Gloucester Kingsholm)

> They were both light-armed and heavy-armed, the former attacked the enemy with javelins, the latter pressed on in close order breaking up the ranks of the Britons as they met them, since these did not have the protection of breast plates or helmets. In fact, if they resisted the auxiliary troops, they were massacred by the swords and spears of the legionaries, and if they turned against these, they met the same fate at the hands of the auxiliaries with their broadswords and lances. (*xii.35*, with reference to Caractacus' last stand)

> They surrounded the legionary cohorts who had been left behind under a senior officer to build defences in Silures territory. So, if help had not been sent from the neighbouring forts to the besieged men ... they would have been utterly slaughtered. *(xii.38*, referring to the Silurian fightback)*

Ostorius then sent his light-armed cohorts against the attackers, but even by this strategy he would not have stopped the rout if the legions had not joined in the battle. (*xii.39*, also about the Silurian fightback)

The message here is clear: the Roman Army's approach to fighting in the uplands of Britain was to combine the hitting power of the heavy infantry of the legions with the flexibility of the more lightly armed auxiliaries. But did Scapula have sufficient auxiliary units to get the job done?

As noted above, a characteristic of this early phase of the conquest of Britain is the use of fortresses, smaller than a full legionary fortress of 16–20 hectares but much larger than even large forts of 2–4 hectares. They are often called vexillation fortresses, but this is misleading as it can be taken technically to be just a legionary vexillation (named after the flag or *vexillatio*). They are sometimes termed *hiberna* or *aestiva*, that is, winter or summer bases, but are probably better called campaign bases, since they could house combined forces of legionaries and auxiliaries and seem to be occupied for more than part of a campaign season.

These types of campaign bases for combined arms are to be found across Britain in the two decades after the invasion of AD 43. At a size of between 8 and 12 hectares, they provided bases for combined task forces operating into, and in some cases deep inside, enemy territory. A base of this size could hold two to four legionary cohorts supported by several auxiliary units, possibly an infantry *cohors* and a cavalry *ala*. This would provide for an effective and flexible combined-arms force.

Probable and possible Scapulan forts

Listing the forts and fortresses for which there is reasonable evidence of foundation in the Scapulan era, we can see how the campaign developed on the ground (Figure 2.10). When these sites are plotted onto the physical geography and map of tribal occupation, we can start to work out the shape of Scapula's plan of campaign. Three elements emerge:

1. the framework of strategic roads built around Watling Street, the Fosse Way and Akeman Street;
2. rear areas protection in the 'triangle' between Watling Street and the Fosse Way;
3. four Lines of Penetration (LOPs):
   a. one into North Wales to conquer the Deceangli from Scapula's campaign in 48;
   b. one into South Wales to attack the Silures along the River Wye;
   c. one along the Coast in 50;
   d. a massive thrust into eastern Ordovices territory, probably dating to the campaigns against Caractacus in 51.

Scapula's Strategy of Aggression
47-52AD
Fortresses and Forts

Camp-aign	System	Purpose	Desription	Id	Name	Phase	Roman Name	Size Ha	Size Code	Strength Factor	First Unit	Approx Manpower	Unit if Known	Build Code	Start Date	End Date	RM	IM	Km
SCAPULA'S CONQUEST OF THE SILURES & ORDOOVICES																			
SCA	WAT	LOP	CONQUEST	1.0	Wigston Parva (H Cross)			0.7	SFT	0.6		240		Scap	55		0.0	0.0	0.0
SCA	WAT	LOP	CONQUEST	2.0	Mancetter		Manduessedum	9.0	VEX	8.0		2,000	XIV GEM	Scap	55		11.2	10.6	17.0
SCA	WAT	LOP	CONQUEST	3.0	Wall		Lectocetum	Vex	VX	6.0		2,000		Scap	55		19.1	18.0	29.0
SCA	WAT	LOP	CONQUEST	4.0	Kinvaston (Water Eaton)	1	Pennocrucium	7.8	VX	6.0		2,000		Scap	55		16.4	15.5	25.0
SCA	WAT	LOP	CONQUEST	5.0	Redhill		Uxacona	0.7	SFT	0.6		240		Scap	55		13.2	12.4	20.0
SCA	WAT	LOP	CONQUEST	6.0	Wroxeter		Viroconium	2.20	LFT	2.0	CQE	500	coh I Thracum eq	Scap	55		13.8	13.0	21.0
SCA	WAT	LOP	CONQUEST	6.1	Leighton (nr Wroxeter)			8.1	VEX	8.0	LEG+AUX	2,000	XIV GEM	Scap	55		0.0	0.0	0.0
SCA	WAT	LOP	CONQUEST	7.0	Rhyn Park			17.2	LEG	12.0	LEG+AUX	5,000	XIV GEM	Scap	55		28.3	26.7	43.0
SCA	WAT	LOP	CONQUEST	8.0	Chester			10.0	VEX	8.0		2,000		Scap	55		26.3	24.9	40.0
Watling Street Line of Penetration (Decangi and Ordovices)										43.2		13,980					102.0	96.3	155.0
SCA	DOB	AREA	CONTROL	1.0	The Lunt Baginton			Vex		6.0		2,000		Scap	55				
SCA	DOB	AREA	CONTROL	2.0	Alcester					1.0		500		Scap	55				
SCA	DOB	AREA	CONTROL	3.0	Droitwich		Salinae	5.0	SLF	4.0		1,500		Scap	55				
SCA	DOB	AREA	CONTROL	4.0	Metchley			4.4	SLF	4.0		1,500		Scap	55				
SCA	DOB	AREA	CONTROL	5.0	Greensforge	1		1.6	FRT	1.5		500		Scap	55				
Area Control of Northern Dobunni (W Midlands Triangle)										16.5		6,000					0.0	0.0	0.0
SCA	WYE	LOP	CONQUEST	1.0	Cirencester			1.8	FRT	1.5	AQ	500	ala Galliorum Indiana	Scap	55		0.0	0.0	0.0
SCA	WYE	LOP	CONQUEST	2.0	Gloucester	1	Glevum	10.0	VEX	10.0		3,000		Scap	55		18.4	17.4	28.0
SCA	WYE	LOP	CONQUEST	3.0	Canon Frome			1.8	FRT	1.5		500		Scap	55		23.7	22.4	36.0
SCA	WYE	LOP	CONQUEST	4.0	Kenchester?					1.0		500		Scap	55		15.1	14.3	23.0
SCA	WYE	LOP	CONQUEST	5.0	Clifford	1		6.5	VX	6.0		2,000		Scap	55		14.5	13.7	22.0
Wye Line of Penetration (N Silures/Dobunni Border)										20.0		6,500					71.7	67.7	109.0
SCA	WYE	LOP	CONQUEST	1.0	Gloucester	1	Glevum	10.0	VEX	10.0		2,000		Scap	55		0.0	0.0	0.0
GAL	WYE	LOP	SUP	2.0	Chepstow							-		Scap	55		31.6	29.8	48.0
GAL	WYE	LOP	SUP	3.0	Caerleon							-		Scap	55		15.1	14.3	23.0
Vale of Gamorgan Line of Penetration (S Silures)										0.0		2,000					46.7	44.1	71.0
TOTAL: GALLUS' CONTAINMENT SYSTEM										79.7		14,500							

Fig 2.10. The database of fortresses and forts in Wales and the Marches dating from Scapula's campaigns.

1: The road baseline

The road network provided the baseline to launch the campaign. The Fosse Way was not, as we have seen, a defended linear frontier; rather, it was a jumping-off point for future offensive operations. It provided lateral communications between legionary task forces for the military, provided the opportunity to move troops between 'fronts' and to supply the forces, and enabled Scapula to keep in communication with his forces.

2: Rear area protection: forts and roads in the 'West Midlands triangle'

Rear area protection was provided by a grid of four early forts in the West Midlands in the triangle between the Fosse Way, Watling Street and the Severn Valley. The purpose of this heavy deployment of force was to secure the fertile zone which lay between the northern Dobunni centred on Cirencester and the Cornovii of Shropshire. The Dobunni were, as we have seen, a coin-issuing tribe and appear to have developed a cohesive tribal organization, whilst the Cornovii were less economically developed and seem to have been formed of smaller sub-tribal groups with their own leaders centred around hillforts (Cunliffe, 2006, p.210). Whether the West Midlands was a territory of the Dobunni or the Cornovii (or even both) is far from clear, but whatever the allegiance, here was a population with fertile territory in the rear of the planned area of operations that needed to be controlled. This was achieved by three military roads with large but conventional-sized forts:

- a road between Kinvaston/Water Eaton on Watling Street, through Greensforge and Droitwich (*Salinae*) with its valuable salt extraction facility, down to Gloucester;
- a north–south road which ran from Watling Street through Metchley to Alcester;
- a third east–west road from the Fosse Way through Alcester to the salt works at Droitwich.

In addition, there may have been a campaign base under the Neronian fort at The Lunt near Coventry, which could be associated with the 'triangle' (Figures 2.7 and 2.8).

3: The Lines of Penetration

The third element is a startling series of no less than nine 'campaign bases' (sometimes termed vexillation fortresses).

3a: Scapula's campaign against the Deceangli of North Wales in AD 48

The first of these is an early campaign base site at Rhyn Park on the upper River Dee. Positioned on the southern borders of the territory of the Deceangli, it is usually associated with Scapula's first campaign. The first fort on this site is a truly massive 17.2 hectares in size, large enough to accommodate all of *XIV Gemina* or alternatively four or five legionary cohorts supplemented by several auxiliary cohorts. Rhyn Park I is therefore a strong candidate as the means by which Scapula secured the mineral wealth of the Deceangli shortly after his arrival in the province.

Whilst we are in the north of Wales, it has been suggested that there is another campaign base under the later legionary fortress at Chester. Whilst there is no firm evidence at the moment, the strategic position of Chester on the Dee, dominating the Cheshire Plain and the coast of North Wales, makes this a possibility.

3b: Scapula's campaign against the Silures in AD 50

In the south, we can see the outlines of Scapula's campaigns against the Silures. As headlined by Tacitus, the campaign base was at Gloucester Kingsholm, built by *Legio XX* (not yet *Valeria Victrix*). Significantly, this was only 10 hectares in size; in other words, although it seems to have been the command base of the legion, it was only of campaign base size, sufficient for five or six of the ten cohorts. This is further evidence of the campaign base philosophy adopted by Scapula. The other cohorts were presumably deployed into the other campaign bases.

There is a clear LOP starting from the Fosse Way fort at Cirencester, heading west through the new legionary fortress at Gloucester and aiming at northern Silurian territory, via an early intermediate 'normal-sized' fort at Canon Frome; and then up the Wye Valley to a campaign base of 6 hectares at Clifford (near Clyro, Picture 2.1). This is the first of three large forts built in this position penetrating into the heart of the Silurian uplands through the fertile and navigable river valleys. The Wye could easily accommodate supply barges at this point.

3c: Scapula's South Wales coast campaign in AD 50

There is another possible LOP down the Severn estuary and along the coastal plain, where you might expect to find forts guarding the crossings of the lower Wye at Chepstow and the lower Usk at the site of the future fortress at Caerleon. There is, it must be stressed, little evidence for such early forts. We should also expect the navy operating out of Sea Mills on the other side of the Bristol Channel to support the army on the Welsh side.

3d: Scapula's campaign against Caractacus in AD 51

There are no less than four campaign bases lined up along Watling Street: Mancetter (8 hectares), Wall (unknown size), Kinvaston/Water Eaton (6 hectares) and Leighton near Wroxeter (8 hectares). They are set out one after the other, all apparently pointing directly at the Ordovices of North Wales along the valleys of the upper River Severn and River Vrynwy. Mancetter is usually seen as the HQ of *XIV Gemina*, as Gloucester Kingsholm was in the south.

To calibrate the four Midlands campaign bases, a permanent legionary fortress of the mid-first century was 16–20 hectares in size; therefore, these campaign bases are about half-size for a full legion. This would be large enough for:

- four or five full-strength legionary cohorts (*c.* 2,000–2,500 men) or
- two legionary cohorts plus one auxiliary cavalry *ala* plus an auxiliary infantry cohort (*c.* 1,000 + *c.* 500 + *c.* 500 = *c.* 2,000 men).

It is possible that some or even all of these bases were used as the assembly point for Scapula's campaign of AD 51 that brought Caractacus to battle. On the assumption that both sides would have seen this as the decisive battle for the control of southern Britain and not just Wales, then we should expect to find, as well as *XIV Gemina*, vexillations (detachments) from *Legio XX* and possibly *II Augusta* in the field with their auxiliaries. This hypothetical force could therefore amount to:

- *Legio XIV Gemina* (5,000 men);
- *a vexillatio* of *Legio XX* of four cohorts (2,000 men);
- *a vexillatio* of *II Augusta* of four cohorts (2,000 men);
- supporting auxiliaries at a ratio of 1:1, amounting to eighteen units (9,000 men).

This force, with a theoretical total strength of 18,000 men, would be significantly reduced by the rigours of campaigning, but could still be enough to utilize some or all of the campaign bases.

Some of these campaign bases could also have formed the jumping-off point for Scapula's Deceangli campaign, with the route from Wroxeter to the north-west to Rhyn Park and north up the Dee Valley.

Typology of Scapula's aggression

Scapula's conquest strategy is unpacked in Figure 2.8 on the map of Wales and the Marches. The Typology Diagram (Figure 2.11) breaks down Scapula's strategy so that it can be compared with other Roman campaigns.

We can see that for this strategy – which of course started as early as AD 48 – the recently constructed Fosse Way was the baseline, providing lateral communications between the legionary fronts:

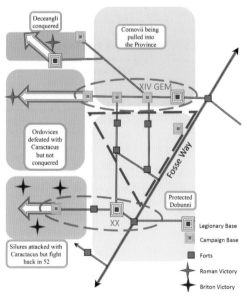

Typology Diagram of Scapula's Strategy of Aggression AD48

- Fosse Way provides lateral communications between the 4 legionary 'fronts'
  - ➤ 'Protects his rear area with forts in the West Midlands Triangle
- AD48 Scapula attacks and defeats Decangli and Romans start exploiting Silver and Lead
- AD49 LEG XX VV moves to Gloucester Kingsholm
- AD50 Scapula attack Caractacus and Silures
  - ➤ Caractacus and his Comitatus moves to Ordovices
- AD51 launches the 'final assault' on Caractacus
  - ➤ Forces assemble along line of Watling Street
  - ➤ Apparent decisive victory
  - ➤ Caractacus flees to Cartimandua and is handed over for Claudius Triumph in Rome
  - ➤ AD52 Silures fight back and inflict defeats on Roman troops building forts and plundering
  - ➤ AD52 Scapula worn out by his exertions dies

Fig 2.11. Typology diagram breaking down Scapula's strategic approach in the 'West Midlands triangle'.

- *II Augusta* operating from Exeter against the Dumnonii and still keeping watch over the Durotriges;
- *XX* operating from Gloucester Kingsholm and other campaign bases;
- *XIV Gemina* from the bases along Watling Street;
- *IX Hispana* operating in the East Midlands.

Scapula had protected his rear by disarming the tribes 'inside' the province, no matter whether they were under military occupation or notionally allied. He then extended formal control over the northern Dobunni and the southern Cornovii in the West Midlands triangle with a grid of forts and roads.

As we have seen, Scapula then launched his offensive into Wales, starting first with the Deceangli of north-east Wales. This was an interesting choice given this was a long reach, but it was a relatively small tribe with considerable mineral wealth to be exploited – an insight into the priorities of the governor. Scapula then followed up with an attack on his principal target, Caractacus and the Silures in South Wales, who had by this stage become the focus for all those opposed to Roman rule.

It must have seemed that all was going very much to plan for Scapula as governor, but then it all fell apart. This seems to have happened as the governor moved into

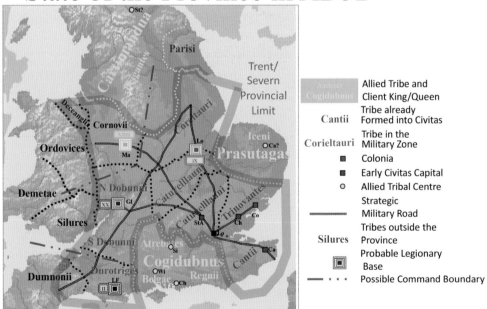

Fig 2.12. Scapula had advanced the province to include the 'West Midlands triangle' and the Deceangli were probably 'protected' so that their mineral wealth could be exploited. His attacks on the Silures and Ordovices had, however, failed to result in lasting occupation.

consolidating his conquests. We have two early forward bases. In the north, the Rhyn Park I fortress is no less than 17 hectares in size and could easily accommodate several legionary cohorts and their accompanying auxiliaries. In the south there is a series of marching camps and three large forts clustered along the middle Wye at Clifford/Clyro. The current interpretation of the sequencing is that Clifford I was first and was placed in a position close to the river that is liable to flooding and waterlogged in winter (Picture 2.1). Clifford I is 6 hectares in size and could have held some of the cohorts of *Legio XX* not stationed at the *c.* 10-hectare Gloucester Kingsholm fort. Kingsholm is connected by an apparent road, and a 'normal-sized' fort at Canon Frome, that then leads to the middle Wye Valley. Could Clifford be the fort under construction when the tribune and eight centurions were lost? We can only speculate.

In addition to these forward bases there are, although much more tentatively identified, early invasion period positions potentially at Chester on the Dee, on the Severn at Wroxeter, and at Chepstow and Caerleon in the south. All of these are speculative. Standing back to look at the overall intent, though, Scapula's objective here appears to reach into and start to dominate the tribes of the interior. This

Pic 2.1. The first campaign base on the middle River Wye at Clifford, established under Scapula. As can be seen, the siting was miserably poor, being too close to the river and liable to flooding. It was succeeded by a better sited base a kilometre upstream. (*Photo by author*)

Pic 2.2. Clyro campaign base on the River Wye, successor to the two bases at Clifford. Founded in the mid-50s as part of Gallus' forward policy of containment, it is 8ha in size and sits on a rounded hilltop in the middle of the valley. (*Photo by author*)

was a strategy that the Silures certainly opposed, as recorded by Tacitus, and it is noteworthy that the heartlands of the Ordovices were not troubled by these early campaign bases. What we have here is therefore the next phase of the conquest – foundations intended to enable future incursions. Effective resistance by the Silures stopped Scapula short in his plans, however.

Vital statistics of Scapula's conquest policy for Wales and the Marches

If we marshal the vital statistics from the modelling of Scapula's campaigns in Wales and the Marches, we can get a 'bottom up' view of the forces he deployed to defeat Caractacus and the 'freedom fighters' from the southern and eastern tribes, and to conquer the Silures and Ordovices, presented in Figure 2.14. This of course incorporates the many assumptions enumerated above about how the Roman Army was deployed and where. This is a theory built upon a hypothesis built on assumption and interpolation. Notwithstanding this, such a reconstructive model can give us useful insights which can be debated and tested by future excavators and researchers.

There were two legions fully committed to the 'Welsh Front' – an anachronistic term but, although we do not know what the Roman Army called it, this was effectively what it was. These were the *XIV Gemina* based in Mancetter and the *XX* brought forward to Gloucester Kingsholm. Each had ten cohorts and four *turmae* of cavalry, primarily for escort duty and messages, nominally of about 5,000 men. After years of campaigning in Britain, however, their actual strength and effectiveness

Scapula's Attempted Conquest of Wales Deployment Analysis Chart

Scapula's Attempted Conquest of the Silures and Ordovices - Category	Size from (ha)	Size to (ha)	Code	SFs	Possible Garrison	Number in Cat	SFs in Cat	Fort Names
Legionary Fortress	16.00		LEG	12.0	Full legion + support	1	12.0	Rhyn Park,
Small Legionary Fortress	12.00	15.99	LG	10.0	Most of legion			
Campaign Base (Vexillation)	8.00	11.99	VEX	8.0	Legionary cohorts + support	4	32.0	Mancetter, Leighton, Chester? Glouceester Kingsholm
Small Campaign Base (Smal Vex)	6.00	7.99	VX	6.0	Legionary cohorts + support	4	24.0	Wall, Kinvaston, The Lunt? Clifford,
Super Large Fort	4.00	5.99	SLF	4.0	Auxiliary task force	2	8.0	Droitwich, Mtchley,
Extra Large Fort	3.00	3.99	ELF	3.0	AM			
Very Large Fort	2.50	2.99	VLF	2.5	CME			
Large Fort	2.00	2.49	LFT	2.0	AQ or CMP	1	2.0	Wroxeter,
Standard Fort	1.60	1.99	FRT	1.5	CQE	3	4.5	Greensforge, Cirencester, Canon Frome,
Small Standard Fort	1.20	1.59	FOR	1.0	CQP			
Small Fort	0.80	1.19	SFT	0.6	part of a cohort	2	1.2	Wigston Parva, Rdhill,
Large Fortlet	0.40	0.79	lft	0.3	2 x centuries or numerus			
Small Fortlet	0.10	0.39	sft	0.1	1 x century			
Micro Fortlet		0.09	mic	0.0	1 x conturbernia			
Turret/Signal Station			tur					
Naval Base			NAV		fleet detachment			
Unknown Size or ?			???	1.0		3	3.0	Alcester? Kenchester? Chepstow?
Total						20	86.7	

Fig 2.13. The total of forts constructed in Scapula's campaigns, categorized by size, using the data-led analytical method (D-LAM).

would depend on how recent new recruitment had been from its *coloniae*, where old soldiers had settled and had sons, and from new drafts of citizens.

There now follows an assumption, which is no more than this. On the basis that the campaign bases we find so liberally deployed in this period consisted of a garrison of at least 2,000 men – half legionaries and half auxiliaries, that is two cohorts of each – we need to find another 6,000 legionaries and an equal number of auxiliaries to garrison them. It should be stressed that many of the campaign bases are of a size that could accommodate many more than the four cohorts or 2,000 men postulated here. It is therefore unlikely that they were all occupied at the same time, so perhaps these factors offset each other.

If each of the other two legions in Britain under Scapula – *IX Hispana* and *II Augusta* – deployed vexillations for the 'Welsh Front', then this level of force would have been temporarily possible. The total requirement, adding together the auxiliaries required for both campaign bases and also the 'normal-sized' forts, could be as high as some twenty-seven regiments of auxiliaries.

If we look next at the strength of the deployments, using the Strength Factors (SFs) as a proxy for the force deployed, we arrive at a total of about eighty-eight SFs for the whole campaign in the west. The bulk of these are to be found in the north with the overwhelming force deployed to attack Caractacus and the Ordovices in AD 51.

For the 'West Midlands triangle', assuming that there was a campaign base under the Lunt and that it was occupied at the time, we have sixteen SFs. In the south, with the axis of Gloucester/Clifford/Collen Castle, we have eighteen SFs.

The Vital Statistics of Scapula's Policy of Conquest in Wales and the Marches

	No of Forts (excluding duplicates)	Road Length	Nominal Garrison Manpower	Strength Factors	Ave Distance Forts
Watling Street LOP High Cross to Chester	1 LegF + 5 CBs + 3 Forts	155 kms	5,000 leg + 5,000 vex + 6,000 aux = 16,000 men	12.0 Leg + 36.0 CBs + 3.2 Forts = 51.2 SFs	17 kms
Area Control W Midlansd Triangle	1 CB + 4 Forts	250 kms	1,000 vex + 5,000 aux = 6,000 men	6.0 CBs + 10.5 Forts = 16.5 SFs	50 kms
N Silures LOP (Severn/Wye)	1 LegF + 1 CB +3 Forts	109 kms	3,000 leg + 2,000 leg + 1,500 aux =6,500 men	8.0 Leg + 6.0 CBs + 4.0 Forts = 18 SFs	24 kms
S Silures LOP (Vale of Glam)	2 Forts	71 kms	1,000 aux = 1,000 men	= 2.0 SFs	22 kms
TOTALS	2 LegFs + 7 CBs +11 Forts	625 kms	10,000 leg + 6,000 vex + 13,500 aux =29,500 men	= 87.7 SFs	28 kms

Key:
LegF = Legionary Fortress with HQ
CB = Campaign Base
leg = legionaries with own legion
vex = legionary detachments
aux = auxiliary troops
Leg = SFs in home Legionary Fortress

Notes: it has been assumed here that the Campaign Bases in North were manned with 2 Legionary Cohorts and 2 Auxiliary Cohorts totalling c2,000 men – this will have differed considerably depending on local circumstances. For Gloucester Kingsholm although the HQ of Legio XX, was not large enough to hold more than 6 Legionary Cohorts or 3,000 men at most, so the other 2,000 have been assumed deployed at Clifford.

Fig 2.14. The vital statistics – number of forts, road lengths, garrison and strength factors – of Scapula's campaigns summarized by component.

These are the raw numbers, and they seem very large at nearly 30,000 men and eighty-eight SFs in total. So whilst, as noted above, it was entirely possible for Scapula to assemble forces of this size, we should not expect these forces to be present 'in theatre' for the full five years of campaigning. The forces will have been changed and evolved, so stripping this back we can postulate a sequence along the following lines:

- AD 48: *XIV Gemina* plus auxiliaries against the Deceangli (maybe thirty to forty SFs);
- AD 50: *XX* moves to Gloucester plus auxiliaries, against Caractacus and the *Silures* (maybe thirty to forty SFs);
- AD 51: *XIV Gemina* and *XX* plus legionary vexillations of *IX Hispana* and *II Augusta*, plus full auxiliary force, against Caractacus and the Ordovices (maybe the full 30,000 men and more than eighty SFs);
- AD 52: *XX* plus legionary vexillations and auxiliaries against the Silures (maybe 15,000 men and thirty to forty SFs).

In this scenario, the reinforcements assembled along Watling Street are pulled together for the climatic confrontation with Caractacus in AD 51, and then returned to their donor legionary commands in the south-west (*II Augusta*) and north Midlands (*IX Hispana*) after the victory. The same could also be the case with some or all of the putative Lunt, Rhyn Park and Chester campaign bases that would have been abandoned by the end of Scapula's governorship. This would leave the West Midlands and the northern Marches garrisoned largely by auxiliaries in 'normal-sized' forts that we would expect from later campaigns.

Assessment of Scapula's strategy

Ultimately, Scapula's policy of aggression was a complete failure. Although the provincial perimeter did advance beyond the Severn and Trent line to incorporate the northern Dobunni and the Cornovii, the only part of Wales that seems to have been consolidated into Roman occupation was the territory of the Deceangli in the north-east, where the silver and lead mining and refining were the prize. The exploitation of mineral deposits had been rapid after conquest: the Mendips were producing lead and silver by AD 49, and Welsh lead and silver was in production by the reign of Vespasian at the latest. Indeed, we know that Britain was undercutting Spanish metal producers because they lobbied against its development. Tacitus noted that 'Britain yields gold, silver and other metals, the fruits of victory' (Tacitus, *Agricola* 12).

The Ordovices and Silures may have been defeated in pitched battle but they were in no sense out of the field, let alone incorporated into the formal province. Indeed, they inflicted serious tactical defeats on Roman forces, and even the construction of forts in their territory was a risky enterprise. They continued to fight on for another quarter of a century.

What had gone wrong? The answer surely lies in Scapula's approach to defeating the tribes of Wales. It was a strategy and mode of operations that was all about conquest rather than sustained occupation. Scapula's army, from the evidence of the forts and fortresses that can be dated to the late 40s and early 50s, was to operate in large multi-role task forces built around the legionary heavy infantry, supported by auxiliary infantry and cavalry. We can see this in the large number of campaign bases, seven across the West Midlands and North and South Wales. Even the new home base of *Legio XX* at Gloucester Kingsholm was only 10 hectares in size, enough for just half the legion and possibly an attached cavalry *ala* (Figure 2.13).

This approach of using overwhelming force was no doubt conditioned by the effectiveness of the Silures in taking on and defeating Roman detachments. It meant that in any pitched engagement, the Romans could be reasonably certain of victory, although even then, as Tacitus reports, serious defeats could happen. These immensely strong task forces were, however, of little use in consolidating the Roman hold on territory and in occupying hostile lands. As soon as the Roman task force had passed through their valleys, the Silures and Ordovices could emerge again, probably more determined than ever to oppose Rome if a scorched-earth policy had been followed by the occupiers.

In this, the Roman Army of the late AD 40s was little different from other, more technologically advanced states encountering determined opposition in their homelands: there are many examples from history, whether nineteenth-century colonial occupiers like the French in Morocco and the British on the North-West Frontier of India, the French and US in twentieth-century Vietnam or more recently the Russians and the US-led coalition successively in Afghanistan.

The tribes of Wales were challenging for the Roman Army to deal with because, unlike organized Greek and Eastern kingdoms – and indeed the more developed tribes of the majority of Gaul and Spain and the south-east of Britain – there was simply not much to get hold of and 'no throat to choke'. There were no *oppida* (nascent Iron Age towns) in Wales, as there had been at Colchester, Silchester and St Albans. A largely pastoral society could move its possessions out of harm's way on the hoof. There was no elite eager for the comforts and luxuries of Mediterranean civilization, and no monetary economy of any kind. The Romans were offering, at best, the prospect of forced 'taxation in kind' of animals and foodstuffs, and at worst, settlement burning and enslavement for anyone who offered any resistance – or even appeared to do so.

How the Roman arrival was experienced, what was offered and what was sought, was very different for the Silures and Ordovices and their leaders compared to the collaborators Kings Cogidubnus and Prasutagus and Queen Cartimandua and their followers. It is fascinating to note that Caractacus came from as exalted and as materially developed a background as the collaborators, but chose the path of resistance. For some there was a real choice, and possibly the speech of Caractacus at the start of this chapter is not so far-fetched a representation of his views. As we have seen, this negative view of the impact of Roman civilization was shared by Tacitus, who put those words into the voice of Caractacus and those attributed to Calgacus on the eve of Mons Graupius in AD 83:

> These plunderers of the world, after exhausting the land by their devastation, are rifling the ocean, stimulated by avarice, if their enemy be rich; by ambition, if poor; unsatiated by the East and by the West: the only people who behold wealth and poverty with equal avidity. To ravage, to slaughter, to usurp under false titles they call empire; and where they make a desert, they call it peace. (Tacitus, *Agricola* 29–32)

Chapter 3

Failed Conquest in Wales Becomes Containment under Gallus

A quarter century of fruitless struggle

The Emperor on hearing of the death of his representative [Scapula] appointed Aulus Didius [Gallus] in his place, that the province might not be left without a governor. Didius, though quickly arrived, found matters far from prosperous, for the legion under the command of Manlius Valens had meanwhile been defeated, and the disaster had been exaggerated by the enemy to alarm the new general, while he again magnified it, that he might win the more glory by quelling the movement or have a fairer excuse if it lasted. This loss too had been inflicted on us by the Silures, and they were scouring the country far and wide until Didius hurried up and dispersed them… For Didius burdened with years and covered with honours, was content with acting through his officers and merely holding back the enemy. (Tacitus, *Annals* 12.40)

Aulus Didius, the Emperor's legate, had merely retained our existing possessions, and his successor Veranius, after having ravaged the Silures in some trifling raids, was prevented by death from extending the war. (Tacitus, *Annals* 14.29)

Fort building programme of Didius Gallus 52–57 – a policy of containment

Gallus gets a poor press from Tacitus. The new governor had, however, inherited a difficult situation from Scapula, who died in office, exhausted by the conflict with Caractacus and the British tribes. The Silures were in revolt and had defeated foraging and construction parties – and even a legionary detachment – before his arrival, an event so significant as to be noted by Tacitus.

In addition to the Silures, Gallus was having trouble with the Brigantes, where the pro-Roman Queen Cartimandua was challenged by her anti-Roman husband Venutius. This required the dispatching of Roman troops on at least two occasions to preserve her collaborationist regime and stabilize the northern limits of the province. This will have occupied the first two years of Gallus' governorship, together with campaigning on the 'Welsh Front' to restore the situation.

In AD 54, Emperor Claudius was in all probability murdered by his wife Agrippina, and her son Nero gained the imperial purple. The new province of *Britannia* – troublesome and costly in terms of military resources – was Claudius' imperial legacy, and it is more than possible that Nero and his advisers in the new regime contemplated abandoning the project. After all, now more than a decade into the project, Rome's grip on the west and north of *Britannia* was still tenuous, while the tribes supposedly defeated alongside Caractacus were patently very capable of inflicting defeats on the Roman occupying forces. Was Claudius' vanity project still worth the cost and effort?

The orders from Rome were probably to refrain from further profitless military adventures in the Welsh mountains and hills; and this was therefore the context of Gallus' fort-building programme of containment in the mid-50s.

Gallus' line of forts in the Marches and South Wales

How to find Gallus' forts? This is not easy, as the dating of forts from this period is far from secure, since mid-first-century forts often underlie later forts, like Chester and Cardiff, or have not been excavated, such as Whitchurch or Jay Lane. Consequently, the process followed here has been to list the forts built (or possibly built) in the 50s and to plot them on the map of Wales and the Marches (Figures 3.2). There are self-evident problems here with circularity of argument and confirmation bias, but this approach gives us at the very least an interesting hypothesis that future archaeological investigation can challenge (Figure 3.6).

The anchors of Gallus' containment strategy were the two new legionary fortresses he built in the 50s at Wroxeter and Usk. *Legio XIV Gemina* moved forward from its campaign base in Mancetter along Watling Street to Wroxeter. This was a carefully considered strategic position which dominated and protected the Cornovii, and from where the legion could threaten intervention with the Ordovices by marching further up the Upper Severn and Vyrnwy Valleys. From here, the legion could also move north into the Cheshire Plain and south into the Marches.

Legio XX moved its base from Gloucester Kingsholm, which seems to have been occupied by auxiliary units in the meantime, to a highly aggressive position in the heart of east Silurian territory at Usk on the River Usk (Figure 3.4). The message could not have been clearer that the Roman Army was here to stay inside Silures territory. From Usk, the legion could march straight up the River Usk into the hills, where resistance perhaps continued. It is also possible that this positioning was to protect the Silures of the coastal plain, who had much to lose from Roman campaigns and may have partially reconciled themselves to Roman occupation. The positioning of forts in the second century suggests that the uplands still required garrisons even when the *civitas* of the Silures had been established.

Taking the legionary fortresses as the anchors and plotting the forts between them, and then extending north and south, we can see a chain of forts likely to have been founded by Gallus. In the north, an early fort beneath the later legionary fortress at Chester has long been suspected. The same is true for the intermediate fort at Whitchurch on the road south to Wroxeter. There is a road between Wroxeter and Usk which follows the foothills of the Welsh mountains; heading south of the new legionary fortress, there are three candidate forts at Stretford Bridge, Jay Lane and Hindwell Farm, which run broadly along the presumed western boundaries of the Cornovii and Dobunni. At the crossroads of our north–south road and the east–west road running from Gloucester Kingsholm up to the valley of the River Wye we do not find a fort, but the converted hillfort of Credenhill, which has been interpreted as a supply base. The road from Gloucester then heads west into the Wye Valley to a forward position at Clifford II, of which more below. Heading south, we find another large fort at Castlefield Farm. A further 19km south there is what looks like a massive early fort at Monmouth, almost 12 hectares in size. Then we have the Usk fortress itself of 20 hectares, and south of there the road leads to Cardiff, where another massive fort is suspected, this time possibly covering 11 hectares (Burnham and Davies, 2010, p.42).

What we have here is a 222km road with fortresses and forts along its length at an average spacing of 25km. There are three sections:

- a lightly held northern extension to the Irish Sea at Chester along the border between the Cornovii and Deceangli;
- a central section along the western borders of the Ordovices and Dobunni with some large (at least by later standards) forts;
- a southern section held by a major force detaching the eastern Silures and the Silures of the South Wales coast from their brethren in the South Wales valleys.

A particular characteristic of the strategy adopted by Gallus is the forward elements of forts and fortresses that project force ahead of the main north–south road line into the interior of the uplands. There appear to be five of these:

1. In the north there is a very large fort of 6 hectares built as a successor to Scapula's campaign base at Rhyn Park, at the point where the River Dee turns west into the Welsh mountains (Burnham and Davies, 2010, p.280). This is located to continue the domination of the Deceangli and protect supplies of silver and lead from the mines here (Figure 3.1). We have lead pigs from these mines, albeit from twenty-five years later stamped with the name of the then governor, Agricola.

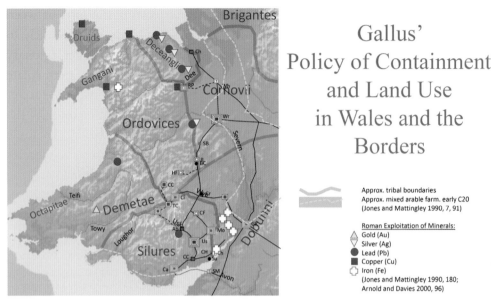

Fig 3.1. Although Gallus' policy looks like timidity in the extreme, if the forts at Rhyn Park and Usk were occupied by the Roman Army, then much of the mineral wealth known to the Romans was inside the temporary frontier and could be exploited: note the lead and silver of the Clywdian Range and the iron of the Forest of Dean. The largest fortresses and forts are shown.

2. There is a large fort at Hindwell Farm some 24km west into the uplands from Jay Lane in the central sector (Burnham and Davies, 2010, p.248).

3. There are early campaign bases up the River Wye Valley, first at Clifford II, which was replaced around AD 55 by the 8-hectare campaign base at Clyro (Picture 2.2). From the campaign base at Clyro there were two routes: one led north-west even further up the Wye to Colwyn Castle, where there is another (probably Neronian) fort (Frere, 2004). The other route leads south-west through a newly discovered fort at Three Cocks and then over the hills to link up with the River Usk Valley at Cefn-Brynich – both large forts (Davies and Driver, 2015, p.267). This network of forts and roads would be well positioned for patrolling up and down the Wye and Usk Valley. Further, the River Wye may have been the southern extent of the Ordovices, so this could have been an important strategic objective containing people and arms from the Silures moving northwards.

4. Further south on the River Usk north-west of Usk fortress itself there is an early fort at Abergavenny, providing a forward base for punitive expeditions into the Silurian uplands. One of the most exciting discoveries of recent years has been the discovery of the early fort at Cefn-Brynich even further up the River Usk (Davies and Driver, 2015, p.267).

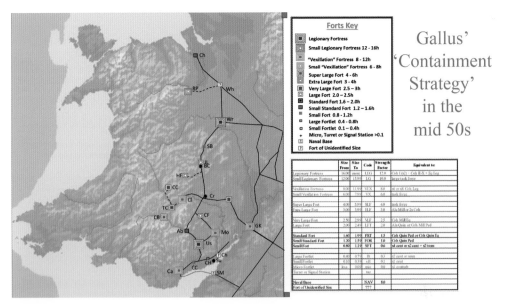

Fig 3.2. Here the forts from the database are plotted onto the physical geography of Wales and the Marches.

5. Finally, along the south coast there is a campaign base at Cardiff dominating the fertile Vale of Glamorgan and the Silures along the coast. Other recent discoveries include a line of forts stretching down the Welsh side of the Severn estuary from Gloucester, through a strongly presumed fort at Chepstow (where Claudian coins have been found) to a fortlet at Carrow Hill close to the future site of Caerwent, and a 1-hectare fort at Coed-y-Caerau overlooking the River Usk near Caerleon (Driver *et. al.*, 2020, p.117).

Typology of Gallus' containment

Gallus had much else to deal with in his newly conquered and still only tenuously pacified province, with its patchwork of new native states, clients, allies, hostile tribes, a new colony and a military zone. The well-practised train of tax collectors, money lenders and traders that followed the Roman Army's expansion was no doubt changing life in the 'wild west' towns with trading posts growing up across the south and east of *Britannia*. The threat and opportunity of the new world would have been dramatic and life-changing for many.

Gallus determined on a policy of containment (Figure 3.3.) This required the deployment of two legions, with two legionary fortresses founded as anchors. The first was at Wroxeter in the middle Severn Valley, where the *Legio XIV* watched the Ordovices and protected, and also supervised, the Cornovii. The second fortress

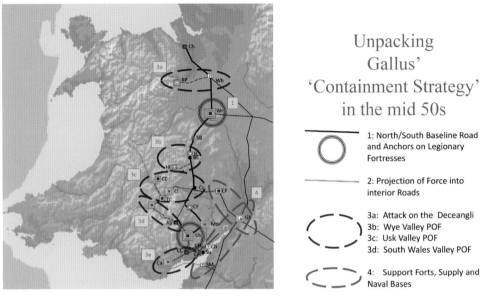

Unpacking
Gallus'
'Containment Strategy'
in the mid 50s

1: North/South Baseline Road
and Anchors on Legionary
Fortresses

2: Projection of Force into
interior Roads

3a: Attack on the Deceangli
3b: Wye Valley POF
3c: Usk Valley POF
3d: South Wales Valley POF

4: Support Forts, Supply and
Naval Bases

Fig 3.3. Gallus' containment strategy unpacked into its strategic component parts.

demonstrates that this was not a defensive strategy: this was still about expanding the empire's reach, but now in a considered and achievable way. Gallus moved the *Legio XX* forward from Gloucester Kingsholm to Usk in the valley of the River Usk. A fort was positioned further up the valley of the Usk at Abergavenny. Gallus also placed a campaign base in Cardiff. Together, these large bases 'bit off' a substantial chunk of the best Silures territory around the lower Usk and along the South Wales coast in the Vale of Glamorgan (Figure 3.5).

In the north, Gallus had continued Scapula's supervision of the Deceangli and the mining operations with a smaller but still substantial installation at Rhyn Park, together with a probable (but not proven) fort at the strategic position of Chester on the River Dee – to control the Lower Dee Valley and to supervise communications between Wales and northern England, which had been Caractacus' escape route in the AD 40s.

Finally, there is a large fort forward of the north–south road at Hindwell Farm which feels anomalous and not part of any wider system – perhaps it was for keeping an eye on the southern Ordovices or a local threat.

Vital statistics of Gallus' conquest policy for Wales and the Marches

Standing back and taking the strategic view generated by our database, we can see that the forces committed by Gallus were still substantial to contain the tribes of Wales and the Marches, amounting to maybe two-thirds what Scapula had

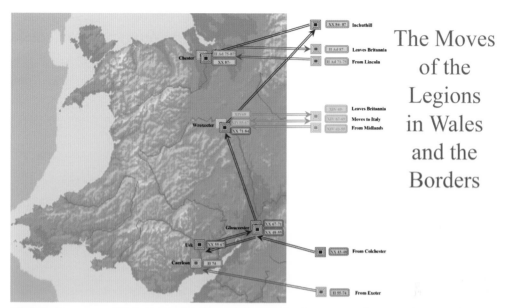

Fig 3.4. Summary of the moves of the legions during the first century. Most moves and the broad dates are secure, but the sequence and occupation of the two Gloucester legionary fortresses, Usk and Wroxeter are not definite to exact years.

deployed: two legions with their accompanying auxiliaries, some 23,000 men and fortresses and forts, amounting to about seventy Strength Factors (Figure 3.8).

The bulk of these troops were committed to the north–south baseline road that ran for over 200km from Chester through Wroxeter to Usk. There were projections of force in front of the baseline, with major concentrations – probably still consisting of combined detached legionary cohorts and auxiliaries – at Rhyn Park and Cardiff and at the forward forts at Hindwell Farm and Abergavenny. The ratio of force on the baseline road to forward forces, calculated by Strength Factors, was 4:3.

The spacing of the installations was very much as we would expect, being the normal day's march of between 23 and 28km. Perhaps the most interesting element in Gallus' system was in the south. The history of the fortress at Gloucester Kingsholm is not well understood; the move forward to Usk by *Legio XX* in the mid-50s is on the face of it extraordinary, however, given that the new fortress on the Severn had only been in existence for barely five years. This starts to make sense when we observe that at 10 hectares it was sub-scale for a full legion and that half the legion was posted elsewhere, probably in the Wye Valley. What happened to the Kingsholm fortress between the mid-50s, when *Legio XX* moved to Usk, and the construction of the new full-scale fortress at Gloucester around 67? A logical hypothesis is that it initially served as the HQ while Usk was built in hostile territory; two years is usually seen as the time required. After that it could have

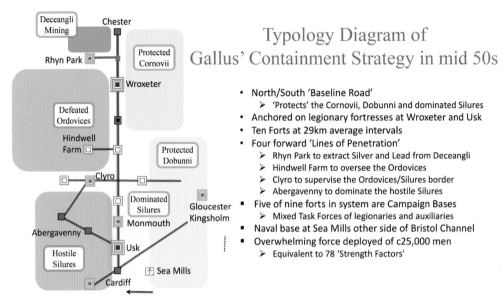

Typology Diagram of Gallus' Containment Strategy in mid 50s

- North/South 'Baseline Road'
  - ➢ 'Protects' the Cornovii, Dobunni and dominated Silures
- Anchored on legionary fortresses at Wroxeter and Usk
- Ten Forts at 29km average intervals
- Four forward 'Lines of Penetration'
  - ➢ Rhyn Park to extract Silver and Lead from Deceangli
  - ➢ Hindwell Farm to oversee the Ordovices
  - ➢ Clyro to supervise the Ordovices/Silures border
  - ➢ Abergavenny to dominate the hostile Silures
- Five of nine forts in system are Campaign Bases
  - ➢ Mixed Task Forces of legionaries and auxiliaries
- Naval base at Sea Mills other side of Bristol Channel
- Overwhelming force deployed of c25,000 men
  - ➢ Equivalent to 78 'Strength Factors'

Fig 3.5. The standard typology diagram produced for Gallus' time as governor. The importance of the Wroxeter–Usk baseline and its extension north to the Dee and south to the Bristol Channel is clearly visible.

become the supply base for the *Legio XX* battle group on the South Wales Front. From Gloucester, the *Legio XX* could support its forces on the upper Usk, at Usk itself, and then down the Severn estuary at the new campaign base at Cardiff. Operations on the south coast would have been supported by the Roman Navy operating out of its bases in the Bristol Channel.

Defensive frontier or stop line?

What Gallus constructed here was a patrolled north–south road with outpost forts forward into enemy territory – a concept familiar from many periods and places in Roman military history. Was this a frontier? Certainly not in the terms that we think of a frontier, like Hadrian's Wall or the Upper German *Limes*. The context was that Roman forces in Britain had suffered some significant defeats inflicted by the Silures, and enthusiasm for further – costly in every sense – British conquests had greatly dimmed in Rome with the change of regime to Nero.

Debates over whether a road line is or is not a frontier miss the point. In hostile territory, the Roman Army protected its lateral lines of communication with regularly spaced forts. This enabled supplies, reinforcements and orders to flow in one direction, and submission of returns to the governor's staff to travel safely in the other, with overnight protection provided by the forts along the way. These strategic roads would have been regularly patrolled. When the army was conquering new

Gallus' Containment Strategy in the mid AD50s Fortresses and Forts

Camp-aign	System	Purpose	Desription	Id	Name	Phase	Roman Name	Size Ha	Size Code	Strength Factor	First Unit	Approx Manpower	Unit if Known	Build Code	Start Date	End Date	Distance. RM	IM	Km
GALLUS CONTAINMENT SYSTEM WALES & MARCHES																			
GAL	N/S	BASE	CONTAIN	1	Chester	1	Deva	1.6	FRT	1.5		500		Gal	55	71	0.0	0.0	0.0
GAL	N/S	BASE	CONTAIN	2	Whitchurch	1	Mediolanum	1.6	FRT	1.5		500		Gal	55	??	21.7	20.5	33.0
GAL	N/S	BASE	CONTAIN	3	Wroxeter	2		16.0	LEG	12.0		5,000		Gal	55		25.0	23.6	38.0
GAL	N/S	BASE	CONTAIN	4	Stretford Bridge			1.5	FOR	1.0		500		Gal	55		23.0	21.7	35.0
GAL	N/S	BASE	CONTAIN	5	Jay Lane			2.2	LFT	2.0	AO	500		Gal	55	E Flav	7.9	7.5	12.0
GAL	N/S	BASE	CONTAIN	6	Credenhill			na	sup			na	hillfort supply base?				24.3	23.0	37.0
GAL	N/S	BASE	CONTAIN	7	Castlefield Farm	1		2.3	LFT	2.0		500		Gal	55		18.4	17.4	28.0
GAL	N/S	BASE	CONTAIN	8	Monmouth	1	Blestium	11.9	VEX	8.0		2,000		Gal	55		12.5	11.8	19.0
GAL	N/S	BASE	CONTAIN	9	Usk	1	Burrium	19.5	LEG	12.0		5,000		Gall	55		13.2	12.4	20.0
Total Gallus Baseline										40.0		14,500					146.1	137.9	222.0
GAL		POF	METAL	2.1	Rhyn Park	2		6.0	VX	6.0		2,000		Gal	55		17.8	16.8	27.0
GAL		POF	CONTAIN	5.1	Hindwell Farm			2.3	LFT	2.0		500		Gal	55		15.8	14.9	24.0
GAL		POF	WYE	6.1	Clyro	3		8.0	VEX	8.0		2,000		Gal	55		18.4	17.4	28.0
GAL		POF	WYE	6.11	Colwyn Castle	1		2.8	VLF	2.5		500		Gal	55		11.2	10.6	17.0
GAL		POF	WYE/USK	6.1	Clyro	3		8.0	VEX	8.0		2,000		Gal	55		18.4	17.4	28.0
GAL		POF	WYE/USK	6.2	Three Cocks (Gwernyfed)	1		2.5	VLF	2.5		500		Gal	55		5.4	5.1	8.2
GAL		POF	WYE/USK	6.4	Cefn-Brynich	1		5.5	SLF	4.0		1,500		Gal	55		11.8	11.2	18.0
GAL		POF	USK	9.1	Abergavenny	1	Gobannium	1.3	FOR	1.0		500		Gal	55		11.8	11.2	18.0
GAL		POF	USK	9.2	Cefn-Brynich	1		5.5	SLF	4.0		1,500		Gal	55				
Total Forward Forts										26.0		7500.0					344.2	325.1	523.2
GAL		LOC	SUP	1	Gloucester Kingsholm	2		10.0	sup?	0.0								0.0	0.0	0.0
GAL		LOC	SUP		Chepstow			1.6	FRT	1.5		500		Gal	55		31.6	29.8	48.0
GAL		POF	CONTAIN	3	Carrow Hill	1		0.2	1ft	0.3		160					5.7	5.4	8.7
GAL		POF	CONTAIN	4	Coed-y-Caerau (nr Caerleon)	1		1.0	SFT	0.6		500					5.9	5.6	9.0
GAL		POF	CONTAIN	5	Cardiff	1		10.5	VEX	8.0		2,000		Gall	55		21.7	20.5	33.0
Total Severn Estuary and South Coast Forts										10.4		3,160					64.9	61.3	98.7
GAL		LOC	SUP	1	Gloucester Kingsholm	2		10.0	sup?	0.0								0.0	0.0	0.0
GAL		LOC	SUP	2	Canon Frome	1		1.8	VLF	2.5		500		Gal	55		23.7	22.4	36.0
GAL	SEV	LOC	SUP	1	Sea Mills				NAV			500		Gal	55				
Total Support Forts										2.5		500					22.4	22.4	36.0
TOTAL: GALLUS' CONTAINMENT SYSTEM										78.9		25,660					577.6	546.7	879.9

Fig 3.6. An extract from the database in relation to Gallus' campaigns, with vital statistics for the fortresses and forts likely to have been occupied.

territory, these military roads would have pointed into the hostile lands as Lines of Penetration (LOPs). Here we have a lateral route acting as the baseline for future campaigns: it is worthy of note that the two legions were not held back but were positioned well and truly in the front line.

This was a policy of forward 'containment', as Tacitus effectively admits, although contemporaries would have seen it as merely a temporary pause in the advancement of the borders of the empire.

In the same way that the roads leading up to the 'front' would be regularly patrolled, and messengers and convoys of supplies would be protected, Gallus' containment baseline north–south road would be patrolled. This would reassure – and remind – those to the east in the province that they were under the 'protection' of Rome, and would warn the Silures and Ordovices to the west that there would be consequences to any attacks on Roman forts and those under Roman protection.

The four projections of force would have done exactly the same. In the north, the Deceangli were supervised to provide mineral tribute, and the mines themselves were perhaps worked by the army. In the centre, the interface between the Ordovices and the Silures was supervised. In the south, the upland Silures had the forts at Abergavenny and Cefn-Brynich 'in their face', while the coastal Silures were similarly supervised by the large new installation on the coastal plain at Cardiff.

Comparison of Scapula's and Gallus' strategies

The pie charts at Figure 3.7 use the Strength Factors in each of Scapula's and Gallus' campaigns and allocate them to a type of fort. We need to make allowance for the fact that we are aggregating the totals of all fortresses and forts through several years. This is very much the sum total of all forts occupied in Wales and the Marches in their respective governorships. What is striking, however, is how significant the concentration of forces is in both periods, with legions committed with forward bases in the front line and campaign bases projected into hostile territory.

This is very different from the dispersal of forces that we find under Frontinus and Agricola, where auxiliaries are used to cover the ground with dispersed but linked networks of forts across the whole of Wales or the Scottish Lowlands.

This gives an insight into the causes of failure of Scapula's approach and Gallus' success, given his probably lesser objectives. Roman legions would always beat the Welsh tribes in a head-on battle, even when the tribes chose the ground: Caractacus could vouch for that. Holding the territory after the battle was the challenge, and large campaign bases like that at Clyro could not dominate more than their immediate vicinity.

A different approach, with more auxiliaries and fewer legionaries, was needed to occupy the territory and stamp out opposition over a period of decades.

Assessment of Gallus' strategy

Gallus' five years of fort building did not at all fit Tacitus' ideal of an aggressive governor using Roman arms to extend the empire, regardless of how barren the land was. However, Gallus was probably obeying 'containment orders' from Nero and the imperial household in Rome. In doing this, Gallus was actually doing the sensible and rational thing after Scapula's aggressive and failed campaigns of conquest. In this interpretation, Gallus' policy of containment achieved:

- continued extraction of mineral wealth from the Deceangli;
- incorporation of the Cornovii into the directly controlled province;
- protection for the loyal Dobunni;
- containment of the recently defeated Ordovices;

Comparison of Scapula and Gallus' Unit Deployment by SFs

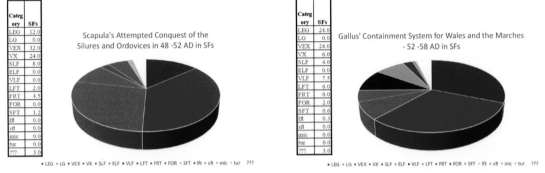

Fig 3.7. Statistical comparison of the types of fort deployed between Scapula in Wales in AD 48–52 and Gallus in 52–58. The preponderance of large installations in both campaigns is clear, with more concentration of force under Scapula.

- incorporation of key parts of the Silures' territory in the valley of the lower and middle Usk and the coastal Vale of Glamorgan;
- containment of the remaining Roman-hating Silures.

It would not be difficult for a member of Governor Gallus' staff – one not imbued with the 'expansion is the end in itself, at whatever cost' ethos of Roman imperialism advocated by Tacitus – to make a pragmatic argument that this gave Rome all that it really wanted or needed in Britain. Even in the traditional territory of the Silures, the Romans now held the best areas. Why should Rome expend blood and silver on conquering several thousand more pastoralists who had no desire to join the empire, were well-armed and could not afford to pay taxes anyway? Tacitus gave the following verdict on Gallus:

> Didius Gallus held onto the land won by his predecessor. He also advanced further into native territory, building just a few forts so that he might win the glory of having increased the area under his control. (Tacitus, *Agricola* 14)

We should see Tacitus' judgement of Gallus as 'harsh but fair' as to what happened – but quite wrong in terms of motivation and achievement. Although his was fundamentally a strategy of containment, Gallus could justifiably argue that the province now contained the leaders and tribes most susceptible to the Roman mission, as well as some of the mineral wealth of Wales.

The Vital Statistics of Gallus' Containment Policy in Wales and the Marches		No of Forts	Road Length	Nominal Garrison Manpower	Strength Factors	Ave Distance Forts
	Baseline Chester to Usk	2 LegFs + 1 CB 5 Forts +1 supply base	222 kms	10,000 leg + 4,500 aux = 14,500 men	24.0 Leg + 8.0 CB + 8.0 Forts = 40.0 SFs	25 kms
	Deceangli POF	1 CB	27 kms	2,000	= 6.0 CB SFs	27 kms
	Central POF (Hindwell)	1 Fort	24 kms	500	= 2.0 CB SFs	24 kms
	Wye Valley POF	1 CB + 2 Forts	71 kms	3,000	8.0 CB + 5.0 Fort = 13.0 SFs	23 kms
	Usk Valley POF	2 Forts	18 kms	2,000	= 5.0 SF	18 kms
	South Wales Coast POF	1 CB + 3 Forts	99 kms	3,160	= 10.4 SFs	20 kms
	Support Forts	1 Fort +1 supply base + 1 fleet base	36 kms	500	= 2.5 SFs	n.a.
	TOTALS	2 LegFs + 4 CBs + 14 Forts	507 kms	10,000 leg + 15,660 = 25,660 men	= 78.9 SFs	22 kms

Key:
LegF = Legionary Fortress with HQ
CB = Campaign Base
leg = legionaries with own legion
vex = legionary detachments
aux = auxiliary troops
Leg = SFs in home Legionary Fortress

Fig 3.8. The vital statistics of Gallus' containment strategy, showing for each component the total number of forts, road lengths, nominal manpower and Strength Factors.

A quarter-century of struggle in Wales; history repeating itself – failed conquest then containment again

> Veranius took over from Didius, but he died within a year. Suetonius Paulinus then enjoyed great success for two years. Conquering tribes and strengthening our garrisons. Confident in these achievements he advanced on Anglesey as this island was supplying the rebels. By such tactics, however, he exposed his rear to attack. (Tacitus, *Agricola* 14)

As noted, in AD 54, Claudius was assassinated, probably by his wife Agrippina in order to put his adopted son, Nero, on the imperial throne. The new regime, led by Seneca and the praetorian prefect Burrus, adopted a more vigorous policy than in the later years of Claudius, both in the East and in Britain. Gallus' successor from AD 57, Quintus Veranius, promised to 'lay the whole province at [the Emperor's] feet', and started with minor operations against the old enemy, the Silures (Burnham and Davies, 2010, p.38). However, he died in office before more could be achieved.

He was succeeded by Suetonius Paulinus, who seems to have had orders to complete the conquest of Wales. He is recorded as conducting two successful campaigns in 58 and 59, 'conquering tribes and strengthening garrisons', presumably defeating the Ordovices and Silures, and reconstructing and building forts in their territories. This led him in 60 to attack the Druids in Anglesey, who are generally presented as the source of the continuing resistance in Britain. Much has been said – and much more speculated – on the role of the Druids in Late Iron Age society. They were clearly important, and this importance seems to have spanned tribal boundaries. They were also implacable enemies of the Romans. Quite how they functioned as spiritual and religious leaders of the tribes is not clear. The question arises: if they were so important to the resistance to Rome, why did it take the Roman Army so long – some seventeen years – to make the connection between a continuing co-ordinated resistance to the occupation and the independence of a nest of sedition on the island of Anglesey? Was it simply too far away from the main Roman bases, and renewed war with the Ordovices something that could not be contemplated until the Silures had been cowed? And is this what Paulinus achieved in his successful first three years as governor?

The absence with Paulinus' expeditionary force of *Legio XIV* and its supporting auxiliaries in the far west, in Anglesey, gave Boudicca the opportunity to start her revolt. The extent that imperial exploitation was a major cause of the revolt is clearly stated by Dio:

An excuse for the war lay in the reclaiming of the money which Claudius had given to the leaders of the Britons. According to Decianus Catus, the

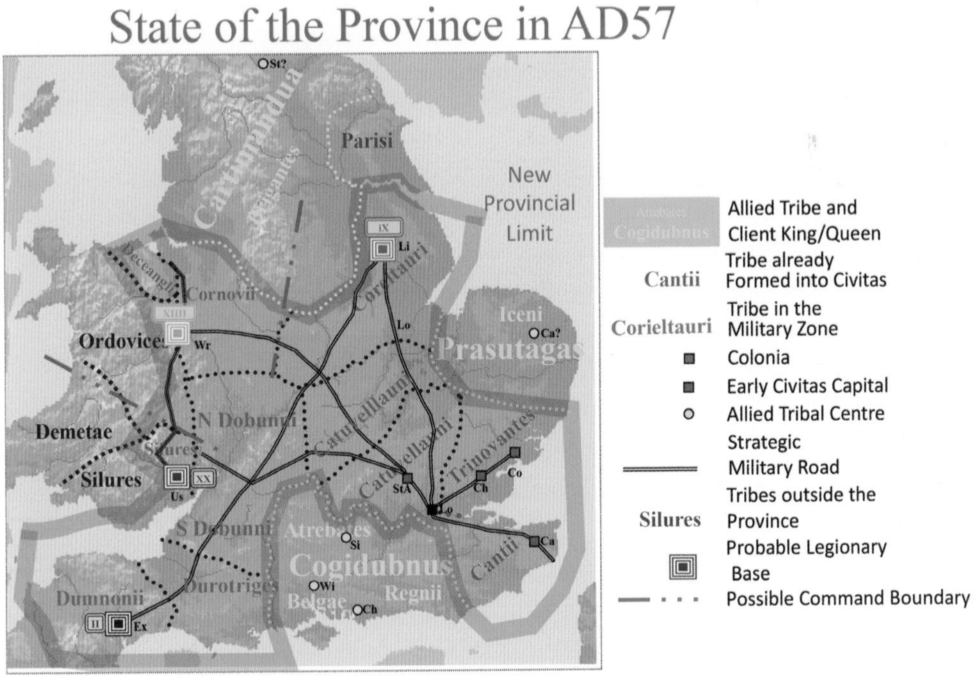

Fig 3.9. When Gallus left the province of *Britannia* it was stable, but apart from progress in the north-west, with the incorporation of the Cornovii, and in the south-west, with the Dumnonii, little had changed from when Scapula left in AD 48.

procurator of the island, that sum had to be given back. It was for this exercise that they rebelled, and because Seneca had lent them several million sesterces, even though they had not requested it, in the hope of making a large amount of interest, and had then recalled all the capital at once, exacting it with considerable harshness. (Dio, *Histories* lxii.2.1)

Although Paulinus had started the occupation of Wales with fort building, presumably in the interior, all was now abandoned when he had to break off from the conquest of the Druids to attempt to rescue London and the south-east of the province, and then stand and fight the pitched battle that finally defeated Boudicca in the West Midlands.

The aftermath of the defeat of Boudicca was the suppression of the rebel eastern tribes (at least the Iceni, Trinovantes and Catuvellauni) and the garrisoning of these areas by auxiliary units transferred back from the fronts in the west and the north. It was probably the case that some territory in Wales was given up at this stage in order to free troops for transfer to the east. We gather that Nero may have at this time contemplated giving up the gains of nearly two decades and even considered the withdrawal of Roman forces from Britain:

He was never driven by any desire or hope of increasing and extending the size of the empire, and he even considered withdrawing the army from Britain. He only gave up this plan out of fear that he might thus appear to detract from the glorious achievements of his father. (Suetonius, *Nero* XVIII)

Britain was not evacuated, however, even though a fully objective balance sheet of the costs so far versus the net gains could have come up with only one answer. It was probably a close call, but the loss of imperial prestige weighed heavily in the decision-making balance.

With the province wrecked and barely subdued, it was out of the question to resume a forward policy, so the next two governors – Petronius Turpilianus (62–63) and Trebellius Maximus (63–69) – pursued no more expansion. They had their hands more than full with a provincial population – following doubtless violent reprisals – still teetering on the edge of revolt, three significant towns needing to be rebuilt after being sacked, the province's economy in tatters and unable to pay its taxes, and a jittery army.

Indeed, it looks likely that as soon as normality was returning after six years of repression and rebuilding in the province, Nero – instead of resuming expansion – was pleased to be able to extract the *XIV Gemina* legion from the western front for his planned Parthian expedition. It is plain that conquering rather small areas of territory and small numbers of primitive if ferocious upland tribes had lost its

State of the Province in AD70

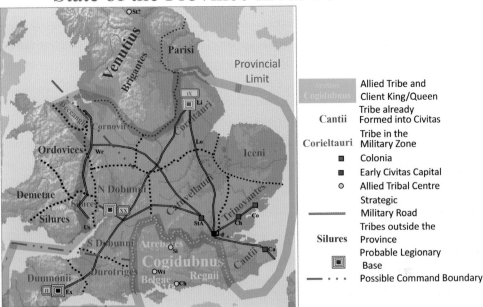

Fig 3.10. The province was in a sorry state in AD 70. Rome's long-standing ally, Queen Cartimandua, had been ejected from the Brigantian Confederation by her estranged husband, Venutius. There were only three legions now after the final departure of *Legio XIV Gemina* in 69. *Legio XX VV* had been pulled back to Gloucester from Usk, leaving the Silures to their own devices, and the legion itself was in a mutinous condition.

attraction in Rome: a relaunch of Nero's 'imperial brand' would be much better served by a Parthian triumph than leading some freshly washed barbarians in chains into the Forum. This applied, of course, whether you looked at the question in terms of imperial glory or costs versus benefits. Emperors still saw Britain as a source of glory and prestige. That they did so reflects the Roman view of Britain as literally 'the ends of the earth' – comparable to a 'moonshot' or a mission to Mars in today's terms – combined with a wish to follow in the footsteps of Julius Caesar and Claudius (Hoffmann, 2015, p.119).

The removal of *XIV Gemina* precipitated a serious reappraisal of the troop dispositions in Wales and the Marches. On the safe assumption that the legion departed with accompanying auxiliary units, at least a quarter of the Roman forces in Britain – some 10,000 men – left for Italy.

Legio XX (now, post-Boudicca, titled *Valeria Victrix*) moved out of Usk in 67, although the site was still occupied by a mixed force of a cavalry *ala* and a vexillation of legionaries (Burnham and Davies, 2010, p.187). There is debate as to where *Legio XX VV* went next. Here, the favoured option is that the legion returned to Gloucester, where it built a new full-sized fortress (dated to 68) south of its former HQ at Kingsholm (Burnham and Davies, 2010, p.42). The logic here is that Maximus was faced with a much-reduced British garrison, with *II Augusta* fully committed in the south-western peninsula based at Exeter and *IX Hispana* watching the restless Brigantian Confederation from Lincoln. He could not afford to leave his third legion deep inside what was – we can infer – still hostile or barely subdued territory at Usk. Consequently, it had to fall back to Gloucester.

The plan was that *XIV Gemina* would return to Wroxeter, which it duly did after the Civil War of AD 69. Maximus' career as governor was ended when the commander of *Legio XX VV*, Roscius Coelus, led a mutiny. Vettius Bolanus was appointed by Vitellius during the 'Year of the Four Emperors' and led *Legio XIV Gemina* back to Britain and its mothballed base at Wroxeter. Vitellius wanted *Legio XIV* out of Italy since it was still loyal to his defeated predecessor, Otho.

Venutius, Queen Cartimandua's estranged husband, now chose his moment well and staged a palace coup. Bolanus, clearly hamstrung by the shaky loyalty of his legions, could only send a snatch force of auxiliaries to rescue Cartimandua. Clearly, her restoration was out of the question, so weakened was the Roman leadership in Britain.

By the end of 69, Vespasian had defeated Vitellius to become emperor and set about restoring discipline and Roman rule in Britain and the west generally. The *XIV Gemina* was withdrawn again to help put down a revolt by Civilis on the Lower Rhine. Coelus was removed as commander of the potentially disloyal *Legio XX VV* in 70 and replaced by the Flavian loyalist Julius Agricola, of whom we will hear much more.

Bolanus was allowed to stay on until 71; the poet Statius speaks of him establishing forts and capturing trophies from a British king, so he was able to restore some of the ground lost since the departure of *XIV Gemina* in 67. The Flavian era in Britain really started with the arrival of Petilius Cerialis in 71, bringing with him – fresh from his victories in *Germania Inferior* against Civilis – *Legio II Adiutrix* with many auxiliary units, the former composed of Flavian loyalist marines of the Ravenna fleet and the latter freshly raised from tribal groups in *Belgica* and *Germania Inferior*. The fortunes of Roman *Britannia* were about to change.

Assessment of the years from Gallus to Cerialis in Wales and the Marches

Gallus had clearly built a strong foundation, at least along the western front; one which Paulinus, who was more than a competent general, was able to build upon. Yet however successfully matters were going in Wales, many of Rome's new subjects were not reconciled to their fate and had not understood how the 'new world order' worked for them.

So not only did the tribes of Wales defeat Scapula, but they kept Gallus at arm's length, made Veranius irrelevant and saw Paulinus stabbed in the back by Boudicca just as he was on the verge of finally defeating them. They were then in a position to ensure that Turpilianus and Maximus gave up all attempts at expansion in order to rebuild the province. Bolanus was reduced by mutinous legions and lack of manpower to a position of impotence. It is likely that the effective border of the empire retreated in the 60s from Gallus' forward defence. The Silures and Ordovices had defeated no less than nine Roman governors and the largest legionary garrison in the empire.

For the decade from AD 60–70, there would have been a *de facto* frontier of the empire running from North Wales to the Clywdian range down through the Marches, east of the Ordovices in the uplands and bisecting the Silures. It appears that the outposts on the Wye and Usk at Clyro and Abergavenny were still held. It is hard to know what relations were like in this frontier region, there being no demarcated border. Under one scenario trade flourished, with foodstuffs flowing in one direction and manufactured goods from the other. However, another scenario would envisage beleaguered forts, as in the American 'Wild West', with supply trains straining to get through. While we cannot be certain what the situation was, it was certainly an unstable and unsatisfactory position from Rome's perspective, which a group of *Britannia* specialists in the new regime determined to solve once and for all.

Chapter 4

Governor Julius Frontinus' Masterclass in Wales

The Flavian conquest, control and occupation – Overwhelming force designed to get the job finished

We are very fortunate that the Roman remains in the area now known as Wales have been intensively studied, excavated and written up. Furthermore, there have been three magisterial syntheses of Roman military history in the area, each entitled 'The Roman Frontier in Wales'. The first was created by the curator at the National Museum of Wales, V.E. Nash Williams (1954), the second by Michael G. Jarrett (1969) and the most recent by Barry Burnham and Jeffery Davis (2010). This latest version chronicles the explosion of knowledge resulting from aerial surveys and rescue excavations in the 1970s and 1980s, and from developer-funded archaeology in the 1990s and 2000s. As a result of their work, and the meticulous survey and dating of sites through pottery and other artefacts on which it is built, we are now able to make good judgements in reconstructing not just where and when Roman forts were built, but how they fit together with the Roman road network, and to describe the tribes they encountered. There are still large areas of ignorance and doubt, where more work is required, but with remarkably little degree of inference and filling-in of gaps, I believe a credible narrative can be constructed.

The sub-title of this chapter is of course anachronistic, since 'Wales' did not exist as a term until the sixth or seventh centuries, when *Cymry* emerged as a self-description by non-Anglo-Saxons. It was only much later that it became the name of a geographical entity. Nevertheless, in this book modern geographical usage has been adopted, along with modern descriptors for rivers, mountains and geographical areas.

This chapter applies the data-led analytical method (D-LAM) detailed in Chapter 8, deploying the tool-kit explained there to unpack the 'Roman way of war' in the first century and how it was applied by Governor Frontinus to the conquest of the tribes of the west. In this way we are able to reconstruct what was a textbook campaign by Frontinus.

Historical context of Frontinus' campaign

The Roman Army had been attempting to conquer the areas we now call Wales since Ostorius Scapula's campaigns in the mid-40s (see Chapter 2). Yet they had very obviously failed in their mission to complete this conquest. Scapula had fought the Silures in South Wales, where they were led by the exiled Caractacus. When Caractacus moved north to join the Ordovices, Scapula defeated him in pitched battle, whence he escaped – only to be handed over by Queen Cartimandua of the Brigantes for display at Claudius' Roman triumph (Tacitus, *Annals* xii.31–40).

The Silures resorted to guerrilla tactics and fought on with some success (Tacitus, *Annals* xii.39), wearing down the Romans in the field and Scapula mentally until he died in office. As we have seen, the next governor, Didius Gallus, adopted a policy of containment along the logical line broadly followed by the future Offa's Dyke. Despite promising to lay the whole province at Nero's feet, his successor as governor, Quintus Veranius, seems to have pursued only minor operations against the Silures.

The next big push against the tribes of Wales came under Suetonius Paulinus, who went all-out to complete the conquest in the west:

> Suetonius Paulinus enjoyed great success for two years, conquering tribes and strengthening our garrisons [probably in Wales]. (Tacitus, *Agricola* 14)

Boudicca seized the opportunity presented by Paulinus' absence with *Legio XX* and its accompanying auxiliaries – who were attempting to exterminate the Druids on Anglesey – by capturing and destroying Roman Camulodunum (Colchester), Londinium and Verulamium (St Albans). The warrior queen even came close to expelling the Romans from the island for good.

Given the post-Boudiccan revolt requirement for repair and reconstruction of the province, and the need for close supervision (and presumably punitive action) in the recently rebellious areas, it is not surprising that governors over the next decade – Petronius Turpilianus and Trebellius Maximus – adopted a care-and-maintenance policy along what had become the *de facto* western frontier of *Britannia*. This policy of caution and retrenchment was reinforced by the departure of *Legio XIV Gemina* for Nero's putative Eastern expedition in AD 66, which decisively removed any capacity for further offensive operations in the province. The emperor's advisers – effectively the Roman Army High Command in Rome – and the governor's staff in *Britannia* had, it seems, a clear rule of thumb: 'You need three legions just to hold Britain and four legions to mount offensive operations; with only two legions the province will be lost.'

We can now see that for almost thirty years, the four tribes of what we now call Wales – principally the Silures and Ordovices – had been able to maintain

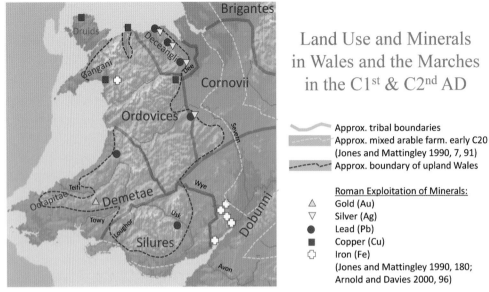

Fig 4.1. Wales is mostly uplands, with the best land around the coasts and in the river valleys. There were considerable mineral resources to be exploited, including the gold mines at Dolaucothi in Carmarthenshire.

their independence from the empire, despite defeats in pitched battle and multiple campaigns directed against them. This was an extraordinary achievement for a native population which probably totalled only some 330,000, equating to a fighting force of 66,000 able-bodied men across the entire area, assuming that fighting-age men accounted for 20 per cent of the total (Burnham and Davies, 2010, pp.135–36).

Vespasian's policy of total conquest of *Britannia*

In AD 69, Vespasian emerged victorious from the Civil War to become emperor. He was of course a specialist on *Britannia*, having led *II Augusta*, one of the legions in the original Claudian expeditionary force. The evidence we have strongly suggests that he decided to complete the conquest of the whole island of *Britannia*. We do not have direct evidence, but his actions as emperor speak clearly, as he posted three of his most capable and loyal governors to *Britannia*:

- Petilius Cerialis from 71–74;
- Julius Frontinus from 74–77;
- Julius Agricola from 77–83.

To support them, he also deployed his new *Legio II Adiutrix* to *Britannia*, bringing the legionary garrison up to the full complement of four and creating sufficient force for offensive operations. We can see from the evidence of later diplomas

State of the Province in AD70

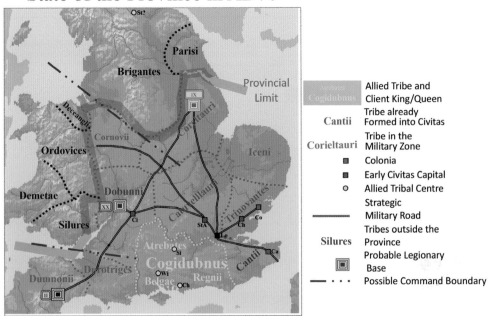

Fig 4.2. The province that Frontinus took over in AD 74 had been expanded by Cerialis to take over the Brigantes, or at least their major centres of population.

awarding Roman citizenship that the auxiliary units were probably also brought commensurately up to complement.

Although we do not have certainty on the size of the auxiliary component of the Roman Army deployed in the province – the *Exercitus Britannia* – we can work backwards from reasonable certainty about the size and composition of the army in Britain in *c.* AD 100 to what it might have been in 70. If the core task had been the conquest of Britain, the legionary and auxiliary force deployed in the late 60s had clearly not been up to the job, either in the basic numbers of legions, their supporting auxiliaries or indeed the army's loyalty to the regime.

Despite the challenges involved – and indeed its ultimate failure – the completion of the conquest of *Britannia* under the Flavians was both a reasonable and a logical imperial policy. Complete conquest and control had been achieved in Gaul, Spain and Illyricum under Augustus and Tiberius, where much larger territories had been comprehensively taken over and incorporated into the empire. This achievement had enabled the substantial and costly forces deployed in holding down those provinces to be moved to the Rhine and Danube frontiers, in the process freeing up legions for the conquest of *Britannia* and the annexation of other client kingdoms.

The Flavian loyalist Cerialis arrived as governor in *Britannia* in 71, fresh from suppressing Civilis' Batavian revolt. He bought with him *II Adiutrix*, together with

Legionary Deployments in Wales and the Marches

	65	70	75	80	85	90	95
Chester					X		
Wroxeter		C X		C C C C C			
Gloucester							
Usk							
Caerleon							

■ II Adiutrix   C = on campaign

■ XX Valeria Victrix   X = leaves Britannia

▨ XIV Gemina

▨ II Augusta

Fig 4.3. The deployment of the legions is critical to the understanding of Roman strategy. This diagram sets out the likely deployments on the Welsh Front from AD 65–100. The largest areas of uncertainty are the occupation of the second legionary fortress at Gloucester during the turmoil of the late 60s, and the length and extent of the occupation of Wroxeter in the 70s and 80s, when Agricola and his successor were campaigning in Scotland (see Chapter 5).

battle-hardened auxiliaries from the Rhine (Figure 4.4). He presumably had orders to finish off the conquest of this rebellious and troublesome province. He was also a British specialist, having been legate of *IX Hispana*, failing to save Camulodunum from Boudicca, losing his infantry and barely escaping with his cavalry in AD 60. For Cerialis, the north and the Brigantes came first, since they had expelled the long-term Roman client and supporter Queen Cartimandua in 69 and were now opposed to Rome (Tacitus, *Histories* III). As was to be expected of an experienced military commander, Cerialis seems to have done an excellent job, founding the new York legionary fortress and penetrating with his army over the Stainmore pass to Carlisle, where he built a fort in 72/73 (Caruana, 1992, p.104).

The next target was Wales, and this task fell to Julius Frontinus, who arrived in the province in 74. On the face of it, this was arguably a lesser and more contained challenge, as Wales probably had a smaller population than the north of Britain tackled previously by Cerialis and by Agricola in his later campaigns in Scotland. The army needed to campaign in the territory of the Silures and Ordovices and defeat any opposition in the field, and then to hold the territory, something that Frontinus' predecessors – Scapula, Gallus and Paulinus – had signally failed to achieve. Frontinus' campaign is described briefly by Tacitus as the prelude to his account of his hero Agricola:

The *Exercitus Britannia* after Vespasian's Reinforcement for Cerialis in AD71

Legiones, Alae & Cohortes

Unit	43?	Type	Cent	Turm	Remarks
Lego II Augusta	y	LEG	64	4	
Lego XX Valeria Victrix	y	LEG	64	4	
Lego IX Hispana Macedonica Triumphalis	y	LEG	64	4	
Lego XIV Gemina Martia Victrix	y	LEG	0	0	0 Left Britain during Civil War
Lego II Adiutrix	y	LEG	64	4	4 Arrived with Cerialis

Unit	43?	Type	Cent	Turm	Remarks
Ala Augusta Gallorum Proculeiana		AQ	0	16	
Ala Gallorum Agrippiana miniata		AQ	0	16	
Ala Gallorum Indiana	y?	AQ	0	16	
Ala Gallorum Petriana		AQ	0	16	16 Came over with Cerialis, drawn from other Provinces
Ala Gallorum Sebosiana		AQ	0	16	16 Came over with Cerialis, drawn from other Provinces
Ala Gallorum Picentiana		AQ	0	16	16 Came over with Cerialis, drawn from other Provinces
Ala Gallorum et Thracum Classiana		AQ	0	16	16 Came over with Cerialis, drawn from other Provinces
Ala I Pannoniorum Sabiniana		AQ	0	16	
Ala I Pannoniorum Tampiana		AQ	0	16	
Ala I Thracum	y	AQ	0	16	
Ala I Hispanorum Asturum	y	AQ	0	16	
Ala II Asturum		AQ	0	16	
Ala I Hispanorum Vettonum	y	AQ	0	16	16 Came over with Cerialis, drawn from other Provinces
Ala I Britannica		AQ	0	16	16 Raised from Gallic militia in 70, came over with Cerialis
Ala I Turgrorum		AQ	0	16	
15 Alae			0	240	

Unit	43?	Type	Cent	Turm	Remarks
Coh I Gallorum Eq	y	CQE	6	4	
Coh II Gallorum Eq	y	CQE	6	4	
Coh III Gallorum Eq	y	CQE	6	4	
Coh IV Gallorum Eq	y	CQE	6	4	
Coh V Gallorum Eq	y	CQE	6	4	
Coh I Pannoniorum Eq		CQE	6	4	
Coh I Delmatarum Eq	y?	CQE	6	4	
Coh II Delmatarum Eq	y?	CQE	6	4	
Coh I Thracum Eq		CQE			Withdrawn by Vitellius
Coh VI Thracum Eq		CQE			Withdrawn by Vitellius
Coh I Afrorum Eq		CQE	6	4	
Coh I Vardullorum Eq		CQE	6	4	
Coh I Aquitanorum Eq		CQE	6	4	
Coh I Batavorum Eq		CQE	6	4	
Coh II Britannorum Eq		CQE	6	4	
Coh III Britannorum Eq		CQE	6	4	
Coh I Hispanorum Eq		CQE	6	4	4 Came over with Cerialis, drawn from other Provinces
Coh I Vascorum Eq		CQE	6	4	4 Came over with Cerialis, drawn from other Provinces
Coh I Asturum Eq		CQE	6	4	4 Came over with Cerialis, drawn from other Provinces
Coh I Vangionum Eq		CQE	6	4	4 Raised from Gallic militia in 70, came over with Cerialis
Coh II Lingonum Eq		CQE	6	4	4 Raised from Gallic militia in 70, came over with Cerialis
Coh III Lingonum Eq		CQE	6	4	4 Raised from Gallic militia in 70, came over with Cerialis
Coh IV Lingonum Eq		CQE	6	4	4 Raised from Gallic militia in 70, came over with Cerialis
22 Cohortes Equitatae			132	88	

Unit	43?	Type	Cent	Turm	Remarks
Coh I Alpinorum		CQP	6	0	
Coh V Raetorum		CQP	6	0	
Coh IV Breucorum		CQP	6	0	
Coh IV Delmatarum	y?	CQP	6	0	
Coh VII Thracum	y?	CQP	6	0	
Coh I Hamiorum Sag		CQP	6	0	
Coh III Bracaraugustanorum		CQP	6	0	
Coh I Celtiberorum		CQP	6	0	
Coh I Baetasiorum		CQP	6	0	0 Raised from Gallic militia in 70, came over with Cerialis
Coh I Batavorum		CQP	6	0	0 Raised from Gallic militia in 70, came over with Cerialis
Coh II Batavorum		CQP	6	0	0 Raised from Gallic militia in 70, came over with Cerialis
Coh IV Batavorum		CQP	6	0	0 Raised from Gallic militia in 70, came over with Cerialis
Coh V Batavorum		CQP	6	0	0 Raised from Gallic militia in 70, came over with Cerialis
Coh VI Batavorum		CQP	6	0	0 Raised from Gallic militia in 70, came over with Cerialis
Coh VII Batavorum		CQP	6	0	0 Raised from Gallic militia in 70, came over with Cerialis
Coh VIII Batavorum		CQP	6	0	0 Raised from Gallic militia in 70, came over with Cerialis
Coh I Cugernorum		CQP	6	0	0 Raised from Gallic militia in 70, came over with Cerialis
Coh I Frisiavonum		CQP	6	0	0 Raised from Gallic militia in 70, came over with Cerialis
Coh I Menapiorum		CQP	6	0	0 Raised from Gallic militia in 70, came over with Cerialis
Coh I Morinorum et Cersiacorum		CQP	6	0	0 Raised from Gallic militia in 70, came over with Cerialis
Coh I Sunucorum		CQP	6	0	0 Raised from Gallic militia in 70, came over with Cerialis
Coh I Tungrorum		CQP	6	0	0 Raised from Gallic militia in 70, came over with Cerialis
Coh II Tungrorum		CQP	6	0	0 Raised from Gallic militia in 70, came over with Cerialis
Coh I Usiporum		CQP	6	0	0 Raised from Gallic militia in 70, came over with Cerialis
Coh I Nerviorum		CQP	6	0	0 Raised from Gallic militia in 70, came over with Cerialis
Coh II Nerviorum		CQP	6	0	0 Raised from Gallic militia in 70, came over with Cerialis
Coh III Nerviorum		CQP	6	0	0 Raised from Gallic militia in 70, came over with Cerialis
Coh IV Nerviorum		CQP	6	0	0 Raised from Gallic militia in 70, came over with Cerialis
Coh V Nerviorum		CQP	6	0	0 Raised from Gallic militia in 70, came over with Cerialis
Coh VI Nerviorum		CQP	6	0	0 Raised from Gallic militia in 70, came over with Cerialis
31 Cohortes Peditatae			186	0	

Fig. 4.4. Cerialis brought (as well as *II Adiutrix*) additional auxiliaries from the Lower Rhine; possibly as many as six *alae*, eight CQE (*Cobors Quingeneria Equitata*) and twenty-four CQP (*Cobors Quingenaria Peditata*). These were possibly reconstructed units from the Batavian Revolt, as well as newly raised units, as the list here suggests.

When however, Vespasian had restored to unity Britain as well as the rest of the [Roman] world, in the presence of great generals and renowned armies the enemy's hopes were crushed. They were at once panic-stricken by the attack of Petilius Cerialis on the state of the Brigantes, said to be the most prosperous in the entire province. There were many battles, some by no means bloodless, and his conquests, or at least his wars, embraced a large part of the territory of the Brigantes. Indeed, he would have altogether thrown into the shade the activity and renown of any other successor; but Julius Frontinus was equal to the burden, a great man as far as greatness was then possible, who subdued by his arms the powerful and warlike tribe of the Silures, surmounting the difficulties of the country as well as the valour of the enemy. (Tacitus, *Agricola* 17)

Julius Frontinus

Vespasian again chose the best man for this job. We do not know much about Frontinus' background: like Agricola, he seems to have been an equestrian from southern Gaul (*Gallia Narbonensis*). Vespasian, who himself was not out of the 'top drawer' of Roman senatorial society, attracted talented and patriotic 'new men'. Frontinus had with Cerialis helped to suppress the Rhineland revolt in 70 and received, he tells us, the surrender of 70,000 of the Lingones tribe (Frontinus, *Strategemata* IV.13.14). He was suffect consul before being appointed to succeed Cerialis in 74. After leaving Britain, he probably accompanied Domitian in Germany in 83 and attained the plum (and very profitable) appointment of Proconsul of Asia in 86.

In 97, Frontinus was appointed *Curator Aquarum* with the vital charge of managing the water supply for the city of Rome. He successfully made the switch from Domitian to the new Nerva/Trajan regime, was suffect consul for a second time and became *consul ordinarius* with Trajan himself in 100. Frontinus wrote two books that have survived. His *De Aquaeductu* is a report to the emperor on his management of the many aqueducts feeding Rome. Frontinus describes the sources, the flow rates and the quality of the water arriving in Rome. He is very concerned about the abstraction of water on the way to Rome and also the problem of drinking water being mixed with lower-grade water suitable only for flushing and irrigation. He sets out for his successors how the system should be maintained in good working order, showing considerable technical and management capability.

Frontinus was clearly a conscientious and systematic man, something of a first-century technocrat and someone who was trusted by four emperors, from Vespasian to Trajan. His second book, *Strategemata*, is a theoretical treatise on military science. It is a collection of examples of military stratagems from Greek and Roman history, and Frontinus draws on some of his own experiences in the field in Germany, but alas not in *Britannia*. One looks in vain for examples that relate to his campaigns in Wales: the warfare exemplified in his book is between ancient states and cities, with the set battles and sieges of the Mediterranean world. This feels a far cry from the guerrilla ambushes, storming of tribal hillforts and punitive burning of indigenous villages that Frontinus led in the Welsh hills, and with Domitian in the German forests. Nevertheless, as we shall see, Frontinus' campaign in Wales was a text-book example both of planning and execution. His writings clearly reflect his devotion to process and system. As he says at the outset of his *Strategemata* (I.1):

> Since I alone of those interested in military science have undertaken to reduce its rules to **system** [emphasis added] and since I seem to have fulfilled that purpose [in a work now sadly lost] I still feel under obligation, in order to complete the task I have begun, to summarise in convenient sketches the adroit operation of generals, which the Greeks embrace under the name of *stratagemata*.

Data-led analytical method (D-LAM) deployed

Unlike Agricola's conquest of what is now Scotland, we do not have a literary account of Frontinus' conquest of Wales, however contested. We must therefore rely on the archaeological record, which is, of course, hard to date precisely to a given year or even governorship. Fortunately, as noted above, the Roman forts of Wales have been studied intensively and brought together in the three successive syntheses. Careful dating of the excavations using pottery remains has enabled the dating and phasing of forts into broad periods such as 'Claudian', 'Neronian', 'early Flavian' and 'Flavian'. This dating, coupled with interpretation of the size and relationships of forts and roads, enables us to model and map the stages of Frontinus' conquest, control and occupation of Wales (Figure 4.9).

The Roman road network has also been traced: although this is both complex and largely impossible to date firmly, it provides valuable insights into how the forts worked as control networks.

Stages of the campaign

The terrain and the people of Wales were extremely well known to the Roman Army, given the previous three decades of unsuccessful campaigning, particularly against the Silures. Indeed, part of the Silures' lands had been occupied in Monmouthshire, with the legionary fortress at Usk, which still left the larger part of the tribal territory free. In the north, the Ordovices of Powys had received their share of attention, as the marching camps testify, but they were also still free. The Deceangli of the north-west, with their lead and silver mineral wealth, seem to have been 'protected' since Scapula's earlier campaign of 47, while the Demetae of Cardiganshire and Pembrokeshire remained untouched. As with all tribal groups on the edge of the Roman Empire, contact would have changed them. Trade and exchange would have occurred, yet the ever-present threat of Roman conquest may have also strengthened tribal loyalties and cultural resistance, even as Roman pots, weapons and luxury goods were traded. The Native American adoption of nineteenth-century American trade goods and weapons, even while resisting the soldiers and settlers of the westward expansion, provides a relevant parallel. We have in Wales the clearest evidence for what are now called discrepant identities, with the tribes of Wales repelling ever more violent attacks on them and resisting incorporation (Mattingly, 2006, p.520). Theirs was an experience and a culture very different from that of the people of the client King Cogidubnus (the Regni, Atrebates and Belgae) with their expanding towns in Chichester, Silchester and Winchester (and no Roman garrisons).

Frontinus took office in 74 and was (using the generally accepted dating) succeeded in late summer 77 by Agricola (Hanson, 1987, pp.44–45). This only provided him with partial campaigning seasons in 74 and again in 77, therefore he had at best only two full campaigning seasons in the field to complete his task.

Analysis of the forts in Wales with reasonably secure early Flavian dating suggests a four-stage process (the four 'C's), each leaving different archaeological traces:

- campaign phase (74 and 75): marching camps;
- conquest phase (75 and 76): building of extra-large forts;
- control phase (76–78): the tight network of forts and roads;
- consolidation phase (80–120): thinning-out of the fort garrisons and eventual creation of self-governing civilian *civitates* for the Silures and Demetae in the south (which is beyond the scope of this book).

The first **campaign phase** is the hardest to trace, since the task forces deployed by Frontinus would have penetrated the territories to be occupied, receiving the submission of prudent tribal groups while attacking those that held out.

The second **conquest phase** has left clear remains and can be traced in the extra-large forts (ELF) between 3 and 4 hectares in size. These first two stages can safely be attributed to Frontinus from 74–76.

The third **control phase** – based on dating of forts to the early Flavian period – consisted of a dense network of forts across the conquered territories. Based on Tacitus' narrative in his *Agricola*, Agricola's campaigns in Wales were explicitly limited to punishing the Ordovices in the late summer of AD 77, including another expedition to exterminate the Druids on Anglesey. Given the limited amount of time taken to move from campaign to conquest to control, however, we should credit Frontinus and his staff with the overall design of the control phase, but attribute the completion of the overall network of forts and roads to Agricola in 77–79. The forts of the north-west could have been Agricolan foundations, although still part of Frontinus' masterplan.

Phase 1: The campaign phase

Frontinus assembled overwhelming force for the final reckoning with the Silures and Ordovices. As with other campaigns of occupation, the Roman Army created a strong baseline to act as the jumping-off point for the invasion to ensure supply and facilitate lateral communications. Here the baseline ran north–south along the effective western border of the province. No less than three of the four legions in Britain were deployed along this baseline, with two new legionary fortresses built from scratch (Figures 4.5 and 4.6):

- A northern task force led by *II Adiutrix* and its accompanying auxiliary units. *II Adiutrix* had been raised for Vespasian in the Civil War from the sailors and marines of the Ravenna fleet and was sent with Cerialis to reinforce the British army of doubtful loyalty with reliable Flavian troops. It originally

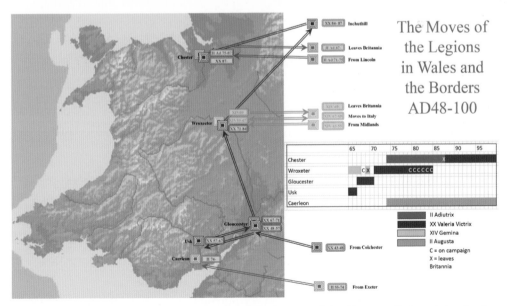

Fig 4.5. Reconstruction of the movements of the legions of the *Exercitus Britannia* in the first century. The dates and sites are still open to debate, especially around Wroxeter and Gloucester (M. Hassall, 2010, pp.51–67).

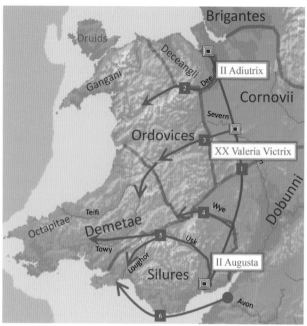

Frontinus Completes the
Conquest of Wales –
the Campaign Phase

Campaigns
AD74-75

1: Baseline
Chester/Wroxeter/Caerleon

2: Northern Force II Adiutrix
Chester >>> the Dee Valley

3: Central Force XX Val Vic
Wroxeter >>> Severn Valley

4: Wye
Buckton >>> Wye Valley

5: Southern Force II Augusta
Caerleon >>> Usk and Towy Valleys

6: Maritime Force
Sea Mills >>> Bristol Channel

Fig 4.6. The alignment of legionary fortresses with the likely Lines of Penetration (LOPs) into the Welsh uplands using the river valleys.

moved into the Lincoln fortress but was then moved forward by Frontinus to its strategic new fortress on the Dee estuary ready for the Wales campaign. Chester was brilliantly situated: from there, *II Adiutrix* was able to threaten the Ordovices up the Dee Valley and also, with the fleet, along the North Wales coast. It was also simultaneously able to dominate the Brigantian tribal groups west of the Pennines, protect the Cornovii of the Cheshire Plain and, when the time came, penetrate up the Lancastrian and Cumbrian coast with the fleet and dominate the northern Irish Sea (Figure 4.8). The marines of *II Adiutrix,* stationed at the fleet base in Chester, were therefore a fundamental part of the mission and a key part of Frontinus' plan. *II Adiutrix*'s symbols were naturally a dolphin and a sea-goat (*capricornus*).

- **A central task force led by *XX Valeria Victrix*** and accompanying auxiliary units. *Legio XX* had been pulled back from Usk to Gloucester in the late 60s in a retreat from Silurian territory. *XX VV* probably moved north into the Wroxeter fortress, which itself had finally been vacated in 69 by *XIV Gemina*'s final departure to fight in the Civil War (Hassell, 2000, p.61). Strategically, Wroxeter had since the mid-50s guarded the Severn Valley, the gateway to mid-Wales, both safeguarding the Cornovii inside the province and at the same time supervising the Ordovices.

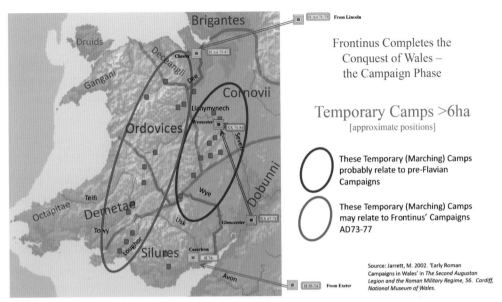

Frontinus Completes the
Conquest of Wales –
the Campaign Phase

Temporary Camps >6ha
[approximate positions]

These Temporary (Marching) Camps
probably relate to pre-Flavian
Campaigns

These Temporary (Marching) Camps
may relate to Frontinus' Campaigns
AD73-77

Source: Jarrett, M. 2002. 'Early Roman
Campaigns in Wales' in *The Second Augustan
Legion and the Roman Military Regime*, 56. Cardiff,
National Museum of Wales.

Fig 4.7. The sites of the larger (more than 6 hectares) marching camps. The more easterly sites probably relate to the campaigns of Scapula, Gallus and Paulinus, while the camps in the upland areas may date from Frontinus' conquest phase.

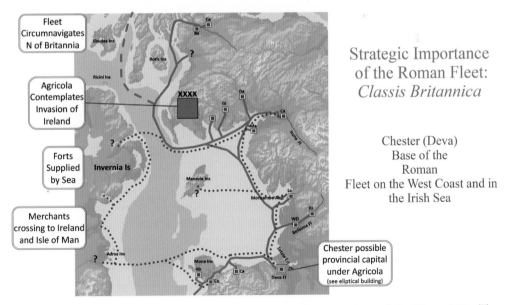

Strategic Importance
of the Roman Fleet:
Classis Britannica

Chester (Deva)
Base of the
Roman
Fleet on the West Coast and in
the Irish Sea

Fleet
Circumnavigates
N of Britannia

Agricola
Contemplates
Invasion of
Ireland

Forts
Supplied
by Sea

Merchants
crossing to Ireland
and Isle of Man

Chester possible
provincial capital
under Agricola
(see eliptical building)

Fig 4.8. The Roman fleet was a major strategic asset in the campaigns of the 70s and 80s. The choice of Chester as a legionary base, and also probably the seat of the governor's administration, was critical. From the Dee estuary, the fleet could dominate the North Wales coast and the coastal areas all the way up to the Scottish Western Isles.

- **A southern task force led by *II Augusta*** and its accompanying auxiliary units. *II Augusta* had been based at Exeter for two decades and had by now completed the pacification of the Dumnonian peninsula, so it could be moved forward to its new base at Caerleon on the lower River Usk. Caerleon was chosen rather than the earlier fortress site at Usk further up-river since Caerleon was in a better position for naval and supply access to the Bristol Channel and closer to the fertile coastal lands of the Silures in the Vale of Glamorgan. This forward placing of the legion was an unambiguous declaration to the Silures that they were now going to become part of the empire, not remain on the fringe. Frontinus was reversing the retreat from Usk and going onto the offensive.

The investment in two new legionary fortresses in forward positions could not have signalled a clearer commitment to the permanent conquest of all of Wales. On the assumption that all three legions were fully present for the campaign, this amounted to 15,000 men at nominal full strength. As a rule of thumb, each legionary would in this period have been accompanied by at least one auxiliary.

When an auxiliary soldier left the Roman Army after serving his twenty-five years, he received an inscribed bronze 'diploma' which proved his service record and his grant of citizenship. Very helpfully for Roman military historians, these diplomas list the units of all the soldiers receiving their honourable discharge (Roxan, 1978, 1985, 1994). Alas, we do not have diplomas from the army in Britain which list units for this period. Nevertheless, we do have them for 98–105, when there was a minimum of thirty-one auxiliary units stationed in the then two Chester and Caerleon commands covering Wales, the Scottish Borders and north-west England. This amounts to a theoretical manpower of 10,000 for the legions and 17,000 for the auxiliaries. It is likely, however, that the Wales garrison had been reduced in the intervening years, given Agricola's campaigns in the North and Scotland, and the transfer of units over the next three decades (*contra* Burnham and Davies, 2010, p.70). Allowing for realistic manning levels, the estimate for the garrison during Frontinus' campaigns with three legions and associated auxiliaries is 25,000–30,000 men. On top of this figure, we must add grooms, slaves and camp followers (Burnham and Davies, 2010, p.135). This is some 10 per cent of the entire empire-wide Roman Army of the period: it appears to be significantly larger than any of the forces which Scapula, Gallus, Cerialis or Agricola deployed in the field, and is probably only comparable with those assembled by Aulus Plautius in AD 43 for the invasion and with Septimius Severus in Scotland in 206–209 (see Chapter 5).

On the face of it, this appears to be enormous overkill, but it is important to remember that the Silures and Ordovices had successfully resisted Roman rule for three decades. Furthermore, 'overwhelming force' was central to the Roman

Army playbook: consider Tiberius in the Illyrian Revolt in AD 6–9 with five legions possibly reinforced by another five (Abdale, 2019); Cerialis against Civilis on the Lower Rhine in 70 with eight legions (Pollard and Berry, 2012, p.66); and Trajan's Dacian War of 101–102 with six full legions and four legionary vexillations (Rankov, 2009, p.168). When it mattered – and the chips were down – the Roman High Command could deploy massive crushing force against tribes who were seen as enemies or threats to the empire. Compared with these assemblages, Frontinus' Wales campaign is almost modest in size. His mission from Vespasian was to complete the conquest of Britain and, given the subjection of the Brigantes by Cerialis and the post-Boudiccan pacification of the province, he could afford to deploy three of his four legions and their accompanying auxiliaries in the final push in Wales.

The challenge that Frontinus faced in the campaign was an enemy which would not for a second time conveniently assemble in a hillfort to be slaughtered by superior Roman tactics and technology. He was facing tribes who were extremely well practised, after three decades of conflict with the Roman Army, in fighting guerrilla warfare. Their fighters knew how to melt into the landscape and were indistinguishable from the inhabitants of Wales, since that is what they were. Consequently, Frontinus' vast force did not advance into Wales in a single army group. Instead, as we have seen above, Frontinus broke the challenge down into different fronts, with each legion tackling a zone. Each zone was probably in its turn broken down into valleys and areas. Therefore, unlike Scotland, we do not find lines of very large (54 hectares) marching camps denoting the course of Frontinus' army in Wales.

Jarrett (2002, p.56) thought that marching camps of more than 6 hectares represent 'campaigning camps', on the grounds that these could hold a force of c.5,000, whereas smaller camps 'may reflect troop movements after [AD] 77'. The camps closer to what we now call the Welsh Borders probably relate to pre-Flavian campaigns from Scapula onwards, and indeed the camps in the interior may do so as well. However, since Frontinus was penetrating into the interior and westwards towards the watershed, then the camps along the upper river valleys of the Dee, Severn, Towy and Loughor are potential candidates for construction by Frontinus' task forces (Figure 4.7).

As noted, the baseline for the campaign was the road linking the three legionary bases at Chester, Wroxeter and Caerleon. The mode of operation would then have been to advance up the major river valleys – the Usk, Severn and Dee – into the interior of Wales and seek the submission of the peoples living there, while making the consequences of resistance very obvious. We should also expect that the fleet played its part along the south coast of Wales, probably operating out

Frontinus Completes the Conquest of Wales –
the Conquest Phase AD75-76
Data-Led Analytical Method [D-LAM]

Campaign	System	Purpose	Description	Id	Name	Phase	Roman Name	Size Ha	Size Code	Strength Factor	First Unit	Second Unit	Approx Manpower	Unit if Known	Build Code	Start Date	End Date	Build Material	Rampart	Buildings	Ditches	Gates	Annex	Controls	Distance RM	IM	Km
FRONTINUS' INVASION OF WALES																											
Frontinus' Invasion of Wales - Baseline																											
FRO	N/S	BASE	CONTROL	1.0	Chester	1	Chester	54.40	LEG	12.0	LEG		3,000	II Adiutrix	Fro	74									0.0	0.0	0.0
FRO	N/S	BASE	CONTROL	2.0	Whitchurch				FOR	2.0	LEG		500		Fro	?4?									22.4	21.1	34.0
FRO	N/S	BASE	CONTROL	3.0	Wroxeter			16.00	LEG	12.0	LEG		3,000	XX Valeria Victrix	???	66	79								25.7	24.2	39.0
FRO	N/S	BASE	CONTROL	4.0	Buckton	1		2.36	LFT	2.0	AQ?		500		Fro?	[80]	110								32.2	30.4	49.0
FRO	N/S	BASE	CONTROL	5.0	Wonnstow	1		1.47?	FOR	1.0	COH??	AQ???	500											46.1	43.5	70.0
FRO	N/S	BASE	CONQUER	6.0	Usk		Usk	???	ELF	3.0	COH??		1,000										Usk Valley	11.2	10.6	17.0
FRO	N/S	BASE	CONTROL	7.0	Caerleon	1	Caerleon	20.50	LEG	12.0	LEG		3,000	II Augusta	Fro	74								8.6	8.1	13.0
Total for Baseline										4.0			1,500											146.1	137.9	222.0
Frontinus' Invasion of Wales - Lines of Penetration																											
FRO	CLY	LOP	CONQUER	1.0	Chester	1	Chester	24.40	LEG	12.0	LEG		5,000	II Adiutrix	Fro	74								0.0	0.0	0.0
FRO	CLY	LOP	CONQUER	3.0	Rhyn Park	2		6.00	VX	6.0	COH??	AQ???	1,000											26.3	24.9	40.0
FRO	CLY	LOP	CONQUER	4.0	Llanfor	1		3.86	ELF	3.0	AQ	LEG COH +	1,000		Fro	74		Timber	Earth		Two	Straight	Supply Base?		30.9	29.2	47.0
																									57.2	54.1	87.0
FRO	SEV	LOP	CONQUER	1.0	Wroxeter	2		16.00	LEG	12.0	LEG		5,000	XX Valeria Victrix	Tre	66	79								0.0	0.0	0.0
FRO	SEV	LOP	CONQUER	2.0	Forden Gaer	1		3.25	ELF	3.0	COH or CQ?	AQ or CQ?	1,000		Fro	74		Timber	Earth		Three	Straight	None	Severn Valley	27.6	26.1	42.0
FRO	SEV	LOP	CONQUER	3.0	Caersws	1		3.90	ELF	3.0	COH or CQ?	AQ or CQ?	1,000		Fro	74		Timber	Earth		Three	Straight	One	Severn Valley	15.8	14.9	24.0
																									100.7	95.1	66.0
FRO	USK	LOP	CONQUER	1.0	Caerleon	1		17.80	LEG	12.0	LEG		5,000	II Augusta	Fro	74								Usk Valley	0.0	0.0	0.0
FRO	USK	LOP	CONQUER	2.0	Usk	2		???	ELF	3.0	COH??	AQ???	1,000											Usk Valley	8.6	8.1	13.0
FRO	USK	LOP	CONQUER	3.0	Abergavenny	2	Gobannium	1.32	FOR	1.0	CQ??		500		Tre	65-70	90-110						One	Usk Valley	11.8	11.2	18.0
FRO	USK	LOP	CONQUER	4.0	Brecon Gaer	1		3.14	ELF	3.0	AQ	CQ?	1,000		Fro	74		Timber	Turf/Clay		Two	Straight	None	Usk Valley	24.3	23.0	37.0
FRO	USK	LOP	CONQUER	5.0	Llandovery	1		3.00	ELF	3.0	COH or CQ?	AQ or CQ?	1,000		Fro	74	140	Timber	Earth		Three			Usk Valley	19.7	18.6	30.0
FRO	USK	LOP	CONQUER	6.0	Llandeilo	1		3.84	ELF	3.0	COH or CQ?	AQ or CQ?	1,000		Fro	74		Timber	Earth		Three?	Two	Surrounding	Heads of Usk and Towy	13.2	12.4	20.0
																									69.1	65.2	118.0
FRO	BRI	LOP	CONQUER	1.0	Sea Mills				Nav	4.0																	
FRO	BRI	LOP	CONQUER	2.0	Neath	1	Nidum	3.30	ELF	3.0	COH or CQ?	AQ or CQ?	1,000		Fro	75	85?	Timber	Earth								
Total for Lines of Penetration										71.0			24,500											227.0	214.4	271.0
TOTAL FOR FRONTINUS' INVASION OF WALES										75.0			26,000											373.0	352.3	493.0

Fig 4.9. Table from the database of Roman forts in Britain, showing the forts thought to be of early Flavian date in Wales. The forts from Frontinus' conquest phase are nearly all extra-large forts (ELF) of more than 3 hectares.

of the early naval base at Sea Mills on the Severn estuary and, potentially, a new base on the River Usk alongside the new fortress at Caerleon. Again, as under Scapula, the defeat of the enemy in the field was assured, but that was not now the real challenge: we can envisage the methodical and technical Governor Frontinus, unlike Scapula, designing a process to follow through systematically with conquest and control.

Phase 2: The conquest phase

The construction of two new legionary fortresses in forward positions proclaimed the determination of Frontinus and the Roman Army to get the job done this time.

We can see how Frontinus split his massive forces into battle groups to cover the key river valleys (Figure 4.11). There are a series of ELFs of between 3 and 4 hectares along the main Lines of Penetration (LOPs) along the river valleys identified as dating to the immediate conquest phase (Burnham and Davies, 2010, p.44).

The northern LOP up the River Dee: it is probable that the large Scapulan campaign base at Rhyn Park was reoccupied with another ELF at Llanfor, where the Dee enters Bala Lake (Figure 4.12). Together with the new legionary fortress being built at Chester, these forts dominated the lands of the Deceangli and the northern Ordovices.

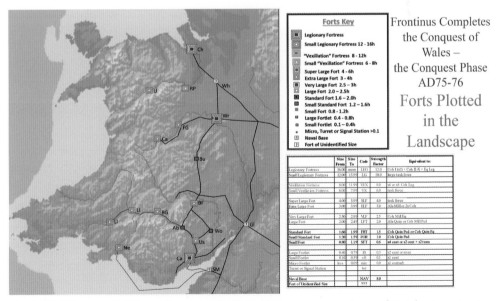

Fig 4.10. The remarkably uniform installations of the conquest phase of 3–4 hectares in size: ELFs situated deep up the major river valleys, projecting Roman force into the interior of Wales.

The central LOP up the River Severn: the principal line of penetration was the upper Severn Valley, with the route running west from Wroxeter to one ELF at Forden Gaer and another towards the Severn headwaters at Caersws, 3.25 hectares and 3.9 hectares respectively in size. This was aimed at the more southerly heartlands of the Ordovices.

The southern LOP up the River Usk: in the south, the line of penetration followed the River Usk up from the new legionary fortress at Caerleon to the former legionary site at Usk itself, which was still occupied by one or two auxiliary units. From there the route led up the Usk Valley to Abergavenny, with a fort of a more conventional 1.3 hectare size, and thence to a line of three ELFs at Brecon Gaer, Llandovery and Llandeilo. Brecon being in the Upper Usk Valley, the route then crossed the watershed into the valley of the Rivers Tywi and Towy. This LOP therefore effectively surrounded the Silures and crossed into the lands of the Demetae in modern Carmarthenshire.

The north–south baseline road: there may have been another new ELF constructed on this baseline at Blackbush Farm, although its dating and size are in doubt. This baseline was strategically placed close to the Upper Wye Valley, which may have formed the border between the Silures and Dobunni, and then further west where the Ordovices met the Demetae.

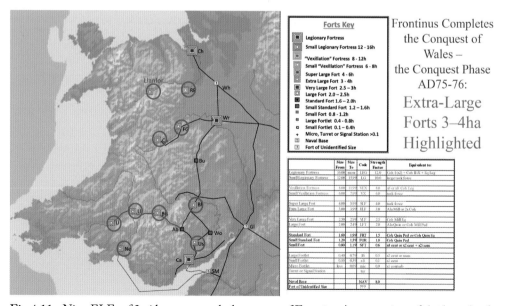

Fig 4.11. Nine ELFs of 3–4 hectares track the course of Frontinus' penetration of the heartlands of the Silures and Ordovices.

Frontinus Completes the Conquest of Wales – the Conquest Phase AD75-76
Diagrammatic Representation of one of Frontinus' ELF c4ha in Size Containing a Task Force of 1½ Legionary Cohorts of and a Cavalry Ala

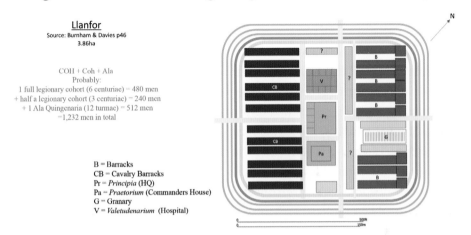

Llanfor
Source: Burnham & Davies p46
3.86ha

COH + Coh + Ala
Probably:
1 full legionary cohort (6 centuriae) = 480 men
+ half a legionary cohort (3 centuriae) = 240 men
+ 1 Ala Quingenaria (12 turmae) = 512 men
=1,232 men in total

B = Barracks
CB = Cavalry Barracks
Pr = *Principia* (HQ)
Pa = *Praetorium* (Commanders House)
G = Granary
V = *Valetudenarium* (Hospital)

Fig 4.12. Standard notation for representing the elements of Roman fort and fortresses, developed to describe and compare occupation-era forts. The ELF of Llanfor at the head of Bala Lake yielded unusually clear geophysical survey results (based on Burnham & Davies, 2010, p.46).

Finally, the fleet would have operated along the northern shores of the Bristol Channel with another early Flavian ELF identified as the first fort at Neath. The full system is set out in Figure 4.11.

What is noticeable here is that in this phase, the river valleys draining eastwards are occupied but the lands over the watershed draining west into Cardigan Bay generally are not; neither is the far north-west of Snowdonia and the Isle of Anglesey, or indeed the North Wales coast. This may generally be explicable in terms of the difficulty of the terrain, although a factor in the omission of Anglesey may be its reputation as the Druidic refuge.

The best interpretation of Frontinus' conquest phase is that these ten or so ELFs – there is a remarkable convergence of size here, from 3–4 hectares – were deliberately deployed to dominate the tribal centres of population of all four tribes in the territory of Wales. By controlling the valleys, these forts controlled the major lines of communication, as well as the bulk of the population. Each of these would have been garrisoned by at least two auxiliary units, and in some cases also a legionary cohort deployed forward with an auxiliary *cohors* or *ala*. An excellent example of this is the early Flavian fort fully excavated at Llanfor, where the barracks could accommodate not just an *ala quingenaria* of twelve *turmae*, each of thirty-two men and their horses, but also one full legionary *cohors* of six *centuriae* and most probably another half legionary *cohors* of three *centuriae*.

Llanfor is 3.8 hectares in area and, whilst it is at the upper end of the range, well demonstrates how much force was concentrated in each of these forts. This force, nominally of over 1,200 men, would pack an enormous punch, with fast-moving cavalry able to patrol deep into the valleys of Snowdonia to the north, west to Cardigan Bay and south into central Wales; together with legionary heavy infantry of *II Adiutrix* able to smash any resistance encountered and storm any hillforts holding out against the Romans (Figure 4.12).

Allowing an average of two units per extra-large fort, there would be some twenty units (including detached legionary *cohortes*) deployed forward up the LOPs by Frontinus. Including the legions, the total Strength Factors deployed comes to thirty-six SFs (three x twelve SFs) in the legionary fortresses and up to thirty-nine SFs in the forts. However, it should be noted that, because of the forward deployment of some legionary cohorts, there is almost certainly significant double counting of Strength Factors here between the legionary bases and the forward ELFs.

Phase 3: The control phase

How long the conquest phase took we cannot be sure, but on the evidence of dating we would expect no more than two years, which is comparable with how long the Flavian and Antonine conquest periods took in Scotland, with two three-year campaigns. Assuming a start to campaigning in the second half of 74, and allowing all of 75 and part of 76, we could see the transition to the control phase beginning towards the end of the campaigning season in 76 and getting into full swing in 77. The latter was Frontinus' handover year to Agricola.

When all of the definite and likely early Flavian forts are plotted onto the map of Wales, we see a remarkable situation revealed (Figure 4.15). There is a high-density network of forts that 'locked down' the whole country (Figures 4.13 and 4.14 for the D-LAM analytics). These are connected by the network of roads, which are harder to date but equally as important to Frontinus' mission of completing the conquest of Wales. This network has clearly been carefully planned to cover the whole of Wales and to bring everyone who lived there into the Roman control framework. Frontinus was determined to pull the four tribes of Wales into the province in a systematic and planned manner.

Standing back from the map of now-occupied Wales, we see a 'textbook' implementation of Roman zonal occupation, with forts spaced along roads at intervals of approximately one day's infantry march (Figure 4.16). It is worth spending time unpacking the process at work here, and in so doing we are reading Frontinus' textbook.

Frontinus Completes the Conquest of Wales – the Control Phase AD76-78

Data-Led Analytical Method [D-LAM] – Part 1

FRONTINUS AND AGRICOLA'S OCCUPATION OF WALES

Frontinus' Occupation of Wales - Baseline

Code				No.	Name			Unit	Date		Garrison	Size		Location	N1	N2	N3
FRO	DEE	LOC	CONTROL	1.0	Chester	1	24.40 LEG 12.00 LEG	II Adiutrix	Fro 74		LEG	5,000	One		0.0	0.0	0.0
FRO	N/S	BASE	CONTROL	2.0	Whitchurch	2	??? FOR? 1.0 ???		Fro ???		???	500			22.4	21.7	34.0
FRO	SEV	LOC	CONTROL	3.0	Wroxeter	2	16.00 LEG 12.00 LEG	XX Valeria Victrix	Fro? 66 79		LEG	5,000	Severn Valley		0.0	0.0	0.0
FRO	N/S	BASE	CONTROL	4.0	Buckton	1	2.36 LFT 4.0 AQ?		Fro? [80] 110		AQ?	500			32.2	30.4	49.0
FRO	BORD	BASE	CONTROL	5.0	Blackbush Farm	1	<3.2 ELF 3.0 CME?				CME?	1,000			31.6	29.8	48.0
FRO	N/S	BASE	CONTROL	6.0	Wonastow	1	1.4?? FOR? 1.0 CQP?				CQP?	500			23.0	21.7	35.0
FRO	USK	LOC	CONTROL	7.0	Usk	2	??? ELF 3.0 COH???	AQ???			LEG	1,000	Usk Valley		8.6	8.1	13.0
FRO	SCST	LOC	CONTROL	8.0	Caerleon	1	17.80 LEG 12.00 LEG	II Augusta	Fro 74		LEG	1,000	Usk Valley		47.4	44.7	72.0
Total for Baseline				**7.0**								**2,500**			**165.1**	**156.0**	**251.0**

Frontinus' Occupation of Wales - South Coast Line of Control

Code				No.	Name			Unit	Date		Garrison	Size		Material	Location	N1	N2	N3
FRO	SCST	LOC	CONTROL	1.0	Glouceste Glevum		Sup 0.0				LEG					0.0	0.0	0.0
FRO	SCST	LOC	CONTROL	2.0	Caerleon	1	17.80 LEG 12.0 LEG	II Augusta	Fro 74		LEG	5,000			Usk Valley	47.4	44.7	72.0
FRO	SCST	LOC	CONTROL	3.0	Cardiff	2	2.18 LFT 2.0 CMP?		Fro 75?		CMP?	1,000				15.8	14.9	24.0
FRO	SCST	LOC	CONTROL	4.0	Caergwanaf	1	1.56 FOR? 1.0 CQP?		Fro 70-75 80-85		CQP?	500	Two Parrot			10.5	9.9	16.0
FRO	SCST	LOC	CONTROL	5.0	Neath Nidum	2	2.30 LFT 2.0 AQ?		Agr 80 90		AQ?	500				27.6	26.1	42.0
FRO	SCST	LOC	CONTROL	6.0	Loughor Leucarum	1	2.15 LFT 2.0 CMP?		Fro 73-80 80-85		CMP?	1,000				13.8	13.0	21.0
FRO	SCST	LOC	CONTROL	7.0	Carmarthen Muridunum	1	2.31 LFT 2.0 AQ?		Fro 74?		AQ?	500				21.1	19.9	32.0
FRO	SCST	LOC	CONTROL	8.0		1	??? FOR?											
Total for South Coast Line of Control				**22.0**								**9,000**				**167.8**	**158.5**	**255.0**

Frontinus' Occupation of Wales - Silures Zone of Control

Code				No.	Name			Unit	Date		Garrison	Size		Material	Location	N1	N2	N3
FRO	SCST	LOC	CONTROL	1.0	Caerleon	1	17.80 LEG 12.0 LEG	II Augusta	Fro 74		LEG	5,000			Usk Valley	47.4	44.7	72.0
FRO	USK	LOC	CONTROL	2.0	Usk	2	??? ELF 3.0 COH???	AQ???	Fro 74		COH???	1,000	One		Usk Valley	8.6	8.1	13.0
FRO	USK	LOC	CONTROL	3.0	Abergavenny Gobannium	2	1.32 FOR 1.0 CQP?		Tre 65-70 90-110		CQP?	500			Usk Valley	11.8	11.2	18.0
FRO	USK	LOC	CONTROL	4.0	Pen y Gaer	1	1.16 SFT 0.6 4 x cent		Agr 80 130		4 x cent	320				10.5	9.9	16.0
FRO	USK	LOC	CONTROL	5.0	Brecon Gaer	1	3.14 ELF 3.0 AQ	ala Hispanorum Vettonum cR?	Fro 74 140		AQ	1,000	Two Straight	Timber Turf/Clay	Usk Valley	14.5	13.7	22.0
FRO	USK	LOC	CONTROL	6.0	Llandovery	1	3.00 ELF 3.0 COH???		Fro 74 130?		COH???	1,000	Three	Timber Earth	Heads of Usk and Towy	19.7	18.6	30.0
												112.5				**106.3**	**171.0**

FRO	SIL	LOC	CONTROL	1.0	Brecon Gaer	1	3.14 ELF 3.0 AQ	ala Hispanorum Vettonum cR?	Fro 74 140		AQ	1,000	Two Straight None	Timber Turf/Clay	Usk Valley	14.5	13.7	22.0
FRO	SIL	LOC	CONTROL	2.0	Coelbren	1	2.25 LFT 1.0 CMP		Fro 74? 130-40		CMP	80	Two	Turf	One	21.1	19.9	32.0
FRO	SIL	LOC	CONTROL	2.5	Hirfynydd	1	0.40 1ft 0.3 1 x cent				1 x cent	80				5.0	4.7	7.6
FRO	SIL	LOC	CONTROL	2.6	Rheola Forest	1	0.11 sft 0.1 4 x con				4 x con	40				5.0	4.7	7.6
FRO	SCST	LOC	CONTROL	3.6	Neath Nidum	2	2.30 LFT 2.0 AQ?		Agr 80 90		AQ?	500				27.6	26.1	42.0
												73.2				**69.1**	**111.2**

FRO	SCST	ZON	CONTROL	1.0	Cardiff	2	2.18 LFT 2.0 CMP?		Fro 75? 100		CMP?	1,000		Earth		8.6	8.1	13.0
FRO	SIL	ZON	CONTROL	2.0	Caerphilly	1	1.70 FRT 1.5 CQE?		Fro 75? 100		CQE?	500		Stones/Clay		7.2	6.8	11.0
FRO	SIL	ZON	CONTROL	3.0	Gelligaer	1	2.40 LFT 2.0 AQ?		Fro 75? 100		AQ?	500				10.5	9.9	16.0
FRO	SIL	ZON	CONTROL	4.0	Penydaren	1	2.30 LFT 2.0 AQ?		Fro 75? 140		AQ?	500	Two	Turf/Clay		42.1	39.8	64.0
Total for Silures Zone of Control				**17.5**								**6440**				**227.8**	**215.1**	**346.2**

Frontinus' Occupation of Wales - Severn Valley Line of Control

Code				No.	Name			Unit	Date		Garrison	Size		Material	Location	N1	N2	N3
FRO	SEV	LOC	CONTROL	1.0	Wroxeter	2	16.00 LEG 12.0 LEG	XX Valeria Victrix	66 79		LEG	5,000			Severn Valley	0.0	0.0	0.0
FRO	SEV	LOC	CONTROL	2.0	Brompton/Pentrehyling	1	2.70 VLF 2.5 CMP? or AQ?	CQ?	Fro 74 120		CMP? or AQ?	1,000		Timber Clay/Grav	Severn Valley	28.9	27.3	44.0
FRO	SEV	LOC	CONTROL	3.0	Caersws	1	3.90 ELF 3.0 COH or CQ?	AQ or CQ?	Fro 74		COH or CQ?	1,000	Three Straight	Timber Earth	One	17.8	16.7	27.0
FRO	SEV	LOC	CONTROL	3.5	Pen y Crochen	1	0.12 sft 0.1 4 x cent				4 x cent	40	None	Turf		32.2	30.4	49.0
FRO	SEV	LOC	CONTROL	4.0	Pennal	1	2.60 VLF 2.5 CME?		Fro 74		CME?	1,000	Three	Timb-Earth	R Dovey	24.3	23.0	37.0
												103.3				**97.6**	**157.0**

FRO	SEV	LOC	CONTROL	1.0	Caersws	1	8.90 ELF 3.0 COH for CQ? AQ or CQ?	Leg Coh from II Adiutrix?	Fro 74		COH or CQ?	1,000	Three Straight	Earth	Severn Valley			
FRO	SEV	LOC	CONTROL	5.0	Cae Gaer	1	1.05 SFT 0.6 4 cent?		Fro 74		4 cent?	320	One	Turf	Traeusg Defile	19.7	18.6	30.0
FRO	SEV	LOC	CONTROL	6.0	Pen-llwyn	1	2.70 VLF 2.5 CME?		Fro 74 125		CME?	1,000	Three	Turf/Gravel	Vale of Rheidol	16.4	15.5	25.0
Total for Severn Valley Line of Control				**23.2**								**9360**				**157.2**	**148.5**	**239.0**

Fig 4.13. Part 1 of the extract from the Forts Database for the Control Phase of Frontinus' Campaign, showing the extent of the forts constructed at this time.

Frontinus Completes the Conquest of Wales – the Control Phase AD76-78

Data-Led Analytical Method [D-LAM] – Part 2

Frontinus' Occupation of Wales – Dee Valley Line of Control

FRO	DEE	LOC	CONTROL	1.0 Chester	1		24.40	LEG	12.00		LEG	5,000		II Adiutrix	Fro	74				Dee	0.0	0.0	0.0
FRO	DEE	LOP	CONTROL	2.0 Rhyn Park		2	6.00	VX	6.0	CQ?	COH?	2,000	CQ??		Fro	74?	90???		Clay	Dee	26.3	24.9	40.0
FRO	DEE	LOP	CONTROL	3.0 Caer Gai	1		1.75	FRT	1.5	CQE?		500			Fro	75-80	120-30	Timber	Turf	Dee	37.5	35.4	57.0
FRO	DEE	LOP	CONTROL	4.0 Tomen y Mur			2.03	LFT	2.0	CMP?		1,000			Fro	75-80	120-30	Timber	Earth/Timb	Two Snowdonia Pr/Pa/2G/6B/1S/4??? Two	19.1	18.0	29.0
Total for Dee Line of Control							21.5					8,500									82.9	78.3	126.0

Frontinus' Occupation of Wales – Central Wales Line of Control

FRO	DEE	LOP	CONTROL	1.0 Caer Gai	1	1.75	FRT	1.5	CQE?	500			Fro	75-80	120-30	Timber	Turf	Two		Dee	37.5	35.4	57.0
FRO	CWL	LOC	CONTROL	1.5 Halen	1	0.48	1ft	0.3	2 x cent	160			Fro				Turf						
FRO	CWL	LOC	CONTROL	1.6 Llanfair Caereinion		0.24	df	0.1	5 x contub	40													
FRO	SEV	LOC	CONTROL	2.0 Caersws	1	3.90	ELF	3.0	COH or CQ?	AQ or CQ?	1,000	Leg Coh from II Adiutrix?	Fro	74		Timber	Earth	Three Straight	One	Severn Valley	17.8	16.8	27.0
FRO	CWL	LOC	CONTROL	3.0 Castell Collen	1	2.04	LFT	2.0	CQE?	500			Fro	74?			Turf/Clay				27.0	25.5	41.0
FRO	CWL	LOC	CONTROL	3.5 Pennuiscæ	1	0.13	sft	0.1	5 x contub	40			Fro				Turf/Clay		Wye		13.2	12.4	20.0
FRO	CWL	LOC	CONTROL	4.0 Cacnu	1	1.90	FRT	1.5	CMP?	1,000			Fro	74?	100		CMP?						
FRO	CHE	LOC	CONTROL	4.5		0.70	lft	0.4	2 x cent	160													
FRO	USK	LOC	CONTROL	5.0 Llandovery	1	3.00	ELF	3.0	COH???	1,000	CQ???		Fro	74	190?	Timber	Earth	Three Surrounding Heads of Usk and Towy	19.7	18.6	30.0
FRO	CWL	LOC	CONTROL	6.0 Llandeilo	1	3.84	ELF	3.0	AQ or CMX?	1,000			Fro	74?			Earth	Three	One		13.2	12.4	20.0
FRO	SUST	LOC	CONQUER	7.0 Carmarthen	1	3.31	LFT	2.0	AQ?	500	Maridunum		Fro	74?							23.1	19.9	32.0
Total for Central Wales Line of Control							7.3				2,900									149.3	141.1	227.0

Frontinus' Occupation of Wales – West Coast Line of Control

FRO	USK	LOC	CONTROL	1.0 Brecon Gaer	1	3.14	ELF	3.0	AQ?	CQ?	1,000	ala Hispanorum Vettonum cR?	Fro	74	140	Timber	Turf/Clay	Two Straight	Two	Usk Valley	14.5	13.7	22.0
FRO	USK	LOC	CONTROL	1.5 Wern-ddu	1	0.13	sft	0.1	5 x contub	40			Fro	74			Bank						
FRO	USK	LOC	CONTROL	2.0 Llandovery	1	3.00	ELF	3.0	COH???	1,000	CQ???		Fro	74	190?	Timber	Earth	Three Surrounding Heads of Usk and Towy	19.7	18.6	40.0
FRO	WCST	LOC	CONTROL	3.0 Pumsaint	1	1.90	FRT	1.5	CME?	1,000			Fro	74	100		Turf/Clay	One	Dolaucothi Gold	9.9	9.3	15.0
FRO	WCST	LOC	CONTROL	3.5 Careg y Bwci		0.04	watch	0.0	1 x contub	8							Bank	One	commands road			
FRO	WCST	LOC	CONTROL	4.0 Llanio	1	1.55	FOR	1.0	CQP?	500	Bremia		Fro	74	120	Timber	Turf/Gravel	One	R Teifi	13.2	12.4	20.0
FRO	WCST	LOC	CONTROL	5.0 Trawscoed	1	2.10	LFT	2.0	CMP?	1,000			Fro	74	90?		Turf/Clay	One 10B*	Ystwyth	13.8	13.0	21.0
FRO	SEV	LOC	CONTROL	6.0 Pen-llwyn	1	2.70	VLF	2.5	CME?	1,000			Fro	74	125		Turf/Gravel	Three	Vale of Rheidol	16.4	15.5	25.0
FRO	WCST	LOC	CONTROL	6.5 Erglodd		0.13	sft	0.1	5 x contub	40			Fro	74			Turf/Clay	One	Exploit lead and silver			
FRO	SEV	LOC	CONTROL	7.0 Pennal	1	2.60	VLF	2.5	CME?	1,000			Fro	74			Turf/Clay	Three	R Dovey	24.3	23.0	37.0
FRO	WCST	LOC	CONTROL	7.5 Brithdir		0.30	sft	0.1	5 x contub	40			Fro	74	80				R Wnion commands road			
FRO	WCST	LOC	CONTROL	7.6 Liety Cunol	1	0.01	watch	0.0	1 x contub	8												
FRO	DEE	LOP	CONTROL	8.0 Tomen y Mur		2.03	LFT	2.0	CMP?	1,000			Agr	78	90		Earth/Timb	Two	Snowdonia	19.1	18.0	29.0
FRO	WCST	LOC	CONTROL	9.0 Pen Llystyn	1	1.80	FRT	1.5	CQE?	500			Agr	77	90		Turf/Gravel	Two	Lleyn Pen	17.8	16.8	27.0
FRO	WCST	LOC	CONQUER	10.0 Caernarfon		2.27	LFT	2.0	CMP?	1,000	Segontium		Agr	77	90		Turf/Gravel	Two		28.3	26.7	43.0
Total for West Coast Line of Control							6.3				3,136									177.0	167.1	269.0

Agricola's Occupation of Wales – North Coast Line of Control

FRO	DEE	LOC	CONTROL	1.0 Chester	1	24.40	LEG	12.00	LEG	5,000	II Adiutrix	Fro	74				Dee	0.0	0.0	0.0
FRO	NCST	LOP	CONQUER	2.0 St Asaph?	1	0.58	ELF?	1.0	CQP?	500	Varis	Agr	77						27.6	26.1	42.0
FRO	NCST	LOP	CONQUER	3.0 Caelinn	1	1.97	FRT	1.5	CQP?	1,000	Canovium	Agr	77			Turf/Gravel	Teo		19.7	18.6	30.0
FRO	NCST	LOP	CONQUER	4.0 Caernarfon	1	2.27	LFT	2.0	CMP?	1,000	Segontium	Agr	77	90					28.3	26.7	43.0
FRO	NCST	LOP	CONQUER	5.0 Llanoghor???		0.23	sft	0.1	5 x contub	40		Agr	77						16.4	15.5	25.0
FRO	NCST	LOP	CONQUER	5.5 Canllyn								Agr							16.4	15.5	25.0
Total for North Coast Line of Control							5.6				2,540								108.6	102.5	165.0

Frontinus' Occupation of Wales – Border Line of Control

FRO	N/S	BASE	CONTROL	1.0 Buxton	1	2.36	LFT	2.0	AQ?	500		Fro?	160?	110				Dee	32.2	30.4	49.0
FRO	BOR	XRT	CONTAIN	2.0 Blackwell Farm	2	2.29	LFT	2.0		500		Goi	55						15.5	14.9	22.0
FRO	BOR	XRT	CONTROL	3.0 Cobrau Castle	2	2.79	VLF	2.5		500		Goi	55						11.3	10.6	22.0
FRO	CWL	LOC	CONTROL	4.0 Castell Collen	1	2.04	LFT	2.0	CQE?	1,000		Agr	74?			Turf/Clay			27.0	25.5	41.0
Border Cross Route							4.0				1,000								86.2	81.4	134.0

TOTAL FRONTINUS' AND AGRICOLA'S OCCUPATION OF WALES	108.1	41,740		1332	1248	2012

Fig. 4.14. Part 2 of the extract from the Forts Database for the Control Phase of Frontinus' Campaign, showing the extent of the forts constructed at this time.

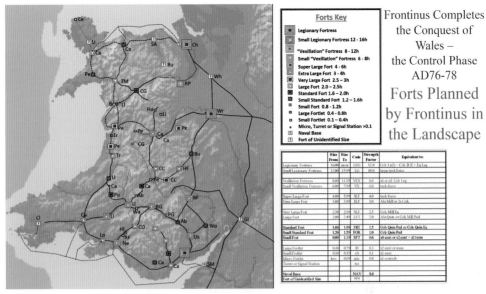

Fig 4.15. The most important map in the chapter – since it reconstructs Frontinus' design as executed by him and Agricola, his successor as governor, for the occupation and final subjugation of what we now know as Wales.

The objective of Frontinus' campaign was the final and complete not just conquest but control and occupation of the territory of what is now Wales. This was but one component of the complete conquest and control of the whole of the island of *Britannia* as ordered, I believe, by Vespasian in Rome in 70.

We have seen in the conquest phase how the baseline was fixed north–south, connecting the three legionary fortresses which acted as the campaign bases for the task forces penetrating the river valleys running westwards into the interior and highland areas. In the control phase, these LOPs became Lines of Control (LOC) reaching westwards from the three legionary fortresses (Figures 4.13 to 4.16). The codes denoting the size of each fort are shown after each reference.

- **The northern task force** led by *II Adiutrix* with its auxiliaries reached south and west from Chester up the valley of the River Dee through Rhyn Park. The extra-large legionary/*ala* fort at Llanfor (Burnham and Davies, 2010, p.259) was probably decommissioned at this time and replaced with a new standard-sized fort at Caer Gai on the River Dee at the other end of Bala Lake (Burnham and Davies, 2010, p.213). Caer Gai was set up as the key nodal point of the northern military road network. It had connecting roads:
  - back to Chester fortress (LEG) down the Dee Valley;
  - two connections west: one over the mountains to Tomen y Mur (LFT) in Central Snowdonia;

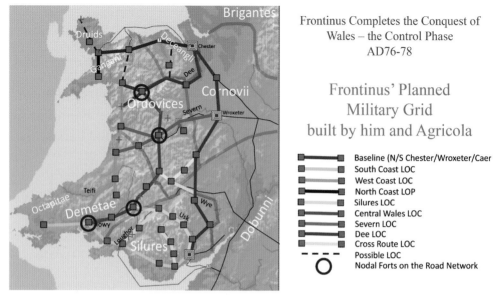

Frontinus Completes the Conquest of
Wales – the Control Phase
AD76-78

Frontinus' Planned
Military Grid
built by him and Agricola

▬▬▬▬▬	Baseline (N/S Chester/Wroxeter/Caer
▭▭▭▭▭	South Coast LOC
▭▭▭▭▭	West Coast LOC
▬▬▬▬▬	North Coast LOP
▭▭▭▭▭	Silures LOC
▭▭▭▭▭	Central Wales LOC
▭▭▭▭▭	Severn LOC
▭▭▭▭▭	Dee LOC
▭▭▭▭▭	Cross Route LOC
– – – –	Possible LOC
◯	Nodal Forts on the Road Network

Fig 4.16. The dense network of forts and roads that Frontinus designed and built to lock-down the territory of Wales.

- ○ another to the fortlet at Brithdir (sft) near Dolgellau on the western coastal road;
  - ○ finally the road south to Caersws (ELF) on the central Wales LOC.
- **The central task force** led by *XX Valeria Victrix* with its auxiliaries reached west up the Severn River Valley, either maintaining the ELF at Forden Gaer or, as above, more likely replacing it with a smaller but still substantial fort at Brompton/Pentrehyling, just 6.5km distant. The next fort west along the Severn was Caersws I (ELF) at Llwyn-y-brain, another extra-large fort from the occupation period. In the control period, Caersws became the key nodal point on the central sector military road network, with five routes:
  - ○ east to Wroxeter fortress (LEG) down the Severn Valley;
  - ○ north to Caer Gai (FRT) on the northern network;
  - ○ west over the mountains to the key fort at Pennal (VLF) situated at the highest tidal point of the River Dovey above Cardigan Bay;
  - ○ the strategic interior north–south road over the uplands leading to Castell Collen (LFT);
  - ○ probably another western route from Caersws. Although the roads do not seem to align, this would have connected through an intermediate small fort at Cae Gaer (SFT), south-west to the west coast fort at Pen-llwyn (VLF), where the west coast road crosses the River Rheidol flowing into Cardigan Bay.

- **The southern task force** led by *II Augusta* with its auxiliaries reached north and west up the Usk Valley through the forts at Usk, Abergavenny, Pen y Gaer and Llandovery established in the conquest phase, thereby putting a ring around the Silures. We should expect these forts to have reduced garrisons in this period. *II Augusta* also established Lines of Control designed to place the Silures under tight surveillance:

  - One ran along the south coast with forts at Cardiff II (a new LFT reoccupying this strategic site), Caergwanaf (FOR?), a new smaller fort at Neath II (LFT) on the river of the same name and new forts at Loughor (LFT) and Carmarthen (LFT), by now well into the territory of the Demetae. This Line of Control continued west with a known road for about 40km, leading to speculation that there is another fort to be found near Whitland or Haverfordwest (Burnham and Davies, 2010, p.47).

  - A second new Line of Control ran along what may have been the western limits of the Silures' territory south-west from Brecon y Gaer to a new fort at Coelbren (LFT) on the River Tawe, then connecting to the coastal fort at Neath. There were in addition two intermediate fortlets at Hirfyndd (lft) and Rheola Forest (sft) on the way down to the coast.

  - A third Line of Control ran north up higher land dominating both the Rhymney and Taff valleys to Caerphilly (FRT), Gelligaer I (LFT) and Pennydaren (LFT), showing the determination at last to dominate the

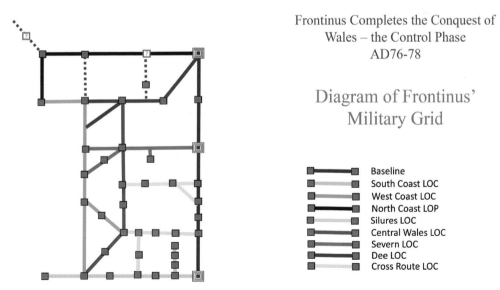

Frontinus Completes the Conquest of
Wales – the Control Phase
AD76-78

Diagram of Frontinus'
Military Grid

Baseline
South Coast LOC
West Coast LOC
North Coast LOP
Silures LOC
Central Wales LOC
Severn LOC
Dee LOC
Cross Route LOC

Fig 4.17. Frontinus' network is even clearer in diagrammatic form: there are forty-two forts and some 2,000km of connecting road.

heartlands of the Silures, presumably sources of continuing resistance in years past.

In order to connect the east–west Lines of Control and complete the 'control grid', it was necessary to run two north–south routes which connected the valleys:

- **A coastal north–south route:** the three Task Forces having traversed the watershed and reached the west coast, it was necessary to run a connecting road along the coast. Starting in the south at Llandovery, the road headed north-west over the hills to a fort at Pumsaint (FRT) to control the gold mines there, then to Llanio (FOR) in the valley of the River Teifi, where a branch road to Carmarthen joined. From there the road headed north to Trawscoed (LFT), Pen-llwyn (Figure 4.22) and Pennal, where, as noted above, the Central LOCs intersected, and thence to Tomen y Mur, where the Northern LOC route joined.

  It is interesting to see that there are many more fortlets and watch towers along this route – at Waun-ddu (sft), Careg y Bwci (watch), Erglodd (sft), Brithdir (sft) and Liety Canol (watch) – than have been found on the other LOCs. This may denote Frontinus starting to run out of troops and economizing on forts or, more probably, a more hostile environment in the far west requiring close surveillance of the roads and the convoys running along them.

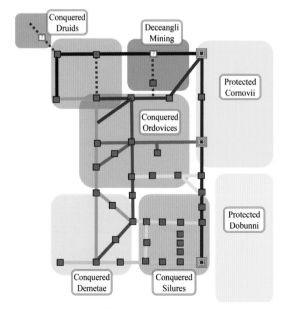

Frontinus Completes the Conquest of Wales – the Control Phase AD76-78

Typology Diagram

- **North/South 'Baseline Road'**
  - ➢ 'Protects' the Cornovii, Dobunni and dominated Eastern Silures
- Anchored on legionary fortresses at Chester, Wroxeter and Caerleon
- Forts at 32km average intervals along grid of roads
  - ➢ South Coast and Silures Control
  - ➢ Severn and Dee Valleys
  - ➢ Central Wales north/south route
  - ➢ West and North Coasts
  - ➢ Marches
- Overwhelming force deployed of >40,000 men in full garrison
  - ➢ Equivalent to 115 'Strength Factors'

Fig 4.18. Typology diagram of the Frontinian occupation of Wales, showing the comprehensive lockdown of all areas and all tribes.

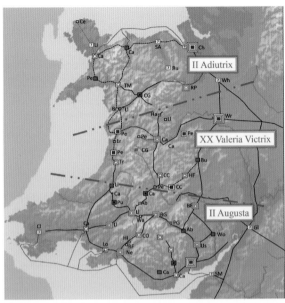

Frontinus Completes the Conquest of
Wales – the Control Phase
AD76-78

Conjectural Army
Command Boundaries

Chester Northern Command
1 Legion
3 large forts >2ha
3 forts
4 possible forts

Wroxeter Centre Command
1 Legion
7 large forts >2ha
2 forts

Caerleon Southern Command
1 Legion
12 large forts >2ha
7 forts
1 possible fort

Fig 4.19. The reconstructed deployment at the completion of the Frontinian System, probably at the start of Agricola's governorship in 77/78. Assuming that the legions controlled their 'sector', this gives a northern, centre and southern command, with the greatest weight of force deployed in the south, supervising the Silures.

- **An interior north–south route:** this second route ran through the interior, also starting in the south in Carmarthen, then running north-east to Llandeilo and on to Llandovery, which was another key nodal fort on the control road network. Continuing north-east over the hills to Caerau (FRT) and then to Castell Collen (LFT), this road connected with the central route on the Upper Severn Valley at Caersws (ELF) and north to the Dee Valley at Caer Gai (FRT).

  Again, we find infilling posts between the major forts at Abererbwll (lft), Penmincae (sft) and Llanfair Caereinon (sft), ensuring security along this strategic road through the central Welsh uplands.

The final piece in the jigsaw of Frontinus' control was back in the Borders, where there was still a need to dominate the other major river flowing out of the Welsh uplands – the River Wye:

- **Wye Valley Route:** this explains the presence of Blackbush Farm (ELF?) and Buckton (LFT) further north, which, as well as controlling the baseline road north–south, would have connected with the forts to the west at Colwyn Castle (VLF) and Hindwell Farm (LFT). These last two forts are typologically similar and may originally date to an earlier Neronian push westward under Paulinus (Burnham and Davies, 2010, p.241). If they were

Auxiliary Units:
Theoretical Alignment Between Manpower and Size of Forts

Auxiliary Unit	Number of Centuriae (80 men)	Number of Turmae (32 men)	Number of Barracks	Manpower	Estimated Size Range	Britannia Type Site	Wales Type Site
Ala Milleria	-	24	24	768	>3.2ha multiplle	Stanwix 3.77ha	
Ala Quingenaria	-	16	16	512	2.3 – 2.4ha 2.3 – 2.7ha	Chesters 2.32ha	
Cohors MiII Equitata	10	8	18	1056	2.7 – 3.2ha 2.7 – 3.2ha		
Cohors Mil Peditata	10	-	10	800	1.8 – 2.27ha 1.8 – 2.3ha	Housesteads 2.02ha	
Coh Quin Equitata	6	4	10	608	1.7 - 1.8ha 1.6 – 1.8ha	Wallsend 1.66ha	
Coh Quin Peditata	6	-	6	480	1.3 - 1.57ha 1.3 – 1.6ha	Gelligaer II 1.4ha	Gelligaer II 1.4ha

Fig 4.20. The complement of the different types of auxiliary units, aligned with different sizes of forts: this is purely indicative, and the practicalities of campaign and troop shortages would have determined what was deployed where.

still held into the early Flavian period, they would dominate both the Wye Valley and the area where the Silures met the Ordovices and the Dobunni: indeed, these four forts seem to be aligned to the inferred tribal interfaces.

What did Frontinus build and what did Agricola finish?

Conspicuous by its absence from the above Lines of Control has been the North Wales coast. Historians have long attributed the forts in this area not to Frontinus but to his successor, Julius Agricola, who arrived in late 77. This is on the basis of Tacitus:

> The Ordovices, shortly before Agricola's arrival, had destroyed nearly the whole of a squadron of allied cavalry quartered in their territory. Such a beginning raised the hopes of the country, and all who wished for war approved the precedent, and anxiously watched the temper of the new governor. Meanwhile Agricola ... collected a force of veterans and a small body of auxiliaries; then as the Ordovices would not venture to descend into the plain, he put himself in front of the ranks to inspire all with the same courage against a common danger, and led his troops up a hill. The tribe was all but exterminated.... he formed the design of subjugating the island of Mona [Anglesey], from the occupation of which Paulinus had been recalled, as I have already related, by the rebellion of the entire province. But, as his plans were not matured, he had

no fleet. The skill and resolution of the general accomplished the passage. With some picked men of the auxiliaries, disencumbered of all baggage, who knew the shallows and had that national experience in swimming … he delivered so unexpected an attack that the astonished enemy who were looking for a fleet, a naval armament, and an assault by sea, thought that to such assailants nothing could be formidable or invincible. (Tacitus, *Agricola* 18)

Tacitus clearly states that the control network in the north-west was still under construction in 77 and the Ordovices were far from subdued. He also states that the Roman units had already dispersed into their winter garrisons when Agricola arrived, so it must have been early autumn.

We know of four forts in the north-west which are probably early Flavian and are likely to date from this period. These form a rough square or 'quadrilateral' surrounding Snowdonia and connected by Roman roads:

- Tomen y Mur (LFT), where the north–south routes met the northern route;
- Pen Llstyn (FRT) dominating the fertile Llyn Peninsula;
- Caernarfon (LFT) on the Menai Straits opposite Anglesey;
- Caerhun (FRT) in the Conwy Valley.

Given the normal mode of operation, we would expect to see a route along the coast with intermediate forts. There is a Roman road inland along the north coast west from Chester, however, which appears to head for Caerhun, and an extension – again initially inland – to avoid the precipitous coast to Caernarfon. Roads have been proposed south from this route up the Clwyd Valley to meet the Dee, and a fort at Ruthin has also been suggested to fill the gap. Another route south from Caerhun heads up the Conwy Valley to cross the mountains at Ffestiniog and reach the nodal fort at Tomen y Mur. The intermediate fort at Bryn y Gefeiliau is almost certainly of a later date, connected with mineral extraction.

Perhaps most surprising is the lack of Flavian forts and sites on Anglesey, given its strategic importance as the refuge of the demonized Druids and its fertility compared to any other part of North Wales. There is a newly identified small fortlet at Cemlyn on the north coast, and it has been postulated that there should be a fort to be found at Llangefni, on what was probably a tidal inlet in the Roman period.

A reasonable theory about the north coast of Wales would be that Frontinus and his staff had conquered most of the territory of modern Wales in 74 and 75, although leaving the north coast and the Druids on Anglesey untouched. Frontinus had completed the plan and had commenced the construction of the control network of forts and connecting roads in the newly occupied zone, including Ordovican territory. These were well under construction in 77 when the Ordovices revolted.

This led to Agricola's urgent and decisive intervention to quell the revolt, followed by his invasion of Anglesey involving his auxiliaries swimming the Menai Straits with their arms and horses.

Analyzing Frontinus' design

Having analyzed the forts, and standing back from Frontinus' design, we can now break it down into its component parts. We can clearly see a dense network of fortresses, forts and roads, tightly overlaying the physical geography and human settlement of what is now Wales. It is essentially a grid built out westwards from the north–south baseline running down the lowlands of what we now call the Borders, which had effectively been the western border of the province for two decades.

There are five east–west LOCs and three north–south LOCs. Completing the grid and dominating important areas of hostile tribal settlement, there are additional Lines of Control in the South Wales valleys, the Wye Valley, the Clwyd Valley and the Conwy Valley.

When shown diagrammatically (Figures 4.17 and 4.18), the systematic planning is clear. It is striking how comprehensive the Lines of Control are. It was once thought that the occupation of Wales concentrated primarily on the long-term

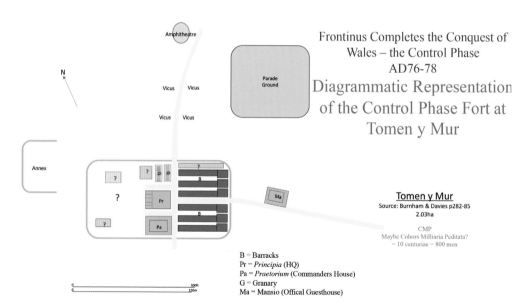

Fig 4.21. The fort at Tomen y Mur built high up on a bleak spur in southern Snowdonia at the junction of strategic roads. Large enough to have accommodated a *Cohors Milliaria Peditata* (CMP), it has a parade ground, an annex to protect supply convoys, a *mansio* for visiting dignitaries and even a military amphitheatre to relieve the boredom with (probably gruesome) entertainment.

Roman enemies, the Ordovices and the Silures. However, whilst there is clear focus on these tribes, the fort and road network also incorporate the Demetae and the Decangli – albeit less thoroughly.

As would be expected, the network – as well as occupying the good lands of the Vale of Glamorgan, the Gower Peninsula and (probably) Pembrokeshire – also covered all the fertile river valleys of the Usk, Wye, Severn, Dee and Clwyd and the coastline of Cardigan Bay. The network also incorporated into the organized province the mining areas for gold at Dolaucothi in the south-west and for silver and lead in the north-west and north-east.

Most strikingly, the grid takes great care to also cover the mountainous zones by providing easy military access to areas where people hostile to Rome could hold out. Snowdonia is compartmentalized with a quadrilateral of forts. The central Wales north–south LOC runs down the spine of Wales, and the three inland Lines of Control do not stop at the end of the Usk, Severn or Dee valleys, but cross the watershed to reach Cardigan Bay.

Neither was the Roman Army afraid of placing garrisons in inhospitable locations. The large fort at Tomen y Mur occupies a remote plateau south of Snowdonia (Figure 4.21). There, the garrison – probably a 1,000-man infantry

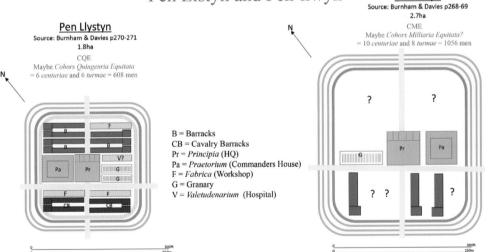

Figure 4.22. Using the standard notation, we can see that Pen Llstyn (extensively excavated ahead of quarrying) appears to be a 1.8-hectare standard-sized fort for a *Cohors Quingeneria Equitata* (CME). The Pen-llwyn plan is far less clear: the central range has the standard HQ and Commander's House, but the remainder is obscure, although at 2.7 hectares there is space for a full CMP.

unit (*cohors milliaria peditata*) – was well connected to north, south, east and west. It was provided with a parade ground, an amphitheatre and a *mansio* for visiting dignitaries, and a *vicus* (civilian settlement) grew up to service the garrison. It would be impossible for this garrison to live off the locality, so the supply trains snaking up from the coast (assuming sea transport supply) would have needed to be frequent. The point here is that Frontinus and his Roman forces had come to complete the job this time. Other forts in isolated upland locations without large contemporary tribal settlements, and so designed to control insurgents, included those at Coelbren and Cae Gaer (Burnham and Davies, 2010, p.68).

The size and deployment of Frontinus' force

Whilst we can estimate the overall size of the forces at Frontinus' disposal in 74, it is challenging to construct the unit composition. It has been said that the force was similar to that found occupying Wales at the turn of the first century (Jarrett, 1969); that is, the two legions and at least the thirty-one auxiliary units (eight AQs, three CMXs and twenty CQXs) in the diplomas. This gives a nominal manpower still over 30,000 men.

However, it is worth stepping back from this assumption to consider whether this is really likely to be the case. The three diplomas we have for Wales date to the turn of the century and align to the two commands of Caerleon and Chester (Figures 4.23 and 4.24). While many of the units were probably still in position three decades later, we should recognize that there were three legions deployed by Frontinus for the campaign, and therefore most probably three commands, as has been set out above. Furthermore, the period from 70–110 was a very active one for campaigning in different theatres in *Britannia* and, providing the general assumption that each legion had a train of attached auxiliaries is correct, it is likely there would have been considerable movement into and out of the theatre of operations. Moreover, the legionary fortress at Wroxeter, active in the 70s, had been converted to civilian use by 100.

The fact that *II Augusta* was fighting in the north of Britain – or indeed in the 120s building a wall and its forts – did not mean that its base in South Wales at Caerleon had to be abandoned. The model of British Army regiments in the late nineteenth century after the Cardwell Reforms of 1868 – of one service battalion (cohort size), with another battalion serving in the empire in India, Africa or elsewhere – is a helpful comparator here. A similar model could be true for a legion's associated auxiliaries, although the frequency that forts were built, modified and abandoned suggests that auxiliaries were much more likely to move theatre and their base than legions in this period.

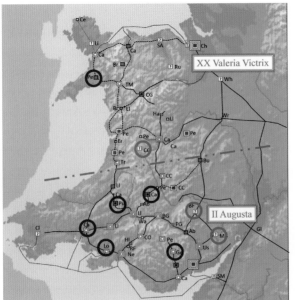

Conjectural Army Group Command Boundary in Wales under Trajan AD 98-105

Chester Northern Command
[10 leg cohorts + 16 auxiliary units]
1 Legion
12 forts
4 possible forts
+ others in North West Britain

Caerleon Southern Command
[10 leg cohorts + 15 auxiliary units]
1 Legion
17 forts
3 possible forts

Fort reduced in size from Flavian period
Fort uncertain occupation in Trajanic period

Fig 4.23. Reconstructed Army Group Commands with conjectural boundary and the known reductions in garrisons between the Frontinus original design and the turn-of-the-century diplomas.

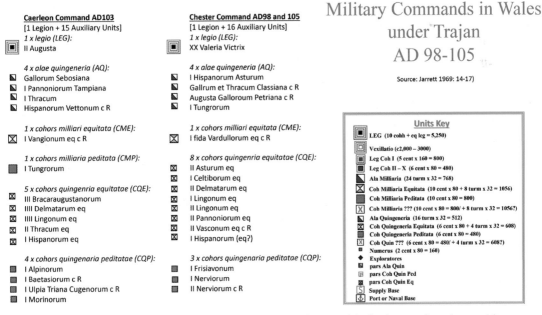

Military Commands in Wales under Trajan AD 98-105

Source: Jarrett 1969: 14-17)

Caerleon Command AD103
[1 Legion + 15 Auxiliary Units]
1 x legio (LEG):
II Augusta

4 x alae quingeneria (AQ):
Gallorum Sebosiana
I Pannoniorum Tampiana
I Thracum
Hispanorum Vettonum c R

1 x cohors milliari equitata (CME):
I Vangionum eq c R

1 x cohors milliaria peditata (CMP):
I Tungrorum

5 x cohors quingenria equitatae (CQE):
III Bracaraugustanorum
IIII Delmatarum eq
IIII Lingonum eq
II Thracum eq
I Hispanorum eq

4 x cohors quingenaria peditatae (CQP):
I Alpinorum
I Baetasiorum c R
I Ulpia Triana Cugenorum c R
I Morinorum

Chester Command AD98 and 105
[1 Legion + 16 Auxiliary Units]
1 x legio (LEG):
XX Valeria Victrix

4 x alae quingeneria (AQ):
I Hispanorum Asturum
Gallrum et Thracum Classiana c R
Augusta Galloroum Petriana c R
I Tungrorum

1 x cohors milliari equitata (CME):
I fida Vardullorum eq c R

8 x cohors quingenria equitatae (CQE):
II Asturum eq
I Celtiborum eq
II Delmatarum eq
I Lingonum eq
II Lingonum eq
II Pannoniorum eq
II Vasconum eq c R
I Hispanorum (eq?)

3 x cohors quingenaria peditatae (CQP):
I Frisiavonum
I Nerviorum
II Nerviorum c R

Units Key
LEG (10 cohh + eq leg = 5,250)
Vexillatio (c2,000 – 3000)
Leg Coh I (5 cent x 160 = 800)
Leg Coh II – X (6 cent x 80 = 480)
Ala Milliaria (24 turm x 32 = 768)
Coh Milliaria Equitata (10 cent x 80 + 8 turm x 32 = 1056)
Coh Milliaria Peditata (10 cent x 80 = 800)
Coh Milliaria ??? (10 cent x 80 = 800/ + 8 turm x 32 = 1056?)
Ala Quingeneria (16 turm x 32 = 512)
Coh Quingeneria Equitata (6 cent x 80 + 4 turm x 32 = 608)
Coh Quingeneria Peditata (6 cent x 80 = 480)
Coh Quin ??? (6 cent x 80 = 480/ + 4 turm x 32 = 608?)
Numerus (2 cent x 80 = 160)
Exploratores
pars Ala Quin
pars Coh Quin Ped
pars Coh Quin Eq
Supply Base
Port or Naval Base

Fig 4.24. From the evidence of diplomas issued in the honourable discharge of auxiliary soldiers after their twenty-five years of service, it is possible to reconstruct with reasonable certainty the units of both the northern Chester Command and the southern Caerleon Command. Many of these units would have been present in these forts twenty years earlier.

The start of the Flavian period saw the arrival of *II Adiutrix* with Cerialis in 71, the construction of the new legionary fortress at York and the conquest of the Brigantes from 71–73, which probably involved two of the province's legions and their auxiliaries. Then Frontinus campaigned in Wales from 74–77, with the construction of two new legionary fortresses at Caerleon and Chester, the abandonment of the Exeter fortress and the move back into Wroxeter. In 78, Agricola consolidated Cerialis' conquest of the Brigantes and drove through into the Scottish Lowlands with, we are told, fort construction. Agricola then penetrated into the Highland zone, with at least two-and-a-half legions present at Mons Graupius, with some 11,000 auxiliaries doing the actual fighting. This was followed by the move forward of *XX Valeria Victrix* from its base at Wroxeter to yet another new Flavian-era legionary fortress at Inchtuthil.

Following the decision by Domitian to withdraw *II Adiutrix* in 87 to reinforce the Danube Frontier, the hard-won Scottish territory was abandoned and a withdrawal in stages back to the so-called Stanegate frontier line on the Tyne–Solway line was implemented. It therefore seems highly unlikely that, amidst all of this legionary campaigning and new deployment, the auxiliary unit deployments in Wales would have remained unchanged for three decades.

Reconstructing the commands in Trajan's time seems to align the known units and the forts, there being the two legions and the thirty-one named auxiliary units, which compares reasonably well with the estimated sixteen forts in the Chester command and twenty forts operational in the Caerleon command at this time (Figures 4.23 and 4.24). Looking at this from the forces required in the 70s under Frontinus, there are three fortresses and thirty-six forts. The difference of five forts can be made up either from other units withdrawn between 78 and the 90s or, more probably, there were legionary cohorts deployed forward in forts, as had definitely been the case at Llanfor.

The effort required and time taken to occupy Wales

The numbers involved in the conquest and occupation of Wales are very large, given the size of the territory. There are three legionary fortresses (two new-builds) and thirty-six forts, the vast majority built or planned under Frontinus, some starting in the occupation phase in 74/75, but most in the control phase during 76/77, with some (especially those in the north-west) being completed under Agricola in 78/79. There is a network of some 2,000km of roads connecting the forts. My belief is that this textbook fort and road network was designed and implemented by the prominent military theorist, Sextus Julius Frontinus, assisted of course by an able staff of legionary surveyors, architects and construction engineers.

The effort required to build all of this is not simple to calculate. The best comparator is the work done on the building of the legionary fortress at Inchtuthil in 84–86 (Shirley, 2011, pp.111–28, and Figure 4.27). The fortress was constructed from timber, tiles, wooden cladding and turf, like the fortresses and forts of Flavian Wales. Shirley calculates that the Inchtuthil system consisting of the fortress and the thirteen surrounding forts would take 1,000 men (or two cohorts) twenty months to construct, that is probably spread over three seasons of work. Alternatively, she calculated that if 5,000 men (a whole legion) was deployed, the construction work could theoretically be done in as fast as four months. This would not of course have been a practicable option for a legion that was actively involved in campaigning.

The forces employed at Mons Graupius were 11,000 auxiliaries and possibly two-and-a-half (probably understrength) legions, amounting to a force of about 23,000 (Tacitus, *Agricola* 35–37). We therefore have a force smaller than that committed by Frontinus to the final conquest of the Silures and Ordovices in Wales.

It is important to note that Shirley's estimates are narrow calculations just for erecting the buildings and ramparts. They do not include the extraction and manufacture of the vast amount of material required for Inchtuthil and the smaller forts. Neither do they calculate the effort required to build the connecting road network, nor are the many and various calls on the army's manpower (including guard duties, training, food supply, cooking for the builders, animal care and those on the sick lists) included. As the Vindolanda tablets and the Egyptian military papyri, together with what we know about eighteenth- and nineteenth-century professional armies, demonstrate, military manpower has to be occupied with many other duties. There are of course many uncertainties about these calculations around the length of the construction season and the extent to which auxiliary manpower was used in building their own forts, which it probably was, given the evidence from inscriptions. Also, it is possible that native labour was impressed for road construction and assembling wood and stone. Therefore, even if we assume a tripling or quadrupling of the manpower required, it looks as if the resources available in the north were sufficient to complete one full legionary fortress and the thirteen subsidiary forts with connecting roads in the period 84–86 (Figure 4.25).

If we apply the same logic to Frontinus in Wales a decade earlier, he had a force of three full legions and at least thirty-one auxiliary units, nominally totalling 32,000 men, to build two full legionary fortresses and thirty-six smaller forts, with connecting routes. Given the enormous size and scope of the Flavian investment in forts and the road network in Wales, the manpower – by analogy with the Scottish campaign less than a decade later – seems to demonstrate that the construction work could be delivered in the three seasons of work available from 75–77, with some hangover into Agricola's governorship.

Frontinus Completes the
Conquest of Wales –
the Control Phase
AD76 onwards

Summary of
Vital Statistics
of the
Lines of Control

	Number of Forts	Road Length	Nominal Garrison Manpower	Strength Factors	Ave Distance Forts
Baseline	8	251 kms	2,500	7.0	32 kms
South Coast LOC	1 leg + 7	255 kms	5,000 leg + 4,000	12.0 leg 10.0	32 kms
Silures LOC/ZON	11	346 kms	6,440	17.5	32 kms
Severn Valley LOC	1 leg + 5	239 kms	5,000 leg + 4,360	12.0 leg + 11.2	40 kms
Dee LOC	1 leg + 3	126 kms	5,000 leg + 3,500	12.0 leg + 9.5	32 kms
Central Wales LOC	7	227 kms	2,900	7.3	32 kms
West Coast LOC	10	269 kms	3,136	6.3	27 kms
North Coast LOC	5	150 kms	2,540	5.6	30 kms
Marches Cross Route	4	134 kms	1,000	4.5	33 kms
TOTALS	3 Leg +36 excluding duplicates	1,997 kms	15,000 leg + 30,376	114.9	32 kms

Fig 4.25. Statistical summary of the Line of Control in the Frontinian system, showing a theoretical maximum of 45,000 troops deployed over some 2,000 miles of military roads, with a SF value of 115 – a very mighty force indeed.

How the troops were deployed in the occupation

Using the analytical tool set, we can calculate the Strength Factors (SFs) deployed along each Line of Control and in each area. There are some 115 SFs in total in the Frontinan system. The weight of the garrisons was strongly skewed to the south for oversight and occupation of the Silures. The main east–west Lines of Control with the legions (each with an SF of twelve), were around ten SFs strong, while the north–south LOCs along the west coast and in Central Wales had around six SFs. The main force of occupation was in the territory of the Silures, with seventeen SFs deployed to keep the Roman Army's old enemy firmly under the military thumb (Figure 4.26).

One of the most striking facts of the deployment is the interval between the forts, which averages at 32km: on no less than seven of the nine routes, the interval averages between 30 and 33km. This is the length of the textbook single day's march between forts, and thus another strong indication for central planning of the system (Figure 4.26).

The total of the Strength Factors for Frontinus in Wales comes to 114.9, which is a very large force. This certainly includes some double-counting because elements of the legions (three x twelve = thirty-six SFs) would have been brigaded with auxiliaries in the new fort network, although probably less than in the campaign period. However, it seems that Frontinus had designed and built a fort and road network that meant the *Exercitus Britannia* soon became too overstretched to garrison all the territory it was taking on when the additional commitments in Northern England and then Scotland are taken into account.

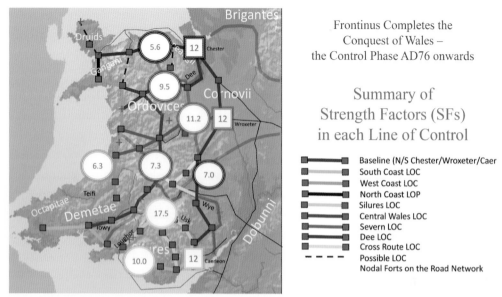

Fig 4.26. The Strength Factors (SFs) shown diagrammatically on the map of Frontinus' masterplan of forts and roads. The three baseline Legionary fortresses are the square '12SF' boxes, and the circles show the SFs for each of the Lines of Control.

Conclusion

What has been described here is as close to a textbook Roman campaign and occupation of a hostile area as can be found.

The Silures and the Ordovices had long been a thorn in the side of the Roman governors of *Britannia*. They had given one governor (Scapula) a fatal breakdown, forced another (Gallus) to effectively withdraw from their territory, made another (Veranius) eat his words, resisted the scorched-earth policy of another (Paulinus) and caused yet another to retreat (Maximus). More than three decades after the Claudian expeditionary force had landed, Wales and its still-resisting tribes remained a very visible sign of unfinished business by the Roman Army.

Cerialis, Frontinus and Agricola had orders to execute the complete conquest of the peoples of Britain. After Cerialis had brought the people of the uplands of England – the confederation of the Brigantes, who had slipped out of the orbit of Rome – into the formal empire, this left those living in modern-day Wales as the next target for Governor Frontinus when he arrived in the province in 74.

Frontinus, both as a military theorist and an able administrator, was a loyal servant of four emperors. He had at his disposal a much increased *Exercitus Britannia*, and he therefore deployed overwhelming force to finish what his predecessors had failed to achieve.

The impact that this amount of military development and demand for supply had on this relatively small and hitherto self-sufficient area would have been immense.

The consumption of timber, turf and clay for construction, and demand for food and forced labour from local populations, would have dramatically changed how society functioned. This time, any resisters and their families would have been killed or enslaved.

In Wales, the Romans had, after three decades, finally and decisively won. This was not just because of their increased and superior numbers – although this was a fundamental component of their success. It was because Frontinus executed the campaign systematically, having recognized that after the military victory, conquest and control were essential. Previous Roman governors tasked with the conquest of Wales were entirely prepared to be ruthless: what made the difference for Frontinus was his systematic approach. He was able to reach the furthest corners of Wales, in the same way Augustus had in Iberia. Frontinus' fort and road grid extended to Cardigan Bay, while his north–south LOCs not only dominated the coasts, they dominated the interior and all the river valleys of the west and the north, whether it was the Conwy or the Rheidol. Once completed by Agricola's surprise occupation of Anglesey, there was nowhere for resisters to retreat.

Frontinus has given us here a masterclass in how to defeat and overawe a population using military 'shock and awe'. This was how the Romans took over and gripped hostile territory. In doing so, Frontinus showed himself to be a master of terrain and physical geography and human settlement, as well as military strategy. He and his staff had surveyed the geography of Wales; they understood where and how the population lived, and deployed forts and garrisons to first conquer and then control these areas. The military surveys both before and during the campaign had to be detailed, comprehensive and up-to-date to construct this intricate network. Here,

The Building of the Legionary Fortress at Inchtuthil
[Source: Shirley 2011 in Britannia XXVII 111-128]

- Calculations by Elizabeth Shirley a Chartered Building Surveyor
- Used Inchtuthil Legionary Fortress to calculate material used and labour
- Fortress considered in construction of fortress
  - i.e. assemblage of materials, groundworks, timber structures etc. – these further sub-divided into, frame, roof coverings and wall cladding etc.
- Estimates made for roof shape and pitch, coverings, eaves, etc.
- Calculations made for each building i.e. 66 barracks etc
- The materials used were calculated:
  - 16,100m3 of main timbers
  - 366,000 tegulae and 375,000 imbrices
  - 800m3 mortar
  - 776,000 shingles
- *Source: Shirley 2011 in Britannia XXVII 111-128*

- Man-hours for groundworks – 32,000
- Man-hours for structural frameworks – 597,000
- Man-hours for turf ramparts – 475,000
- Total including other work = 2.7m man-hours
  - Areas excluded include extraction and manufacture of materials;, guarding, training, food supply, cooking, animal care, sick, detached duty etc.
- The total just for construction of Fortress is 4.7m man-hours
- For the labour force estimating a working day of 8 hours was assumed
- In addition to the legionary fortress some 13 other forts were constructed around this period
  - 587,500 = 5,000 men working for 4 months
  - or 1,000 men for 20 months over 2 or 3 seasons
- Taking Inchtuthil alone
  - 337,500 equivalency of 5,000 men working for 2¼ months
  - or 1,000 men for 11¼ month over 2 seasons

Fig 4.27. Summary of the effort involved in building the Flavian legionary fortress at Inctuthill.

the Roman Army demonstrated its understanding of space and distance, as well as the application of force. They deployed forts not just to control the population, but also to exploit the considerable mineral wealth of Wales: the working of gold mines in Dolaucothi and lead and silver mines in the Clywd range in the north-east, and the iron working of the Forest of Dean.

The failure of the North Wales tribes to develop *civitates* and the arguably stunted growth of the southern two *civitates* (*Venta* and *Moridunum*) demonstrate not just the underdevelopment of the region, but also the lasting effects of five decades of warfare and occupation. They also highlight the less-than-enthusiastic integration into the Roman economy and resistance to adoption of the imperial ideal by some of the tribal leadership and population alike, who continued to value their freedom (Mattingly, 2006, p.523).

It is therefore not surprising that there is a strong comparison to be made with another period and another organization driven by surveyors and engineers, one that was also interested in the centres of population, exploiting the mineral wealth of Wales and acutely aware of the terrain they were traversing. These were the nineteenth-century railway companies, whose strategic network is very similar to that of Frontinus and the Roman Army. Even the major rail junctions closely correspond to the nodal forts, a relationship that was first highlighted by Michael Jarrett (2002) (Fig 7.28).

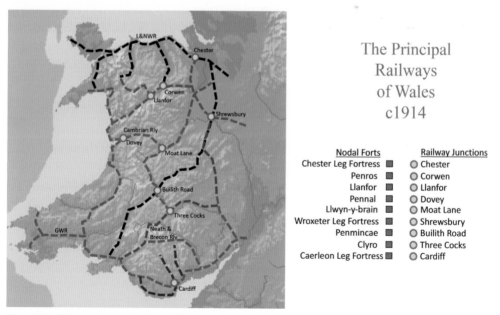

The Principal
Railways
of Wales
c1914

Nodal Forts		Railway Junctions	
Chester Leg Fortress	■	○	Chester
Penros	■	○	Corwen
Llanfor	■	○	Llanfor
Pennal	■	○	Dovey
Llwyn-y-brain	■	○	Moat Lane
Wroxeter Leg Fortress	■	○	Shrewsbury
Penmincae	■	○	Builith Road
Clyro	■	○	Three Cocks
Caerleon Leg Fortress	■	○	Cardiff

Fig 4.28. The railways built in Wales in the Victorian era follow the paths of many of the Roman roads built by Frontinus, and many of the key railway junctions are to be found close to the sites of strategic forts – a correspondence noticed by Jarrett (2002).

Chapter 5

Agricola in Scotland – Rome's First Frontier Followed by Rome's Failure? The Flavian Conquest and Retreat from Scotland

Vespasian's imperial grand design achieved and then thrown away

Method Adopted

The Flavian conquest of what is now the area of Scotland lying north of the Forth/Clyde isthmus is an ideal test case for analysis by the D-LAM method (see Chapters 7 and 8). This is because:

- in Tacitus' *Agricola*, we have the most detailed written record of a Roman campaign in Britain. Whether we regard it as history, hagiography or regime-change ideology, we have it and should make use of it (Hanson, 1987, p.23);
- there has been antiquarian and archaeological investigation of the Roman remains – and more recently the native settlements – in the area for almost three centuries, and most of it is published and readily available, in particular Richmond on Fendoch (1939), Pitts and St Joseph on Inchtuthil (1975) and Hanson on Elginhaugh (2007);
- this Roman occupation was short (possibly as little as six years, and only thirteen at most), which means that the remains are mostly single-phase or have at most two Flavian phases (although some of the forts then have Antonine overlays). British archaeologists are very fortunate: there are few places in the Roman Empire where there is such a snapshot in time and nowhere else that includes such rich diversity, including an almost completed legionary fortress, large and normal-sized forts, fortlets, turrets and strategic military roads;
- the complexity and wealth of the remains have generated some passionate debates as to what they signify, and there is a wealth of published data and analysis (Hanson, 1987; Woolliscroft & Hoffmann, 2010).

But just what needs to go into the analytical 'test tube'? The elements are as follows:

1. the historical context of the campaign;
2. the physical environment which the Roman Army faced in the North;
3. the native population, structures and settlements that the Romans encountered;
4. the archaeological evidence left by Agricola's campaigns;
5. the archaeological evidence left by Agricola's forts and roads;
6. analysis and interpretation of the archaeological system.

On the basis of this analysis, we can pull the strategic story together by applying the analytics tool set (D-LAM) to Agricola's campaigns in the North. This enables us to reconstruct assessments of:

- Agricola's final campaign in 82–83;
- the work done by Agricola's unknown successor in 84–87;
- the abandonment of the North in 87;
- what might have been had not Britain's fourth legion been transferred.

1: The historical context of the campaign

The main force of the Roman Army probably first penetrated the lands north of the Forth/Clyde isthmus at the end of the 70s, although the early 70s have been suggested (Woolliscroft & Hoffmann, 2010, p.185). The Romans held some of this territory north of the isthmus on at least three occasions:

- from 79–86/87 under the Flavians;
- from 142–c.163 as a forward extension of the Antonine Wall;
- during Septimius Severus' assault and ultimately genocidal campaign against the Caledones and Maeatae from 206–209.

A question that deserves to be posed is why the Romans bothered with Britain, in particular with the upland areas, and why they attempted to conquer the north of Scotland, given that it was unhospitable, sparsely populated and (even after taking account of slightly warmer temperatures then) climatically hostile. Part of the answer is that Caledonia and Thule – now securely identified as the Shetland Islands (Wolfson, 2008, p.63) – exercised a powerful hold on the elite Roman imagination. These were the fabled 'Ends of the Earth', the furthest north that Rome ventured. To win battles and conquer peoples in far *Britannia* demonstrated the reach of Rome and power of the emperor who could achieve this, even at so great a distance from Rome. Agricola's campaigns were the first-century equivalent of a 'moonshot'. It is surely no coincidence that Tacitus' narrative practically finishes

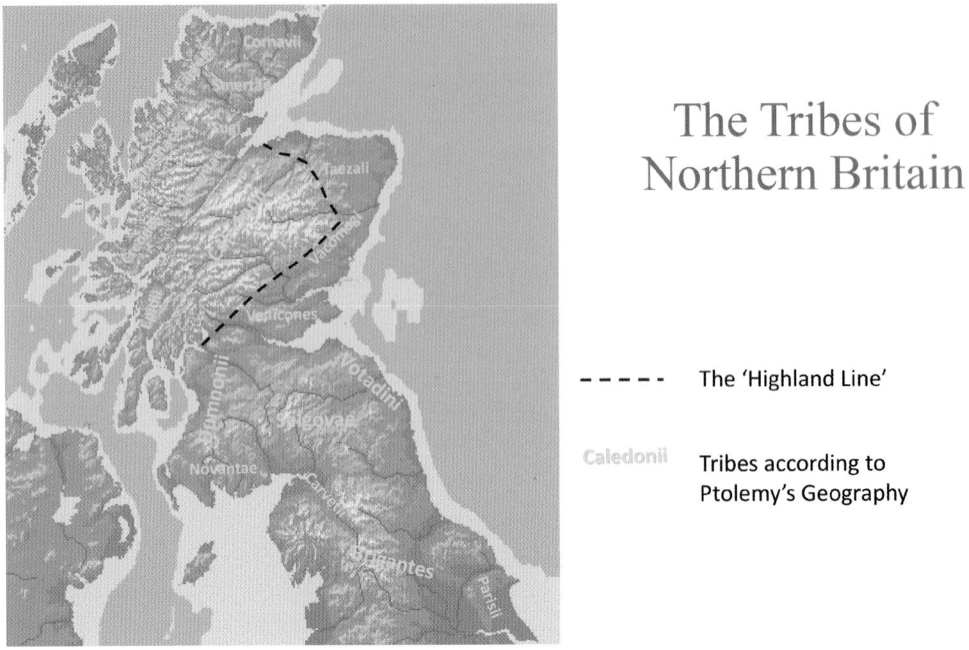

The Tribes of
Northern Britain

- - - - -   The 'Highland Line'

Caledonii   Tribes according to
Ptolemy's Geography

Fig 5.1. The tribes of Northern Britain according to the second-century *Geography* of Ptolemy, itself derived from an earlier document. It probably reflects military surveys carried out during Agricola's campaigns.

with the circumnavigation of Britain, just as Claudius' conquest concluded with the submission of Thule (Hoffmann, 2013, p.119).

This case study is concerned with the Flavian invasion and occupation of the area north of the Forth/Clyde isthmus. This was the culmination of the mission to complete the conquest of *Britannia* that Vespasian set his three governors. The task was paused by his son Titus, then restarted by Domitian before being completely abandoned. We are blessed (although some say misled) with a unique literary source: Tacitus' biography of his father-in-law, Julius Agricola, governor from 77–83.

This Flavian invasion has left, north of the isthmus, the remains of one almost complete legionary fortress, some thirteen smaller forts, six fortlets and many marching camps. Antiquarians and archaeologists have diligently studied these sites over the past three centuries. Many academic studies exist, as well as popular guides to visiting the surviving Roman military remains. Unlike the rest of the empire, where civil life in time reached to the borders, the remains of Roman Scotland are, owing to the transitory nature of the successive occupations, almost exclusively military. This borderland therefore provides us with unique insights and perspectives.

The Roman campaigns tend to be seen as temporary interludes in the long-running continuity of the Iron Age in Northern Britain. This approach is exemplified by

	AD	Emperor	Actions of Agricola as described by Tacitus
Yr1	77	Vespasian	• arrives in Britain late in campaigning season
			• Ordovices had attacked a cavalry *Ala*
			• pursues tribe into Welsh hills and takes Anglesey
Yr2	78	Vespasian	• conquers area usually taken to be that of Brigantes (N. England)
Yr3	79	Vespasian/Titus	• advances as far as the 'Taus' (identified as River Tay)
Yr4	80	Titus	• consolidation and Forth/Clyde isthmus forts
Yr5	81	Titus/Domitian	• amphibious operations in area facing Ireland (Argyll or more probably Galloway)
Yr6	82	Domitian	• combined operations with the fleet north of Forth/Clyde
			• almost loses weak *Leg IX Hispana* when operating in three columns
			• natives get away into the forests and marshes
Yr7	83	Domitian	• Battle of Mons Graupius against 30,000 Caledones led by Calgacus
			• auxiliaries do the fighting; legions sit back and watch
			• 10,000 Caledones killed, 360 Roman dead
			• Agricola recalled after seven years' governorship
			• 'All Britain now conquered but immediately thrown away'

Fig 5.2. The now generally accepted version of the sequencing and dates of Agricola's campaigns during his unprecedented seven-year governorship of *Britannia*.

the way in which the extraordinarily fine and interesting Roman-era finds in the Scottish National Museum are now split up and displayed as various classes of artefacts rather than grouped together as 'Roman'. Interpretations of the Roman invasions and occupations also gets caught up in contemporary Scottish perceptions of English invasion and occupation. For the inhabitants of south, central and eastern Scotland, however, the Roman Army would have been a constant presence for three centuries: as regular patrols beyond the frontier, as occasional occupiers and sometimes, for other tribes such as the Votadini, as 'protectors'.

Tacitus' *Agricola* is the starting point for any discussion of the context and chronology of the Flavian invasion of northern Scotland. Tacitus notoriously gives few military or geographical details, but what he does tell us about Agricola's campaigns in each of his five years in the north is summarised in Figure 5.3. As is now recognized, the *Agricola* is not history in the modern sense, but neither should it be discounted, as some have argued. It was published in 98 by Tacitus, not simply as a biography of his father-in-law but as a literary tour de force, and would have been understood as such by his core audience of fellow senators in Rome. Tacitus thus references other histories such as Caesar's *Gallic Wars*. It is also a political tract supporting the new Galba/Trajan regime, while attacking Tacitus' hated regime of Domitian, which had dominated the Senate. While 'a healthy dose of scepticism is fitting … the story would not have worked at all, had there been no fighting during Agricola's governorship' (Woolliscroft & Hoffmann, 2010, p.202). Senators would have had a good understanding – and even personal recollections – of the Flavian campaigns in Britain because some, like Frontinus, had themselves served in these campaigns.

2: The physical environment that the Roman Army faced in the North

The campaign in the north of Britain was for the Roman Army, as for the Flavian dynasty and the Senate in Rome, the campaign at the 'Ends of the Earth' to the Caledonian forest and mountains, and to furthest Thule (Hoffmann, 2013, p.119). This was to be the proof that the Romans were masters of the world. Jupiter had given the Romans 'rule [*imperium*] with no boundaries' (Vergil, *Aeneid* 1.278–9), and Agricola had been tasked with proving this to be true.

The Roman Army of the first century AD was no stranger to hard campaigning or harsh terrain, as Corbulo in Armenia in the 60s or Germanicus in the German forests early in the century had proved. Nevertheless, the north of Scotland presented some unique challenges, especially when the decision had been taken to stay and occupy, not just to fight in the summer seasons. The long winter nights and cold

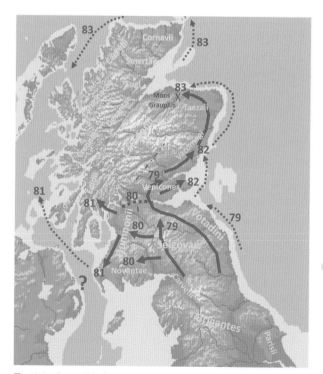

Agricola's
Campaigns
in the North
AD79-83
According to Tacitus

Caledonii   Tribes according to
Ptolemy's Geography

Fig 5.3. Agricola's five years campaigning in Northern Britain, derived from Tacitus' account in his *Agricola*.

at these latitudes would have made this a hard posting for Roman legionaries and auxiliaries alike.

We know that the Roman Army included specialist surveyors, and it appears that one of the first acts of the army upon landing in AD 43 was to survey long-range alignments across the whole of Britain, as far north as lines from Lancaster and Catterick to High Rochester in modern Northumberland (Entwhistle, 2019, p.20). Agricola would thus have had excellent knowledge both of the lands and the people he would encounter on the campaign.

As proof, we have the remains of one of the Flavian military maps, which is the source for the Scottish entries in Ptolemy's *Geography*. This contains tribal, river and place names north of the isthmus. The place names probably relate to Roman forts, and it is tempting to associate *Victoria* with Inchtuthil. Each place had co-ordinates but, as many of these were plotted relative to each other, Scotland was portrayed with a major distortion to the east, which makes identification of places challenging (Jones and Mattingly, 2002, p.19).

There is a distinct difference, still apparent today, between the inhospitable Highlands beyond the Highland Line Fault to the north and west, and the fertile

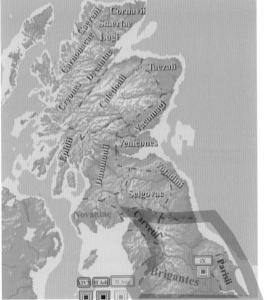

Britain on Agricola's Arrival in AD77

Brigantes   Conquered/occupied
Votadini   Protectorates
Caledonii   Unoccupied
— · — · ·   Notional boundaries

Fig 5.4. Cerialis had recently occupied some of the territory of the Brigantes, having moved *Legio IX Hispana* to a forward base at York in the heart of their best territory. He then built a Line of Penetration up Ermine Street, and then across Stainmore to a fort at Carlisle. Cerialis possibly also had a temporary campaign base in Dalswinton in Galloway on the north side of the Solway Firth.

coastal lands which narrow as they approach the sea at the area known as the Mounth near Stonehaven. This determined both the area worth occupying by a conquering force and also framed the route of any invasion, which had to follow the course taken by the modern A90 road and the main railway line up from the crossing of the Firth at Stirling, north-east through Strathearn and Strathmore. This was the route taken by Agricola in AD 83, Edward I in 1303 and the Duke of Cumberland in 1746 (Jones and Mattingly, 2002, p.76).

Topography dictates the shape of campaigns in the north of Scotland, but three key differences between the present and the first century AD must be recognised. The land today has many trees, some in managed plantations and others in natural woods, whereas pollen analysis from the Late Iron Age and the Roman invasion period strongly suggests that the landscape had then been cleared of trees, except in the river valleys. Furthermore, the fertile lands had been drained over the preceding three centuries to our times, drying out the old marshes and bogs. These would have made moving through the territory much harder for the Roman Army. Finally, although this is a hotly contested subject, the sea level was probably higher than today; by as much as 9m c.2000 BC and possibly still 3m in the first century AD (Davies, 2020, p.39). While further increasing the extent of waterlogged ground, this would have improved access up the river estuaries, an important logistical advantage for a campaign in which combined operations and sea-borne supply were important.

3: The native population, structures and settlements that the Romans encountered

The characteristic settlement of Late Iron Age Scotland was the defended homestead, but this encompassed great variety in its design and construction. In the north and west, there were many brochs (stone towers) and duns (more irregular and smaller stone towers). In the areas we are concerned with – that is, the Forth/Clyde isthmus and the Straths to the north and east – there were by the first century duns and some brochs (Jones & Mattingly, 2002, 61). Beyond the Highland Line north of the Upper Tay, there were large numbers of duns. There were also souterrains (stone-built underground stores).

North of the Forth/Clyde isthmus, Agricola found himself facing a very different enemy from the tribes he had recently conquered in the Lowlands. Whilst there were many substantial hillforts of more than 2.5 hectares in the eastern Lowlands, these were not to be found further north. There were small hillforts with timber ramparts stretching up the east side of the Highland Line, but these seem to have been going out of use before the first century. In the Lowlands, there were major tribal centres – Traprain Law for the Votadini, Eildon Hill North for the Selgovae and Ward Law for the Novantae – but none further north. In the campaign area north of the isthmus, there was only one large hillfort, Bennachie in Aberdeenshire.

There were large numbers of undefended hut settlements. The density of Iron Age sites was particularly high to the north and south of the Tay estuary, with medium levels of settlement over most of the rest of the campaign area, stretching up the fertile lands of the east coast to Aberdeenshire, round to Nairn and the Moray Firth and into the Great Glen (Jones & Mattingly, 2002, p.63). Where there have been detailed studies, sites indicate a well-populated landscape (Woolliscroft & Hoffmann, 2010, p.209).

Pollen analysis suggests that forest clearance in the lowland areas had started in the Neolithic period, and arable farming had spread, so that by the time of the Roman invasion the landscape was cleared of trees, except for alder and willow on the riverbanks. Cereal remains – mostly barley – plus vegetables and fruit are found on Iron Age sites. However, pollen analysis suggests an economy principally based on stock-rearing, with most of the land given over to grazing, interspersed with areas of cultivated fields and orchards (Woolliscroft & Hoffmann, 2010, p.208).

The Flavian Frontier in Scotland
The Forth/Clyde Isthmus and the Gask Ridge

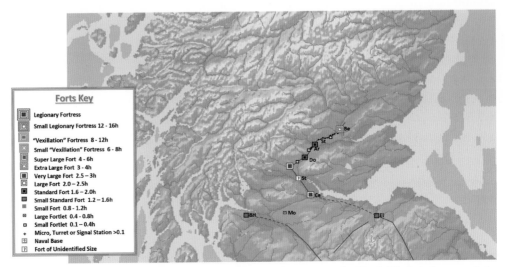

Forts Key

Legionary Fortress	
Small Legionary Fortress 12 - 16h	
"Vexillation" Fortress 8 - 12h	
Small "Vexillation" Fortress 6 - 8h	
Super Large Fort 4 - 6h	
Extra Large Fort 3 - 4h	
Very Large Fort 2.5 – 3h	
Large Fort 2.0 – 2.5h	
Standard Fort 1.6 – 2.0h	
Small Standard Fort 1.2 – 1.6h	
Small Fort 0.8 - 1.2h	
Large Fortlet 0.4 - 0.8h	
Small Fortlet 0.1 – 0.4h	
Micro, Turret or Signal Station >0.1	
Naval Base	
Fort of Unidentified Size	

Fig 5.5. The first two components of the system: the forts across the Forth/Clyde isthmus and the defended road up to Stirling, Ardoch and along the Gask Ridge to the Tay, thus enclosing Fife and the Venicones.

The Flavian Frontier in Scotland
with the addition of the Highland Line Forts and Strathmore

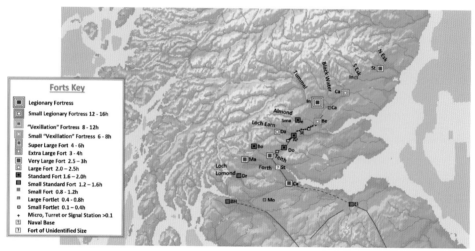

Fig 5.6. The addition of the next three components of the system: the legionary fortress at Inchtuthil; the Highland Line forts; and the extension up Strathmore, thus defending the good lands between the isthmus and the Highland Line as well as providing the jumping-off point for the final conquest of the island of *Britannia*.

Unfortunately, it is not possible to estimate population levels with any degree of certainty, but those of Dalriada and Pictland around AD 500 have been estimated at 10,000 and 80,000–100,000 respectively (Laing, 2006, p.21), so a total of 100,000–200,000 north of the isthmus is a reasonable assumption. This is a number worth remembering when we look at the relatively large size of the Roman forces deployed against them.

Although our knowledge and understanding of the existing tribal inhabitants north of the isthmus is sketchy, and there is much to be discovered and studied, all the indications are of a dispersed society. This is in stark contrast to the stereotype of aristocrat-led warring tribes in Gaul and the south of Britain. The tribes Agricola was now attacking were living in relatively secure conditions with self-sufficient mixed arable and pastoral farming, without the significant social differentiation, external trade and luxury items to be found in the societies further south (Jones & Mattingly, 2002, p.61). Although they were given tribal names by the Romans – the peoples north of the isthmus in Fife and the Straths being called the Venicones – there is no evidence of them acting as a tribe like those in southern Britain. This was therefore a very different social and economic situation that the Romans encountered: no large tribes ruled by kings, no *oppida* that could be captured and no ruling class to be Romanized. This was an area that it would be hard to grip in the tried and tested Roman manner.

The Flavian Frontier System in Scotland
- planned by Agricola and implemented by him and his Successor

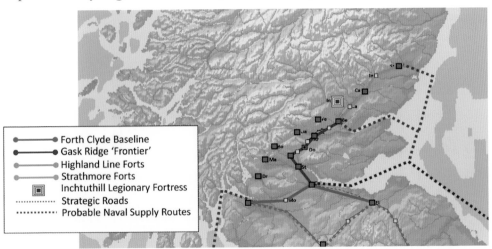

Fig 5.7. The Flavian System split into its five component parts. Note also the marine supply lines.

Our description of how the tribes of the North fought comes from Roman descriptions and from the archaeology. There is also argument by analogy with other less-developed Celtic societies, often from later periods, and also with tribal societies around the world. The central assumption is that the tribes had small numbers of well-armed and experienced warriors attached to the tribal leaders. Young men would be attracted to these bands, since this would be a way to acquire wealth and glory. They would have been supplemented by farmsteaders who fought in kindred groups and could be called to arms when danger threatened or a raid on other tribes was planned (Fraser, 2005, p.42).

If this summary is correct, the 'Caledones' would have been a federation of small tribes and kindred groups living between the Highland Line and the Great Glen.

4: The archaeological evidence left by Agricola's campaigns

The first element of archaeological evidence we encounter is the remains of strings of marching camps which are interpreted as tracing Agricola's campaigns of 82 and 83 against the coalition of the Caledones.

Scotland, like Northern England, is a treasure-trove of what are variously termed temporary or marching camps. Their positions have been used to try to locate Agricola's route to the site of Mons Graupius, without success (except in generating a small publishing industry). Very few of these camps have been excavated, and they have rarely yielded secure dates. A particularly complex gate formation with an

The Flavian Frontier in Scotland
Forth/Clyde Isthmus, Gask Ridge, Highland Line and Strathmore Line

Camp-aign	System	Purpose	Desription	Id / Name	Roman Name	Phases	Size Ha	Size Code	Strength Factor	First Unit	Second Unit	Approx Manpower	Unit if Known	Build Code	Start Date	End Date	Materia l	Buildings	Ditches	Gates	Annex	Controls	RM	IM	Km
FLAVIAN OCCUPATION OF N SCOTLAND																									
AGR	HIGH	FRO	GLENBLK	1.0 Drumquhassle		None	1	1.30	FOR	1.0	1coh?		500					Turf		Double	Parrot	None	Endrick Water, Strathblane	0.0	0.0	0.0
AGR	HIGH	FRO	GLENBLK	2.0 Malling		None	1	2.78	VLF	2.5	2coh or lala/1coh?		1,000					Turf		Double	Eagle	One?	Aberfoyle, Glen of Aird	9.9	9.3	15.0
AGR	HIGH	FRO	GLENBLK	3.0 Bochcastle		None	1	1.90	FRT	1.5	1coh or lala		500					Turf		Double	Parrot	None	Strathyre, Strath Gartney	6.1	5.8	9.3
AGR	HIGH	FRO	GLENBLK	4.0 Dalginross	Antonn?	1	2.43	LFT	2.0	2coh		1,000					Turf		Double	Parrot	Post/Bld?	Glen Artney, Strathearn	13.2	12.4	20.0
AGR	HIGH	FRO	GLENBLK	5.0 Fendoch	Later Fl?	1	1.80	FRT	1.5	1coh or lala		500					Turf	Pr/Pa/2G/V?/10B/4?	Single	Straight	None	Snuf Glen, Glen Almond	11.3	10.7	17.2
Highland Line									8.5			3,500											40.5	38.2	61.5
AGR	HIGH	FRO	ANCHOR	6.0 Inchtuthil	None	1	21.74	LEG	12.0	LEG		5,000	XX Valeria Victrix	Agr	84	86	Wood	Pr/4T/6G/V1F/E/5C/64B/T	Turf/Sto	Single	Straight	Building		96.2	90.9	84.8
Legionary Anchor									29.0			5,000													
AGR	GASK	FRO	ROADLINE	1.0 Camelon		1 2 Fl/3 Aut?	large	SLF	4.0	3coh or lala/1coh?		1,000		Agr	80	88	Wood	Turf		Single	Straight	?	Tay Valley	15.3	14.5	23.3
				2.0 Stirling (King's Knot)?	?	?	?		1.0	1coh?		500			?									0.0	0.0	0.0
AGR	GASK	FRO	ROADLINE	3.0 Doune	None	1	2.25	LFT	2.0	lala or 2coh?		1,000		Agr	84	86	Wood	Turf		Triple				11.2	10.6	17.0
AGR	GASK	FRO	ROADLINE	3.5 Glenbank	None	1	0.07	mic	0.0								Wood	Turf	3H?	Double				9.2	8.7	14.0
AGR	GASK	FRO	ROADLINE	3.7 Greenloaning	None	1		tow	0.0								Wood	Turf	None metalling	Double	Tower					
AGR	GASK	FRO	ROADLINE	4.0 Ardoch	2Ant/3Aut	1 2	3.50	ELF	3.0	2coh?		1,000	Coh 1 Hispanorum				Wd/St	Turf	Pr/Pa/7B/?	Double	Butt-end	None			11.8	11.2	18.0
AGR	GASK	FRO	ROADLINE	4.1 Blackhill Wood	None	1		tow	0.0								Wood	Turf		Double	Butt-end					
AGR	GASK	FRO	ROADLINE	4.2 Shielhill South	None	1		tow	0.0								Wood	Turf		Double	Butt-end					
AGR	GASK	FRO	ROADLINE	4.3 Shielhill North	None	1		tow	0.0								Wood	Turf		Double	Butt-end					
AGR	GASK	FRO	ROADLINE	4.5 Kaims Castle	None	1		mic	0.0								Wood	Turf		Single	Butt-end					
AGR	GASK	FRO	ROADLINE	4.7 Westerton	None	1		tow	0.0								Wood	Turf		Single	Butt-end					
AGR	GASK	FRO	ROADLINE	??? Cuiltburn	???			???									Wood	Turf		Single						
AGR	GASK	FRO	ROADLINE	5.0 Strageath	Ant2/Aut3	1	1.77	FRT	1.5	1coh?		500					Wood	Turf	Pr/Pa/2G/V?/2F/12Bo/1W?	Double	Parrot?	One		7.2	6.8	11.0
AGR	GASK	FRO	ROADLINE	5.01 Parkneuk	None	1		tow	0.0								Wood	Turf		Single	Butt-end					
AGR	GASK	FRO	ROADLINE	5.02 Raith	None	1		tow	0.0								Wood	Turf		Single	Butt-end					
AGR	GASK	FRO	ROADLINE	5.03 Ardunie	None	1		tow	0.0								Wood	Turf		Single	Butt-end					
AGR	GASK	FRO	ROADLINE	5.04 Roundlaw	None	1		tow	0.0								Wood	Turf		Single	Butt-end					
AGR	GASK	FRO	ROADLINE	5.05 Kirkhill	None	1		tow	0.0								Wood	Turf		Single	Butt-end					
AGR	GASK	FRO	ROADLINE	5.06 Muir o'Fauld	None	1		tow	0.0								Wood	Turf		Single	Butt-end					
AGR	GASK	FRO	ROADLINE	5.07 Gask House	None	1		tow	0.0								Wood	Turf		Single	Butt-end					
AGR	GASK	FRO	ROADLINE	5.08 Witch Knowe	None	1		tow	0.0								Wood	Turf		Single	Butt-end					
AGR	GASK	FRO	ROADLINE	5.09 Moss Side	None	1		tow	0.0								Wood	Turf		Single	Butt-end					
AGR	GASK	FRO	ROADLINE	5.5 Midgate	None	1	0.05	mic									Wood	Turf		Single	Butt-end					
AGR	GASK	FRO	ROADLINE	5.6 Westmuir	None	1		tow	0.0								Wood	Turf		Single	Butt-end					
AGR	GASK	FRO	ROADLINE	??? Cuilmuirhead	???			???									Wood	Turf								
AGR	GASK	FRO	ROADLINE	5.8 Peel	None	1		tow	0.0								Wood	Turf		Single	Butt-end					
AGR	GASK	FRO	ROADLINE	5.9 Huntingtower	None	1		tow	0.0								Wood	Turf		Single	Butt-end					
AGR	GASK	FRO	ROADLINE	6.0 Bertha		1	3.90	ELF	3.0	3coh or lala/1coh?		1,000					Wood	Turf		Single	Butt-end			18.4	17.4	28.0
Gask Ridge									14.5			4,500											57.9	54.7	88.0
AGR	SMORE	FRO	LOP	1.0 Bertha		1	3.90	ELF	3.0	3coh or lala/1coh?		1,000					Wood	Turf		Simple				0.0	0.0	0.0
AGR	SMORE	FRO	ROADLINE	2.0 Cargill		1	0.50	lft	0.3	2 cent		160					Wood	Turf		Double	Parrot		Strathmore, Strathtay	8.6	8.1	13.0
AGR	SMORE	FRO	ROADLINE	2.1 Cargill		2	1.94	FRT	1.5	1 coh		500					Wood	Turf		2.3	Parrot		Strathmore, Strathtay	0.0	0.0	0.0
AGR	SMORE	FRO	ROADLINE	3.0 Cardean		1	3.70	ELF	3.0	2 coh		1,000					Wood	Turf		2,1,4,5		Two		9.5	9.0	14.5
AGR	SMORE	FRO	ROADLINE	4.0 Inverquharity		1	0.52	lft	0.3	2 cent		160					Wood	Turf		3,2				11.0	10.4	16.7
AGR	SMORE	FRO	ROADLINE	5.0 Strathcathro		1	2.60	VLF	2.5	2 coh		1,000					Wood	Turf		Triple			S. Esk, Prosen Water, Quharity	14.8	14.0	22.5
Strathmore									6.1			2,000											43.9	41.4	66.7
AGR	GASK	FRO	ROADLINE	1.0 Camelon / Elginhaugh		1 2 Fl/3 Aut	large	S2F	4.0	3coh or lala/1coh?		500		Agr	80	88	Turf	Turf		Triple	Parrot	One		0.0	0.0	0.0
				Mollins		1	0.40	lft	0.3	2 cent		160					Wood	Turf		Single		One?		34.9	32.9	53.0
				Barochan		1	1.30	FOR	1.0	1 coh		500					Wood	Turf		Single		One?		12.5	11.8	19.0
Forth/Clyde Isthmus									2.3			1,160											24.3	23.0	37.0
																							130.4	123.2	109.0

Fig 5.8. The database for the five elements of the system, showing Strength Factors, distances and garrisons where known or inferred.

Pic 5.1. Looking out from the north-east corner of Newstead fort towards the River Tweed, the Roman bridge for Dere Street was between where the rail and road bridges now stand. The military amphitheatre – the most northerly in the Empire – was on the platform in the foreground. (*Photo by author*)

out-turned bank and ditch, and also an internal ditch, is known as a 'Strathcathro' gate. There are fourteen of these marching camps of varying sizes in Scotland, and all but two in the far north are associated with Flavian-era forts (Jones and Mattingly, p.82, and Figure 5.10). Most authorities accept 'Strathcathro' camps as Flavian, and it has been suggested that they were the invention of a particular

Pic 5.2. The boar, symbol of the legion, was proudly displayed on this antefix (roof component) made by Legion XX. From Holt in Clwyd, in the British Museum. (*Photo Wikicommons*)

praefectus castrorum, either of the *XI Hispana* whilst it was campaigning in the north and was attacked in its camp in 82, or of the *II Adiutrix* that left Britain in 87: the attribution is not proven (Jones, 2012, p.127). The 'Strathcathro' camps are shown in Figure 5.9: they are of very varied sizes and do not make up a coherent group of camps that could be linked to a single campaign. Many of them may well relate to the construction detachments for their adjacent forts (Hanson, 1985, p.125).

There are several strings of marching camps north of the Forth/Clyde isthmus which are clearly typologically linked, but none can be securely associated with Agricola's campaigns. Given the Roman Army's commitments in Wales, Northern England and the Lowlands at this time, it seems unlikely that the lines of very large 54-hectare camps are Agricolan. Instead, a Severan date to accommodate the Praetorians and legionary reinforcements seems possible (Jones and Mattingly, 2002, p.83). There is a double line of 25-hectare marching camps running from Ardoch up Strathmore and heading for where the Highlands meet the sea at Stonehaven, together with another line of 25-hectare camps nearer the coast (Figure 5.9). These are squarish in shape, with six entrances and banks outside their gates (*tituli*). It is possible these represent Agricola's army marching up Strathmore and along the coast in two columns or, alternatively, a single force advancing and then returning. In support of this contention, the earlier date of the 25-hectare camps is confirmed by the fact that the 54-hectare phase at

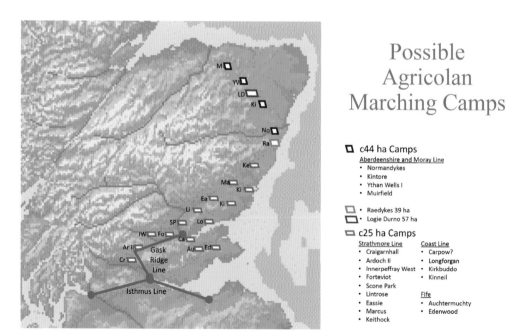

Possible
Agricolan
Marching Camps

□ c44 ha Camps
Aberdeenshire and Moray Line
• Normandykes
• Kintore
• Ythan Wells I
• Muirfield

□ • Raedykes 39 ha
□ • Logie Durno 57 ha

▭ c25 ha Camps

Strathmore Line	Coast Line
• Craigarnhall	• Carpow?
• Ardoch II	• Longforgan
• Innerpeffray West	• Kirkbuddo
• Forteviot	• Kinneil
• Scone Park	
• Lintrose	Fife
• Eassie	• Auchtermuchty
• Marcus	• Edenwood
• Keithock	

Fig. 5.9. The series of 25-hectare camps between the isthmus and Stonehaven may be Flavian in date, based on the sequencing of camps at Ardoch and the Flavian road at Innerpeffray. The 44-hectare camp at Kintore is securely Flavian, so also, therefore, are the other three camps in the sequence.

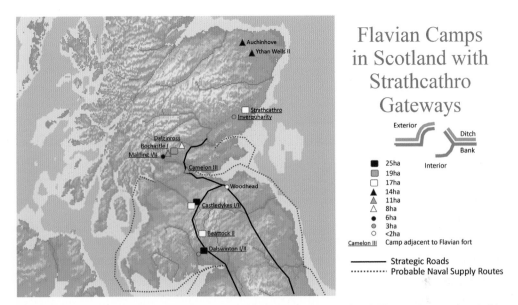

Fig. 5.10. The unique design of 'Strathcathro' gates is closely associated with Flavian forts, and probably indicates construction camps. Unfortunately, the great diversity in fort size and location means they cannot be used to trace Flavian campaigns.

Ardoch overlies the earlier 27-hectare camp. Furthermore, the probable Flavian road at Innerpeffray near Strageath postdates the 25-hectare camp there (Jones, 2012, pp.102, 115).

If we look further into north-east Scotland in Aberdeenshire and Moray, we find there are six marching camps that have been proposed as Agricola's route to bring Calgacus to battle at the still-unidentified site of Mons Graupius. We can be reasonably sure that four of those six are Flavian:

- Normandykes;
- Kintore;
- Ythan Wells I;
- Muiryfold.

These form a clear group since they are all 44 hectares in size, have six entrances protected by *tituli* and are roughly 20km apart. Furthermore, Kintore in Moray is a marching camp that has at last been extensively excavated, securely dating it to the Flavian period, with a later reoccupation in the Severan campaigns (Jones, 2012, p.116; Hoffmann, 2013, p.136). Raedykes, sited at the exit from the pinch point at the Mounth near Stonehaven, is often included in this series, but it is smaller at 39 hectares. Another often proposed addition is the vast 57-hectare camp at Logie Durno, between Kintore and Ythan Wells. This is the equivalent of three-and-a-half legionary fortresses (or eighty football pitches) in size. Durno housed a very large force indeed and was St Joseph's favoured site for Agricola's camp before Mons Graupius, but there is no evidence to support this or indeed any other of the many identifications of the battle site (Frere and St Joseph, 1986; Jones, 2012, p.127).

One myth needs to be demolished, which is that these camps were occupied for only a single night on the march. The excavation of the marching camp at Kintore yielded semi-permanent structures, including ovens, with Flavian radiocarbon dates. This is important because, although the camps are generally one day's march apart, the army could have stayed in the camp, once constructed, for days or even weeks during the campaigning season. We might also expect detachments to remain in occupation, ready for when the army returned on its march back to winter quarters.

In conclusion, we can tentatively propose that Agricola's army, starting from its secure base area behind the Gask Frontier, marched in two columns up Strathmore in 82. They worked closely with the navy, as recounted by Tacitus, who also notes that the army was working in three groups by the end of this year. Then, for the campaign of 83 they retraced their steps through Strathmore, and the army united for the march past Stonehaven and the Mounth for the final climatic battle with

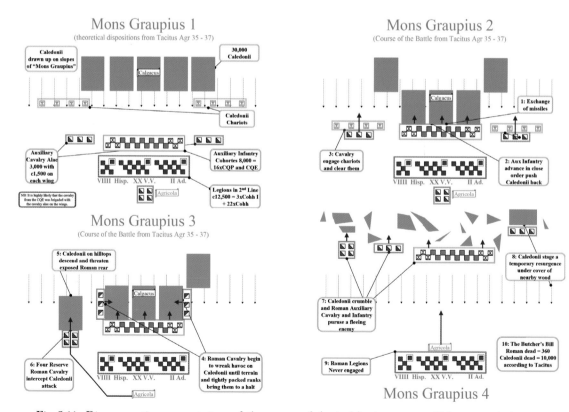

Fig 5.11. Diagrammatic representation of the stages of Agricola's victory over Calgacus and the Caledones at the Battle of Mons Graupius, as narrated by Tacitus in his *Agricola*.

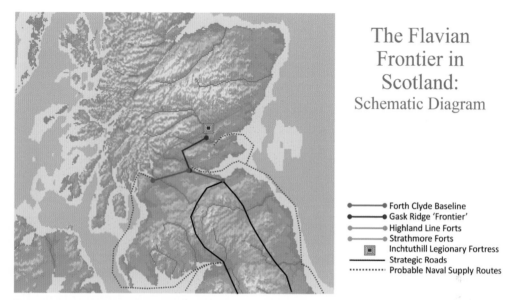

The Flavian
Frontier in
Scotland:
Schematic Diagram

●————● Forth Clyde Baseline
●————● Gask Ridge 'Frontier'
●————● Highland Line Forts
●————● Strathmore Forts
▣ Inchtuthill Legionary Fortress
————— Strategic Roads
············ Probable Naval Supply Routes

Fig 5.12. Pulling the system together, we can see how the army had once again taken over the good lands and provided a secure zone for further campaigning.

the Caledones, whether at Durno or elsewhere, or possibly they marched further still, turning west into Moray or even to the mouth of the Great Glen, where Inverness now stands. In this strategy, we envisage Agricola focusing on the fact that Angus, Moray, Nairn and Buchan represent the largest concentration of good land in Scotland: threatening devastation throughout this area would have meant starvation for the tribes who, as a consequence, united to stand and fight at Mons Graupius (Hanson, 1987, p.128). The large areas of good grazing land taken over by the army for their temporary camps during this and other campaigns suggest that this was a violent campaign of conquest, which would have affected even allied tribes like the Venicones and have severely impacted hostile tribes such as the Vacomagi and Caledones (Jones, 2011, p.122).

5: The archaeological evidence left by Agricola's forts and roads

When we analyze the evidence for a permanent military presence from the Flavian period, it appears to have been built in two stages: before the Battle of Mons Graupius and after. Two elements seem to date from before the battle:

- the three *praesidium* forts across the **Forth/Clyde** isthmus at Barochan, Mollins and Camelon were, according to Tacitus, built by Agricola in 80;
- the **Gask Frontier,** a system of six forts running north from Camelon on the Forth up to the Tay at Bertha, connected by a road protected by a remarkable set of fortlets and watchtowers on its north-easterly route along

the Gask Ridge, with Strathearn to the south. It has been described as 'Rome's first frontier', being the first land frontier as opposed to a defended river line like the Rhine or Danube (Woolliscroft & Hoffmann, 2010, pp.73–148).

After the battle in 83, and probably planned by Agricola but not executed by him, came the three elements added to the Agricolan system in the north:

- At the heart of the system was the legionary fortress at **Inchtuthil**. The fulcrum of the mature system, this sat where three elements met and could be supplied by the navy up the River Tay. Inchtuthil was the most northerly legionary fortress in the Roman Empire and has been the subject of the only complete excavation of such a fortress (Pitts and St Joseph, 1985), and as such, its plan appears in almost every textbook on the Roman Army (Figure 5.15).
- The '**Highland Line**' was another system of forts, this time without a connecting road with fortlets or towers. These five forts sat at the entrance or exit (depending on your interpretation) of all the major and minor routes into and out of the Scottish Highlands. They were placed either to intercept raiders or to invade and launch punitive expeditions into the Highlands (Woolliscroft & Hoffmann, 2010, pp.35–72).
- Finally, the '**Strathmore Line**' was a northern extension of both of these lines of forts running up the principal invasion route to the fertile north-east of Scotland in Moray (a route still followed by the A90 road and ScotRail) and then round to Strathspey and the Great Glen. There were some five forts on this line, running from Bertha to Strathcathro. The large Roman marching camps usually attributed to Agricola (but as yet unprovable) extend this way and stretch north to the possible sites of Mons Graupius. It was on this strategic route that John Balliol in 1296 surrendered to King Edward I in what had been Strathcathro fort.

5.1: The Forth/Clyde isthmus Line

Almost uniquely, there is firm literary evidence for the construction and dating of this line. The political backdrop would seem to be the reign of Titus, who appears to have called a halt to his father Vespasian's forward policy in Britain. It is clearly stated by Tacitus that in Agricola's fourth year as governor (usually taken to be 80), forts were constructed across the Forth/Clyde isthmus:

> If the valour of our army and the glory of Rome had permitted such a thing, a good place for halting the advance was found in Britain itself. The Forth

and Clyde, carried inland for a great distance by the tides of opposite seas, are separated by only a narrow neck of land. This isthmus was now firmly held by garrisons. (Tacitus, *Agricola* 23).

This passage has generated a hunt for Flavian-period forts across the isthmus, but ironically, the archaeological remains themselves are somewhat doubtful and there have been various misidentifications around the Antonine Wall sites. There seems reasonable evidence for Flavian occupation at three forts across the isthmus, and Elginhaugh has been included because that is where Dere Street, descending from the Cheviots, approaches the Forth:

- Elginhaugh, 1.3 hectares (FOR): probably one cohort in garrison;
- Camelon, size unknown but probably very large: three cohorts or one *ala* plus one cohort;
- Mollins, 0.3 hectares (lft) small: probably two centuries;
- Barochan, 1.3 hectares (FOR): probably one cohort.

Therefore, the isthmus was presumably held by the strong fort at Camelon, maybe with three cohorts ready to move north along the Dere Street extension, and two other forts on the Clyde and the Forth, along with a small outpost fortlet at Mollins (possibly garrisoned from Camelon). This only requires a garrison of about 2,000 men (Figures 5.13 and 5.14).

5.2: The Gask Frontier

The 'Great North Road' of Flavian Britain started at York. Traversing the Tyne at Corbridge, it crossed the Cheviots as Dere Street and reached the Forth at Elginhaugh (in the modern suburbs of Edinburgh). It was 195km to the fort at Camelon and skirted what would have been the marshy estuary of the Forth in the Roman era, the height of the Forth being estimated to have been 3m higher in the first century AD (Davies, 2020, p.40). From Camelon, the road headed for a fort at Doune, 30km distant. Almost everyone who has studied this road expects that there will have been an intermediate fort at Stirling, since the distances logically suggest this and it is the historic crossing place of the Forth which the road points to. However, no fort has yet been found.

From there the road turns to the north-east, with forts at Ardoch and Strageath, and finally reaches the Tay at Bertha, 88km from Camelon. The most remarkable element of this system is not the forts but the system of intermediate fortlets and towers. It consists of fortlets at Glenbank, Kaims Castle and Midgate and some seventeen towers identified so far, mostly along the Gask Ridge, starting at Glenbank and stretching for 50km. Unfortunately, the views today are restricted

Agricola's Frontier in AD80

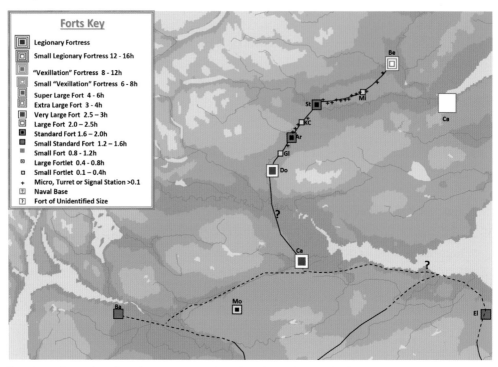

Forts Key

▣	Legionary Fortress
▣	Small Legionary Fortress 12 - 16h
▪	"Vexillation" Fortress 8 - 12h
▫	Small "Vexillation" Fortress 6 - 8h
▪	Super Large Fort 4 - 6h
▫	Extra Large Fort 3 - 4h
▪	Very Large Fort 2.5 – 3h
▫	Large Fort 2.0 – 2.5h
▣	Standard Fort 1.6 – 2.0h
▪	Small Standard Fort 1.2 – 1.6h
▪	Small Fort 0.8 - 1.2h
▫	Large Fortlet 0.4 - 0.8h
▫	Small Fortlet 0.1 – 0.4h
+	Micro, Turret or Signal Station >0.1
⊞	Naval Base
?	Fort of Unidentified Size

Fig. 5.13. A map based on the assumption that when Agricola built the forts across the isthmus, he also protected the Venicones in Fife, thus producing a curious dog-leg frontier line, including the dense Gask Ridge in contrast to the thinly held isthmus. If this was the case, then it reflected where the perceived threat was coming from – that is, tribes to the north and east beyond the 'Highland Line'.

Explanation of Agricola's Frontier in AD80

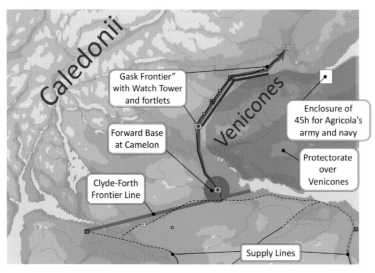

Caledonii

Venicones

Gask Frontier" with Watch Tower and fortlets

Enclosure of 45h for Agricola's army and navy

Forward Base at Camelon

Protectorate over Venicones

Clyde-Forth Frontier Line

Supply Lines

Fig. 5.14. Agricola's frontier of AD 80 provided a protected base for the army and navy campaigning in the north.

by modern planting, but in the largely tree-denuded landscape of the first century, the views both north-west and south-east would have been excellent (Davies, 2020, p.41). The Gask system seems to have been as much concerned with supervising the area of Strathearn to its south as keeping an eye out for 'hostiles' from the north.

The system appears to have operated in the following way, and the four known forts here are all 'large':

- Camelon, size unknown, but probably very large: three cohorts or one *ala* plus one cohort;
- Stirling interpolated fort, unknown size: possibly one cohort;
- Doune, 2.2 hectares (LFT): possibly one *ala* or two cohorts;
- Ardoch, 3.5 hectares (ELF): possibly two cohorts;
- Strageath, 1.77 hectares (FRT): one cohort;
- Bertha, 3.9 hectares (ELF): possibly one *ala* plus one cohort.

There was therefore a significant commitment of force deployed along this road line, with a theoretical strength of over 5,000 men, well able to provide garrisons for the interspersed fortlets and towers as well as for the forts themselves (Figures 5.13 and 5.14).

Despite extensive excavation and study, we are not certain how the towers and the turrets functioned. What we do know is that the towers are sited to allow signalling along the line, both between each other and with the forts. So Ardoch and Strageath can see each other, and Ardoch can see both Glenbank and Kaims Castle and the five towers in between. All seven towers along the Gask Ridge can be seen from Raith, which may have been a fortlet rather than a tower. There is a gap between Midgate and Bertha, which implies a possible lost tower at Cultmalundie (Woolliscroft & Hoffmann, 2010, p.135).

This has the strong look and feel of a system that is designed to be as 'watertight' as possible, with patrols regularly moving along the road to prevent anything other than a few individuals slipping across on a dark night. The fact that it is not a linear barrier should not surprise us, given the investment of time, effort and resources that would require. Furthermore, if the Roman Army's primary purposes were to regulate trade and movement, prevent low-level incursions, cattle rustling or raiding, and to spot any hostile movement, then the Gask towers and road would have achieved this. It is the kind of supervised road line we find on the German *Limes* and on the Eastern frontiers in later years (Steidl, 2019, p.22). It could also be likened to the infamous British control lines across the Veldt in the final phase of the Boer War, designed to interdict movement: the barbed wire and watch towers did not stop a few individuals slipping through, but did very effectively prevent Boer commandos moving or exfiltrating livestock:

The British had constructed so formidable a network of barbed wire, and the blockhouses were so close together and strongly defended, that hitherto our attempts had been abortive. (Viljoen, p.45)

The Roman Army units best adapted to garrison this system would have been the *Cohors Quingenaria Equitata* containing, if at notional full strength, six *centuriae* of auxiliary infantry and four *turmae* of cavalry. A unit such as this would have little difficulty in mounting shift patterns of patrols, with the infantry going out to the towers on a daily basis and the mounted troopers patrolling the roads and bringing rations to the garrisons. There is no evidence of cooking in the towers but, then again, a brazier on a first floor would not leave evidence of a hearth.

The forts along the Gask Ridge are spaced at 17, 14, 18, 11 and 28 (or if there were to be an interpolated fort, 14 plus 14km) kilometres apart. Let us assume that a quick-reaction force with fresh horses was stationed at each fort. So, if a tower saw some 'hostiles' trying to cross the road line with rustled cattle, we should allow five minutes for the alarm to be raised by lighting a beacon at night or a visual sign during the day, then ten minutes for the emergency *turma* to be 'scrambled'. Allowing for a trot at 20km/hr, then the average time it could take for the force to arrive on the scene is about thirty minutes: quite enough to mount a hot pursuit on horseback and thus a major deterrent to raiding.

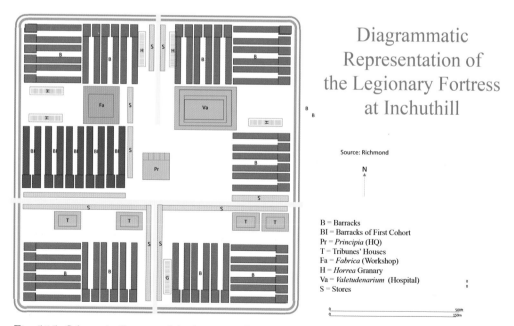

Diagrammatic Representation of the Legionary Fortress at Inchuthill

Source: Richmond

N

B = Barracks
BI = Barracks of First Cohort
Pr = *Principia* (HQ)
T = Tribunes' Houses
Fa = *Fabrica* (Workshop)
H = *Horrea* Granary
Va = *Valetudenarium* (Hospital)
S = Stores

Fig. 5.15. Schematic diagram of the legionary fortress at Inchtuthil. The only completely excavated legionary fortress in the Roman Empire. It was unfinished: the *Principia* was a temporary structure not completely filling the space, the commander's residence has not been started although the site was clear, and only four of the five tribunes' houses had been built.

5.3: Inchtuthil Legionary Fortress

At the heart of the system described above is the legionary fortress of Inchtuthil beside the Tay, which was clearly the anchor for all three lines. This suggests an overall design with the fortress at the core. As we have seen in the earlier campaigns in Britain, the legions with their legate, tribunes and centurions provided the command structure for not just the legion but for its associated auxiliary units. There were some fifteen forts which would have required a similar number of auxiliary units based in the area. This amounts to the typical size for a legionary command, as shown by the diplomas from Chester and Caerleon set out in Chapter 4.

From the Inchtuthil fortress, the distance to the ends of the fort lines are c.120km south-west down the Highland Line, c.85km back along the Gask Ridge to Camelon and c.65km north-east up Strathmore to Strathcathro. Given the effectiveness of visual communications along Roman military installations, the legion is ideally placed to command at the centre of the whole system.

5.4: The Highland Line

To the west of the Gask Frontier is another chain of forts from the Flavian era which runs along the geological divide of the Highland Line. Each fort sits where a highland glen or glens meet the more open and fertile country to the east. Five forts are known in this position, running from south-west to north-east, garrisoned as follows:

- Drumquhassle facing Strathblane, 1.3 hectares (FOR): one cohort;
- Malling facing Aberfoyle, 2.8 hectares (VLF): two cohorts, or one cohort plus one *ala*;
- Bochcastle facing Strathyre, 1.9 hectares (FRT): one cohort or *ala*;
- Dalginross facing Strathearn, 2.4 hectares (LFT): two cohorts;
- Fendoch facing Sma'Glen and Glen Almond, 1.8 hectares (FRT): one cohort or *ala*.

Again, this was a substantial commitment, notionally 4,000 men. There should possibly be a fort on the Clyde to complete the line in the south; the Rock of Dumbarton would be a possibility. Arguably, however, Barochan – high above the Clyde on the south side – performed this role. In addition, the fortress at Inchtuthil itself covers the major route of the Tay Valley.

The traditional explanation of these is that they are 'glen-blocking' forts designed to protect the occupied territory. In contrast to the Gask Ridge, these are generally standard-sized forts. Was such a substantial force really just for defensive purposes, sited simply to block invasion or raiding routes, as the descriptor 'glen-blocking'

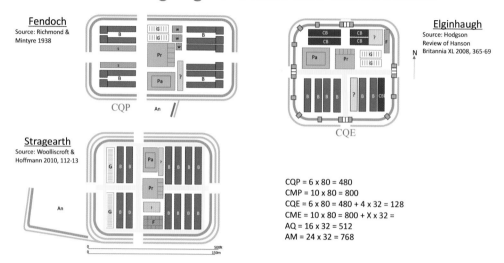

Diagrammatic Representation of
Forts Along Highland Line and Gask Frontier

Fendoch
Source: Richmond &
Mintyre 1938

CQP   An

Stragearth
Source: Woolliscroft &
Hoffmann 2010, 112-13

An

Elginhaugh
Source: Hodgson
Review of Hanson
Britannia XL 2008, 365-69

N

CQE

CQP = 6 x 80 = 480
CMP = 10 x 80 = 800
CQE = 6 x 80 = 480 + 4 x 32 = 128
CME = 10 x 80 = 800 + X x 32 =
AQ = 16 x 32 = 512
AM = 24 x 32 = 768

Fig. 5.16. Fendoch fort was completely excavated by Richmond between the world wars using trenching techniques. Although the plan appears in many standard textbooks on Roman forts, it has been challenged more recently as potentially conflating several phases.

implies, or did it have an aggressive purpose? The Roman Army of the Flavian era was on an expansion mission to complete the conquest of Britain. During the 70s, Roman forces had completed the conquest of Wales, Northern England and the Scottish Lowlands: why would they stop now?

Vespasian had ordered the completion of the conquest of *Britannia* and sent three of his best and most trusted marshals to do this: Cerialis, Frontinus and Agricola. It is therefore improbable that the army switched to a defensive mode immediately after Agricola's victory at Mons Graupius. Would the army really deploy a force of this size merely to block Caledonian raids, particularly by raiders from the tribes so recently defeated?

It seems much more likely that the forts along the Highland Line are designed to dominate those Highland glens within patrol reach. Assuming a day's march by auxiliary infantry of 30km and by cavalry patrol of 60km a day (which is what US cavalry expected in the nineteenth century), then patrols even out as far as the Great Glen some 150km away could easily have been mounted over a five-day patrol period. An aggressive forward policy like this would also have had the additional benefit of protecting recently occupied lands to the south and east.

Pic 5.3. The impressive multiple ditches of successive forts at Ardoch – one of the forts possibly founded around AD 80/81 as part of the creation of the Gask Frontier by Agricola. Forts in the North were usually surrounded by multiple ditches to deter attack. (*Photo by author*)

Pic 5.4. The ditch of the Marching Camp Ardoch II, found north of the permanent fort. This is one of the series of 25ha Camps that may be of Agricolan date, and it appears to underlie a much larger Severan Marching Camp. (*Photo by author*)

Pic 5.5. Two of the vast hoard of 875,400 complete iron nails buried when the construction of the legionary fortress at Inchtuthil was abandoned in AD 87. The hoard was elaborately concealed and in total weighed 7 tons. (*Photo by author*)

5.5: The Strathmore Line

The final element in this system is a line of forts running in a north-west direction up Strathmore from Bertha on the Tay. So far, five forts – counting the two at Cargill as one site – have been identified:

- Bertha, 3.9 hectares (ELF): possibly one *ala* and one cohort;
- Cargill, 0.5 hectares (lft): possibly two centuries;
- Cardean, 3.7 hectares (ELF): possibly two cohorts;
- Inverquharity, 0.5 hectares (lft): possibly two centuries;
- Strathcathro, 2.5 hectares (VLF): possibly two cohorts.

It has been assumed that the original standard-sized fort at Cargill of 1.9 hectares was superseded by the fortlet of 0.5 hectares when the legionary fortress was erected at Inchtuthil, although there is no clarity about sequencing here. This would, however, produce a pattern of three large forts with two fortlets in the gaps, and is a reasonable supposition.

This line of forts therefore had a garrison of up to ten auxiliary units stationed along the road line, with a notional manpower of some 2,800 men. At the start of this line there is evidence of the continuation of the Gask Ridge road. This is then effectively another Line of Penetration road extending for 80km along the classic invasion route leading to the north. As with the Highland Line forts, this looks like an offensive deployment – one which, like the legionary fortress, is probably unfinished, with the line potentially extending further towards the north-east.

5.6: Summary of the forces deployed in the system

Adding these five elements together, we can see that a very considerable military force was deployed north of the Forth/Clyde in the Flavian period. Counting the garrison of forts that appear in two lists only once, the force may have amounted to:

- Forth/Clyde isthmus: two auxiliary units, 1,200 men;
- Gask Ridge: six auxiliary units, 4,500 men;
- Highland Line: five auxiliary units, 4,000 men;
- Inchtuthil Fortress: one legion, 5,000 men;
- Strathmore: four auxiliary units, 2,000 men.

To hold all these elements of the system at a single time would therefore require the substantial force of one legion and up to seventeen auxiliary units, amounting to a theoretical strength of $c.16,700$ men (Figure 5.17). To these can be added some nine forts on the Lowland system with a garrison of $c.4,500$. Are these all part of a single complete system, or are we seeing different phases of occupation?

6: Analysis and interpretation of the archaeological system

There are a number of very different interpretations of how the five elements fit together which turn around how long the Flavian occupation lasted. Fortunately, there is no argument about the end of the Flavian occupation in 87; there are no coins later than 87 found in any of the Flavian forts (Woolliscroft & Hoffmann, 2006, p.166). The legionary fortress at Inchtuthil had plainly been abandoned when it was close to completion: the *Principia* is a small temporary installation unsuitable for a fortress; the *Praetorium* is completely missing, whereas there is what looks like a building for the legionary legate in one of the adjoining work compounds; space for another four granaries is unused; and only four of the houses for the tribunes have been built. Furthermore, the external bathhouse stoke-holes have been constructed but not fired (Hanson, 2007, p.28).

These were dramatic events: the construction of a full-scale permanent legionary fortress was as definitive a statement as could be made that the Roman Army was here to stay in northern Scotland. Compare Inchtuthil with the fortresses planted at Mainz or Nijmegen, or even Severus' fortresses in newly conquered Mesopotamia in 197. The apparently sudden abandonment of so much high-quality construction work was a painful strategic U-turn in imperial policy. Inchtuthil had taken at least two years' work by the legionaries, and now they had to dismantle it and bury many thousands of hand-wrought nails to prevent them from falling into enemy hands. No longer was Caledonia to be the scene of glorious imperial expansion, because the

Summary of Military Dispositions after Mons Graupius in the North

	Number of Forts	Road Length	Nominal Garrison Manpower	Strength Factors	Ave Distance Forts
Lowland Occupation	9	620 kms	4,500	???	59 kms
Forth/Clyde Isthmus	3	109 kms	1,160	2.3	36 kms
Gask Frontier	6	88 kms	4,500	14.5	15 kms
Inchtuthill Fortress	1 leg	na	5,000 leg	12.0 leg	na
Highland Line	5	62 kms	3,500	8.5	12 kms
Strathmore Line	4	67 kms	2,000	6.1	17 kms
TOTALS	1 Leg +18+9 excluding duplicates	326 +620 kms	5,000 legg + 11,160 +4,500	43.4 +???	18 kms 32 kms

Fig. 5.17. Standard metrics for the campaign, showing numbers of fortresses and forts, miles of road in the system, theoretical manpower and Strength Factors. There is no known Roman road between the Highland Line forts and Inchtuthil, although one has been inferred here.

situation on the Danube had become critical with the eruption of the Dacians into the empire. One of Britain's four legions, *II Adiutrix*, with its associated auxiliary units, had to be withdrawn as part of an imperial response to a very real threat to Italy and the heart of the empire. The decision to remove 10,000–15,000 men from Britain can only have come from Emperor Domitian himself, and the result was, as Tacitus so pithily put it, that 'Britain was conquered and immediately lost' (*Histories* 1.2).

6.1: When did the Romans reach Northern Scotland?

The conventional approach has been to rely on Tacitus and to date the first military advance into the area to 79 – Agricola's third year, when he advanced '*ad Taum*', which is usually taken to be the River Tay. In 80, Agricola constructed a temporary frontier across the Forth/Clyde isthmus, which is interpreted as a pause put on the advance by the new Emperor Titus, a hiatus which continued into 81 when Agricola launched amphibious assaults, possibly in Argyll. He took his army to the western coast to face Ireland and contemplated an invasion. In 82, after the death of Titus and the succession of his brother Domitian, the advance into Caledonia was renewed, with combined operations supported by the navy. We hear about the near loss of the *Legio IX Hispana*, yet in 83 the decisive Battle of Mons Graupius was won and the Caledonians defeated. At that point, after an unprecedentedly lengthy governorship, Agricola was recalled by Domitian.

Earlier chapters have shown that there was a logical sequence to Roman conquest and occupation:

- reconnaissance, contact and survey of the land and the people;
- treaties with friendly or simply prudent tribes;
- invasion and defeat of hostile tribes, leaving transitory remains of temporary or marching camps as an often hard-to-date record;
- construction of permanent roads and forts for occupation, leaving sometimes substantial remains which can usually be dated with reasonable accuracy;
- taxation and regulation, with 'Romanization' of elites;
- establishment, with local self-government as an integral part of the empire, leaving substantial material remains of urbanization and growth of villa economies.

In northern Scotland, we can see at least the first four of these phases being compressed into a very short period of five years at most (82–86), but the process was then abandoned. This timescale does not leave much time for the construction of as many as twenty-seven forts; seven years at most for the Gask Ridge frontier line; the near completion of a complete legionary fortress at Inchtuthil; and the final three years after the victory at Mons Graupius for the creation of the Highland and Strathmore Lines.

The generally accepted interpretation is that, because the forts from Camelon to Bertha and the Gask Ridge towers exhibit two structural phases, they were started in 79 when Agricola marched to the Tay. Possibly it was one of these forts that was attacked by the Caledonians in 82 (Breeze, 1996, p.57). In the eighteenth century, General Roy postulated Dalginross as the site of this attack. In this scenario, Agricola decides to protect the Venicones of Fife because this gives him a fertile protected base zone for operations to complete the conquest of Britain. This could be after the campaign of 79 and as part of the halt on the isthmus directed by Emperor Titus in 80 (Hanson, 2007, p.22). The forts along the isthmus and the Gask Ridge line produce an interestingly shaped protected zone running west–east and then back north-west to the Forth at Stirling, with a right-angle turn to the north-east up the Gask Ridge to the Tay (Figures 5.18 and 5.19). Interestingly, this is exactly the frontier line that includes the better lands and the apparently friendly tribes, and which would be delineated by the Antonine Wall and its outpost forts in the 140s and 150s.

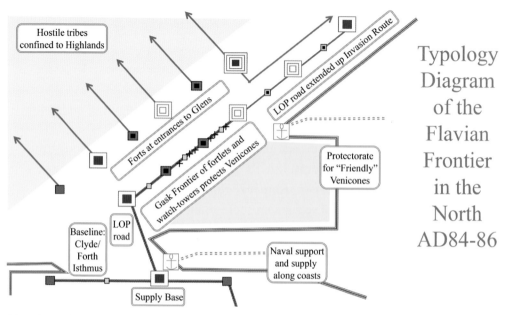

Fig. 5.18. Schematic of the Flavian frontier in the North, showing the five elements of the system: the Clyde/Forth isthmus Line, the Gask Frontier with Inchtuthil at the centre, the Highland Line forts south-west of the legionary fortress and the Strathmore Line of forts heading north-west.

The Flavian Frontier System in Scotland
- planned by Agricola and implemented by him and his Successor

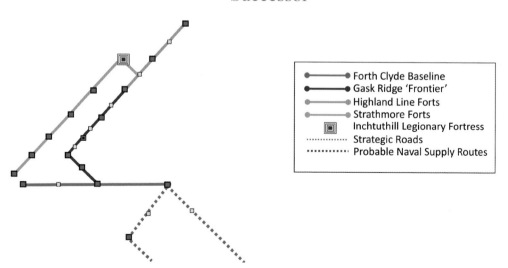

Fig. 5.19. The Flavian Frontier shown in diagrammatic and simplified format, with the five elements and how they relate to each other.

6.2: Alternative timescales for the Flavian occupation

Because of the compressed timescales, there have been suggestions that the Romans penetrated the North earlier than 81/82. The poet Statius refers to Vettius Bolanus campaigning in the 'Caledonian Plains', which would suggest penetration to the Central Belt of Scotland in the very early 70s, and Pliny the Elder mentions in his *Naturalis Historia*, published before 79, that it was then thirty years since the Roman invasion of Britain but that knowledge of the island had not progressed beyond the fringes of the *Caledonia Silva*, which, whether interpreted as forests or – less credibly – as mountains, surely means the fringes of the Highlands (Hoffmann, 2019, p.121). The discovery of wood in the fort at Carlisle with a dendrochronology date of 72 firmly places the Roman army under Cerialis on the borders of Scotland.

There is clear evidence for multiple structural phases in definitely four – and possibly six – Gask towers (Woolliscroft & Hoffmann, 2010, p.179), and there are no Antonine finds in the Gask towers. We are therefore looking at substantial rebuilds, including replacement of the upright timbers and recutting of ditches after silting. There is some evidence of pre-Flavian pottery and glass from forts in Lowland Scotland such as Newstead, Camelon, Strageath and Cardean (Woolliscroft & Hoffmann, 2006, pp.175–202).

Extrapolating from this, it has been suggested that the Roman Army had been campaigning deep into Scotland – and may have built the Gask forts and towers – under Frontinus in 74–77, Cerials in 71–74 or maybe even Bolanus in 69–71 (Woolliscroft & Hoffmann, 2006, p.189; Hoffman, 2019, p.126). The argument is that the evidence is far from conclusive and that, whilst Agricola indeed campaigned on the Tay and in the North, Tacitus 'talked up' Agricola's achievements – including Mons Graupius – and failed to credit previous Flavian governors with the 'softening up' of the region during their times in office.

6.3: The Elginhaugh debate

When the report on the excavation of the entire site at the fort of Elginhaugh was published in 2007, the timing of the start of the Flavian occupation was fixed. A hoard of 45 *denarii* had been found in the foundations of the *Principia*: in it there were many Republican coins, but the two latest were from 74/75 and 77/78, and the pottery and glass were consistent with that dating. This gave a foundation date firmly in Agricola's governorship – probably 79 – and a strong case was made that this implied the same date for all the forts south of Elginhaugh down Dere Street to Corbridge Red House (Hanson, 2007, pp.29–31). The date of Elginhaugh was also taken to decisively undermine claims that the forts north of the Forth had

Pic. 5.6. The line of the Gask Ridge Frontier Road near Kirkton looking north-east. One of the watchtowers has been identified in the field just to the left of the track. (*Photo by author*)

been undertaken by Agricola's predecessors (Hodgson, 2009, P.366). Hanson's conclusions have since been challenged, however, on the basis that the hoard had been disturbed and partially scattered (Hoffmann, 2019, p.131).

6.4: Conclusions on dating the Flavian presence in the North

Given the sequence of reconnaissance, invasion, conquest and occupation operated by the Roman Army, the proposition that there was at least some degree of pre-Agricolan presence in the Central Belt and even further north has some force. No doubt Roman surveying and military reconnaissance teams penetrated the North before Agricola and the main force of his army. This was reconnaissance, however, not occupation, and does not in my view invalidate the statements at the heart of the *Agricola* about Agricola leading the decisive campaigns in the North and the construction of the 'first frontier' from the Clyde to the Forth and thence north along the Gask Ridge to the Tay.

Pic. 5.7. The site of Ardunie Watch Tower: its ditch is visible as a slight depression and when excavated revealed four large postholes as tower foundations. (*Photo by author*)

The 'second frontier' along the Highland Line and the line of forts up Strathmore, with the legionary fortress at Inchtuthil at the fulcrum, were the work of Agricola's unknown successor from 83–87. The whole looks like a planned system, and was presumably one mapped out by Agricola for implementation after his victory.

When evaluating Tacitus, it is important to distinguish bias from inaccuracy. Tacitus was writing in 98 for a senatorial audience who were not only well aware of the military successes and reverses on the frontiers, but had in many cases personally participated in campaigns, as had their sons and other relatives. Certainly, lauding of Agricola's achievements would have been understood and expected. Significant distortions of what Agricola had and had not achieved would have undermined Tacitus' credibility, however, especially if he was thereby stealing the glory from other senatorial families.

6.5: A model of invasion, conquest and assimilation

The process of Roman campaigning in the first century can be characterized in six stages:

- **reconnaissance**: surveying the land, rivers and coasts, and contact with potentially friendly tribes or factions of tribes;
- **invasion**: attack on the *oppida* and hillforts of tribes deemed hostile, defeat of the enemy in open battle if they challenged the army, and construction of so-called marching camps (often occupied for weeks or even months, not just overnight) connected by campaign routes;
- **occupation** of the area: construction of permanent forts, initially of turf and timber, connected by roads often built along the campaign routes, domination of hostile tribes and their eviction from hillforts and strongholds, protection of friendly tribes, the arrival of merchants to supply the army and the purchase of military supplies;
- **incorporation** of the conquered area into the empire: some forts reconstructed in stone for longer occupation and other forts evacuated as opposition ebbed away; inhabitants pulled into the Roman economy by providing supplies for the army, being taxed and purchasing basic goods from merchants; settlements growing up around forts; tribal elites encouraged to adopt Roman ways and to speak Latin, frequent baths, wear togas, consume luxuries and build villas;
- **revolt**: when the tensions between collaborating 'Romanizing' elites and tribes versus 'resisters' occurred and had to be put down by the army;
- **assimilation**: over time: with peace and stability and the payment of taxes; tribes gaining the status of a *civitas* with a capital town (usually a converted fortress or fort) granted self-government with its own council; and the army's withdrawal from the area.

The speed of this whole process – and indeed whether it was completed at all – varied greatly. In Britain, the leadership of the Catuvellauni and their tribal centre at Verulamium embraced Roman 'civilization' within a decade of the invasion. Other areas took much longer to go through this process: the Silures, after decades of resistance, had Venta Silurum (Caerwent), as did the Brigantes with Isurium Brigantum (Aldborough). Other areas, such as the Ordovices in north-west Wales as we have seen, never reached this stage. Interestingly, in the long run the outcome seems to have been determined more by the levels of economic potential and development and less by the level of resistance. The Iceni become a *civitas* surprisingly quickly in the 70s after Boudicca had been defeated, and even the Silures – inveterate resisters to Roman rule over the first thirty years of Roman occupation

– supported Venta Silurum (Bowden, 2020). A similar sequence is recognizable in early twentieth-century colonial Africa, for instance with the foundation of district capitals and trading centres like Fort Hall (modern Murang'a) amongst the Kikuyu in Kenya.

Even when everything ran to the Roman plan, the reconnaissance, invasion, occupation and incorporation took several seasons of campaigning at the minimum. The archaeological remains from the latter stages are much more visible, but for Flavian Scotland we not only have extensive 'marching camps' detectable but also, for all its faults as a narrative history, Tacitus' year-by-year account of Agricola's campaigns.

Pulling the strategic story together

Agricola inherited a province which had lived through conquest and colonization for more than three decades, as Pliny the Elder observed (*Natural Histories* iv.102). The tribes of the south and east were well on the way to becoming 'civilized' in Roman terms, much assisted by collaborationist client kings and queens and by pro-Roman elites easing the transition.

By now it was seventeen years since the defeat of Boudicca and the army was no longer needed in the south: Frontinus had finished the long-delayed and hard-fought conquest of Wales started by Scapula in the late 40s, and Cerialis had conquered Northern England and begun the occupation process in the North (witness the dendrochronology date of 72 from Carlisle). The process of incorporation and assimilation in all three areas was far from complete, however.

Upon his arrival, Agricola had to suppress another revolt by the Ordovices of North Wales and repeat Suetonius' invasion of the Druid stronghold of Anglesey. He also felt it important to spend part of his second year (78) in 'Romanizing' the elites of the south of Britain:

> His object was to accustom them to a life of peace and quiet by the provision of amenities. He therefore gave official assistance to the building of temples, public squares and good houses. He educated the sons of the chiefs in the liberal arts and expressed a preference for British ability as compared to the trained skills of the Gauls. The result was that instead of loathing the Latin language they became eager to speak it effectively; in the same way, our national dress came into favour and the toga was everywhere to be seen. And so the population was gradually led into the demoralising temptations of arcades, baths and sumptuous banquets. The unsuspecting Britons spoke of such novelties as 'civilisation', when in fact they were only a feature of their enslavement. (Tacitus, *Agricola* 21)

This is as good a description of colonial enrolment of conquered elites through the ages as you could find.

Tacitus' description of Agricola's 'conquest of the Brigantes' was formerly taken at face value, but is now questioned. Short of precisely datable evidence from forts, it is impossible to say with precision which Flavian governor founded any given fort. We can confidently assume that Cerialis oversaw the building of the new legionary fortress at York and occupied at least some of the lands of the Brigantes – probably best regarded as a confederation of several sub-tribes – up to Carlisle (Cunliffe, 2005, pp.211–14). We should therefore also attribute to Cerialis the forts north from York through Stainmore to Carlisle to. There is also a strong case to be made for the forts up the west coast, and possibly up the east to the Tyne, being his achievement. Cerialis' campaigns may also have reached into the Lowlands of Scotland, and it is possible that Dalswinton north of the Solway was built by him (Hanson, 1987, p.61); however, Phase 1 of Dalswinton has recently been interpreted as a temporary campaign base rather than a permanent fort (Hanson *et. al.*, 2019, p.285). The process of occupation took time; Cerialis' conquest of the Brigantes probably covered 30,000km^2, much of which was hard-to-control upland.

A balanced view of what Cerialis and Agricola achieved is that Cerialis largely undertook the conquest, along with building the fortress at York, the north–south roads and major forts, whilst Agricola – in his second year as governor in 78 – completed the task, constructing the east–west routes and consolidating Cerialis' conquest.

Resolving the issue of which governor conquered which area or tribe is not essential since, as the Roman Army recognized, this was a multi-year process. Thus, Agricola finished off Frontinus' conquest of the Ordovices and Cerialis' conquest of the Brigantes, in the same way that Agricola's unknown successor built Inchtuthil and the forts of the Highland Line.

When Agricola moved north in 79, he was occupying new territory, although the invasion routes and tribal areas would already have been thoroughly surveyed by scouts. The only evidence of Agricola founding particular forts which is comparable to the dendro-date for Cerialis' foundation of Carlisle is Hanson's interpretation of the Elginhaugh hoard found under the *Principia* there, which ties the Lowland Flavian forts to Agricola.

There seem to be three sets of forts that we can attribute to Agricola, and Tacitus explicitly refers to fort construction in 82, his sixth year as governor (*Agricola* 25).

Forts of the Scottish Lowlands – Agricolan

The first set of forts reflects the Flavian occupation of the Lowlands following Agricola's campaign of 79 that reached the River Tay. These forts stretch in the east from the major base at Corbridge up Dere Street to Elginhaugh near the Forth, and in the west from Carlisle up through Annandale over Shap and then north-east to Elginhaugh. These strategic Lines of Penetration are, as in the north of England, connected by cross-routes in the Lowland Dales. The area consolidated is much less than the whole landmass between the two isthmuses of Tyne/Solway and Forth/Clyde, reflecting the practicalities of dominating a partly hostile zone. The forts could have been started in 79 and completed in 80 (see Figure 5.18).

Forts across the Forth/Clyde isthmus – Agricolan

The second set of forts is the frontier constructed in AD 80 on the Forth/Clyde isthmus when the Emperor Titus apparently ordered a halt to further expansion, as is inferred from Tacitus (*Agricola* 23). This was probably when construction of the Gask Frontier forts and watchtowers began, incorporating the Venicones of Fife into the province. Whilst this looks on the map like an illogical configuration for a frontier, it incorporated some of the most fertile areas yet encountered in the North and was the same configuration adopted by the army in the 140s when the Antonine Wall was built across the isthmus.

Forts in the western Lowlands – Agricolan

Agricola, possibly due to an order to halt expansion from Emperor Titus, devoted 81 to further consolidation: if the forts and watchtowers of the Gask Frontier do date to this period, a sizeable part of the army would have been engaged in construction work. Tacitus tells us that Agricola campaigned in the west of Scotland facing Ireland. This may have led to the construction of a fort in Nithsdale, facing the Novantae of Galloway, and possibly a road to a port at Ayr where a marching camp has been recently found (*Current Archaeology* 353, July 2019).

The years 82 and 83 were taken up with campaigning, culminating in the victory at Mons Graupius. If we take the fort building in 82 to be the completion of the Gask Frontier, this then left the final three elements of the system to be completed by Agricola's successor as governor in Britain.

The legionary fortress at Inchtuthil – Agricola's successor

The key element is the move of the *XX Valeria Victrix* from Wroxeter to Inchtuthil. Some or most of this legion had probably been serving in the field with Agricola in the northern campaigns, but after the victory over the Caledones, the decision was taken to permanently move the legion's base to the North. This would still have left two legions at Chester and Caerleon watching the recently conquered tribes of Wales, but if the North was to be held and permanently incorporated into the province, then the transfer of a legion was essential. The construction of a fortress so far north and so close to the theatre of operations is the clearest possible statement of the intent to continue with campaigning and to permanently occupy the North.

The Highland Line forts – Agricola's successor

The fourth set of forts were those at the glen entrances (the misnamed 'glen-blocking forts') and along Strathmore, with Inchtuthil in their centre. These appear to have been part of the consolidation phase following Agricola's campaigns of 82/83. On the basis of the sequencing analyzed above, they are probably the work of Agricola's unknown successor as governor. Unlike the Forth/Clyde and Gask Ridge forts, which form a definitive frontier line, these are emphatically not a frontier. The forts at the entrances to the glens are, in my view, not defensive in intent. Whilst the forts do block access to the fertile lands of the Straths, they are more likely to have been aggressive in intent; by penetrating the glens, Roman patrols could reach as far west as the Great Glen.

The Strathmore Line forts – Agricola's successor

The Strathmore line of forts is not defending a line on the ground but, rather, points straight up the only invasion route to the North. Furthermore, rather like Inchtuthil, it also looks like a work-in-progress. The forts seem to be filling in the line of temporary camps built by Agricola that stretch further north into Aberdeenshire and Nairn. Indeed, several fort sites have been identified further north (Keillar, 2005, pp.90–94), although none of these has as yet been fully confirmed.

Applying the analytics toolset to Agricola in the North

Taking this reconstructed chronology and phasing of the campaigns and fort construction, we can now analyze Agricola's approach to the campaign and the size and shape of the eventual deployment.

The table in Figure 5.17 shows the disposition of the forces in the post-Mons Graupius period, with each of its five elements. If our analysis is correct, there was one legion, the *XX Valeria Victrix*, and eighteen forts in the system garrisoned by some 16,000 men, provided the units were up to complement. The overall road length of the system was some 326km and the average fort spacing only 18km. Calculating the notional Strength Factors, we arrive at 43.4 SFs.

This analysis suggests that, compared with the Frontinan settlement in Wales less than a decade earlier, there were fewer troops to go round. This also reflects the likelihood that, whilst in Wales the aim was complete coverage of the area, here the initial focus was on holding the isthmus and then the good lands up the eastern seaboard.

Looking at each component, there are some surprises. Notwithstanding Tacitus' comments about holding the isthmus with forts (*praesidia*), despite great efforts to find them, there are only three forts that have been identified as Agricolan on the isthmus itself. There is the massive base at Camelon on Dere Street by the Forth in the east and Barochan overlooking the Clyde in the west, but only the fortlet at Mollins in between. This was in no sense a defended or even rigorously controlled frontier line, in stark contrast to the so-called 'Gask Frontier' which had no less than four forts (probably five with the putative Stirling fort) and three fortlets with multiple watchtowers along the road on the Gask Ridge itself, constituting a true defended and patrolled line with 14.5 SFs (Figure 5.20).

The isthmus and the Gask Frontier forts built between 79 and 81 provided the protected base for Agricola's successful campaign in the North. Following victory, his staff designed the deployment of the army to occupy the eastern seaboard. The heart of the system implemented by Agricola's unknown successor was the positioning of the new legionary fortress in the Tay Valley at Inchtuthil.

The Flavian Frontier System in Scotland
- Strength Factors in each Line

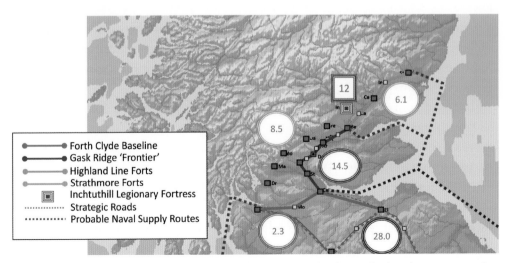

Forth Clyde Baseline
Gask Ridge 'Frontier'
Highland Line Forts
Strathmore Forts
Inchtuthill Legionary Fortress
Strategic Roads
Probable Naval Supply Routes

Fig. 5.20. Using Strength Factors (SFs) as the proxy for the forces deployed, we can see that Agricola had to expend much of his force on his lines of communication through the Lowlands. This left him with a similar force of auxiliaries to deploy in the North.

The system was completed with the five forts along the Highland Line at the entrances of the glens leading into the Highland interior, amounting to 8.5 SFs. These were not defensive in nature but represented or reflected an offensive posture for active patrolling into the interior and for moving forward in later campaigning seasons. Forces of this size would easily have prevented incursions by the Caledones.

Finally, there were four forts leading up the optimal route for invading the Highlands up the east coast, set 7km apart and with 6.1 SFs. Again, this was not a defensive strategy but a Line of Penetration facing directly along the best route to the north-east (Figure 5.20).

Assessment I: Agricola's final campaign in the North in 82–83

As Tacitus succinctly observed, as soon as Britain had been conquered it was given up. Agricola had brought Vespasian's objective of total conquest of Britain within reach. The Flavian sequence of capable military governors – Cerialis, Frontinus and Agricola – had effectively defeated all remaining serious opposition to Rome in the island of *Britannia*.

In 71, Cerialis, when he arrived as governor with his fresh army of new auxiliaries from the Rhine and Belgica, faced a province whose population had revolted a decade earlier and destroyed all traces of Roman 'civilization' they could lay their hands on. The Silures and Ordovices of Wales had shown that vigorous resistance could keep the Romans at bay; the long-term client kingdom of the Brigantes holding down the tribes of Northern England was now hostile under Venutius; and in the Scottish Lowlands, the Selgovae and Dumnonni of Clydesdale were untouched, as were the Caledones of the Highlands. All of these had by 83 been defeated in battle if they offered it, and their territories, save only that of the Caledones, had been occupied. Amongst the tribes in the province were protectorates over the Demetae in Cardiganshire and Pembrokeshire, the Votadini in Northumberland and Berwickshire, and the Votadini in Fife.

The benefits of completing the conquest would in time be the ability to reduce the very large garrison of what is now Scotland – as of course actually happened in Wales – over the next fifty years. This is what had been achieved in Iberia (Hispania) and in Dalmatia, Noricum and Pannonia following their final conquest, pacification and incorporation. In Iberia, there were eight legions at their peak in 28 BC; the garrison stabilized at four legions by the turn of the century, then gradually decreased to just one by the 60s. The same process occurred along the Upper Danube following the Augustan conquest of Dalmatia and Pannonia, with six legions in garrison – twelve during the Illyrian Revolt – reducing to three legions facing outwards along the defended Danube line in the 60s and 70s.

Comparisons of Theoretical Military Force Deployed in First Century Britannia		Number of Forts	Road Length	Nominal Manpower	Strength Factors	Ave Distance Forts
	Scapula's Wales Campaign AD47-52	2 Leg Ft + 7 Camp Base + 11 forts	625 kms	10,000 leg+ 6,000 vex+ 13,500 aux = 29,600 men	87.7	28 kms
	Gallus' Frontier in Wales AD52-57	2 Leg Ft + 4 Camp Base + 14 forts	507 kms	10,000 leg+ 15,660 aux = 25,660 men	78.9	22 kms
	Cerialis in Nth England AD71-74	2 Leg Ft + 19 forts?	tbd	10,000 leg+ 11,000 aux = 21,000 men?	63?	tbd
	Frontinus in Wales AD74-77	3 Leg Ft + 36 forts	1,997 kms	15,000 leg+ 30,376 aux = 45,376 men	114.9	32 kms
	Agricola in the Far North AD80-83	1 Leg Ft + 18 forts	326 kms	5,000 leg+ + 11,160 aux = 16,160 men	43.4	18 kms

Source: see previous chapters

Fig. 5.21. Using the standard metrics for each campaign, this table compares the number of forts, length of roads, theoretical total manpower and Strength Factors used to compare deployments in campaigns in first-century Britain.

So, how should we judge the final campaign and the following period from 82–87? It was clearly a complete and costly strategic failure; since not only was the fortress of Inchtuthil abandoned before completion and the eighteen forts dismantled in AD 87, but the effective limits of empire over the next twenty years fell back to the Stanegate Line on the Tyne/Solway, giving up 20,000km² of territory, six tribes – two of whom were allies – and the best opportunity to 'finish the job' in *Britannia*.

However, I think we can judge Agricola's campaign and the work of his unknown successor a brilliant tactical success, before the strategic withdrawal of the legion, which brought the whole northern strategy tumbling down and turned success into a major failure.

It is worth pausing to compare Agricola's achievements with that of his predecessors. The reaction against Tacitus' hagiographical approach has been necessary and, as emphasized above, given that the Roman Army's approach to conquest and colonisation was an extended process, no one governor can ever be said to have finally and completely conquered a particular area or tribe. Thus, Agricola finished Frontinus' work in Wales, not just in putting down the Ordovices and occupying Anglesey, but also completing the forts started by his predecessor: not an action worthy of Tacitus' narrative but nonetheless very necessary. Furthermore, he completed Cerialis' occupation of the lands of the Brigantian confederation. Therefore, Agricola's successor was in the expected manner continuing Agricola's work in the North. However, it is worth recognizing that Agricola's achievement of these conquests was achieved with considerably less force at his disposal than

Comparisons of Campaigns in Britain
Number of Fortresses/Forts and Manpower

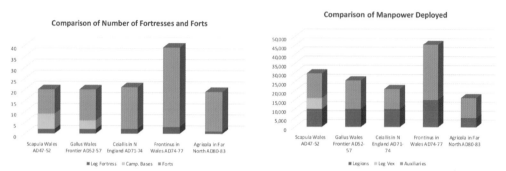

Fig. 5.22. Graphs comparing the results of first-century campaigns in Britain, showing the number of installations constructed and manpower deployed.

his predecessors had available in the South. This was because of the need to hold down the newly won territories in the South, and also the tribes he was encountering had not been worn down by three decades of Roman campaigning involving village burning, crop confiscation and enslavement, as the Silures and Ordovices had been.

If we compare the theoretical forces deployed in different campaigns in first-century *Britannia* (Figure 5.22), we can see that Agricola was operating with a force about half what Scapula and Gallus were able to deploy in their earlier Welsh campaigns. It was only a third of the overwhelming force assembled by Frontinus to complete the conquest of Wales, and significantly less than Cerialis had deployed in 72/73 against the Brigantes in Northern England. The key point here is that the Roman Army by the 80s was getting close to overstretch, unsurprising given the Flavian surge was back in 71, since when many new territories had been taken and needed to be held. The Army was nevertheless still winning both battles and new territory, and was still expanding the empire. It was therefore also still winning booty for itself in the form of moveable wealth – animals and possessions – and also taking slaves.

Assessment II: the work of Agricola's successor in 84–87

As noted above, the dispositions of the systems operated by Agricola and his successor are not defensive. The line south-west of Inchtuthil is not 'blocking the exits' from the glens. Having just won a decisive battle, is the Roman Army of the first century, with an aggressive and ambitious governor, going to retreat into

The Status of Tribes in Britain after *Mons Graupius*

Brigantes   Conquered/occupied
Votadini   Protectorates
Novantae   Bypassed
Caledonii   Conquered/unoccupied
Caledonii   Unoccupied
– · – · – ·   Notional boundaries

Fig. 5.23. The Battle of Mons Graupius reconfigured the political geography of the North.

a defended redoubt? This is importing Hadrian's thinking back forty years. The army is defending its base area and friendly protected tribes. The dispositions are all about dominating the recently defeated Caledones beyond the Highland Line, and mounting patrols deep into Caledonia. Neither is the Strathmore Line a defensive line like the Gask Ridge. It is a classic Line of Penetration through the lands of the Vacomagi in Angus, which then becomes a Line of Control. It follows as we have seen the only viable invasion route to the far north, along the coast and past the Mounth at Stonehaven, leading to the fertile lands of the north-east in modern Aberdeenshire, Moray and Nairn, and thence to the northern mouth of the Great Glen where Inverness now stands.

The placing of the legionary fortress in the front line is exactly what the Roman Army did when preparing for a new campaign of conquest. The *XX Valeria Victrix* moved forward to Gloucester Kingsholm under Scapula to conquer the Silures, the *IX Hispana* to York under Cerialis to conquer the Brigantes, the *II Adiutrix* to Chester to conquer the Ordovices and western Brigantes, and so *XX Valeria Victrix* moved to Inchtuthil to conquer the far north.

This new system was therefore designed to be the jumping-off point for the final campaigns into the far north and the incorporation of all the tribes in Britain. This is signalled by the circumnavigation of *Britannia* by the Roman Navy in the final year of Agricola's governorship:

> Agricola led back his army into the territory of the Boresti. He received hostages from them, and then ordered the commander of the fleet to sail round Britain. A force for this purpose was given him, which great panic everywhere preceded. Agricola himself leading his infantry and cavalry by slow marches, so as to overawe newly conquered tribes by the very tardiness of his progress, brought them into winter-quarters. (Tacitus, *Agricola* 38)

This was not just Roman bravado – although this was clearly part of the motivation; it was surveying the coasts to be occupied. The more it echoed the surrender of Thule to Claudius in AD 43, the better it would have resonated.

Assessment III: the Roman abandonment of the North in 87

In AD 87, *II Adiutrix* – the amphibious warfare experts – were withdrawn from Britain to prop up the Lower Danube Frontier which had just collapsed under pressure from a Dacian invasion that had overwhelmed the provincial defences. This meant that the new fortress at Chester, with its governor's HQ, was empty, and therefore *XX Valeria Victrix* was pulled back. The Roman High Command – in Rome with Domitian – was clearly acutely conscious of the risk of overstretch and knew that in 87, when a whole legion and its auxiliaries (10,000–15,000 men) had to be withdrawn to the Danube, this meant that territory had to be given up. To their credit, they acted swiftly and decisively, pulling back although trying to hold as much territory as they could. Most northern forts were evacuated (Shotter, 1996, p.40). This is positive proof of 'controlling governance' at the top of the Roman government. We do not need to postulate a General Staff in a modern or even nineteenth-century sense, but there were advisers to the emperor in the imperial household who not only understood the situation at the front in Northern Britain, but were both capable of calculating the chances of success against Rome's enemies and then executing actions for the greater good of the empire. In this case, an action was decided on that reversed the central provincial policy set by Vespasian, squandered three years of hard work and investment, and was a major local loss of face and prestige. But it had to be done.

What might have been? Total conquest and occupation

Was there a grand strategic plan for final conquest? What follows is complete speculation, based on the previous campaigns, but it does serve to illustrate the dispositions of 83–86 (Figure 5.23). We can speculate that the final push was planned for 87 or 88, when the construction work had been completed. Why did the army wait? I think that the governor and the Roman High Command were by

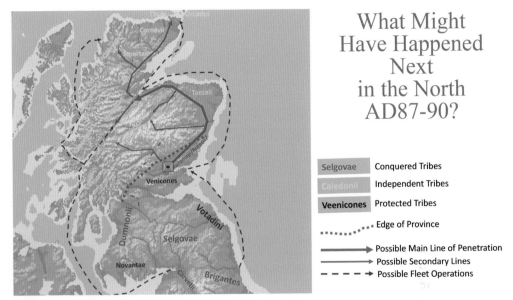

What Might
Have Happened
Next
in the North
AD87-90?

Selgovae	Conquered Tribes
Caledonii	Independent Tribes
Veenicones	Protected Tribes
....	Edge of Province
——→	Possible Main Line of Penetration
——→	Possible Secondary Lines
– – – →	Possible Fleet Operations

Fig. 5.24. Map suggesting what might have happened in the years 87–90 if the *II Adiutrix* had not had to be withdrawn from *Britannia* in order to serve on the Danube Frontier against the Dacians, resulting in strategic overstretch in Northern Britain.

this time acutely aware that they were close to overstretch and had been bitten too many times in Britain by pushing ahead too quickly. Agricola had come close to losing a legion in 82, so they had respect for the fighting qualities of their enemies and would recall that although Caractacus had been defeated in battle in 51, the Ordovices and Silures had carried on effective resistance for two more decades. So even after the defeat of Calgacus, they would expect the Caledones to keep fighting. Also, their scouts had identified eight more tribes beyond the Great Glen, and the ultimate source for Ptolemy's *Geography* was a military map relating to the Flavian conquest and occupation of the regions when military surveyors were making astronomical observations on Midsummer's Day (Jones & Mattingly, 2002, pp.19–20). The Roman High Command would also have had great respect by now for the difficult terrain and climate, and short campaigning season, that the soldiers faced in the far north. The Roman Navy, as before in Britain, would have been central to the tactics adopted.

All of this assumes that Domitian does not withdraw *II Adiutrix*. The most likely future Line of Penetration would have been Agricola's probable route of 83, that is, an advance beyond the Mounth into the north-east and thence along the coast toward to the Great Glen. This is the only route capable of supporting the size of force we would expect: the *Legio XX VV* accompanied by vexillations from at least two of the other three legions in *Britannia*, plus supporting auxiliaries. This would amount to a force of some 18,000 men, plus the *Classis Britannica* (British fleet) providing surprise, supply and close support.

The route was well surveyed and there were marching camps to be reactivated. We might therefore envisage the army splitting into two or three parts, with one task force heading down the Great Glen to meet another force moving up from the south delivered by the Navy. The other part of the army would move up the east coast towards Caithness and Thule. Meanwhile, auxiliaries would fan out north and west, and naval forces would take the submission of the tribes on the Western Isles. In this way, Vespasian's mission to Cerialis of 70 would have been completed by 90. But it was not to be.

Chapter 6

The Antonine Wall – Military Overstretch and Policy U-Turns on Rome's North-West Frontier

The Roman reoccupation of the Scottish Lowlands and the building of a new wall

The reoccupation of the Scottish Lowlands, starting around 139 and ending in evacuation sometime after 158, forms the perfect 'laboratory' to examine how the Roman Army operated – campaign, conquest, occupation and, in this case, evacuation, possibly followed by reoccupation and another evacuation and withdrawal. What is more, the Antonine campaign is tightly bound in space and time: the whole episode lasted for just twenty years and covered a contained area of no more than 20,000km², roughly a quarter of the area of present-day Scotland. It was bound by the Irish Sea and North Sea between the two isthmuses of Tyne/Solway and Forth/Clyde, plus the area between the Tay and Forth estuaries on the east coast which is is now Fife.

The imperial Roman Army in the mid-second century still had great power to impress, as a glance at the mountain of books on its campaigns, uniforms, arms and conquests published in just the last five years will show. The army of this period is seen, in both popular and academic histories alike, as being at the height of its powers. Its impressive remains across Europe, North Africa and the Middle East – reinforced by museum displays and re-enactors, films and documentaries – still dazzle visitors and historians alike, but can blind us to the army's real record and obscure its objectives, behaviour and failings.

This is why the Antonine interlude in Central Scotland is so illuminating. We see appearing here major cracks in the ideology of invincibility cultivated both by emperors and the Roman Army itself. Over the twenty-plus years from 139 to 162, we see – despite a classic 'shock and awe' initial conquest – Rome's failure to pacify tribes and hold territory, failure to incorporate this land into the province or to counter effective native resistance, and the effects of military manpower overstretch. We witness not just one, but potentially four fundamental reversals of frontier policy, culminating in evacuation of the densest major frontier line ever constructed in the empire, followed by the reactivation of Hadrian's Wall.

The reoccupation of the Scottish Lowlands was led by the new governor of *Britannia*, Lollius Urbicus, on the orders of the new emperor, Antoninus Pius. Roman forces invaded and then built permanent forts in what is now Scotland on at least three occasions – the Agricolan, Antonine and Severan invasions – and later fought significant punitive campaigns there on at least three further occasions in the fourth century, under Constantius I, Count Theodosius and Stilicho. Roman military interaction with the peoples of Southern and Eastern Scotland was continuous, lasting for more than three centuries. The Lowlands of Scotland and Fife were incorporated into the empire at least twice, and a protectorate was exercised over several tribes of the area for much of the time.

The experience of Rome for the tribes living here differed radically between friends of Rome and resisters. For some, this encounter with Rome brought wealth, wine and fine dining; but for many others it meant defeat and destruction, enslavement or death. The Antonine army destroyed the broch at Leckie, evidenced by a ballista bolt and burning (Picture 6.5), a site which had enjoyed friendly relations with Rome during the Flavian and early Antonine periods (Hanson, 2020, p.220).

Comparisons with the British (and latterly Americans) in Afghanistan – where there were three Anglo-Afghan Wars in 1839–42, 1878–80 and 1919, and latterly from 2001 to 2021 – are not so far-fetched. The first Afghan War ended in the defeat of the British, the second in the establishment of a British Protectorate and the third in Afghan independence. During the period of occupation of the North-West Frontier and adjacent tribal areas by the East India Company and then the British Raj, control was sketchy at best. The British-led Indian Army's forts were isolated and often beleaguered: large parts of the territory were in no sense effectively controlled. Throughout this period, frontier policies changed back and forth, both in terms of occupation or the protectorate over Afghanistan and whether a 'forward defence' strategy or loose supervision over the frontier tribal areas was the best policy. However far advanced the technology deployed, the British and later the Americans could not subdue the tribes or effectively hold the territory, a situation very similar to Scotland in the three centuries of the Roman era.

We are fortunate that the Antonine campaign took place in an area which has benefited from historical, archaeological and aerial surveys over many generations, from eighteenth-century antiquaries to modern archaeological theoreticians. Furthermore, although the conurbation of Glasgow lies over the west of the Antonine Wall, much of the higher ground has not been developed or subjected to modern agriculture; thus, many remains – including even marching camps, as well as more permanent installations like forts – are still visible or detectable (Jones, 2011; Keppie, 2004).

The political and ideological background in Rome

Within months of becoming emperor, Antoninus had earned the epithet 'Pius' by convincing the Senate, although decidedly hostile to Hadrian, to deify their deceased persecutor. Antoninus conciliated the Army by re-embarking on imperial expansion, a policy that had been explicitly halted by his predecessor. Indeed, the reversal of Trajan's expansion had been Hadrian's hallmark policy. There are clear parallels with Claudius, another distinctly non-military emperor in need of a quick victory in the distant province of *Britannia* (Maxwell, 1981, p.69). Antoninus was expanding the empire, not just on any frontier but in *Britannia*, where Hadrian had personally designed and supervised the construction of a hard stone-wall edge to Roman-held lands.

The exact moment at which the ever-expanding Roman dominion evolved into a defended frontier line is debatable, from Tiberius eventually calling a halt after the Varian disaster in Germany in AD 9, through the defences along the Danube in the mid-first century to the Stanegate Line under Trajan. However, all of these had still been created within the overall Roman ideology of conquest and dominion. So, whilst Trajan himself had called a pause in *Britannia*, this had been done to enable wars of conquest in Dacia and Parthia which had massively expanded the empire: such wars were rewarding to the Roman Army, whether legate or auxiliary trooper.

There is a fundamental difference between a road with forts strung along it, like the Stanegate Line – which could be regarded as a baseline for further advances when the time was right – and Hadrian's Wall, as almost completed at the emperor's death in 138. With its linear ditch, wall and *vallum* (rampart), forts, mile-castles and turrets, Hadrian's Wall was clearly intended to be the final and permanent 'edge' to the Roman Empire. It took seventeen years – and the efforts of three legions and their auxiliaries – to build, and was clearly intended to be the lasting frontier. Given Hadrian's immediate withdrawal from Trajan's new provinces of Armenia and Mesopotamia, and his empire-wide mission to solidify the borders, time had very obviously been called on further wars of expansion.

Although the decision to position the forts on the line of Hadrian's Wall ('Plan B' in David Breeze's scheme – see below) as opposed to behind the line is very much a forward-looking defence in its intent, and whilst the Army would still have taken an uncomfortably close interest in the tribes north of the wall, there could have been no denying that Hadrian intended the wall to mark the final frontier. There had been frontier lines before, like the Gask Ridge, but an 8ft-wide stone and turf wall with twenty-five forts, 101 mile-castles and mile-fortlets, and 202 turrets and towers stretching for over 117km of wall, ditch and *vallum*, with a garrison of some 10,000 men along the line of the wall, was completely unprecedented.

Whilst Hadrian's Wall, in modern terms, 'cost' the Roman state nothing to build – since they employed the military workforce anyway, could conscript forced labour from the local tribes and would certainly not have paid for the land – it was still an enormous investment in terms of military time and effort. Hadrian had put the whole weight and force of his imperial prestige and reputation into the construction of 'his' wall bearing his name.

Consequently, Antoninus' decision, with indecent haste on assuming the purple, to abandon Hadrian's Wall, to slight the *vallum*, to remove the gates in mile-castles and to abandon or mothball the newly constructed forts, could not be a clearer or more publicly visible renunciation of Hadrian's signature frontier policy. We have no evidence, but we can speculate that the news would have been received with acclaim by officers and men who looked back fondly – and with rose-tinted spectacles – at Trajan's wars of expansion and the opportunities for advancement and loot they had furnished.

Antoninus entrusted the campaign to one of his most experienced marshals, Lollius Urbicus. Urbicus was by origin a Berber from Numidia (Algeria), who had been a tribune with *XXII Primigenia* in Mainz, legate to the Proconsul of Asia and commander of *X Gemina* at Vienna, and had served with distinction in the Jewish War of 132–35, after which he became Governor of *Germania Inferior*. This was a classic progression up the *Cursus Honorum* (CIL VIII, 6706). Urbicus' career had been shaped for this moment – when he was made Governor of *Britannia* and charged with expansion. He made an immediate start, attested by an inscription by the *II Augusta* at Corbridge, the supply base set up for the campaign, recording work done under his orders as early as 139.

A key advantage for the new emperor and new governor was that the Roman Army had been this way before, all the way north to the Highland Line and Strathmore forts under Agricola and his successor (see Chapter 5). The land would already have been carefully surveyed, in terms not only of its physical geography but also its tribal dispositions, with the sites for supply roads, camps and hillforts noted. Moreover, the most easterly tribe in the Lowlands, the Votadini, were long-term Roman allies, whilst in the west, even after the building of the wall, the Romans had protected the Brigantes north of the Solway with three outpost forts. Of the other tribes in the Lowlands, the Selgovae in the valleys of the Upper Tweed, Annan, Nith and Upper Clyde were equally long-term 'hostiles' and resistors to the Romans. In all probability, the Dumnonii of the Lower Clyde Valley and both sides of the Clyde were also hostile, while the Novantae in the south-west may have been broadly neutral (Figure 6.1). These polarized reactions and discrepant experiences of Roman power were typical of the highly disruptive impact of the Roman Army on peoples on the margins of the formal empire (Mattingly, 2006, p.523). As with the Honourable East India Company's expansion in India at the start of the nineteenth century, or British colonial expansion in East and West Africa later in the century, colonisers sought out local leaders they could do business with, creating new alliances and loyalties which then precipitated other tribes into opposition.

The Roman Army's pre-existing knowledge of the terrain would have assisted fast planning and mobilization for the reconquest: the routes of Flavian roads and sites for forts that could be reactivated had already been identified. The army had integral specialist surveyors and engineers and, as the Vindolanda tablets show, was an inveterate record keeper. We can therefore safely assume that the Roman 'military memory' functioned here, and that records from Agricola's and subsequent Flavian campaigns on the siting of forts, watch-towers and military roads would have been carefully considered. The reuse of sites and alignments, but with improvements (such as giving up the Elginhaugh site for Inveresk, where Dere Street reached the Forth), supports this.

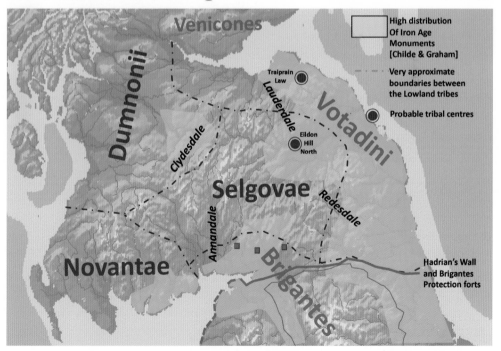

The Lowlands before the Antonine Re-occupation

Fig. 6.1. The Lowlands had been well known to the Roman Army since the late 70s in terms of both physical and human geography. The attitudes of the various tribes were well understood (on the 'my enemy's enemy is my friend' principle), and Roman agents would have been active in the territory as soon as the decision to advance was made.

As we have seen, the sequence of a Roman campaign of conquest was first scouting, then engagement and defeat of the enemy, followed by construction of the network of forts and roads to lock down the newly conquered peoples. Urbicus' campaign began with preparations at Corbridge – recommissioned as the base of operations – for an offensive up Dere Street towards the north. Two legionary cohorts from *Legio II Augusta* (*Coh. III and IV*) from Caerleon moved into the forward garrison there. With little need for new surveying, the years 140 and 141 were occupied in defeating or overawing the enemy. In this case the targets were the Selgovae and Dumnonii, given the friendly stance of the Votadini of the east coast and probably also the Venicones of Fife. The Lines of Penetration (LOP) were well known by the army. The line of temporary marching camps with sizes of 17–23 hectares aligning with Dere Street, and of 8–13 hectare camps on the western LOP have been tentatively identified as dating to Urbicus' offensive (Figure 6.2).

Roman forces quickly and easily penetrated to the Forth and Clyde, very much as Agricola had done in the 80s. The support provided by the Roman Navy and marines leaves few archaeological traces, but we know from Tacitus (*Agricola* 25)

Urbicus' Plan of Campaign

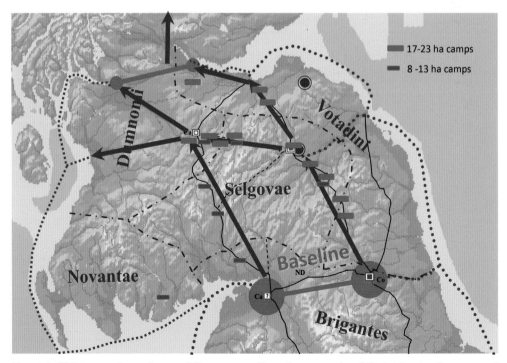

Fig. 6.2. Urbicus used two Lines of Penetration: Dere Street north of Corbridge in the east, and Annandale in the west, leading to the Upper Clyde. Marching camps possibly dating from this period mark these routes.

that combined operations were very much the order of the day in Northern Britain with its estuaries and rivers. We should also expect that the navy operated from ports on the Solway and Tyne, up the coasts to the estuaries of the Clyde, Forth and Tay. Roman scouts and agents will have been active across the Lowlands ever since the decision to move north again was taken in 139.

Permanent occupation of the Lowlands – fort construction

The initial occupation of the land and subjugation of the tribes between the Tyne/Solway and Forth/Clyde seems to have been accomplished quickly and easily. The next task, which would have been planned before the columns set out north, was to lock down the area with a network of forts and roads, as we have seen in previous campaigns.

It is worth analyzing the pattern and approach, which was essentially Agricola's plan of the late 70s, improved in places and modified to reflect tribal dispositions. The two LOPs stand out clearly: the road we call Dere Street was refurbished with forts spaced at one day's march from the base at Corbridge to the line of the new wall. Dere Street ran west of the Votadini, through the lands of the eastern Selgovae, with a major military base at Newstead and a very large fort garrisoned by no less than another two legionary cohorts. Newstead was positioned adjacent to the tribal centre of the Selgovae at Eildon Hill. There could not have been a clearer statement of domination and control by the Roman Army.

The west coast LOP was very different to Dere Street: what leaps out from the map (Figure 6.3) is the different – but still intensely close – attention paid to the western Selgovae. Instead of one massive base, there are six forts deployed along the valleys of the rivers Nith and Annan, with a network of two fortlets and eight lonely small fortlets deployed along the roads cutting through the Selgovae territory. In addition, the three outpost forts in the west, protecting the Brigantes from the Selgovae north of the line of Hadrian's Wall, still appear to have been maintained.

In between the LOPs there was a network of three cross-routes radiating from the forts at Newstead and Castlesteads. The key routes ran between these two major forts from Tweedale to Upper Clydesdale. Another important route ran north-east from Crawford to the Forth at Inveresk, and finally there was a south-west route from Newstead across the hills with a fortlet at Raeburnfoot (Figure 6.4). These would have been regularly patrolled by the troops of the mixed cavalry and infantry cohorts which were ideally suited to this work. The cavalry were able to scout and pursue, and the infantry were capable of standing and fighting when required as well as searching and assaulting defended villages and hillforts. This again raises comparisons with British efforts to control a hostile population in the Afghan Wars on the North-West Frontier of India.

Antonine Occupation of the Lowlands AD 139 - 142

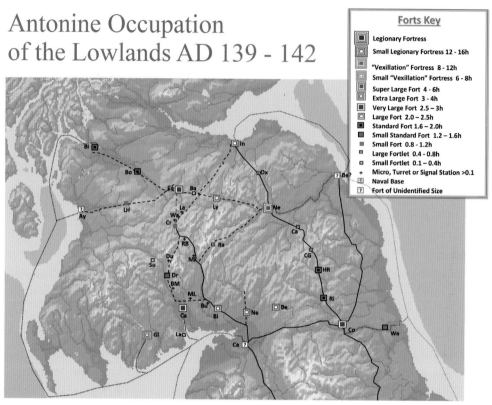

Forts Key

▣	Legionary Fortress
▣	Small Legionary Fortress 12 - 16h
▣	"Vexillation" Fortress 8 - 12h
▣	Small "Vexillation" Fortress 6 - 8h
▣	Super Large Fort 4 - 6h
▣	Extra Large Fort 3 - 4h
▣	Very Large Fort 2.5 – 3h
▣	Large Fort 2.0 – 2.5h
▣	Standard Fort 1.6 – 2.0h
▣	Small Standard Fort 1.2 – 1.6h
▪	Small Fort 0.8 - 1.2h
▫	Large Fortlet 0.4 - 0.8h
▫	Small Fortlet 0.1 – 0.4h
+	Micro, Turret or Signal Station >0.1
⊞	Naval Base
?	Fort of Unidentified Size

Fig. 6.3. This map plots all the forts of the Antonine occupation south of the Forth/Clyde isthmus. These were probably completed by 142.

Schematic of the Antonine Occupation of the Lowlands AD 142 -

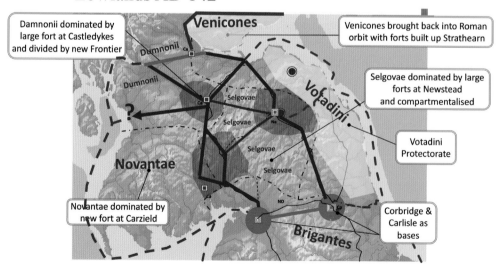

Damnonii dominated by large fort at Castledykes and divided by new Frontier

Venicones brought back into Roman orbit with forts built up Strathearn

Venicones

Dumnonii

Dumnonii

Selgovae dominated by large forts at Newstead and compartmentalised

Selgovae

Selgovae

Votadini

Selgovae

Votadini Protectorate

Novantae

Selgovae

Novantae dominated by new fort at Carzield

Corbridge & Carlisle as bases

Brigantes

Fig. 6.4. This map turns Figure 6.3 into a schematic breakdown of the elements of the Antonine occupation of Lowland Scotland.

The contrasting Roman approaches in the east and west are clear: the Votadini were trusted allies and needed no garrison; the Brigantes needed protection; the Selgovae and Dumnonii were held down with a network of forts, fortlets and patrolled roads. In this way the lines of communications were kept open, allies watched and protected, and enemies kept under the thumb (Figure 6.4).

In total there were twenty forts and fourteen fortlets of assorted sizes covering some 500km of patrolled roads. It is important to recognize that this is almost twice the weight of force deployed on the line of the Antonine Wall itself, even when its outposts are included.

The building of the Antonine Wall

It appeared that the fighting was all over by 142, when Antoninus was acclaimed *Imperator* for his victory in *Britannia* (Maxwell, 1981, p.134). By 143 – the fourth year of the campaign – the army could get down to the hard work of road and fort construction, including laying out a new wall line along the Forth/Clyde isthmus.

The Antonine Wall is just 61km in length, about half that of Hadrian's Wall at 117km, and, as Tacitus first noted (*Agricola* 23), is in the best place geographically to build a barrier from sea to sea in Britain. The wall itself, based on projections from surviving sections, was composed of a rampart about 3m high and made of turf on a stone base. In front of the wall was a *c.*6m berm with a ditch between 6m and 12m wide and 3.7m deep. Between 36m and 46m behind the wall ran a communications road – the 'military way' – itself 5m in width and composed of compressed gravel above rough stones (Hanson & Maxwell, 1983, pp.75–84; Breeze & Hanson, 2020).

Calculations of the labour required suggest 1.75 million man-days for the turf wall, ditch and 'military way', together with fortlets (Maxwell, 1981, p.133). It is thought that of the three British legions, *II Augusta* was there in full force together with vexillations of possibly 2,000 men or four cohorts each from *VI Victrix* and *XX Valeria Victrix*. Their work is commemorated in the nineteen splendid distance slabs now in the Hunterian Museum in Glasgow (Pictures 6.2, 6.3 and 6.4). Although manpower calculations are far from an exact science, especially since inscriptions show that auxiliaries also did some of the construction, the Antonine Wall could have been constructed over about eight months or maybe two campaigning seasons after 142 (Maxwell, 1981, p.134). We should always beware of over-optimistic assessments of Roman military delivery, however, given many other potential administrative and military distractions at the time.

What was the original plan – and was it changed?

We now come to the much-debated questions: what was the original plan for the Antonine Wall and why did it end up being built as it did? One-hundred-and-fifty years of excavations have left us something which, when listed out or plotted on a map, looks like an incoherent jumble of seventeen forts, many too small to hold a whole unit, set out at what seem to be imprecise intervals (Figure 6.7). At first sight, this could not be more different from Hadrian's Wall or the systematic approaches seen on the linear frontiers in Germany. The Antonine Wall itself was made of turf, like the original western length of Hadrian's Wall. To those historians who admire the systematic planning by the Roman military mind, this appears as positively un-Roman, almost a disgrace! So, what happened here?

Three fundamental debates continue to rage around the Antonine Wall:

- What was the design of the wall? Was there an original masterplan for a wall like Hadrian's Wall, with 'proper forts' at normal intervals, that was changed?

The Antonine Wall as Planned

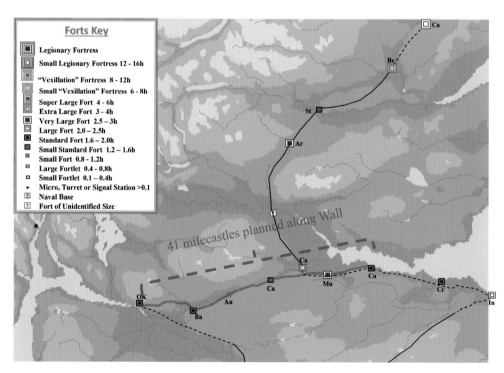

Fig. 6.5. The probable original plan devised by Urbicus for the Antonine Wall: ironically it was very similar to Hadrian's Wall (Breeze's Plan B) that had been so recently finished and had just now been abandoned.

Antonine Wall as Planned?

Camp-aign	System	Purpose	Desription	Id	Name	Phase	Roman Name	Size Ha	Size Code	Strength Factor	First Unit	Second Unit	Unit if Known	Build Code	Start Date	End Date	Distance. RM	IM	Km
ANTI	ANTW	WAL	8PRIM	1.0	Carriden			1.60	FRT	1.5				Urb	141	158	Base		
ANTI	ANTW	WAL	8PRIM	2.0	Mumrills			2.60	VLF	2.5				Urb	141	158	7.8	7.1	11.4
ANTI	ANTW	WAL	8PRIM	3.0	Castlecary			1.40	FOR	1.0				Urb	141	158	9.1	8.4	13.5
ANTI	ANTW	WAL	8PRIM	4.0	Auchendavy			1.10	SFT	0.6				Urb	141	158	8.2	7.5	12.1
ANTI	ANTW	WAL	8PRIM	5.0	Balmuidy			1.60	FRT	1.5				Urb	141	158	7.1	6.5	10.5
ANTI	ANTW	WAL	8PRIM	6.0	Old Kilpatrick			1.70	FRT	1.5				Urb	141	158	9.2	8.5	13.7
ANTI	ANTW	WAL	8PRIM	na	41 planned milecastles			0.03	sft	[0.1]									
Antonine Wall as Planned Primary Forts (PRIM)										**8.6**							**41.4**	**38.0**	**61.2**

Fig. 6.6. Extract from the database for what would have been the original design for the Antonine Wall, starting in the west at Old Kirkpatrick and stretching east to Carriden.

- Were there two occupations of the Antonine Wall, as seems apparent at some of the forts, based on their reconstruction and occupation by different units?
- When and why was the wall abandoned?

We shall look at each of these debates in turn, using the latest thinking on the wall (Hanson & Breeze, 2020; Hanson, 2020, pp.203–23).

The Antonine Wall as Built
17 forts and 4 outpost forts

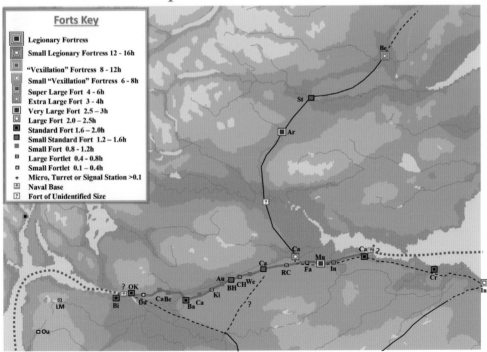

Fig. 6.7. The Antonine Wall as actually built, with seventeen forts along the line. Abandoning the high-level plan of equally spaced forts, additional forts of variable sizes were crammed in to strengthen the line, especially in the west. This is the most densely held frontier line in the Roman Empire.

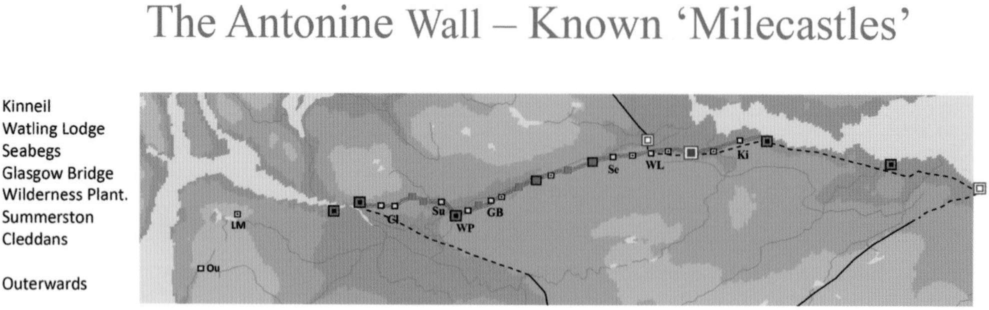

The Antonine Wall – Known 'Milecastles'

Fig. 6.8. There are seven identified 'mile-castles' along the Antonine Wall, with more expected to be discovered. These appear to be placed in relation to the original plan of the wall, leading to some anomalous positions very close to the forts as positioned in the revised design.

Until 1975, the Antonine Wall was seen as a single concept, very different from Hadrian's Wall that it had supplanted. In that year, John Gillam advanced the idea that the Antonine Wall had been originally designed along the lines of Hadrian's Wall 'as completed Plan B Model' (Gillam, 1975, pp.51–56; Breeze, 2019, p.74): that is, there were six 'primary' conventional forts spaced at half-day's march intervals (12km), as on Hadrian's Wall, with forty-one mile-castles spaced in between (Figures 6.5 and 6.6). The 'primary' forts were identified as:

- Carriden;
- Mumrills;
- Castlecary;
- Auchendavy (or possibly Bar Hill);
- Balmuidy;
- Old Kilpatrick.

Hadrian's Wall was at this time deliberately abandoned: mile-castle gates were removed and crossing points put in at intervals across the *vallum*. Clearly, Hadrian's Wall was no longer intended to be a barrier of any kind. One can only imagine the feelings and expressions of the legionaries who had laboured for almost two decades to build the wall, the forts and the *vallum*.

We have noted above that the Antonine Wall was made of turf, but there is evidence that the original plan was for a barrier built in stone, equally as impressive as Hadrian's Wall. Balmuidy and Castlecary forts were constructed of stone, and Balmuidy has wing walls which look to be 2.1–2.4m wide, which matches the width of the stone replacement of the western turf section of Hadrian's Wall. Balmuidy is also the only fort with inscriptions including Urbicus' name. The original intention therefore looks to be a shorter but otherwise very similar replacement of the more southerly barrier, built in stone with regularly spaced forts (Hodgson, 2020, p.302), a suitable monument to the new emperor's forward policy and his first victorious campaign.

Pic 6.1. Distance slab inscribed '*For the Emperor Caesar Titus Aelius Hadrianus Antoninus Augustus Pius, Father of the Country, a detachment of the Twentieth Valiant and Victorious Legion built [this] over a distance of 3,000 feet*'. Under a triumphal arch Britannia gives a laurel wreath to the eagle on a standard held by a legionary. On either side are naked captives down on one knee and beneath is the boar emblem of Legio XX VV. Hunterian Museum, Glasgow University. (*Photo by author*)

Pic 6.2. Antonine Wall distance slab featuring two winged Victories, an officer and a standard bearer. (*Photo by author*)

What actually happened?

The Antonine Wall was built out of turf with non-standard forts at apparently irregular intervals. So whatever happened to Roman planning and order? We have described what seems to have been the easy conquest of the Lowlands by Urbicus, followed by his triumph in 142. The commander of the *Legio II Augusta* was a favoured Greek historian with no previous military experience, Aulus Claudius Charax (Hodgson, 2020, p.307), who seems to have 'come along for the ride' and most probably to write an account of Antoninus' successful campaign against the barbarians. Hodgson argues that shortly after the campaign had been completed and the new wall started, and Urbicus was safely back in Rome, things began to fall apart during 143 and 144.

Urbicus' immediate successor as governor after his triumph in 142 is unknown, and his name has been erased from the milestone from Ingliston. Did he suffer *damnatio memoriae* (damnation of memory) as a result of serious trouble about and around the new wall (Hodgson, 2020, p.308)? The resonances with the First Afghan War in 1839–42, the Coalition invasion of Afghanistan in 2002 and the US occupation of Iraq in 2003 are clear: a successful invasion utilizing 'shock and awe' followed by a popular uprising that a technologically more advanced but overstretched army has great difficulty in holding down. The distance slabs certainly depict ferocious fighting between the Roman Army and the native population. Although traditional in theme, the distance slabs are memorials carved by the units that actually did both the fighting and the building (Picture 6.3).

Did the urgency of the situation dictate not just a change to turf as a faster building material but also a complete reworking of the plan? Was the redesign a haphazard strengthening of the wall line, or was this a different approach but still planned, yet in a different way?

The Antonine Wall as built

There was an intensification of the number of forts along the course of the wall as actually built, with some seventeen of varying sizes spaced out along its course. Furthermore, unlike Hadrian's Wall where the forts were added to the barrier well into the construction phasing, it seems that the fort sites were chosen first for their positions in the landscape, with carefully surveyed connecting site lines and defensible positions, and then the turf wall was built to link them. Turf was used because speed and ease of construction was now imperative in what had become a very hostile environment (Graafstal, 2020, pp.142–85).

If some double spacing in the east between Carriden and Inveravon – where the Forth estuary and the friendly Venicones in Fife would have aided defence – is discounted, the forts are actually, although not perfectly, but quite evenly spaced at 3.7km. The remaining major anomaly is around Bearsden, where plans were seemingly changed late in the day (see below). The spacing does not have the obsessional and arguably irrational uniformity of the original Hadrian's Wall plan, where mile-castle gates overlooked precipices. The Antonine forts were carefully sited within the landscape. However, many of these new forts were sub-scale in size, with some garrisons having to be shared between fort locations.

Work over the last fifty years has gradually discovered, sited between the forts, seven definite and five more suspected fortlets, which we should really call mile-castles, by analogy with Hadrian's Wall (Hanson, 2020, p.208; Figure 6.8). Unlike the forts, they almost all seem to be placed at 1.5km along the course of the wall. This means that in several places forts and mile-castles are placed close together, as if they relate to separate 'systems' with different purposes. There are no observation turrets on the Antonine Wall, however, as there were in both the original and built designs of Hadrian's Wall (Breeze Plans A and B). Therefore, what we have is a high density of forts with mile-castles in between. It looks as if the Roman leadership sacrificed uniformity of fort size and garrison in order to maximize available force

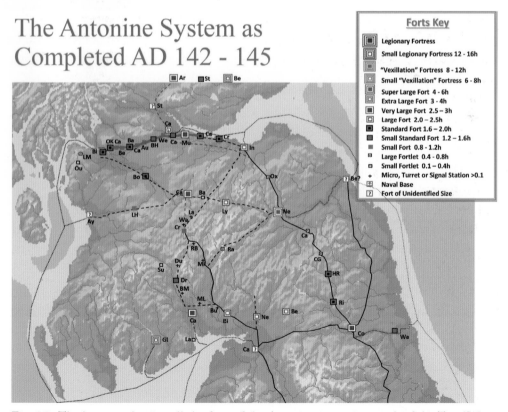

The Antonine System as Completed AD 142 - 145

Forts Key

▣	Legionary Fortress
▣	Small Legionary Fortress 12 - 16h
▣	"Vexillation" Fortress 8 - 12h
▣	Small "Vexillation" Fortress 6 - 8h
▣	Super Large Fort 4 - 6h
▣	Extra Large Fort 3 - 4h
▣	Very Large Fort 2.5 - 3h
▣	Large Fort 2.0 - 2.5h
▪	Standard Fort 1.6 - 2.0h
▪	Small Standard Fort 1.2 - 1.6h
▪	Small Fort 0.8 - 1.2h
▫	Large Fortlet 0.4 - 0.8h
▫	Small Fortlet 0.1 - 0.4h
+	Micro, Turret or Signal Station >0.1
⊞	Naval Base
?	Fort of Unidentified Size

Fig. 6.9. The key map showing all the forts of the Antonine occupation north of the Tyne/Solway isthmus plotted onto the landscape.

The Garrison of the Antonine Wall

No	Fort	Unit	Centuriae	Turmae	Infantry	Cavalry
1	Carriden	CQX	6		480	
2	Inveravon	1x cent detach	1		80	
3	Mumrills	AQ		16		512
4	Falkirk	3x cent detach	3		240	
5	Rough Castle	2x cent detach	2		160	
6	Castlecary	pars CMP	8		640	
7	Westerwood	2x cent leg det	2		160	
8	Croy Hill	1.5x cent leg det	1.5		120	
9	Bar Hill	CQP sag	6		480	
10	Auchendavy	3c cent leg det	3		240	
11	Kirkintilloch	CQP	6		480	
12	Cadder	CQP	6		480	
13	Balmuidy	pars CME	4	4	320	128
14	Bearsden	4x turm+1x cent	1	4	80	128
15	Castlehill	pars CQE	5		400	
16	Duntocher	1x cent det	1		80	
17	Old Kilpatrick	CQE	6	4	480	128
	TOTAL		61.5	28	4920	896

Table after Breeze 2020, 292

Adjustments: 8 barrack blocks at Castlecary for CMP, no troops of cavalry
1) 8 barrack blocks at Castlecary for CMP, no troops of cavalry
2) CQE at Old Kilpatrick on basis of barrack layout (Hodgson 2020,310)
3) Part of CME at Balmuidy since commanded by Tribune (Hodgson 2020, 310)

Carriden (CQX)
Inveravon
Mumrills (AQ)
Falkirk
Rough Castle
Castlecary (CMP)
Westerwood
Croy Hill
Bar Hill (CQPs)
Auchendavy
Kirkintilloch (CQP)
Cadder (CQP)
Balmuidy (CME)
Bearsden
Castlehill }(CQE)
Duntocher
Old Kilpatrick

Fig. 6.10. The garrison of the Antonine Wall, as built. The strength with which the central sector is held is very apparent, as is the concentration of cavalry unis at the eastern end, ready to deploy out to protect their most vulnerable allies.

along the actual wall line. Legionary centuries were even pressed into service on the frontier line, although this was generally not the usual frontier practice.

The fortlets predate the addition of extra forts, as shown by the fact that four forts probably replace primary fortlets: Duntocher, where the fortlet is subsumed in the layout of the secondary fort; Croy Hill, where the original fortlet is only 80m to the west and the fort overlies an Antonine enclosure; Castlehill; and Bar Hill (Hanson, 2020, pp.203–23; Picture 6.7).

This, therefore, was a replanning and has every appearance of being a rushed reaction to a presumably unexpected threat appearing in the central and western sectors. Hanson proposes that the building of the Antonine Wall stimulated a hostile local response from the Dumnonii, who did not submit willingly to being divided by a new Roman wall and had risen up in resistance. The burning of the broch at Leckie may have happened at this time. Urbicus had left *Britannia* in 142, so his successor reacted to the resistance by building faster in turf and strengthening the force along the barrier itself. The addition of another eleven forts plus the outposts in the east would have added at least another construction year to the wall-build, which therefore would have been completed by 144 (Maxwell, 1981, p.143). The result was one of the most heavily defended frontiers anywhere in the Roman Empire (Hanson, 2020, pp.203–23).

Rushed response or state-of-the-art frontier design?

Historians conditioned by Hadrian's Wall's logical and almost obsessional rigidity of design have seen the Antonine Wall as an 'unsystematic' and possibly panicked response to renewed threats. Unlike nearly all Trajanic and Hadrianic forts in Britain and Germany, many of the Antonine Wall forts are sub-scale, built for parts of units, and irregularly spaced (Figure 6.11). The wall itself is built of turf and zigzags across the hills of the Forth/Clyde isthmus. It looks rushed, unplanned and inferior in many ways. Nevertheless, I believe that the Antonine Wall, as modified and built, should in fact be seen as a realistic and pragmatic response to local resistance and a shortage of troops on the frontier.

Graafstal has recently seen the Antonine Wall as a planned response. This is in my view overstated. He argues that the design change came very early in the building of the wall, when just Balmuidy and Castlecary had been laid out in stone by Urbicus, and at that point the original plan was abandoned, reflecting local opposition (Graafstal, 2020, pp.142–80). In my view, he goes too far when he rejects the distinction between 'primary' and so-called 'secondary' forts and sees all seventeen forts as integral to the new design as implemented.

However, Graafstal has done a great service by analyzing the relationship of the components of the wall to each other and to the landscape. He demonstrates that all the fort sites were placed, so far as possible, to be:

- intervisible with their neighbours;
- close to valleys so that the forts would block hostile penetrations;
- built on plateaus (although this was negotiable);
- between 3 and 4.5km apart.

Given the levels of intervisibility between the forts, Graafstal argues that the fort sites were selected first. Furthermore, most of the main wall installations fall along

Antonine Wall as Built

Camp-aign	System	Purpose	Desription	Id	Name	Phase	Roman Name	Size Ha	Size Code	Strength Factor	First Unit	Second Unit	Unit if Known	Build Code	Start Date	End Date	RM	IM	Km
ANTI	ANTW	WAL	9ANTI	1.0	Carriden			1.60	FRT	1.5	CQP				144	158	Base		
ANTI	ANTW	WAL	9ANTI	2.0	Inveravon			small	lft?	0.3	1x cent detach				144	158	5.3	4.9	7.8
ANTI	ANTW	WAL	9ANTI	3.0	Mumrills			2.60	VLF	2.5	AQ		ala I Tungrorum quin		144	158	2.4	2.2	3.6
ANTI	ANTW	WAL	9ANTI	4.0	Falkirk			???	lft?	0.3	3x cent detach				144	158	2.0	1.8	3.0
ANTI	ANTW	WAL	9ANTI	5.0	Rough Castle			0.50	lft	0.3	2x cent detach				144	158	3.3	3.0	4.9
ANTI	ANTW	WAL	9ANTI	6.0	Castlecary			1.40	FOR	1.0	pars CMP	pars cohors I Tungroroum mill ped		Urb	142	158	3.9	3.6	5.8
ANTI	ANTW	WAL	9ANTI	7.0	Westerwood			0.80	SFT	0.6	2x cent leg det		LEG?		144	158	2.1	1.9	3.1
ANTI	ANTW	WAL	9ANTI	8.0	Croy Hill			0.60	lft	0.3	.5x cent leg det		LEG?		144	158	1.9	1.7	2.8
ANTI	ANTW	WAL	9ANTI	9.0	Bar Hill			1.30	FOR	1.0	CQP sag		coh I Hamiorum quin [sag]		144	158	2.0	1.8	3.0
ANTI	ANTW	WAL	9ANTI	10.0	Auchendavy			1.10	SFT	0.6	3c cent leg det		LEG?		144	158	2.2	2.0	3.3
ANTI	ANTW	WAL	9ANTI	11.0	Kirkintilloch			???	lft?	0.3	CQP				144	158	2.0	1.8	3.0
ANTI	ANTW	WAL	9ANTI	12.0	Cadder			1.10	SFT	0.6	CQP				144	158	2.6	2.4	3.8
ANTI	ANTW	WAL	9ANTI	13.0	Balmuidy			1.60	FRT	1.5	CQE			Urb	142	158	2.5	2.3	3.7
ANTI	ANTW	WAL	9ANTI	14.0	Bearsden			0.90	SFT	0.6	4x tumm+1x cent		ala???		144	158	3.0	2.8	4.4
ANTI	ANTW	WAL	9ANTI	15.0	Castlehill			1.00	SFT	0.6	pars CQE		Coh IV Gallorum		144	158	1.6	1.5	2.4
ANTI	ANTW	WAL	9ANTI	16.0	Duntocher			0.20	sfl	0.1	1x cent det				144	158	2.1	1.9	3.1
ANTI	ANTW	WAL	9ANTI	17.0	Old Kilpatrick			1.70	FRT	1.5	CQP				144	158	2.5	2.3	3.7
Antonine Wall as Completed (ANT1)										13.6							41.4	38.1	61.3

Fig. 6.11. Extract from the database of the Antonine Wall forts as actually built.

The Antonine Wall
East and West Extensions
Outpost Forts

Camp-aign	System	Purpose	Desription	Id	Name	Phase	Roman Name	Size Ha	Size Code	Strength Factor	First Unit	Second Unit	Unit if Known	Build Code	Start Date	End Date	Distance. RM IM Km
ANT1	ANTW	WAL	9ANTIE	1.0 Inveresk				2.30	LFT	2.0				Urb	142	158	
ANT1	ANTW	WAL	9ANTIE	2.0 Cramond				1.90	FRT	1.5				Urb	142	158	
ANT1	ANTW	WAL	9ANTIW	20.0 Bishoptom				1.60	FRT	1.5					144	158	
ANT1	ANTW	WAL	9ANTIW	21.0 Lurg Moor				0.05	lft	0.3					144	158	
ANT1	ANTW	WAL	9ANTIW	22.0 Outerwards				0.02	sft	0.1					144	158	
Antonine Wall as Completed East and West Extensions (ANT1E&W)										5.4							

Camp-aign	System	Purpose	Desription	Id	Name	Phase	Roman Name	Size Ha	Size Code	Strength Factor	First Unit	Second Unit	Unit if Known	Build Code	Start Date	End Date	Distance. RM IM Km
ANT1	ANTW	WAL	9ANTIOUT	23.0 Camelon				2.40	LFT	2.0	CMX or AQ						Base
ANT1	*ANTW*	*WAL*	*9ANTIOUT*	*24.0 [Stirling]*				*1.50*	*FOR*	*1.0*	*CQX?*						
ANT1	ANTW	WAL	9ANTIOUT	25.0 Ardoch				2.50	VLF	2.5	AQ???	CQX???					21.8 20.0 32.3
ANT1	ANTW	WAL	9ANTIOUT	26.0 Strageath				1.50	FOR	1.0	CQE	CQP					6.9 6.3 10.2
ANT1	ANTW	WAL	9ANTIOUT	27.0 Bertha				3.60	ELF	3.0	AQ???	CQE???					14.9 13.7 22.0
Antonine Wall as Completed with Outposts Forts (ANT1)										9.5							43.6 40.1 64.5

Fig. 6.12. Extract from the database showing the outpost forts running along Strathmore and the forts at the east and west ends of the main wall.

three long-distance survey alignments (Graafstal, 2020, p.154). Working from excavation sequencing evidence, he argues that the north faces of the forts were marked out first, and that these were then connected by marking out the line of the wall rampart, which was followed by the 'military way'.

The fortlets (or mile-castles in Hadrian's Wall terms) were in Graafstal's view probably part of the plan from the outset but were measured at intervals of almost exactly a Roman mile (1.5km) along the course of the rampart and were therefore surveyed and built as part of this stage. He envisages a system of seventeen forts on the wall sited at between 3 and 4.5km spacing, coupled with a rampart (and 'military way') constructed to connect them, and the regularly spaced fortlets. This then produced 'collisions' like those at Croy Hill, Duntocher and Castlehill, where the two spacing logics deliver a fort and a fortlet close to, or even on top of, each other. While I think that Graafstal is wrong in rejecting the two-stage build thesis, his central point that there is careful planning in the Antonine Wall is important.

In analyzing the building sequence, Graafstal – using excavation sequencing – sees the 30km of the central sector, which was the most vulnerable to attack from the north, as having been started first. After this sector was well on the way, there was a decision to add defended annexes to most of the forts, probably for the protection of supply trains and stores. A fort annex was much more easily defensible than the military zone defined by the *vallum* on Hadrian's Wall. Work on building the western sector seems to have started at this point, together with a decision to downscale Bearsden fort that was already in construction and to upscale Duntocher.

A major difference with the recently abandoned Hadrian's Wall is that the Antonine Wall has no turrets. Turrets were complex and time-consuming to build, and were seen as no longer required since observation could be done as effectively from the mile-castles with regular patrols. Furthermore, the absence of corner towers and complex gateways on the Antonine Wall suggests a lack of suitable mature timbers in the area by the 140s.

The completed Antonine Wall had fortlets at every mile and, for its distance, three times more forts than its predecessor. Graafstal (2020, p.180) sees this as resulting from a combination of the two primary purposes of a linear frontier (*limes*): observation and response. Manning the five mile-castles and fifteen turrets on Hadrian's Wall between each fort would have taken about 200 men, or two-fifths of each fort garrison. The two mile-castles between forts on the Antonine Wall would have required possibly as few as forty men. Even allowing for three times more frequently placed forts, the Antonine Wall would have been both faster to build and more economical with the available forces.

The positioning of the forts and the excellent lines of sight for overseeing hostile lines of infiltration gave the army the ability to manage the low-intensity threat of rustlers and smugglers and to counter larger bands of raiders by pulling in forces from other nearby forts along the 'military way'.

It is clear that three sectors were designed into the Antonine Wall: the west was protected by the Kilpatrick Hills and the east by the Forth and its marshy hinterland, which stretched much further inland with a higher sea level in the second century, while the key sector was the centre, which was held strongly from Mumrills to Castlehill. This was where the first season of works took place and where major raids would have come down from the north.

The Antonine Wall, as completed, is superior to Hadrian's Wall in many respects – including economy of force, sight lines and ability to respond to threats. However you still do have to ask why a Roman Army that was obviously short of manpower would build a new wall with very closely spaced forts, each with a locally optimized position, in a hostile environment; and at the same time build fortlets at fairly rigid intervals, resulting in overlaps and indeed overlays?

The Roman Army was admittedly capable of some deeply illogical actions in the name of uniformity – the siting of Hadrian's Wall mile-castles being one – but the planned simultaneous execution of two different defence systems is surely unlikely. The fact that some of the Antonine forts overlie the fortlets strongly supports this sceptical stance.

There is not as much distance between the positions of Hanson and Graafstal as might be thought: all we need do is to accept the original Gillam thesis of an early change in plan, with the original evenly spaced 'six forts plus fortlets' conception

Pic 6.3. *To the goddesses of the Parade Ground and to Britannia, Quintus Pisentis Justus, prefect of the Fourth Cohort of the Gauls, willingly, gladly and deservedly fulfilled his vow.* Altar to the Goddesses of the Parade Ground from Castlehilll Fort. Hunterian Museum, Glasgow University. (*Photo by author*)

Pic 6.4. *For the Emperor Caesar Titus Aelius Hadrianus Antoninus Augustus Pius, Father of his Country, a detachment of the Sixth Victorious Loyal and Faithful Legion [built this] over a distance of …. thousand paces.* This stone is flanked by *peltas* (light shields) the ends of which are griffin head terminals. The legion forgot to insert the actual length built! Hunterian Museum, Glasgow University. (*Photo by author*)

being replaced by seventeen forts closely spaced and optimized within the landscape. This decision would have resulted in the removal of fortlets/mile-castles where they were no longer necessary, but their retention where that made sense.

Graafstal's major contribution is to demonstrate that the Antonine Wall as built is not an unsystematic response to things falling apart on the northern frontier (Hodgson, 1995), but a flexible and sophisticated reaction to the need to hold a linear barrier running through hostile territory. The change in design is an effective, planned and logical response to threats from the north and to native unrest inside the new border. The fact that it is not rigidly regular is not a weakness but a strength.

The garrison of the Antonine Wall

The seventeen 'forts' along the course of the Antonine Wall were, using size-based definitions:

- one very large fort (VLF) at Mumrills;
- three standard forts (FRT) at Carriden and Old Kilpatrick, at either end on the Forth and Clyde, and at Balmuidy;
- two small standard forts (FOR);
- five small forts (SFT);
- six fortlets (lft) in the sense of sub-scale forts reflecting the manpower shortage.

In addition, up to twelve further fortlets (often called mile-castles in an Antonine Wall context, by analogy with those on Hadrian's Wall) have been definitely or tentatively identified (Figure 6.11).

By the strength calculation method, this amounts to 13.6 SFs overall. We know the original garrisons of only four of the seventeen forts with certainty (Figure 6.10):

- Mumrills: *Ala I Tungrorum* (AQ);
- Castlecary: *Cohors I Tungrorum milliaria* (CMP), not complete;
- Bar Hill: *Cohors I Hamiorum sagittaria* (CQP archers);
- Castlehill, and probably Bearsden: *Cohors IV Gallorum* (CQE).

Breeze has calculated the likely units and sub-units which were deployed along the line of the wall (Breeze, 2020, pp.286–99). The most important unit was the cavalry *ala* based at Mumrills on Dere Street leading to the north of the Wall at the east end. In addition to the cavalry *ala*, there was the equivalent of ten standard cohorts consisting at full strength of *c.*5,000 infantry:

- there was a double-strength *cohors milliaria peditata* based at Castlecary, the *cohors I Tungrorum milliaria*, which had been at Housesteads on Hadrian's

Wall – these count as 'two' as a double unit; there was space for eight of its centuries at Castlecary, allowing for two centuries to be posted out at the smaller forts and mile-castles;

- another possible double-strength unit was a *cohors milliaria equitata*, since it was commanded by a tribune at Balmuidy, one of the original forts where there was space for eight barrack blocks, suggesting that up to six *centuriae* and four *turmae* more were stationed elsewhere;
- unusually we find the equivalent of a legionary cohort with its six centuries split between three different forts at Westerwood, Croy Hill and Auchendavy;
- two or three hybrid *cohors quingenaria equitata* with infantry and integral cavalry were at Old Kilpatrick, making an inference from the barrack layout (Hodgson, 2020, p.310), possibly at Carriden and another one split between Bearsden and Castlehill owing to the late design change in the west;
- the remaining three units were standard infantry *cohors quingenaria peditata*, one of which was the Hamian archers at Bar Hill, and again we can expect these to have had centuries bedded out at the remaining smaller forts and fortlets.

We can see here the Roman Army making the most of the limited forces at its disposal. It was impossible to find units for every fort, so units were split and legionaries were also called into the front line. As a result, even after the redesign and 'thickening up' of the frontier, this total of ten units with a SF of 13.6 compares favourably with the sixteen *alae* and *cohortes* with a combined SF of 25.0 that the recently vacated line of Hadrian's Wall had needed for its garrison (Figure 6.10).

Unlike Hadrian's Wall with its extension forts, mile-forts and towers down the Cumbrian coast facing Galloway, there was no extension to the Antonine Wall down the coast facing the Firth of Clyde. There was, however, one fort – Bishopton – on the south bank in visual contact with Old Kilpatrick, and two fortlets – at Lurg Moor and Outerwards – placed where they could in good weather see raiders and traders crossing the Firth of Clyde (Figure 6.12). Although there has been no confirmation through excavation, we can safely assume the construction of supply ports and bases for the *Classis Britannica* on the Clyde and Forth, possibly at Old Kilpatrick and Carriden. Making further assumptions, given the excellent sight lines and signalling systems, the fortlets would have been able to signal to the fleet to intercept incursions.

Dere Street and the forts ahead of the Antonine Wall

Dere Street reached the sea at Inveresk, where a large fort had been built. From there the road headed west to a standard-sized fort at Cramond, an easy day's march away, and thence to the east end of the wall at Carriden. Dere Street then passed behind the wall until it turned north again, passing through the new wall not at a fort but at the mile-castle/fortlet at Watling Lodge west of Falkirk. It almost immediately reached the large fort at Camelon which was closely integrated into the wall's signalling relay system.

The reinstated Flavian road stretched for a further 65km north through the Lowlands of Strathearn to another reinstated Flavian fort at Bertha, some 64.5km north of Camelon, a distance longer than the wall itself. There were at least two intermediate forts at Ardoch and Strageath, also on well-established Flavian sites one-day's march (21km) apart. Looking at the spacing, there must surely have been another fort near Stirling still to be discovered, covering the road crossing of the Upper Forth (Figure 6.7). These four (or five) powerful forts provided a strong protective screen for the Roman allies, the Venicones of the modern Kingdom of Fife. They had probably been long-term Roman allies since the time of Agricola and the Gask Ridge frontier. There is no evidence for a reinstatement of the Gask frontier of watch towers and fortlets at this time. This whole arrangement also had the advantage of ensuring that the Antonine Wall itself could finish when it met the Forth at Carriden and did not need to have a coastward extension to guard against cross-Firth of Forth raiders.

The line of Dere Street north of the wall is another intriguing example of a Roman frontier line – this time protecting the Venicones, presumably with a constantly patrolled road-line. The force deployed along this road was large, with 9.5 SFs, equivalent to two-thirds of the entire force along the Antonine Wall line. It is thought that the Ardoch and Bertha forts were large enough to contain two units, possibly a cavalry *ala* and a mixed *cohors* (CQE). Camelon potentially held another cavalry *ala*. This would have ensured the ability to regularly patrol the road north to check for infiltration and rustlers, while also providing a strike force that could be assembled quickly to ride north to intercept large raiding forces or pursue warbands escaping with their booty.

Analysis of the Antonine occupation of the Lowlands of Scotland – the 'Antonine System'

The Antonine invasion of what is now the Scottish Lowlands was speedily and well executed, almost a textbook operation of conquest and occupation. The Lowlands appear to have been relatively quickly and easily occupied, and then the army started to build a wall like the one they had just abandoned between the Tyne and Solway. They then ran into unexpected challenges – possibly Dumnonii resistance to being cut in half – which necessitated an urgent revision of plans. The concept of a shorter, more northerly version of Hadrian's Wall built out of stone was replaced, and in its stead was a densely occupied preclusive turf-built barrier between the Firths.

Too much emphasis is placed on the Antonine Wall and not enough notice is taken of the whole integrated 'Antonine System' and its design (Figures 6.13 and 6.14). This section analyses that system and the distribution of the Roman Army using the SFs method. We can break the system down into six sections. Starting with the Lines of Penetration that became Lines of Communication, we can see that there were roughly fifteen SFs deployed along each line, although in different ways:

1. The principal line along Dere Street (the 'East Coast Mainline') was held by legionary cohorts: two garrisoned at Corbridge running the campaign base there, and another two legionary cohorts in the Cheviots at Newstead controlling the eastern Selgovae in Upper Tweedale. There was probably another fort or base at Berwick-upon-Tweed to supply Newstead some 44.5km up the Tweed. Back on Dere Street there were auxiliary forts at the usual day's march intervals until the Forth was reached at Inveresk. We should look for a supply port and naval base at one of the forts along the Forth, or even at Camelon which would have had water access with the higher sea level (Davies, 2020, pp.37–46). The Dere Street deployment served a dual purpose: functioning as the spinal column of the 'Antonine System' that linked the key bases and command centres at Corbridge and Newstead, as well as nailing down the Selgovae and protecting long-term Roman clients the Votadini.

2. The other LOP/LOC (the 'West Coast Mainline') was configured very differently, with only eight SFs along its mainline. Carlisle was apparently emptied as an active fort, although it was still probably a supply base for the northern campaings. The 'West Coast Mainline' mostly followed the Flavian route up Annandale and was anchored on a very large fort (VLF) of about 3 hectares at Castledykes, over the watershed into Clydesdale. From there the LOP ran down to the Clyde at Bishopton, opposite the end of the wall at Old Kirkpatrick. Along this route there was the standard fort at a single day's march. There may also have been routes to the first anchor wall forts at Balmuidy and Castlecary. The major difference in the west with Dere Street was the branch road up Nithsdale that rejoined the mainline south of Castledykes: here we find numerous fortlets and lonely turrets (amounting to another seven SFs) constructed to control this branch of the western Selgovae. The very different deployment pattern here is clear, reflecting the need to lock down an area that presumably had resisted and continued to resist Roman control (Hodgson, 2020, pp.300–12).

3. In the south, the Brigantes' protection zone appears to have been maintained. This had been set up as part of the Hadrian's Wall system, with three fearsomely large forts at Birrens, Netherby and Bewcastle to protect the Brigantes from the Selgovae north of Hadrian's Wall, another indication that the Selgovae were not willing additions to the *Imperium*.

4. In order to hold down the inhabited dales between the walls, there were cross-routes running west from Newstead though Tweedale and possibly through Loudon Hill to an as-yet-undiscovered fort or port at Ayr; and another cross-route running south-west from Newstead through a fortlet at Raeburnfoot to Milton. We should expect these roads, like the mainlines, to have been regularly patrolled by the infantry and cavalry of the mixed cohorts.

5. There were fourteen SFs along the new wall, which provided a very solid garrison line (pulled at the expense of other areas), between the Forth and Clyde, designed to prevent unauthorized crossing and well-equipped to meet threats emerging north of the wall or to launch punitive responses.

6. Finally, there will have been ten SFs in the outpost forts protecting the friendly Venicones in Fife.

The whole defence system deployed maybe 9,000 men (the *II Augusta* plus two vexillations from *Legios VI* and *XX*) from the British legions to build and up to a further 30,000 auxiliaries, equivalent to sixty-three SFs.

Standing back and looking at the 'Antonine System', we can see that only fourteen SFs were actually on the line of the wall, with ten SFs along the far north line of the Dere Street extension north the nall. This will have left as much as forty SFs on the lines of communication with their associated cross-routes to hold down and police the tribes newly brought into the empire (Figure 6.9). This is an important perspective, with nearly two-thirds of the Roman Army strength holding down the newly reoccupied territories between the two walls and less than one-quarter on the actual line of the Antonine Wall itself (Figure 6.13).

The deployment of units after the Antonine invasion

Because the occupation period was short, we are fortunate in being able to identify many of the units deployed during this period (Figure 6.17). Where this is not possible, the size of forts and their finds has led excavators and historians to propose likely garrisons. This enables us to map the probable deployment of auxiliary and legionary units in the period 142–157.

The Roman Army of the second century was still a determinedly offensive weapon with a doctrine that took the fight to the enemy. The Antonine Lowlands offensive was an exercise in taking and then holding more territory by offensive action. We should not see the wall or its supports as a defensive structure, but rather an element of a major offensive system. The objective was to pacify the tribes once again inside the empire while also taking action against the tribes further north beyond the new wall, deterring raids by penetrating far into the north and preventing them communicating with tribes inside the empire. The evidence for this attitude can be seen on other frontiers.

Examining the garrison, it is important to recognize that the types of troops deployed had very different purposes:

- cavalry *alae* were the elite of the auxiliaries who could be used to react to trouble by the tribes inside the wall or to threats from outside, with a reasonable patrol radius of 50km in one day, or more with a forced march;
- auxiliary cohorts of combined infantry and cavalry were the workhorses of the army, able to patrol the road network for up to 30km in one day, keeping

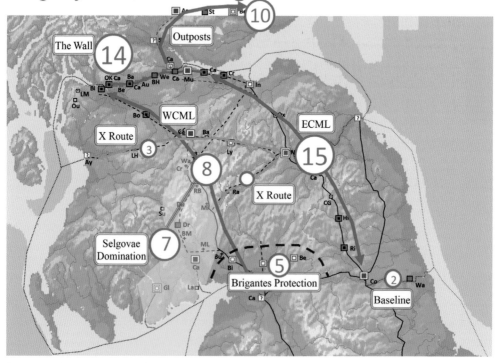

Fig. 6.13. Strength Factors (SFs) show how the Roman Army deployed its forces in the Antonine reoccupation of Lowland Scotland: fifteen SFs on the Dere Street LOC, fifteenSFs in the west, fourteen SFs on the wall itself and ten SFs on the advanced forts along Strathmore.

Campaign Typology: Urbicus Conquest of the Lowlands and Construction of the Antonine Wall

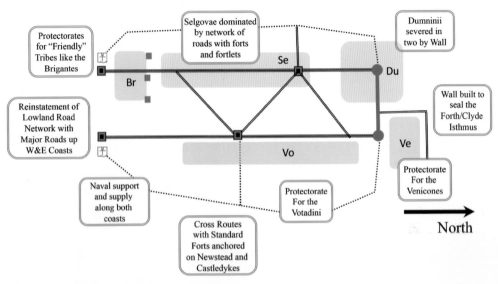

Fig. 6.14. Typology diagram unpacking the strategy of Urbicus' reconquest of the Lowlands, broken into its component parts.

the road network open for messengers and supply convoys and attacking quickly with cavalry and support with infantry when punitive action was needed;

- legionary cohorts were deployed ahead of the main legionary bases of York, Chester and Caerleon; at Corbridge, Newstead and even in some Antonine Wall forts. They provided overwhelming force for deployment in support of the above units when serious opposition was encountered.

If we look at the deployment of each type of unit through this lens, we can see that five of the six cavalry units were on the wall or north of it on the outpost line (Figure 6.15). Clearly, they were positioned there to reach swiftly into hostile territory, to scout beyond the frontier and to intercept hostile forces well beyond the wall. As many as 2,500 cavalrymen from the forts north of the wall, who could, when necessary, have been deployed together, would have provided a formidable mobile striking force (Figure 6.16). The other cavalry unit south of the wall was probably part of the Selgovae supervision forces and would have enabled quick reaction to the source of any problems.

Turning now to the *cohortes quingenaria equitata* (CQEs), these hybrid combined arms auxiliary cohorts were stationed at intervals to patrol and keep open the road network between the old frontier and the new, along Dere Street, along Annandale in the west and along the cross-routes.

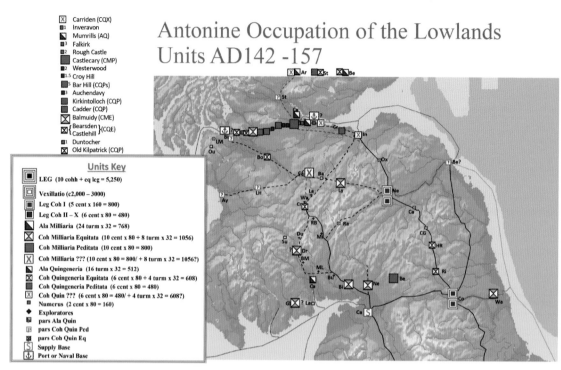

Carriden (CQX)
Inveravon
Mumrills (AQ)
Falkirk
Rough Castle
Castlecary (CMP)
Westerwood
Croy Hill
Bar Hill (CQPs)
Auchendavy
Kirkintolloch (CQP)
Cadder (CQP)
Balmuidy (CME)
Bearsden
Castlehill } (CQE)
Duntocher
Old Kilpatrick (CQP)

Units Key

LEG (10 cohh + eq leg = 5,250)

Vexillatio (c2,000 – 3000)

Leg Coh I (5 cent x 160 = 800)

Leg Coh II – X (6 cent x 80 = 480)

Ala Milliaria (24 turm x 32 = 768)

Coh Milliaria Equitata (10 cent x 80 + 8 turm x 32 = 1056)

Coh Milliaria Peditata (10 cent x 80 = 800)

Coh Milliaria ??? (10 cent x 80 = 800/ + 8 turm x 32 = 1056?)

Ala Quingeneria (16 turm x 32 = 512)

Coh Quingeneria Equitata (6 cent x 80 + 4 turm x 32 = 608)

Coh Quingeneria Peditata (6 cent x 80 = 480)

Coh Quin ??? (6 cent x 80 = 480/ + 4 turm x 32 = 608?)

Numerus (2 cent x 80 = 160)

Exploratores

pars Ala Quin

pars Coh Quin Ped

pars Coh Quin Eq

Supply Base

Port or Naval Base

Fig. 6.15. Map showing the units known or supposed to be deployed in the forts occupied during the Antonine period.

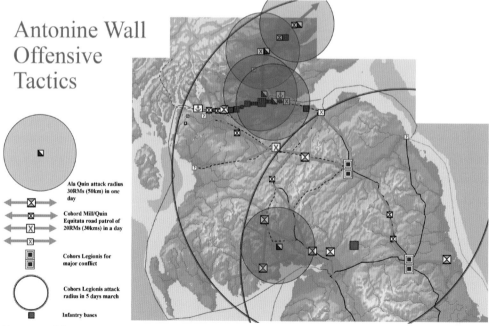

Antonine Wall
Offensive
Tactics

Ala Quin attack radius
30RMs (50km) in one
day

Cohord Mill/Quin
Equitata road patrol of
20RMs (30kms) in a day

Cohors Legionis for
major conflict

Cohors Legionis attack
radius in 5 days march

Infantry bases

Fig. 6.16. The positioning of cavalry units on the new Antonine Wall: they were concentrated to intervene quickly and effectively with the tribes of the Maeatae and Caledones situated north of the wall.

Pic 6.5. Ballista ball fired by a Roman catapult. Found in the destruction levels of the Leckie broch, it shows heat cracking pattern seen on stones made red-hot and then suddenly cooled. Perhaps the shot was fired into the broch and the defenders threw cold water onto it to prevent fire spreading. Hunterian Museum. (*Picture Peter Manson*)

One of the most interesting aspects is the forward deployment of the four legionary cohorts (*c.*2,000 men) at Newstead and Corbridge. Allowing 29.5km a day for each fort interval, the Corbridge legionaries could have covered most of the Lowlands and reached the Forth to repulse attacks on the wall in six days. The two legionary cohorts at Newstead could in the same six days have reached anywhere in the whole theatre of operations, including beyond the outpost fort at Bertha.

What was the purpose of the Antonine Wall as actually constructed?

Much ink has been spilt on arguments over the purpose of Hadrian's Wall, but less so on the Antonine Wall. The latest consensus on the more southerly wall is that, as designed – Breeze's 'Plan A' – it was a barrier to control and channel movement into and out of the frontier. We can see modern parallels in the Israeli security wall on the West Bank or former US President Trump's part-built wall along the US/Mexican border (Breeze, 2019). It was not completed in this form, but had seventeen forts added 'along the line of the wall' (*per lineam valli*) so that the Roman Army could actively patrol to the north and, of course, to the south. This frontier – Breeze's 'Plan B' – extended down the Cumbrian coast and in its completed version was about forward defence. In the third century, after Hadrian's Wall had been reoccupied, its turrets were unmanned, mile-castle gates partially blocked and the Cumbrian coast abandoned. The forts and their garrisons were upgraded with cavalry, however, and the wall appears to have become an intervention platform

Possible Identified Units on the Antonine Wall

Fort	Early Antonine Unit (or Antonine I)		Later Antonine Unit (or Antonine II)	
Carriden	*cohors quingenaria?*	CQX		
Mumrills	ala I Tungrorum	AQ	cohors II Thracum (tombstone)	CQP
Rough Castle	coh VI Nerviorum detach (com leg cent)	CQP		
Castlecary	cohors I Tungrorum milliaria peditata (det)	CMP	cohors I Fida Varullorum milliaria peditata (det)	CMP
Westerwood	Leg detach VI Victrix (wife of cent. tomb)	LG		
Croy Hill	Legionary detach VI Victrix	LG		
Bar Hill	cohors I Baetasiorum quingenaria ped cR ovf	CQP	cohors I Hamiorum quingenaria peditata	CQP
Balmuidy	*cohors milliaria equitata?* (com by tribune)	CME		
Castlehill	cohors IV Gallorum quing equitata (detach)	CQE		
Old Kilpatrick	*cohors quingenaria equitata?*	CQE	cohors I Baetasiorum quingeneria ped cR ovf	CQP

Fig. 6.17. The units on the Antonine Wall identifiable from epigraphic evidence.

for potentially powerful punitive expeditions and shows of strength to the north – Breeze's 'Plan C' (Breeze, 2019).

We can see elements of all three of these conceptions in the Antonine Wall and the associated troop deployments in the Lowlands of Scotland. The original 'Antonine Plan A' is effectively 'Hadrian's Wall Plan B' with forts spaced along the wall, with fortlets/mile-castles in between. This was swiftly abandoned for a more

Forts Evacuated for the Move North AD139-44

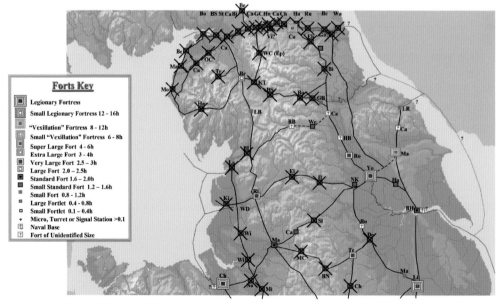

Fig. 6.18. Forts in Northern England that archaeological evidence suggests were evacuated during the Antonine reoccupation from *c.*142.

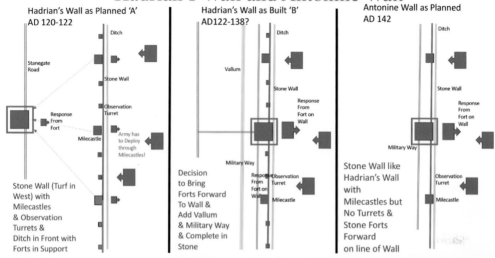

Fig. 6.19. Comparison of the original design of Hadrian's Wall (Plan A) with Hadrian's Wall as completed (Plan B) and the original design for the Antonine Wall as planned (AD 142).

flexible 'Antonine Plan B' with a very high density of forts of varying sizes supported by fortlets/mile-castles, but without turrets (Figures 6.19 and 6.20). The density of the forts and fortlets/mile-castles along the line of the Antonine Wall was clearly designed to preclude and regulate movement into and out of the new province. The

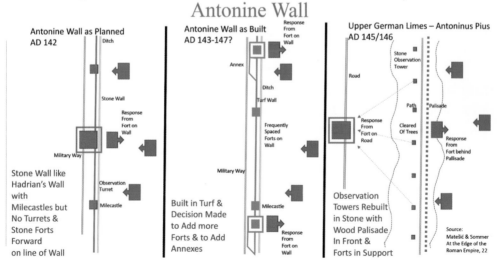

Fig. 6.20. Comparison of the Antonine Wall as planned and as completed with the contemporary Upper German *Limes*.

strong cavalry forces positioned ahead of the wall resonate with 'Hadrian's Wall Plan C': these were not just protecting the Venicones, but enabled the Romans to intercept hostile forces massing and to inflict punitive pain deep into enemy territory. These were intervention forces for use against the tribes further to the west and north – the Maeatae and Caledones as they are called – a few years later. The Romans' aggressive stance here probably helped to drive the previously disparate tribes of the Flavian era together into larger and more threatening confederations, as was to happen on the Rhine and Upper Danube frontiers.

So it is important not to just think about the design of the wall itself: some of the troops were ready to intervene in the far north, while others were protecting the Votadini and Venicones and forcibly incorporating the Selgovae and the southern Dumnonii into the formal province of *Britannia* with, as we shall see, only limited success.

Where did all the units for the Antonine System come from?

The whole enterprise required the construction of some forty new forts across the Lowlands, across the isthmus and up Strathearn. Where did their garrisons come from? The obvious answer is from the abandoned Hadrian's Wall, but this would only have yielded fifteen or so units. We need look no further than the forts of Northern England, where a further twenty-five to thirty forts appear to have been abandoned in the Antonine period (Figure 6.18). The extent to which Northern England was pacified – let alone assimilated – is hotly debated. Certainly, by the 140s the Brigantes had been held inside the empire for seventy years, with a legionary fortress at York and their own *civitas* at Aldbrough (*Isurium Brigantum*). It is likely that only the lowland areas around these centres were fully pacified and integrated into the economy and values of the province, with the upland areas having a discrepant and still largely separate identity (Mattingly, 2006, p.491). However, Urbicus judged that the area was in a condition where the garrison could safely be moved forward to the Scottish Lowlands. It has long been thought that the unreconciled elements of the Brigantes rose in revolt in the late 150s, precipitating the abandonment of the Antonine Wall and various territorial gains: however, the evidence is far from clear. Certainly, the wholesale departure of the garrison from the north of England to the Lowlands and the new wall could have opened the gates for rebellion.

The Mauritanian expedition

Local pottery with strong North African influences – that is, pots made to stand on a small brazier – have been found at Mumrills, Croy Hill, Bar Hill, Bearsden, Duntocher and Old Kilpatrick. This indicates the presence of troops, dependants or slaves – or all of these – who originated in that region. This is regarded as evidence for the return of an expeditionary force that had served in Antoninus' Mauritanian War, that began in the late 140s and was in progress into the 150s. Two soldiers from British units were discharged in North Africa in 152/153, one of whom was from the *cohors I Baetasiorum* stationed at Bar Hill. There is also a Moorish freedman, Victor, who was buried at South Shields, and we find a *numerus Maurorum Aurelianorum* (unit of Aurelian Moors) at Burgh-by-Sands, which probably arrived there at the end of the second century having moved back from being a garrison on the Antonine Wall.

There is therefore a strong probability that a detachment was sent from Britain, including units from the Antonine Wall, to take part in the Mauritanian War of Antoninus Pius in 145. It would be natural for the returning British units to have brought with them additional troops recruited in Africa (Breeze, 2006, pp.197–99).

Was there a second period of occupation on the Antonine Wall?

There are no written records of serious trouble on or behind the new wall, although we can infer problems with the Selgovae in Annandale and Nithsdale in the south-west from the density of fortlets and roads. At some point around AD 160, the decision was taken to evacuate the wall: why was there another reversal of frontier policy, indeed a retreat? This was the second retreat from a well-established permanent frontier in Britain, the first having been from Inchtuthil and the Gask frontier built by Agricola and his successor in the 80s. Once again, the Romans suffered a major reversal and loss of prestige.

This brings us to the second major debate about the Antonine Wall: following Hanson and Maxwell (1984, p.143), the accepted position was that in 157 the decision was taken to evacuate the wall. Their contention was that forts were systematically dismantled, as shown by the archaeological record, which also indicates that after a very short interval – months at most – the forts were reactivated.

There are no historical references to this reversal – and then a reversal of the withdrawal – so any explanations are based on rival interpretations of the excavated sites. There has since Haverfield (1904, pp.454–59) been a hypothesis that there was a 'Brigantian Revolt' around 155 which led to destruction of forts in the North, including Birrens and Newstead. This 'revolt' theory then became linked with the apparent abandonment of the Antonine Wall *c*.155. Apart from an increase in the deposition of coin hoards in the 150s/160s (Maxwell, 1981, p.146), evidence that there was trouble across the north of *Britannia* is scarce. But a substantial vexillation of British troops from *Germania Inferior* and *Superior* arrived back at Newcastle under Julius Verus at around this time (Roman Inscriptions of Britain, RIB 1322): could this indicate serious trouble in the North and/or the Antonine Wall zone?

We can confidently infer that there was ideological conflict between two schools of thought in the High Command of the Roman Army in *Britannia*, and possibly empire-wide. We could call one school the 'Antonines', who would have favoured the forward policy of Antoninus with a wall closer to the likely origins of trouble and a forward interventionist patrolling policy. The other could be termed the 'Hadrianic' school, who would have preferred withdrawal to the rearward line of Hadrian's Wall, with the Lowlands acting as a kind of defensive glacis of friendly and/or cowed tribes. We have already seen that there was resource overstretch explicit in the design of the Antonine Wall, with forts built sub-scale and legionary cohorts pressed into the front-line garrisons.

Under this scenario, the governor since 155, Julius Verus – given continuing resistance from the Dumnonii and Selgovae, and a revolt by the Brigantes to his rear – decided around 157 on a strategic withdrawal. When the now 71-year-old Emperor Antoninus heard about this in Rome, he immediately countermanded this reversal of his trophy conquest, and Verus himself was withdrawn in 158. After the North had been subdued, the Antonine Wall was reoccupied and many of the forts were rebuilt.

After Antoninus' death in 161, however, the reoccupation was reversed around 164. The forts that had just been reoccupied and reconstructed were once again systematically vacated and destroyed, and the army pulled back to Hadrian's Wall, only retaining outpost forts at Newstead and Birrens. Under this scenario, the 'Hadrianic' school eventually won the day, at least until Septimius Severus revived the forward policy in 207.

This interpretation has led to the search for two wall periods – Antonine I and Antonine II after 157, accompanied by different garrisons in the key forts. It would have been instructive to hear the comments of long-serving soldiers on this reversal of policy and two rounds of destruction and reconstruction! Not that different to comments from the US forces following the US withdrawal from Afghanistan in September 2021.

It is therefore possible that there were no less than four fundamental reversals of policy over the course of only twenty-five years:

- Antoninus abandons Hadrian's Wall in 138 to occupy the Lowlands and build the new wall;
- Verus takes a local decision to abandon the Antonine Wall in 157;
- Antoninus orders the reoccupation of the Antonine Wall shortly afterwards in 158;
- Marcus Aurelius finally decides to abandon the Antonine Wall and reoccupy Hadrian's Wall in *c.*164.

If the Roman Army could give up the recently completed Hadrian's Wall in 138, could this scenario of 'marching up the hill and down again' perhaps be credible?

The single-period argument

Did it really happen this way? Hodgson (1995, p.29) has argued that there is no unequivocal excavated evidence for a second period on the Antonine Wall in 157–63. Out of the thirty-six Antonine sites in Scotland which had been excavated by 1996, Hodgson (1996, p.31) found only five that had unequivocal evidence for a second rebuild during the Antonine period. Of these, Birrens, Cappuck and Newstead were future long-term outpost forts for the reoccupied Hadrian's Wall. Strageath on the outpost line was, however, definitely rebuilt with twelve barracks instead of eight (Hodgson, 1995, p.49). The same rebuilding is true of the fortlet at Outerwards, the outpost south of the Clyde to the west of the wall, which was also rebuilt (Hodgson, 1996, p.46).

The resurfacing of internal roads at Bothwellhaugh, Carzield, Castledykes, Rough Castle, Croy Hill, Balmuidy and Old Kilpatrick can be seen not as evidence of two phases of occupation, but as normal care and maintenance, given the need for constant upkeep of drainage systems in a rainy climate. Furthermore, the changes to wooden barracks at Old Kilpatrick, Duntocher, Cadder and Mumrills, plus barracks passing out of use at Cadder and Old Kilpatrick, can be seen as normal fort changes over almost two decades of occupation (Hodgson, 1995, p.32). Such piecemeal changes would normally be expected as part of the maintenance of timber installations in the harsh Scottish climate.

The second element of the two-stage Antonine argument depends on the garrison changes identified as the second-phase occupation. At Mumrills, the *principia* and *praetorium* were rebuilt to a smaller plan; a change associated with the *ala Tungrorum* being replaced by the *cohors II Thracum*. At Castlecary, there is a building inscription (RIB 2155) made by the original garrison – the *cohors I Tungrorum* – who were then replaced by the *cohors Vardullorum*, both units being *milliaria peditata* (CMP). Since both were of the same complemented size and had outposts elsewhere along the wall, this would not have necessitated large-scale rebuilding and indeed suggests continuity of occupation rather than demolition and rebuilding.

The original garrison at Bar Hill were the Hamian archers (*cohors I Hamiorum*), who were replaced by the *cohors I Baetasiorum*, both *quingenaria peditata* (CQP). Excavations there found modifications to the headquarters building but no evidence for a break in occupation (Hodgson, 1996, p.47). The *cohors I Baetasiorum* reappear probably as a detachment at Old Kilpatrick. Hodgson suggests that these unit movements could be associated with the decision to abandon the original primary forts. This is unlikely, however, since the 'original design' was abandoned much earlier, but under the 'single occupation' thesis, these could be seen as normal evolutions and garrison rotations (Hodgson, 1996, pp.34–35).

The biggest problem with the 'single occupation' argument, in my view, is the long period of ramp-down of the garrison from *c.*158–164 which it requires, during which the thinned-out wall fort line and outposts would have been very vulnerable. Undoubtedly, some forts were rebuilt at Outerwards and Strageath, as were Birrens, Cappuck and Newstead. There were unit changes, in the few cases where we know of the units, and headquarters buildings were altered as a result. At present this debate seems too close to call, but perhaps both theses could be true: in other words, in response to the troubles in Germany and the north of England, troops had to be substantially thinned out to suppress the rebels, and this led to temporary abandonment and changes in some but not all of the forts. This need not have required complete abandonment of the wall line or its forts, especially if the intention was that the garrisons would return. Thus, full or partial mothballing followed by recommissioning on the return of the vexillations from the Germanies could be what is being seen. Some garrisons were therefore moved, and some forts were substantially rebuilt, whilst others remained in occupation, albeit at reduced strength.

This hybrid mothballing approach would again be a pragmatic response to threats in Germany and Northern England and the resulting urgent need to pull troops out. It would also have avoided Antoninus having to reverse his own conquest. I do not believe the army would have given up the emperor's conquest without clearance. Then, after Antoninus' death – and in response to the Eastern War – Marcus Aurelius would have taken the logical and pragmatic decision to reduce the army's overstretch and to fall back to the Tyne/Solway line.

The final withdrawal from the Antonine Wall

The archaeological record shows that, whenever the time came, there was a systematic dismantling of the forts on the Antonine Wall and on the outpost road through Strathearn, together with most of the forts in the Lowlands north of the Tweed. This was dismantling, not destruction by an enemy, and, as with Inchtuthil in 87, was therefore a strategic withdrawal conducted in an orderly manner on the orders of the Roman High Command. Buildings were taken down and distance slabs buried. There was burning at Birrens, but this was tidied up, and excavators found a broken spade blade in a post-hole of the second Antonine fort at Strageath (Maxwell, 1981, p.150), proof of systematic – and no doubt heartbreaking – work for a Roman 'squaddie'. Construction work can be seen at Corbridge, Vindolanda and Carvoran on the reoccupied Hadrian's Wall at this time, and also behind the wall at Brough-on-Noe and Ribchester (Maxwell, 1981, p.142).

Date of the withdrawal

The actual date of withdrawal is debated and closely related to the arguments about whether there was a two-stage occupation – the Antonine I and Antonine II thesis. Under that view, the final evacuation of the Antonine Wall is dated to 163 or 164, after the end of Antoninus Pius' reign and following a short second-period occupation. Furthermore, the latest dateable Samian ware and a stratified coin on the wall dates to 164 (Hanson & Maxwell, 1984, p.66). In this scenario, the governor, Calpurnius Agricola, who served from 162–166, administered the evacuation. The *Historia Augusta* notes that early in Marcus Aurelius' reign, war was threatening and Calpurnius Agricola was sent against the Britons.

If, however, Hodgson's view of a single Antonine occupation is accepted, the evacuation could have started as early as 155–158 (Hodgson, 1996, p.38). He suggests that after the main withdrawal had taken place, there was a period of Roman military interest in the Lowlands, which could explain coins of the 170s from Bar Hill and Kirkintilloch, and a gradual evacuation of forts, which would explain coins from 160 at Cadder and 164 at Old Kilpatrick. Indeed, an altar and pottery from Castlecary are taken as evidence of its survival as an 'outpost fort' (Hodgson, 1996, p.39).

Hodgson sees troop transfers away from Britain in the period 151–155 as leading to the necessity of abandoning the advanced Antonine frontier. It was in this period, from 155 onwards, that the Upper German and Raetian frontiers were sealed with the moving forward of the Upper German *Limes* and the construction of the continuous line along the Raetian frontier. The return of the three legionary vexillations (RIB 1322) of the British legions from the two Germanies under Julius Verus as the new governor between 155 and 159 is therefore interpreted as part of the reactivation of Hadrian's Wall. Hodgson therefore sees the completion of the Upper German and Raetian frontier as precipitated by unrest on that frontier and associated with the withdrawal from Scotland, also in the face of military challenges. The Roman High Command was having to make some difficult choices with finite resources.

The nature of the withdrawal

Whenever it happened, the nature of the withdrawal was dramatic. In the west, it went right back to the three Hadrianic forts protecting the Brigantes north of the line of Hadrian's Wall at Birrens, Netherby and Bewcastle. Might there even have been some kind of formal treaty with the Brigantes to this effect? In the east, in an example of Roman Army history repeating itself, Dere Street was probably held all the way up to the fortress of Newstead (and even possibly up to Castlecary,

Pic 6.6. The deep and well-preserved Antonine Wall bank and ditch west of Rough Castle. (*Photo by author*)

now alone on the Antonine Wall), with the outpost forts at Risingham and High Rochester along Dere Street occupied as well (Maxwell, 1981, p.142). This situation appears to have lasted until the 180s, when Roman forces left Newstead in some haste, probably at the time of a serious break-in of the northern tribes through Hadrian's Wall and the devastation of the interior of the province (Trimontium Trust, 1994, p.14).

Pic 6.7. Looking eastward down the hill from the site of Croy Hill milecastle towards Croy Hill fort along the line of the Antonine Wall. (*Photo by author*)

Was the Antonine Wall successful?

The Antonine Wall, for the fifteen years (142–157) of its definite operation, appears to have achieved its aims. The Lowlands were incorporated into the province, and the fact that the fortlets and turrets in Annandale, Nithsdale and Clydesdale became unoccupied at the end of the 150s or early 160s strongly suggests that the Selgovae were pacified, if not reconciled. Although the open country of Northumberland and north of Berwick, Clydesdale and Tweedale, and around Ayr was desirable and exploitable economically, it was always going to be an impossible task to 'Romanize' the Lowlands. In the same way that the uplands of the Silures and the Brigantes seem not to have joined the Roman economy, so it would be in the Lowlands of

Scotland. There was never going to be a viable *civitas* capital, even with the modest pretensions of Aldborough, Carmarthen or Carlisle: this remained the uncivilized North-West Frontier of the Empire. The military amphitheatre at Newstead was strictly for garrison use, and the only native participation would have been as victims for slaughter and entertainment (Picture 5.1). Furthermore, although there appears to have been gold, lead and copper to be mined, these do not seem to have been significantly exploited (Jones & Mattingly, 2002, p.179).

The deployment of aggressive forces supported active intervention north of the wall from the outpost line. It is possible that, whilst being totally in line with the traditional Roman Army doctrine of active offence, this stirred up a hornet's nest of trouble and stimulated the formation of the Maeatae as a single confederated tribe from the mass of small tribes described by Tacitus that Agricola had faced sixty years before.

In the end, Tacitus was right when he castigated Domitian for recalling Agricola in AD 84 after Mons Graupius: if you were going to campaign in the far north of *Britannia*, you had to be ready to finish the job properly.

The fact that the 'Hadrianic' school of thought won in the end, and the new wall and the forts forward and behind it were given up – however you try to spin it – marks the Antonine campaign out in the end as another costly Roman failure, doubly so if the putative strategic *volte face* of 157/158 actually occurred. Although the Romans did not think in terms of public expenditure in a modern sense, the consciousness that massive resources and large sums from the imperial treasury had been deployed on abortive military installations that had now been (possibly twice) dismantled could not have been translated as a glorious triumph of Roman arms, however it was dressed up.

Conclusions about the Antonine Wall

For the size of territory occupied, the force deployed was large, amounting to some sixty-three SFs over 20,000km². As Maxwell and Hanson concluded:

> [T]he Roman grip was assured by the densest and most comprehensive network of forts and similar installations ever constructed in the military zone of the British Province. (Maxwell & Hanson, 1983, p.70)

A textbook campaign by Urbicus was initially followed by a textbook implementation of Roman territorial domination, with incorporation of territory into the formal empire using a grid of forts linked by military roads. This was delivered on plan and the new wall was started – then it all started to go wrong. The design of the Antonine Wall had to be modified very soon after construction had started because of local and possibly more widespread resistance. This result was not the *ad hoc* mess the Antonine Wall is sometimes depicted as; rather, it was a rational, planned and pragmatic response to the challenge, maximizing the forces available. This was the Antonine system. It stabilized the situation in the North for a decade or so, and it was even possible for troops to be sent on the Mauritania expedition and for the supervision of the western Selgovae to be eased off. Built into the Antonine system was strong forward intervention deep into the northern tribes, which provoked them to come together in mutual support. In the late 150s, the situation deteriorated, troops were needed in Germany, the upland Brigantes may also have risen in revolt and pressure from the far north possibly intensified, leading Governor Verus to temporarily mothball forts and remove some troops. Antoninus was not going to let his first and only substantial conquest go, however. This step had to wait for the new emperor, Marcus Aurelius, who, with troops needed for the Parthian War, did the cost-benefit analysis and took the logical decision to pull back from the Antonine Wall and refurbish Hadrian's Wall. This was done in an orderly manner under cover of a campaign by the new governor, Calpurnius Agricola. Fundamentally, the Antonine system as a whole, not just the wall, was judged to be unsustainable; or at least that it was not worth the cost in manpower (and maybe continuing casualties) of holding on.

As set out above, we can see here evidence of an argument inside the Roman High Command, both on the ground in *Britannia* and in Rome in the imperial household. I have termed this 'Antonines versus Hadrians'. The former were clinging to the glory days of the Flavians and Trajan, believing that the Roman Army should and could expand the empire where and when it wanted to, and should dominate the tribes far beyond the formal frontier. Hadrian, meanwhile, saw this as no longer practical and too much of a drain on already stretched resources; better to concentrate on assimilating the peoples the empire already had conquered rather than acquiring more. In this respect, it's worth noting that the final drive for new *civitates* in Britain occurred when Hadrian was emperor and can be attributed to his desire to consolidate what the Romans held and not to keep expanding into hard-to-hold territory with tribes who resisted Roman culture, economy and ideology.

Finally, this tension – which we can see with Agricola, with Hadrian, with Antoninus, with Severus and Caracalla – had the impact of fatally undermining Roman military policy in *Britannia*. The Roman High Command simply could not make up its mind and stick to a policy in *Britannia* and follow it through. An inherent weakness of the imperial system was that it partly depended on the will and competence of the emperor of the day. We have in the Antonine campaign strong evidence of excellent and detailed planning, rigorous record keeping in the army, good intelligence and the ability to analyze challenges and improvise solutions when faced with new challenges. However, we also see the result of fundamental U-turns in policy and approach at the very highest level.

This does not mean that the Roman Army did not have a grand strategy or that it was not a systematic and learning organization. It did have a grand strategy, or rather two competing grand strategies, in the second century. The combination of these competing strategic approaches with manpower overstretch led to another initially brilliantly executed campaign ultimately failing, with all the gains being given up.

Part 2

The Method

Chapter 7

A New Digital and Cartographical Approach

How Roman forts are mapped obscures rather than elucidates Roman strategy

T he way Roman forts are mapped in even some scholarly works obscures rather than elucidates Roman military strategy (Figures. 7.1 and 7.7). More often than not, maps show Roman forts of all sizes, and often all periods, as an undifferentiated square – usually a red square, following British Ordnance Survey conventions dating back to the 1950s. In popular histories, and also in many museum or site displays, there is usually a map of Roman Britain with forts shown, with little attempt made to distinguish the occupation periods of the forts. This is despite the fact that for Britain, Germany and increasingly other frontiers of the Roman Empire, there are now granular and well-established chronologies. Furthermore, there is rarely any attempt to distinguish between fort sizes, although legionary fortresses – at around 16 hectares some ten times larger than most forts – are usually shown differently, again following Ordnance Survey tradition. To be fair, small forts are sometimes indicated by smaller squares and are termed fortlets. There is rarely any attempt made to show what units occupied the forts, however, even when this is known from inscriptions, or whether the garrisons were cavalry, infantry or mixed cavalry/infantry units.

The problem with most maps of Roman forts

As a result of these habits, maps of Roman Britain or of Roman forts in Britain can be highly misleading in depicting the Roman military occupation. They have uniform symbols densely plotted across Northern England and Lowland Scotland. This is understandable and perhaps forgivable in popular histories of the Roman Army that retell the same familiar material. The extraordinary thing is that the same practice occurs not only in serious works by museums and English Heritage, but also in many scholarly works. Even the Roman Army Museum at Carvoran on Hadrian's Wall – while excellent in every other way – has an undifferentiated map of all the Roman forts that ever existed in Britain (Figure 7.1).

There are of course some honourable exceptions. Particularly noteworthy in this respect are David Breeze's maps of Northern Britain, Hadrian's Wall and the Antonine Wall (Figure 7.2), which are widely used in scholarly works (Breeze & Hanson, 2020, p.11). These have excellent topographical bases showing the major rivers, mountains and hills, and the twenty-first-century coastline. They show forts, fortlets, the walls and roads, with probable forts and roads distinguished separately, and respect known chronologies of occupation. This is the example to follow.

The opportunity for a different approach

Northern England, Wales and Scotland (along with the parts of the Rhineland and southern Germany) have, thanks to their agriculturally marginal uplands, preserved forts, roads and marching camps for study by generations of diligent antiquaries, historians and archaeologists. That study has produced unparalleled volumes of published data and analysis, for example in *Britannia* Volumes 1–51, that allow us to start to map these areas more intelligently, in ways that can shed light on how the Roman Army operated and developed its campaigning techniques and processes.

A cartographic manifesto for Roman military studies

Our aim should be to produce maps and illustrations that are as cartographically and diagrammatically sophisticated as the archaeological and historical research in the scholarly articles they illustrate. To fulfil this objective, our maps should have:

- Clear **topographical backgrounds** that illustrate the challenges faced by Roman generals in campaigning in the area. This requires – as Breeze's map-backgrounds show – major rivers, mountains and hills, and coastlines:
  - ideally these should indicate the historic coastlines and landscape setting of the period in terms of forest, cultivated and grazed areas, and so forth;
  - however, because these are topics where our knowledge is generally still developing and there is considerable scope for debate as historical environmental studies progress, this is best done as an overlay or with annotations on the approach that has been adopted and why.
- Separate **icons for different sizes of forts** and for different types of units, such as cavalry and infantry, based on excavation and epigraphic studies:
  - the standard military unit designators should be used, where applicable and modified as necessary for the first-century Roman Army.
- Tracking of known **Roman roads**, and probable roads, that link sites:
  - given that roads are usually impossible to date with certainty, care must be taken here to show probability.

- Development of a **standard diagrammatic notation** for Roman forts to allow comparison of excavated results:
  - use of standard symbols for barracks, *principia*, granaries etc.

What are the right categories to map?

As noted above, three vital pieces of information are often known but not clearly distinguished on maps of Roman military installations:

- the standard red square is used to denote a fort of 'normal' size of roughly 1 hectare, as well as a large installation five times – or even ten times – the size;
- there is no indication of the unit stationed at the fort or fortress, whether they are legionaries or auxiliaries or indeed a *numerus* of irregulars, or whether they are cavalry, infantry or a hybrid unit;
- sometimes there is no attempt to recognize that many forts went out of occupation for periods and were replaced, abandoned and in some cases rebuilt on the same site years or decades later.

So we are looking for cartographic standards that enable us to show the **sizes** of the forts, the **garrison** of the forts and the **periods** the forts were occupied.

Sizes of the forts

Categories for fortresses, forts and fortlet symbols

I have grouped the fortresses, forts and fortlets into six major categories and sub-categories:

- **legionary fortresses** above 12 hectares;
- **campaign bases** or so-called 'Vexillation fortresses', from 6–12 hectares;
- **super-large and extra-large forts** from 3–6 hectares;
- **large forts** from 2–3 hectares;
- **forts** from 0.8–2 hectares;
- **fortlets** below 0.8 hectares.

I have sub-divided these six categories into groups to enable them to be plotted onto terrain maps and to clarify distinctions for analysis. I have developed a three-letter code for each of the size categories, for example 'LEG' for legionary fortress, 'VLF' for very large fort and 'lft' for large fortlet. The groups are:

Legionary fortresses 12 hectares and above in size:

- Legionary fortresses over 16 hectares (LEG) – the vast majority of the classic first to early third-century legionary bases are over this size, and there were also some double legionary fortresses in the Augustan period on the Rhine (LEGG).
- Small legionary fortresses 12–16 hectares (LG) – there are a few small fortresses that are probably like legionary bases but smaller, either because of constrained sites or of permanently detached cohorts – Gloucester Kingsholm at 10 hectares is an extreme example.

Vexillation fortresses (or campaign bases) from 6–12 hectares:

- Vexillation fortresses or campaign bases from 8–12 hectares (VEX) – the bases of the task forces used in the conquest of Britain from the invasion of AD 43 to the 'Flavian surge' of the AD 70s. These probably held the HQ and

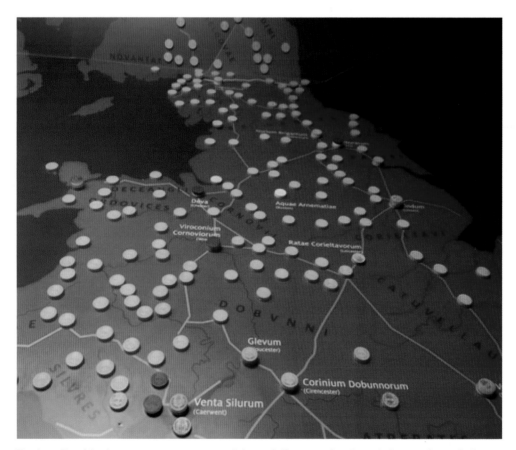

Fig. 7.1. Possibly the most extreme version of the undifferentiated style with Roman forts of all sizes and of all periods simply plotted onto a map, in the Roman Army Museum at Carvoran, part of the Vindolanda Trust. (*Photo by author*)

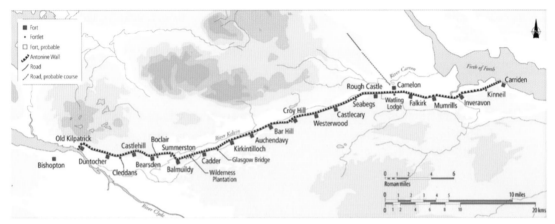

Fig. 7.2. One of David Breeze's exemplary maps: the Antonine Wall, showing forts occupied at the same time in the landscape, differentiating between forts and fortlets and also showing roads (Breeze & Hanson, 2020, p.20).

from four to six cohorts of a ten-cohort legion, allowing the other cohorts to garrison detached forts and bases. It is likely that auxiliaries were also present.
- Small vexillation fortresses or campaign bases of 6–8 hectares (VX) – the bases of smaller task forces composed of mixed legionaries and auxiliaries.

Super-large and extra-large forts from 3–6 hectares:

- Super large forts of 4–6 hectares (SLF) – unusually large forts for brigaded auxiliary forces of several units.
- Extra-large forts from 3–4 hectares (ELF) – the largest 'normal' fort size, which could hold an *Ala Milliaria* (AM), the largest cavalry unit of auxiliaries, some 800 men and more horses strong, or two other normal-size cohorts or other combinations.

Large forts from 2–3 hectares:

- Very large forts from 2.5–3 hectares (VLF) – could hold a *Cohors Milliaria Equitata* (CME), the largest 'mixed' unit of 256 cavalry and 800 infantry, or two other normal cohorts or other combinations.
- Large forts of 2–2.5 hectares (LFT) – large enough to hold an *Ala Quingenaria* (AQ) of 512 cavalrymen and more horses, or a *Cohors Quingeneria Equitata* (CQE) of 480 infantry and 128 cavalry, or other combinations.

Forts from 0.8–2 hectares:

- Standard forts of 1.6–2 hectares (FRT) – of a size to hold the standard auxiliary units in the Roman Army of the first and second centuries, the *Cohors Quingenaria Peditata* (CQP), with 480 infantry, or the *Cohors*

Quingenaria Equitata (CQE), with 480 infantry supplemented by 120 cavalry.

- Small standard forts from 1.2–1.6 hectares (FOR) – which could at a pinch also hold the *Cohors Quingenaria Peditata* (CQP) but could not accommodate the additional horsemen of the larger mixed cohort (CQE).
- Small fort from 0.8–1.2 hectares (SFT) – the size of which meant probably that it could only accommodate a detachment of a normal auxiliary unit; possibly four out of the six centuries of a CQP or CQE, or one of the barbarian irregular *Numeri* units raised under Hadrian.

Fortlets below 0.8 hectares:

- Large fortlets from 0.4–0.8 hectares (lft) – a small detachment of possibly two to four centuries or a *Numerus*.
- Small fortlets of 0.1–0.4 hectares (sft) – possibly two centuries or other detachments.
- Micro fortlets under 0.1 hectares (mic) – garrisoned by part of a century or other detail.
- Turret or signal stations (tur) – of small size but part of the defence system.

Naval and Supply Bases of various sizes:

- We know the Roman Navy operated in support of the Army, and various bases have been proposed (Mason, 2003, pp.77–104). Campaigns require supply, and military installations seem to have been used as supply bases – Corbridge being an example for most of its life, and also Carlisle during the Antonine push to the north.

I have allocated a symbol to each fort category that grades them based on size and colour, the aim being to provide as many visual prompts as possible to the relative importance and role of the installation (as set out in Figure 7.9). To support this approach, it is very helpful that the size of a Roman fort or military installation is one of the pieces of knowledge that we have about nearly all identified forts. This is because over the last seventy years, most forts have been discovered and their overall dimensions have at least been surveyed from the air and now by satellite and LiDAR (Light Detection and Ranging). Often, however, we have very little information except the dimensions of the fort, together with the number of ditches surrounding it and whether it had an annex.

Another method is to identify – through survey, geophysics, cropmarks or excavation – the layout of a Roman fort with its HQ, commander's house and granaries in the central section, and barrack blocks, stables and workshops behind and in front. The designs are well established. We know from the Vindolanda

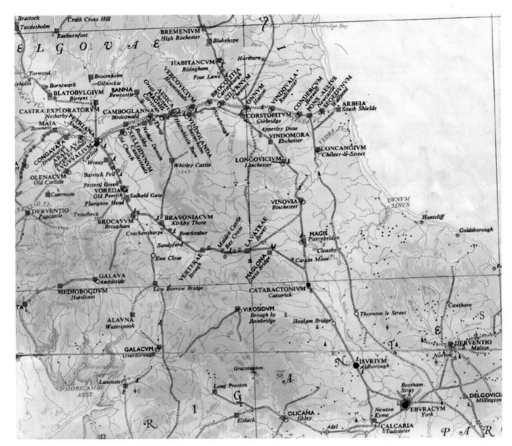

Fig. 7.3. The classic Ordnance Survey map of Roman Britain in its older more detailed format (3rd edition, 1956) showed all Roman forts of whatever date as red squares. It did, however, distinguish between legionary fortresses and fortlets.

strength returns and military papyri from Egypt that – like modern armies – Roman Army units posted men away for other duties and training and sent large detachments to garrison other posts or on campaign. Notwithstanding this, it is clear from the excavated evidence that permanent Roman forts were built to a standardized format for different units: the HQ with its shrine to the unit's standards, the secure cellar for pay and savings, and rooms for clerks and records, as well as the splendid house for the commander and his family. The key here is the number and design of the barracks, which are clearly related to the units in the garrison. Figure 9.20 illustrates a standard method for denoting the layout of Roman forts to enable comparison and typologies to be constructed.

Our ability to identify the purposes of buildings within forts has developed considerably in recent years, notably the discovery that cavalry horses were kept in the same barracks as their riders, and the recognition of two-storey barrack blocks. We are therefore better able to confidently identify garrisons at a few forts and

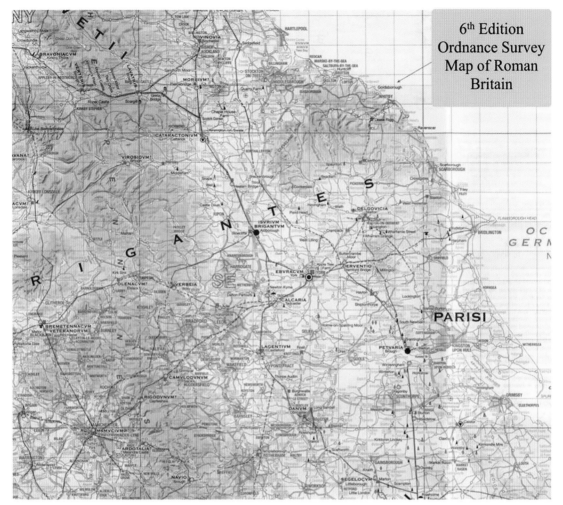

Fig. 7.4. The later Ordnance Survey map (6th edition, 2016) overprints a modern map and still uses the red square (virtually invisible against the background) for the 'generic fort' of any size, garrison and period.

to make informed judgements at many more. We have excellent plans for a few fully excavated forts (e.g., Wallsend/*Segedunum*); reasonable ones for some (e.g., Chesters and Birdoswald); partial plans for many (e.g., Brough-by-Bainbridge); and just outlines of others from photographs and landscape surveys (e.g., Dalswinton and Whitley Castle *Epiacum* near Alston). This information, combined with inscriptions and the knowledge that the basic plans were similar, enables us to estimate the size, type and strength of the unit or units of a combined garrison (Daniels, 2016; Hanson *et. al.*, 2019; Went & Ainsworth, 2009).

We are dealing here with the Roman Army of the first and second centuries, an organization that was capable of building a fort in the Arabian Desert to exactly the same plan as one on the Highland Line in Scotland. This was one of the most standardized organizations that has ever existed, certainly in the pre-industrial age.

Although we do not, of course, possess such a document, the remarkable uniformity of fort and fortress plans across geography and eras demonstrates that a standard building plan for different units existed in Rome. This was presumably held in the HQ of each legion for its architects and engineers to use. What we need to do, therefore, is to apply logic – as far as the evidence will bear – to the evidence we have.

As a result of the desire of unit commanders and emperors to leave records of their achievements in building fortresses, roads and walls, as well as repairing headquarters, baths and granaries, we have excellent epigraphic records which allow us – often with certainty, and sometimes with some margin of doubt – to identify the garrison of a particular fort in a period. There is certainty as to the placing of most legions across the empire during the whole of our period (Bishop, 2012, pp.129–30), although the thirty years after the invasion of Britain in AD 43 presents major challenges owing to the practice of splitting legions into battle groups and task forces. The location of auxiliary units is less certain, but there is reasonable certainty about the garrison of Hadrian's Wall for much of its life, some

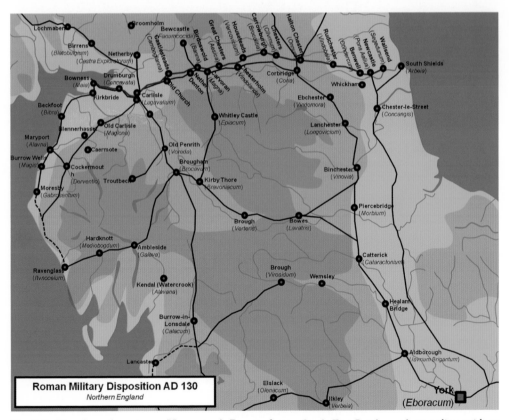

Fig. 7.5. Map from the entry on Housesteads Roman fort in *CastlesFortsBattles.co.uk*, an online guide to castles, forts and battles sites 'that shaped Britain', aimed at the historically interested tourist. Although immense care has been taken to plot forts precisely across Northern England, there is no differentiation between any of the forts by size or garrison where known.

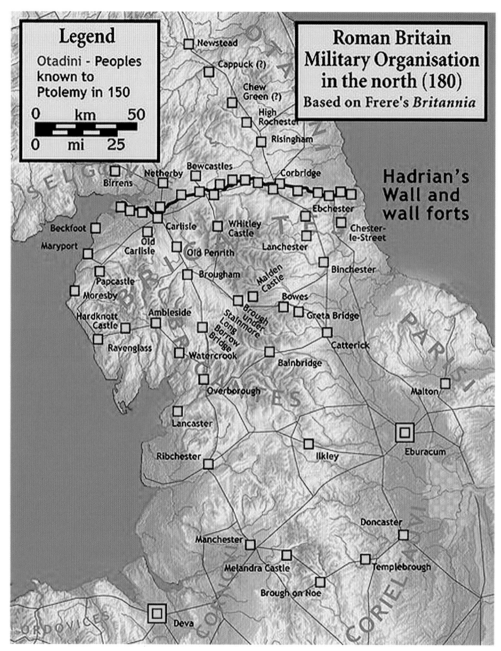

Fig. 7.6. Another example of the undifferentiated fort square marker based on Sheppard Frere's *Britannia*.

understanding for the two decades of the Antonine Wall and patchy coverage for garrisons across *Britannia* for the second, third and the end of the fourth century from the *Notitia Dignitatum*. Alas, our knowledge of the first-century conquest era garrisons is much less secure, given the movement of units between timber and turf forts with an initial life expectancy of less than thirty years.

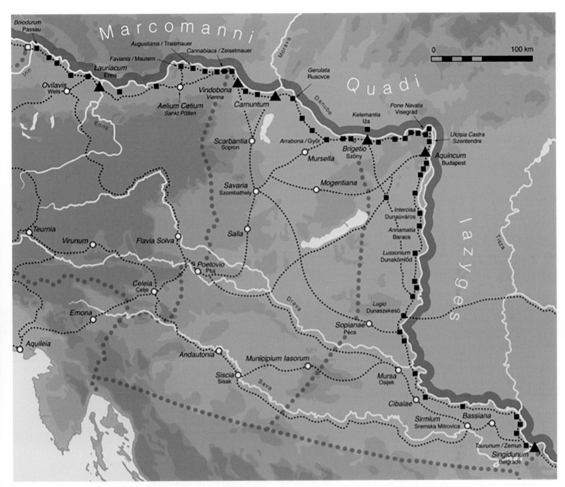

Fig. 7.7. Map from 'The Value of Studying Roman Frontiers' (*Theoretical Roman Archaeology Journal* 1(1), 1). Although legionary fortresses are as usual distinguished (in this case by larger triangles), all other forts of whatever period are undifferentiated.

The legions

The place to start is with the permanent legionary fortresses which are easy to identify: their occupation dates are generally known from their inscriptions and tile stamps. During the Augustan period, the Roman legion standardized on ten cohorts, each composed of six centuries of eighty men each, together with legionary cavalry of four *turma* totalling 120 cavalrymen, forming a total theoretical complement of around 5,000 men. This meant that each first- and second-century legion required a massive 16 hectares-plus fortress as its permanent base. Each fortress was surrounded by both official and semi-official settlements supplying the legion's necessities. The economic and social shock caused by the establishment of multiple legionary fortresses along the frontiers of the West and the impact on the tribal peoples and the environmental landscape is hard to overestimate.

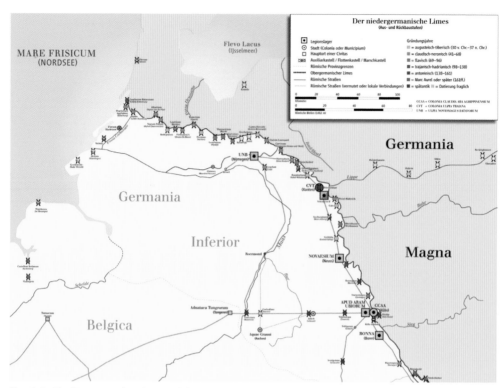

Fig. 7.8. In Germany, the phases of fort-building tend to be shown clearly by colour coding, although the size is not differentiated except at the fortress level. The Lower German *Limes* by Ziegelbrenner – Eigenes Werk (own work), https://commons.wikimedia.org/w/index.php?curid=6350328.

While the home bases of the British garrison legions can be worked out from inscriptions and archaeological excavations, the wider situation is not that simple: when on campaign, each legion was the heart of a larger task force. These task forces would, when on campaign, leave a skeleton HQ, reinforcement and training cadre at their permanent base and occupy forward campaign bases. Also, for tactical reasons, a legion would often be broken up into its constituent cohorts (480 men), double cohorts (960 men) or larger detachments known as vexillations. These troops were brigaded with auxiliaries in task forces and deployed into what are sometimes termed vexillation fortresses but are better called campaign bases, set up to oversee the campaigns in a particular region or tribal area.

Garrisons of the forts: the auxiliaries

In the first century, auxiliary units were of three types, in descending order of pay and prestige, but not necessarily of military utility:

- *Alae* – cavalry wings used for scouting and long-range patrolling. In a pitched battle, they would protect the wings of the legionary and auxiliary infantry and aim to defeat any opposing cavalry, performing the classic role of main battle cavalry, comparable to Napoleonic cavalry regiments.

- *Cohortes Equitatae* – mixed infantry and cavalry cohorts. The cavalry could have been used as mounted infantry, as well as genuine cavalry, to protect their own infantry elements in small actions, and brigaded as line cavalry in pitched battles, as they were at Mons Graupius. A good comparison is with Imperial Yeomanry in the Boer War. The *Cohortes Equitatae* were ideal units for holding newly conquered tribal areas, combining the reach of cavalry with the punch of the infantry for low-intensity 'policing operations' as well as 'search and destroy' punitive missions.
- *Cohortes Peditatae* – infantry cohorts. These were generally less heavily equipped than the legionary infantry and cheaper to maintain, being non-citizens and recruited from recently conquered people such as the Tungrians stationed at Vindolanda in the AD 90s. The so-called 'warlike races' recruited by the British Indian Army in the Punjab Frontier Force in the late nineteenth century are a good analogy.

By the later first century, and certainly by the reign of Vespasian, the auxiliary units came in two sizes:

- *Quingenaria* ('the five hundred');
- *Milliaria* ('the thousand', employed much more rarely) to pack a heavier punch.

As we know from strength returns on the Vindolanda tablets – as with all armies down the ages – the actual front-line fighting strength of Roman units on the battlefield varied greatly due to detachments, training details, sickness and

The Categories of Fortresses and Forts

➤ Fortresses and Forts are divided into five categories:
  ➤ The first is legionary fortresses (>12 ha in size)
  ➤ The second are 'vexillation fortresses' better termed Campaign Bases (6 – 12 ha)
  ➤ The third are super and extra large forts (3– 6 ha)
  ➤ The fourth large and very large forts (2 – 3 ha)
  ➤ The fifth is small and standard size forts (0.8 – 2 ha)
➤ There are then a group of small installations split into
  ➤ Large fortlets (0.4 – 0.8 ha)
  ➤ Small fortlets (0.1 – 0.4 ha)
  ➤ Turrets and signal stations
➤ Finally there naval and supply bases
➤ Forts that are suspected or inferred are shown by ???

	Size From	Size To	Code
Legionary Fortress	16.00	more	LEG
Small Legionary Fortress	12.00	15.99	LG
Vexillation Fortress	8.00	11.99	VEX
Small Vexillation Fortress	6.00	7.99	VX
Super Large Fort	4.00	5.99	SLF
Extra Large Fort	3.00	3.99	ELF
Very Large Fort	2.50	2.99	VLF
Large Fort	2.00	2.49	LFT
Standard Fort	1.60	1.99	FRT
Small Standard Fort	1.20	1.59	FOR
Small Fort	0.80	1.19	SFT
Large Fortlet	0.40	0.79	lft
Small Fortlet	0.10	0.39	sflt
Micro Fortlet	less	0.09	mic
Turret or Signal Station			tur
Naval Base			NAV
Fort of Unidentified Size			???

Forts Key

- Legionary Fortress
- Small Legionary Fortress 12 - 16h
- "Vexillation" Fortress 8 - 12h
- Small "Vexillation" Fortress 6 - 8h
- Super Large Fort 4 - 6h
- Extra Large Fort 3 - 4h
- Very Large Fort 2.5 – 3h
- Large Fort 2.0 - 2.5h
- Standard Fort 1.6 – 2.0h
- Small Standard Fort 1.2 – 1.6h
- Small Fort 0.8 - 1.2h
- Large Fortlet 0.4 - 0.8h
- Small Fortlet 0.1 – 0.4h
- Micro, Turret or Signal Station >0.1
- Naval Base
- Fort of Unidentified Size

Fig. 7.9. The breakdown of forts and fortresses by categories, showing the symbols used for each.

The Categories Roman Army Units of the 1st and 2nd Century AD

➢ The different categories of units are colour coded:
  ➢ Legions and parts of legions (*legiones*) = purple
  ➢ Cavalry units (*alae*) = blue
  ➢ Infantry units (*cohortes*) = red
  ➢ Mixed infantry and cavalry units (*cohortes equitatae*) = orange
  ➢ Irregular units (*numeri*) = green
➢ They are size co-ordinated
  ➢ Full legions at c5,000 men are the largest symbols with three squares surround
  ➢ Legionary cohort is a single purple box with one surrounding square
  ➢ The large notionally a thousand (*milliaria*) strong units whether alae or cohorts are larger than the smaller five hundred (*quingeneria*) units
  ➢ In addition there are smaller symbols to show part of an auxiliary unit
  ➢ 'X' is shown when it is not known whether it is Equitata or Peditata
  ➢ Finally there are symbols for naval and supply bases

Units Key
- LEG (10 cohh + eq leg = 5,250)
- Vexillatio (c2,000 – 3000)
- Leg Coh I (5 cent x 160 = 800)
- Leg Coh II – X (6 cent x 80 = 480)
- Ala Milliaria (24 turm x 32 = 768)
- Coh Milliaria Equitata (10 cent x 80 = 800 + 8 tur x 32 = 1056)
- Coh Milliaria Peditata (10 cent x 80 = 800)
- Coh Milliaria ??? (10 cent x 80 = 800/ + 8 turm x 32 = 1056?)
- Ala Quingeneria (16 turm x 32 = 512)
- Coh Quingeneria Equitata (6 cent x 80 + 4 turm x 32 = 608)
- Coh Quingeneria Peditata (6 cent x 80 = 480)
- Coh Quin ??? (6 cent x 80 = 480/ + 4 turm x 32 = 608?)
- Numerus (2 cent x 80 = 160)
- Exploratores
- pars Ala Quin
- pars Coh Quin Ped
- pars Coh Quin Eq
- Supply Base
- Port or Naval Base

Fig. 7.10. The different categories of Roman Army unit in the first and second centuries.

casualties. It would have been logistically and practically impossible to keep all units up to book strength on campaign. However, the nominal manpower in each type of unit in the first century is shown in Figure 7.11.

As with the fort sizes, I have developed symbols for each type of unit. Therefore, an *Ala Quingenaria* is AQ and a *Cohors Milliaria Equitata* is CME: standard identification codes for each kind of unit are shown in Figure 7.10 and standard abbreviations in Figure 7.12.

Auxiliary Units: Theoretical Manpower and Forts Size

Auxiliary Unit	Number of Centuriae (80 men)	Number of Turmae (32 men)	Number of Barracks	Manpower	Estimated Size Range	Britannia Type Site	Wales Type Site
Ala Milleria		24	24	768	>3.2ha *multiple*	Stanwix 3.77ha	
Ala Quingenaria		16	16	512	2.3 – 2.4ha *2.3 – 2.7ha*	Chesters 2.32ha	
Cohors Mil Equitata	10	8	18	1056	2.7 – 3.2ha *2.7 – 3.2ha*		
Cohors Mil Peditata	10		10	800	1.8 – 2.27ha *1.8 – 2.3ha*	Housesteads 2.02ha	
Coh Quin Equitata	6	4	10	608	1.7 - 1.8ha *1.6 – 1.8ha*	Wallsend 1.66ha	
Coh Quin Peditata	6		6	480	1.3 - 1.57ha *1.3 – 1.6ha*	Gelligaer II 1.4ha	Gelligaer II 1.4ha

Fig. 7.11. Theoretical manpower of Roman Army auxiliary units in the first and second centuries. As the Vindolanda, Egyptian and Dura Europos surviving documents show, the actual strength numbers would vary according to other postings and local circumstances.

Standard Classifications and Abbreviations

Fort Size	
Legionary Fortress	LEG
Small Legionary Fortress	LG
Campaign Base (Vexillation)	VEX
Small Campaign Base (Smal Vex)	VX
Super Large Fort	SLF
Extra Large Fort	ELF
Very Large Fort	VLF
Large Fort	LFT
Standard Fort	FRT
Small Standard Fort	FOR
Small Fort	SFT
Large Fortlet	lft
Small Fortlet	sft
Micro Fortlet	mic
Turret/Signal Station	tur
Unknown Size or ?	???
Naval Base	NAV

Type of Unit	
Legio	LEG
Cohors Legionis	coh
Ala Quingenria	AQ
Ala Milliaria	AM
Cohors Quingenria Equitata	CQE
Cohors Milliaria Equitata	CME
Cohors Quingenaria Peditata	CQP
Cohora Milliariea Peditata	CMP
Numerus	Num

Period		
41-54	Claudian	CLA
54-68	Nronian	NER
69-81	Early Flavian	EFL
81-96	Leter Flavian	LFL
97-106	Early Trajanic	ETR
107-117	Later Trajanic	LTR
117-138	Hadriianic	HAD
138-161	Antonine	ANT
161-180	Marcus Aurelius	MAU
180-192	Commodus	COM
193-211	Severan	SEV

Fig. 7.12. Summary of the abbreviations used for fort sizes, types of unit and each period in the databases and maps that follow.

Defining the unit symbols to use on the maps

In order to show these units on the maps, we need standardized unit symbols. Fortunately, this is a well-developed area of military cartography and we can use established standards, with a few adaptions (Figure 7.10). I have retained the traditional legion symbol of a filled square, with one or more surrounding squares. This enables the full legion to be indicated by surrounding their square, and legionary cohorts operating independently to be shown with one or two squares. The units have also been colour-coded to ensure immediate recognition of the type of unit:

- legions as purple;
- auxiliary cavalry as blue;
- auxiliary infantry as red;
- irregulars as green.

There were also mixed auxiliary units of infantry and cavalry: it is generally agreed that either four (for *quingenaria* units) or eight (for *milliaria* units) *turmae* of cavalry were added to the standard infantry cohorts to produce these hybrid units. It is thought that on campaign, the cavalry from several mixed units were brigaded together to form the equivalent of another cavalry *ala*. Whether this was the case or not, these units – when garrisoned in forts – provided magnificently flexible units for the Roman Army in Britain for holding down newly conquered regions.

The symbols used for each unit are as follows:

- infantry are shown as solid squares;
- cavalry, as is conventional, as diagonally bisected;
- mixed infantry and cavalry units as 'crossed';
- naval bases with an anchor;
- supply bases with an 'S'.

Occupation periods of forts

The final stage of analysis is to separate forts and military installations by time period and to ensure that these do not overlap, but this is of course easier said than done. The tendency of Roman soldiers to mislay coins is enormously helpful here, and there has been brilliant work done using pottery and other artefacts to allow dating within quite precise time periods, although there is also judgement involved and the context (and publication) of finds is critical.

The time periods that are generally recognized in archaeological excavations are aligned with emperors of the first and second centuries. These are also summarized in Figure 7.12.

The creation of new cartographical standards

In summary, I have created the following new tools to use in cartographic analysis of Roman military strategy:

- six high-level **fort groups** by size, divided into **fifteen types** from legionary fortress down to turret, with **standard codes** for each fort group, e.g., FOR represents the standard fort size with a standard cohort;
- **cartographical symbols** for each standard unit type of the first- and second-century Roman Army, with standard codes allocated to each unit type, e.g., CQE for *Cohors Quingenaria Equitata*, AM *for Ala Milliaria*.
- **time periods** for fort occupation, with standard codes for time periods, generally aligned to imperial reigns.

Standard classification and abbreviations

Standardizing these classifications and abbreviations enables quick comparisons to be made between campaigns, regions and timeframes. A standardized approach also enables the faster and more-robust construction of hypotheses. This provides a framework for describing the activities and deployment of the Roman Army. If we can relate – even at an approximate level – the type, or at least the relative strength, of unit which occupied the forts at each period of their occupation, then we can start to develop new and deeper insights into the strategy of the Roman Army in the first and second centuries.

The next step is the creation of analytical techniques to exploit the data and the creation of a graphical toolbox to aid understanding.

Chapter 8

The New Data-led Analytical Method (D-LAM)

Creating the analytical techniques to exploit the data

The application of database management to Roman military studies

I n order to populate the maps, we need consistent and easy-to-use access information on the fortresses, forts and other installations in the areas under study.

This requires the creation of a standardized database of the roads, forts, fortresses and fortlets constructed and occupied in Wales, Scotland and Northern England during the first and second centuries AD. The aim of the database is to hold in a standard format the key information we need to know about that installation to understand its role in the wider picture. This is set out in Figure 8.1.

I have therefore created a **Forts Database** with five sets of **factual** fields for each fort:

- **Factual category 1: basic data**
  - **name**;
  - **Roman name**, if known;
  - **phase** − most forts were reconstructed several times, and this is to align with the phase of each fort as identified by the excavators or those surveying it. Deciding exactly what constitutes a 'reconstruction' involves a large degree of subjectivity based on how much of the fort has actually been excavated, and the judgements of the excavators;
  - **size** in hectares: even this apparently obvious measurement has its challenges, including whether the site is measured from inside or outside the ramparts. Ideally measured from outside corner of the ramparts. This information is generally available from detailed excavations, survey and/or aerial photography.
- **Factual category 2: unit deployed**
  - **type of unit** using the three-letter code (see Fig 7.12). Sometimes, as with a legionary fortress or where there is a surviving and dateable inscription, this is certain. Where this is uncertain, but a type of unit can be inferred, this is indicated by a '?';
  - **name of the unit** or units, when known;

An Example of the Forts and Fortresses Database in Action:

Frontinus in Wales: Conquest Phase AD75-76

Campaign	System	Purpose	Description	Id	Name	Phase	Roman Name	Size Ha	Size Code	Strength Factor	First Unit	Second Unit	Approx Manpower	Unit if Known	Build Code	Start Date	End Date	Build Material	Rampart	Buildings	Ditches	Gates	Annex	Controls	Distance IM	Km	RM Km
FRONTINUS' INVASION OF WALES — Baseline																											
FRO	N/S	BASE	CONTROL	1.0	Chester	1		24.40	LEG	12.0	LEG		5,000	II Adiutrix	Fro	74									0.0	0.0	0.0
FRO	N/S	BASE	CONTROL	2.0	Whitchurch	2		???	FOR	1.0	???		500		Fro	74?									22.4	21.1	34.0
FRO	N/S	BASE	CONTROL	3.0	Wroxeter	2		16.00	LEG	12.0	LEG		5,000	XX Valeria Victr	???	66	7								25.7	24.2	39.0
FRO	N/S	BASE	CONTROL	4.0	Buckton	1		2.36	LFT	2.0	AQ?		500		Fro?	[80]	11									32.2	30.4	49.0
FRO	N/S	BORD	CONTROL	5.0	Buckbush Farm	1		<3.2	ELF	3.0	CME?		1,000													31.6	29.8	48.0
FRO	N/S	BASE	CONTROL	5.0	Monastow	1		1.4??	FOR	1.0	CQP?		500													23.0	21.7	35.0
FRO	N/S	BASE	CONTROL	6.0	Usk	2		???	ELF	3.0	COH??		1,000											Usk Valley	11.2	10.6	17.1
FRO	N/S	BASE	CONTROL	7.0	Carleon	1		20.50	LEG	12.0	LEG		5,000	II Augusta	Fro	74									8.6	8.1	13.0
Total for Baseline										**4.0**			**1,500**												154.6	146.0	235.0
Frontinus' Invasion of Wales – Lines of Penetration																											
FRO	CLY	LOP	CONQUER	1.0	Chester	1		24.40	LEG	12.0	LEG		5,000	II Adiutrix	Fro	74									0.0	0.0	0.0
FRO	CLY	LOP	CONQUER	3.0	Llyn Park	2		6.00	VX	6.0	COH??	AQ???	1,000		Fro	74									26.3	24.9	40.0
FRO	CLY	LOP	CONQUER	4.0	Llanfor	1		3.86	ELF	3.0	AQ	LEG COH +	1,000		Fro	74		Timber	Earth			Two Straight	Supply Base?			30.9	29.2	47.0
																									57.2	54.1	87.0
FRO	SEV	LOP	CONQUER	1.0	Wroxeter	2		16.00	LEG	12.0	LEG		5,000	XX Valeria Victri	Tre	66	7								0.0	0.0	0.0
FRO	SEV	LOP	CONQUER	2.0	Forden Gaer	1		3.25	ELF	3.0	COH or CQ?	AQ or CQ?	1,000		Fro	74		Timber	Earth		Three Straight		None	Seven Valle	27.6	26.1	42.0
FRO	SEV	LOP	CONQUER	3.0	Caersws	1		3.90	ELF	3.0	COH or CQ?	AQ or CQ?	1,000		Fro	74		Timber	Earth		Three Straight		One	Seven Valle	15.8	14.9	24.0
																									100.7	95.1	66.0
FRO	USK	LOP	CONQUER	1.0	Caerleon	1		17.80	LEG	12.0	LEG		5,000	II August	Fro	74								Usk Valle	0.0	0.0	0.0
FRO	USK	LOP	CONQUER	2.0	Usk	2		???	ELF	3.0	COH??	AQ???	1,000		Tre	65-70	90-11							Usk Valle	8.6	8.1	13.0
FRO	USK	LOP	CONQUER	3.0	Abergavenny	2		1.32	FOR	1.0	CQP?		500		Fro	74	14				Two Straight		One	Usk Valle	11.8	11.2	18.0
FRO	USK	LOP	CONQUER	4.0	Brecon Gaer	1		3.14	ELF	3.0	AQ	CQ?	1,000		ala Hispanorum Vettonum cR	Fro	74		Turf/Clay		Three		None	Usk Valle	24.3	23.0	37.0
FRO	USK	LOP	CONQUER	5.0	Llandovery	1		3.00	ELF	3.0	COH or CQ?	AQ or CQ?	1,000		Fro	74		Timber	Earth		Surrounding		leads of Usk and Tow	19.7	18.6	30.0
FRO	USK	LOP	CONQUER	6.0	Llandeilo	1		3.84	ELF	3.0	COH or CQ?	AQ or CQ?	1,000		Fro	74		Timber	Earth		Three Two	Parrot?			13.2	12.4	20.0
																									69.1	65.2	118.0
FRO	BRI	LOP	CONQUER	1.0	Nidum	1	Nidum	3.30	ELF	3.0	COH or CQ?	AQ or CQ?	1,000		Fro	75	83	Timber	Earth								
FRO	BRI	LOP	CONQUER	2.0	Neath				Nav																			
Total for Lines of Penetration									**67.0**				**24,500**												227.0	214.4	271.0
TOTAL FOR FRONTINUS' INVASION OF WALES									**71.0**				**26,000**												381.6	360.4	506.0

Judgemental		Factual Category 1:		Judg		Factual Category 2:		Fact. Cat. 3:		Factual Category 4:		Fact.
Category A:		Basic Data		Cat B:		Unit Deployed		Dating		Basic Data		Cat. 5
Fort Code Class.				SF.								

Judge		Fact.
Cat C:		Cat. 5
Control		Distance

Fig. 8.1. Factual and judgemental categories included in the fields of the Roman forts database (explained above).

- sometimes a **second unit** is present or has been inferred;
- approximate **manpower** assuming full strength (which is very much the upper limit of what was possible).
- **Factual category 3: dating of the fort or installation**
  - **build code** relating to a particular emperor or governor's campaign;
  - projected **start date** for the fort build;
  - projected **end date** for when that phase of the fort went out of commission or was either abandoned or rebuilt.
- **Factual category 4: physical characteristics**
  - number of **ditches**;
  - **gateway** design – some forts have very distinctively different designs, e.g., the Strathcathro, named after the first site where this distinctively curved bank approach was adopted;
  - building **materials** – from the start, for instance timber or stone for the buildings and turf or stone for the ramparts;
  - whether there was any **annex** and, if so, how many.
- **Factual category 5: distance**
  - **distance between forts** along a known Roman road (or an inferred road when one is not known, following a reasonable communication route). This measures the spacing both in distance (by kilometres, Roman miles and Imperial miles) and in time: roughly one day's march for infantry was 25km.

The Relationship of Fort Size and the Strength Factor (SF)

➤ The base for the Strength Factor (SF) is the Small Standard Fort (Code FOR), which has a size of between 1.2ha and 1.6ha

➤ This has a SF of 1.0

  ➤ This reflects a 'basic' garrison of a single cohort *cohors quingeneria peditata* (CQP) 8

    ➤ 6 centuriae x 80 men = 480 men

➤ At the other extreme the Legionary Fortress has a SF of 12.0

  ➤ This reflects the 9 'normal' sized cohorts each of 480 men plus the double strength First Cohort plus legionary cavalry of 4 x *turmae*

➤ The other SFs are judgemental between these values

  ➤ So a Campaign Base of 6 ha has a value of 6 SFs and Super Large Fort of 5 ha has a value of 4 SFs

	Size From	Size To	Code	Strength Factor	Equivalent to:
Legionary Fortress	16.00	more	LEG	12.0	Coh I (x2) + Coh II-X + Eq Leg
Small Legionary Fortress	12.00	15.99	LG	10.0	large task force
Vexillation Fortress	8.00	11.99	VEX	8.0	x6 or x8 Coh Leg
Small Vexillation Fortress	6.00	7.99	VX	6.0	task force
Super Large Fort	4.00	5.99	SLF	4.0	task force
Extra Large Fort	3.00	3.99	ELF	3.0	Ala Mill or 2x Coh
Very Large Fort	2.50	2.99	VLF	2.5	Coh Mill Eq
Large Fort	2.00	2.49	LFT	2.0	Ala Quin or Coh Mill Ped
Standard Fort	1.60	1.99	FRT	1.5	Coh Quin Ped or Coh Quin Eq
Small Standard Fort	1.20	1.59	FOR	1.0	Coh Quin Ped
Small Fort	0.80	1.19	SFT	0.6	x4 cent or x2 cent + x2 turm
Large Fortlet	0.40	0.79	lft	0.3	x2 cent or num
Small Fortlet	0.10	0.39	sft	0.1	x1 cent
Micro Fortlet	less	0.09	mic	0.0	x1 conturb
Turret or Signal Station			tur		
Naval Base			NAV	8.0	
Fort of Unidentified Size			???		

Fig. 8.2. Summary table showing the Strength Factors.

I have also included in the database three sets of **judgemental** fields which cover the classification of the fort, enabling it to be sorted in the database, and the Strength Factor.

- **Judgemental category A: fort code classification**
- there are four codes allocated to each fort in the database which enable the forts to be sorted by combinations of the codes:
  - first, a code for the **campaign**, e.g., SCA denoting Scapula's campaigns as governor in Britain from AD 47–52;
  - secondly, a code denoting the **system** the forts belong to, e.g., WYE denoting forts built along the River Wye Valley in Gallus' governorship;
  - thirdly, the **purpose** of the forts in terms of the role they principally played, e.g., WAL as part of Hadrian's or the Antonine Wall or LOP for Line of Penetration;
  - fourthly, a **descriptor** of how this group of forts is thought to have been used, e.g. CONTROL or CONQUER.
- **Judgemental category B: Strength Factor classification**
  - sometimes a legionary or auxiliary unit can be matched to a given fortress or fort, but this is not possible for most instances in most periods. Therefore, I have devised the **Strength Factor**, which is a proxy for the number and force of the units deployed in each fortress, fort or fortlet. Its purpose is to enable broad comparisons to be made between forces deployed in a system of forts, or in a campaign, without having exact data on which units and forces these were.
- **Judgemental category C: control**
  - often a fort is positioned to dominate a location such as a river valley or a tribal area; and this is what is reflected here. In an upland area like Wales or Northern England, the forts and roads were built to dominate a valley or dale.

Each of these categories is shown overlaid onto an example of an actual database in Figure 8.1.

Purpose of the fort

The descriptor for the **purpose** of the fort is an important tool for classification, and I have developed some standard definitions to support the use of this field. I envisage that these classifications can be developed to suit different areas under study and as understanding of the Roman Army's approach to campaigning develops.
These are generally one of the following:

- **BASE** = Baseline for the campaign: this is the starting point, such as Gallus' road along the Marches from Chester, through Wroxeter to Caerleon; or the Trajanic-era Stanegate line from Carlisle to Corbridge, used by Agricola as his campaign baseline;
- **LOP** = Line of Penetration: this is the presumed invasion line used in the campaign, such as the Upper Severn Valley for Frontinus in Wales in AD 73, or the line of Dere Street for Agricola in 79;
- **LOC** = Line of Control: this is a fort and road line with the presumed role of dominating a key axis, such as the Usk River line after Frontinus' campaigns;
- **XRT** = Cross-Route: this usually runs between Lines of Penetration and Control and is part of a strategy to control an area with a network of roads and forts, such as the Flavian network across Northern England and Lowland Scotland which consists of cross-routes between the Western and Eastern north–south routes;
- **ZON** = Zonal Control: forts with the presumed purpose of dominating an area, such as the forts within Silurian territory also set up by Frontinus.

Where the evidence for a fort is not strong, this is indicated by a database entry in italics and green lettering. Where a fort or fortress has already appeared in a previous fort system – as is common when roads meet at a fort or fortress – the duplicate entry is denoted by italics and red lettering.

Strength Factors (SFs)

Strength Factors are directly linked to the size of the fort as a proxy for strength: the relationship is set out in Figure 8.2. For each of the seventeen types of installation, a Strength Factor (SF) has been determined.

There is no claim here that matching Strength Factors to types of units is an exact science. It is, however, a useful way of broadly estimating the fighting force that could be accommodated in the forts built in any given campaign. It is therefore a reasonable and useful proxy for calculating the size and nature of a force deployed in a particular place and period.

The base unit is the small standard fort (FOR) of 1.2–1.6 hectares, typically accommodating a *Cohors Quingenaria Peditata* (CQP), notionally of 480 infantry in six centuries, which has a Strength Factor (SF) of **one**. SFs proportionate to size have then been allocated to each group of forts.

The largest is the legionary fortress (**LEG** or **LG**, depending on size) of over 16 hectares, with nine cohorts each of 480 men amounting to fifty-four centuries, plus a first cohort with five double centuries consisting of 800 men and four *turmae* amounting to 128 legionary cavalry, amounting to a notional manpower of *c.*5,000. Its SF is **twelve**.

A campaign base or vexillation fortress (**VEX** or **VX**, depending on size) of 8–12 hectares has a SF of **eight**. This reflects its capacity for four legionary cohorts, a cavalry *ala* and an auxiliary infantry cohort.

A super large fort (**SLF**) is 4–6 hectares in size and has a SF of **four**, It could accommodate a mixed task force of units, such as a *Cohors Milliaria Peditata* (CMP) and a *Cohors Quingenaria Equitata* (CQE).

An extra large fort (**ELF**) of 3–4 hectares has a SF of **three**, reflecting its capacity for one of the elite *Ala Milliaria*, a cavalry unit of a thousand (of which there were only seven in the whole empire) or two auxiliary cohorts.

A large fort (**LFT**) of 2–2.5 hectares has a SF of **two**: such a fort could accommodate an *Ala Quingenaria* (AQ) or a *Cohors Quingenaria Equitata*.

A standard fort (**FRT**) is 1.6–2 hectares and has a SF of **1.5**: it could accommodate a *Cohors Peditata Quingenaria* (CPQ) or a *Cohors Quingenaria Equitata*.

A small standard fort (**FOR**), which is 1.2–1.6 hectares in size, has a SF of **one**: such a fort could accommodate a single *Cohors Peditata Quingenaria*.

A small fortlet (**sft**), which is 0.1–0.4 hectares in size, has a SF of **0.1**: such a fortlet could accommodate a single *centuria*.

Where the entry for a category is doubtful or speculative, this is indicated by an entry in italics followed by '?'.

Mapping as a tool for analysis?

If we can map the size of fort – and the relative strength of the unit or units deployed there – at each period of their occupation, then we can gain new insights into the strategy of the Roman Army in the first and second centuries.

It is essential to place the Roman remains in the context of the period. Placing the known forts, roads and naval bases on the map and in the context of the topography and contemporary vegetation, rivers and coastline of the British Isles – and of what is known of the British tribes – is a great aid to understanding Roman strategic thinking.

This is easy to state but hard to do, since knowledge of land-use in pre-Roman and Roman times is fast evolving, given improving environmental analysis. Furthermore, river courses have moved or been canalized over two millennia, marshes and fens have been drained and sea levels have changed substantially. Our knowledge of the human landscape of late Iron Age Britain is also developing fast, with very different levels of knowledge in different localities and a growing recognition of the sophistication of those societies at or beyond the edge of the Roman world.

By using the database of forts and their associated Strength Factors and plotting the Roman deployment onto the physical landscape and human environment, a picture of the Roman military strategy for the area under analysis starts to emerge.

Chapter 9

A New Graphical and Cartographic Tool-set

Analytical techniques to exploit the forts database

Applying the toolset to the database of Roman military campaigns

W e have now developed a database to hold the data on the Roman forts in an area in the given campaign and time period. We have also devised standard conventions to describe and sort forts by size and to identify wherever possible the units deployed there.

The next stage is to populate it with data. As noted, there is no shortage of information available about areas such as Wales, Scotland and Northern England; likewise, the Lower Rhine frontier and the *limes* of Upper Germany and Raetia have wonderful resources that can be used to populate databases for these areas. Filling in the campaign database has proved relatively quick and easy to do, with syntheses having been produced for an area that pull together excavation reports and research from many sources. The three magisterial reviews of the Roman frontier in Wales exemplify this approach (Nash-Williams, 1954; Jarrett, 1969; and Burnham & Davies, 2010), as does the synthesis of the Gask Ridge and associated works for the north of Scotland in the first century (Woolliscroft & Hoffmann, 2010) and the guide to the Raetian frontier (Matešić & Sommer, 2015) produced for the XXIII *Limes* Congress in 2015.

Having populated the campaign database, the next stage in the process is to analyze this data by displaying it on maps, diagrams and graphs in order to illustrate how the Roman Army approached its campaign.

To do this analysis, I have developed twenty-three analytical tools, some or all of which can be applied to understanding Roman campaigns of the first and second centuries. Some of them are map-based, while others are diagrams, graphs or combinations of these. All of them are built from the core resource, which is the database of forts. These tools are designed to be flexible and are a 'pick-and-mix'. They are not meant to be rigid, and can be modified, expanded or omitted depending on the campaign or battle under scrutiny.

What follows is a short description of what each tool is and suggestions as to when and how it can best be used. The full toolbox is illustrated in Figures 9.1 to

9.23, using examples from the chapters that follow. The five broad categories of tools are:

- context tools;
- overall campaign tools;
- tools to map the campaign;
- tools to analyze the campaign;
- tools for making comparisons.

Context tools

1. Written sources
Depending on the campaign, there can be reasonably extensive written sources, such as we have from Tacitus for Scapula's travails in Wales or for Paulinus tackling Boudicca's revolt. Unfortunately, for most campaigns we have sketchy references or none.

2. Political and provincial context
The political context map describes the state of the province, showing which tribes had been incorporated into the province, which had become *civitates* or were still under military occupation, which independent tribes were Roman allies and which were hostile or resisting. Known Roman urban developments and strategic roads are also shown.

3. Population and settlement context
The population map looks at the type of settlement, as far as is known from archaeological investigation, for instance areas with hillforts or enclosed farmsteads.

4. Land-use and minerals context
This sets out what is known about land-use in terms of arable or pastoral, or mixed cultivation. It also shows what is known about exploitation of mineral resources in Roman times, which appears to have been a high priority with the Roman Army.

5. Tribes and peoples context
This map sets out the tribal areas, as far as these are known, by combining ancient geographers with evidence such as the coin distribution of currency-issuing tribes. Boundaries shown are indicative.

Overall campaign tools

6. Legionary fortress sequence
The core of the Roman Army in our period were the legions. These acted on their own, or legionary cohorts were the central component of task forces, with auxiliaries attached. Tracking the movement of the legions and the sites of their home fortresses gives important insights into the Roman High Command's strategic priorities.

7. Legionary deployments
A graph of legionary bases over time is key to understanding Roman strategic priorities.

Tools to map the campaign

8. Map of the course of the campaign
This is an overview map designed to break a campaign into its component parts – usually year by year.

9. Map of marching camps
During the initial invasion phase, Roman armies built temporary marching camps which can be linked by their size, shape and entrance type.

10. Extract from the database
This is the foundation of the analysis and shows the vital statistics of the known fortresses, forts, fortlets, naval and supply bases which are part of the campaign under analysis. It shows when they were built, their relationship to each other, their purpose, building materials, known buildings, whether they have an annex and so forth.

11. Map of the fort locations with military roads
This takes the forts database and maps the forts showing their size and position, connected by the military road network.

12. Map of unit deployments
This maps the known units by type (LEG, AM, AQ, CQP etc.) onto the forts to unpack how the Romans were thinking about the next stages of the campaign.

13. Map of unit patrol zones
By analyzing which unit is deployed where in the campaign, it is possible to start drawing conclusions in terms of the objectives of the individual units that were deployed.

Tools to analyse the campaign

14. Map of the forts and roads as a system
This takes the relationships of the forts in the campaign and turns it into a system or grid, which is overlaid on the map of the area under analysis.

15. Diagram of the fort and road system as a grid
This takes the map of the fort and road system and turns it into a grid.

16. Typology diagram
All the above elements come together in the typology diagram, which takes the analysis and presents it diagrammatically for ease of understanding and for comparative purposes.

17. Strength Factors
Each fort of a given size has a Strength Factor noted above. This is used in the case studies as a proxy for the unit and its 'strength' or force deployed there, even though we cannot in many cases know what sort of unit it is.

18. Summary table of campaign elements
This summarizes all the elements analyzed above and presents the key elements in a comparative table – including the number of forts, road lengths built, garrison in suggested manpower, what this represents in Strength Factors and the average spacing between forts.

Tools for comparisons

19. Comparative graphs
These take the statistical analysis summarized in the table above and present the results graphically to compare between campaigns and commanders.

20. Comparison of forts
This graphic using a set of standard graphics and colour-coded symbols for Roman forts of the first and second centuries enables easy comparison between forts that have been fully or partially excavated.

21. Comparison of battles
Also using a standardized set of symbols and a diagrammatic approach, this enables us to decode and visualize the often sketchy and formulaic descriptions of battles in ancient sources.

22. Campaign scorecard
This is a device to evaluate the success or failure of an individual campaign against the inferred mission from the emperor.

23. Contemporary comparators
This is used when there is a clear resonance between our campaign and another historical period, as there is for instance between the nineteenth-century railway map of Wales and the network of forts designed by Frontinus.

The best way to demonstrate how the tools work is to show them in action. The examples following are extracted from the case studies in Chapters 2–6 in Part 1. Not all the techniques should or need to be used in each study.

> In order, by a taste of pleasures, to reclaim the natives from that rude and unsettled state which prompted them to war, and to reconcile them to quiet and tranquillity, he incited them ... to erect temples, courts of justice, and dwelling houses... [H]e provided a liberal education for the sons of their chieftains... [T]he toga was frequently seen... [T]hose luxuries ... in reality constituted a part of their slavery. (Tacitus, *Agricola* 21)

> He transferred the scene of his conflict to the territory of the Ordovices. He recruited from those who dreaded the establishment of the Roman peace and staked his fate on one last confrontation. (Tacitus, *Annals* xii.33)

Fig. 9.1. Written sources.

State of the Province in AD47

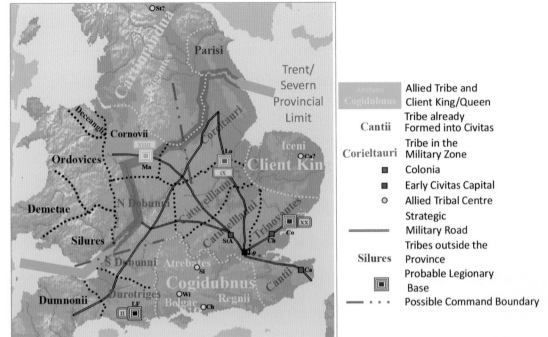

Fig. 9.2. Political and provincial context.

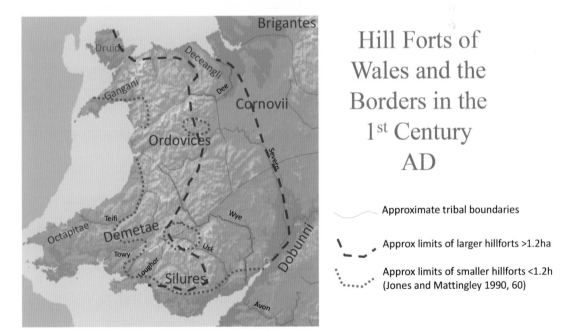

Fig. 9.3. Population and settlement context.

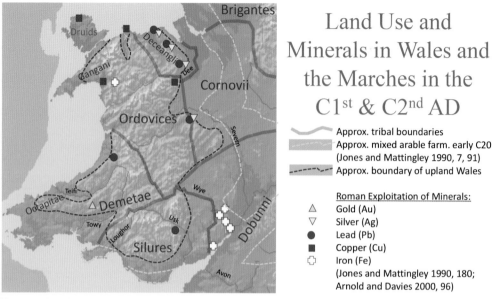

Land Use and Minerals in Wales and the Marches in the C1st & C2nd AD

∿ Approx. tribal boundaries
▬ Approx. mixed arable farm. early C20 (Jones and Mattingley 1990, 7, 91)
---⌐ Approx. boundary of upland Wales

Roman Exploitation of Minerals:
△ Gold (Au)
▽ Silver (Ag)
● Lead (Pb)
■ Copper (Cu)
⊕ Iron (Fe)
(Jones and Mattingley 1990, 180; Arnold and Davies 2000, 96)

Fig. 9.4. Land-use and minerals context.

The Lowlands before the Antonine Re-occupation

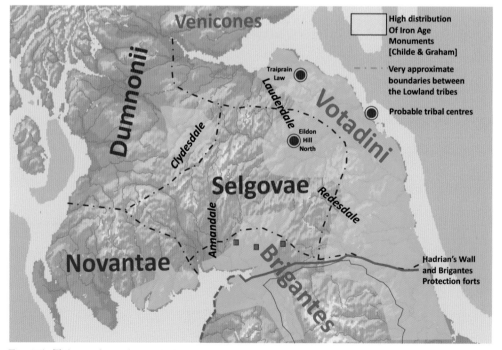

□ High distribution Of Iron Age Monuments [Childe & Graham]

--- Very approximate boundaries between the Lowland tribes

● Probable tribal centres

Hadrian's Wall and Brigantes Protection forts

Fig. 9.5. Tribes and peoples context.

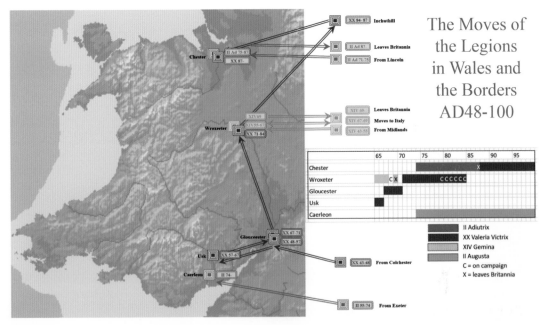

Fig. 9.6. Legionary fortresses sequence.

Legionary Deployments on the Welsh Front

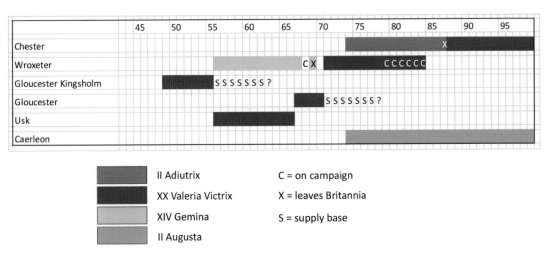

Fig. 9.7. Legionary deployments.

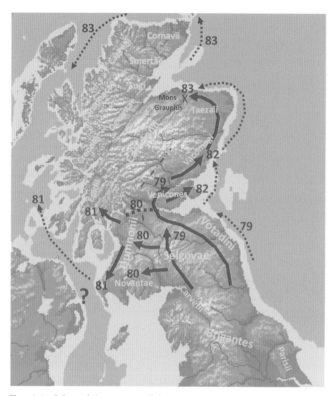

Fig. 9.8. Map of the course of the campaign.

Agricola's
Campaigns
in the North
AD79-83
According to Tacitus

Tribes according to
Ptolemy's Geography

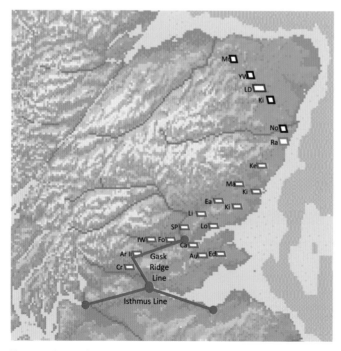

Fig. 9.9. Map of marching camps.

Possible
Agricolan
Marching Camps

◻ c44 ha Camps
Aberdeenshire and Moray Line
• Normandykes
• Kintore
• Ythan Wells I
• Muirfield

◻ • Raedykes 39 ha
◻ • Logie Durno 57 ha

◻ c25 ha Camps

Strathmore Line	Coast Line
• Craigarnhall	• Carpow?
• Ardoch II	• Longforgan
• Innerpeffray West	• Kirkbuddo
• Forteviot	• Kinneil
• Scone Park	
• Lintrose	Fife
• Eassie	• Auchtermuchty
• Marcus	• Edenwood
• Keithock	

Scapula's Strategy of Aggression
47-52AD
Fortresses and Forts

Camp-aign	System	Purpose	Desription	Id	Name	Phase	Roman Name	Size Ha	Size Code	Strength Factor	First Unit	Approx Manpower	Unit if Known	Build Code	Start Date	End Date	Distance. RM	IM	Km
SCAPULA'S CONQUEST OF THE SILURES & ORDOOVICES																			
SCA	WAT	LOP	CONQUEST	1.0	Wigston Parva (H Cross)			0.7	SFT	0.6		240		Scap	55		0.0	0.0	0.0
SCA	WAT	LOP	CONQUEST	2.0	Mancetter		Manduessedum	9.0	VEX	8.0		2,000	XIV GEM	Scap	55		11.2	10.6	17.0
SCA	WAT	LOP	CONQUEST	3.0	Wall		Lectocetum	Vex	VX	6.0		2,000		Scap	55		19.1	18.0	29.0
SCA	WAT	LOP	CONQUEST	4.0	Kinvaston (Water Eaton)	1	Pennocrucium	7.8	VX	6.0		2,000		Scap	55		16.4	15.5	25.0
SCA	WAT	LOP	CONQUEST	5.0	Redhill		Uxacona	0.7	SFT	0.6		240		Scap	55		13.2	12.4	20.0
SCA	WAT	LOP	CONQUEST	6.0	Wroxeter		Viroconium	2,20	LFT	2.0	CQE	500	coh I Thracum eq	Scap	55		13.8	13.0	21.0
SCA	WAT	LOP	CONQUEST	6.1	Leighton (nr Wroxeteer)			8.1	VEX	8.0	LEG+AUX	2,000	XIV GEM	Scap	55		0.0	0.0	0.0
SCA	WAT	LOP	CONQUEST	7.0	Rhyn Park			17.2	LEG	12.0	LEG+AUX	5,000	XIV GEM	Scap	55		28.3	26.7	43.0
SCA	WAT	LOP	CONQUEST	8.0	Chester			10.0	VEX	8.0		2,000		Scap	55		26.3	24.9	40.0
Watling Street Line of Penetration (Decangi and Ordovices)										43.2		13,980					102.0	96.3	155.0
SCA	DOB	AREA	CONTROL	1.0	The Lunt Baginton			Vex		6.0		2,000		Scap	55				
SCA	DOB	AREA	CONTROL	2.0	Alcester					1.0		500		Scap	55				
SCA	DOB	AREA	CONTROL	3.0	Droitwich		Salinae	5.0	SLF	4.0		1,500		Scap	55				
SCA	DOB	AREA	CONTROL	4.0	Metchley			4.4	SLF	4.0		1,500		Scap	55				
SCA	DOB	AREA	CONTROL	5.0	Greensforge	1		1.6	FRT	1.5		500		Scap	55				
Area Control of Northern Dobunni (W Midlands Triangle)										16.5		6,000					0.0	0.0	0.0
SCA	WYE	LOP	CONQUEST	1.0	Cirencester			1.8	FRT	1.5	AQ	500	ala Gallиorum Indiana	Scap	55		0.0	0.0	0.0
SCA	WYE	LOP	CONQUEST	2.0	Gloucester	1	Glevum	10.0	VEX	10.0		3,000		Scap	55		18.4	17.4	28.0
SCA	WYE	LOP	CONQUEST	3.0	Canon Frome			1.8	FRT	1.5		500		Scap	55		23.7	22.4	36.0
SCA	WYE	LOP	CONQUEST	4.0	Kenchester?					1.0		500		Scap	55		15.1	14.3	23.0
SCA	WYE	LOP	CONQUEST	5.0	Clifford	1		6.5	VX	6.0		2,000		Scap	55		14.5	13.7	22.0
Wye Line of Penetration (N Silures/Dobunni Border)										20.0		6,500					71.7	67.7	109.0
SCA	WYE	LOP	CONQUEST	1.0	Gloucester	1	Glevum	10.0	VEX	10.0		2,000		Scap	55		0.0	0.0	0.0
GAL	WYE	LOP	SUP	2.0	Chepstow							-		Scap	55		31.6	29.8	48.0
GAL	WYE	LOP	SUP	3.0	Caerleon							-		Scap	55		15.1	14.3	23.0
Vale of Gamorgan Line of Penetration (S Silures)										0.0		2,000					46.7	44.1	71.0
TOTAL: GALLUS' CONTAINMENT SYSTEM										79.7		14,500							

Fig. 9.10. Extract from the database.

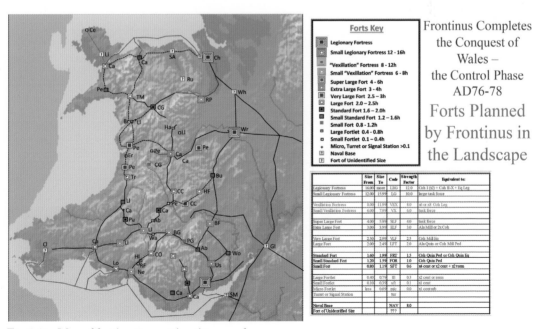

Forts Key

- ▣ Legionary Fortress
- ▣ Small Legionary Fortress 12 - 16h
- ▣ "Vexillation" Fortress 8 - 12h
- ▣ Small "Vexillation" Fortress 6 - 8h
- ▣ Super Large Fort 4 - 6h
- ▣ Extra Large Fort 3 - 4h
- ▣ Very Large Fort 2.5 - 3h
- ◰ Large Fort 2.0 - 2.5h
- ■ Standard Fort 1.6 - 2.0h
- ▪ Small Standard Fort 1.2 - 1.6h
- ▪ Small Fort 0.8 - 1.2h
- ▨ Large Fortlet 0.4 - 0.8h
- ▫ Small Fortlet 0.1 - 0.4h
- + Micro, Turret or Signal Station >0.1
- ⊞ Naval Base
- ⍰ Fort of Unidentified Size

	Size From	Size To	Code	Strength Factor	Equivalent to:
Legionary Fortress	16.00	more	LEG	12.0	Coh I (x2) + Coh II-X + Eq Leg
Small Legionary Fortress	12.00	15.99	LG	10.0	large task force
Vexillation Fortress	8.00	11.99	VEX	8.0	x6 or x8 Coh Leg
Small Vexillation Fortress	6.00	7.99	VX	6.0	task force
Super Large Fort	4.00	5.99	SLF	4.0	task force
Extra Large Fort	3.00	3.99	ELF	3.0	Ala Mill or 2x Coh
Very Large Fort	2.50	2.99	VLF	2.5	Coh Mill Eq
Large Fort	2.00	2.49	LFT	2.0	Ala Quin or Coh Mill Ped
Standard Fort	1.60	1.99	FRT	1.5	Coh Quin Ped or Coh Quin Eq
Small Standard Fort	1.20	1.59	FOR	1.0	Coh Quin Ped
Small Fort	0.80	1.19	SFT	0.6	x4 cent or x2 cent + x2 turm
Large Fortlet	0.40	0.79	IO	0.3	x2 cent or num
Small Fortlet	0.10	0.39	sfl	0.1	x1 cent
Micro Fortlet	less	0.09	mic	0.0	x1 cent sub
Turret or Signal Station			tur		
Naval Base			NAV	8.0	
Fort of Unidentified Size			???		

Frontinus Completes the Conquest of Wales –
the Control Phase AD76-78

Forts Planned by Frontinus in the Landscape

Fig. 9.11. Map of fort locations with military roads.

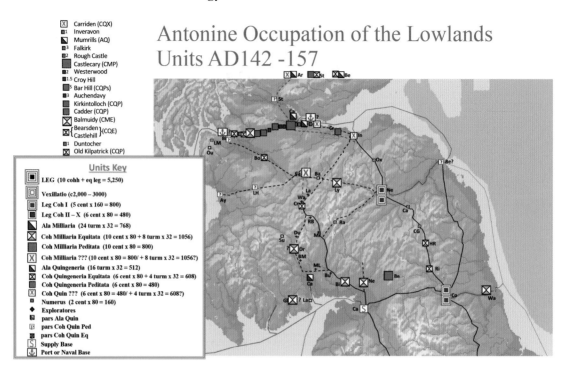

Fig. 9.12. Map of unit deployments.

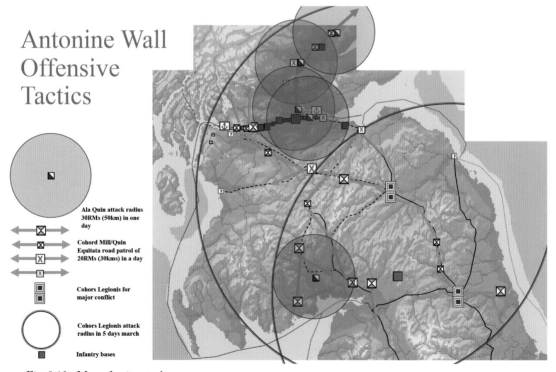

Fig. 9.13. Map of unit patrol zones.

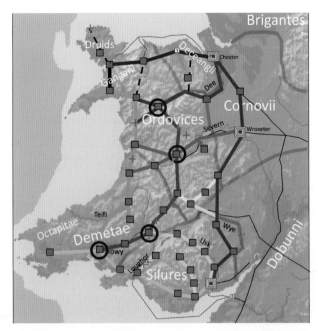

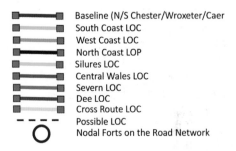

Frontinus Completes the Conquest of
Wales – the Control Phase
AD76-78

Frontinus' Planned
Military Grid
built by him and Agricola

▣━━━▣	Baseline (N/S Chester/Wroxeter/Caer
▣━━━▣	South Coast LOC
▣━━━▣	West Coast LOC
▣━━━▣	North Coast LOP
▣━━━▣	Silures LOC
▣━━━▣	Central Wales LOC
▣━━━▣	Severn LOC
▣━━━▣	Dee LOC
▣━━━▣	Cross Route LOC
▣- - -▣	Possible LOC
O	Nodal Forts on the Road Network

Fig. 9.14. Map of forts and roads as a system or grid.

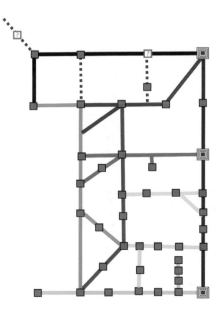

Frontinus Completes the Conquest of
Wales – the Control Phase
AD76-78

Diagram of Frontinus'
Military Grid

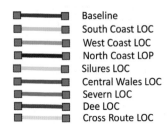

▣━━━▣	Baseline
▣━━━▣	South Coast LOC
▣━━━▣	West Coast LOC
▣━━━▣	North Coast LOP
▣━━━▣	Silures LOC
▣━━━▣	Central Wales LOC
▣━━━▣	Severn LOC
▣━━━▣	Dee LOC
▣━━━▣	Cross Route LOC

Fig. 9.15. Diagram of fort and road grid.

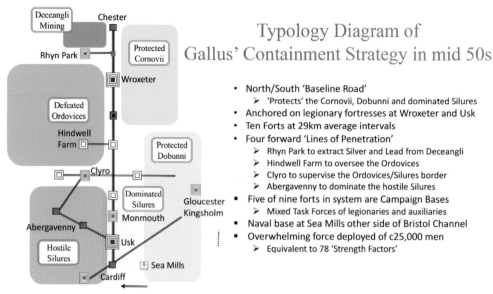

Typology Diagram of Gallus' Containment Strategy in mid 50s

- North/South 'Baseline Road'
  - ➢ 'Protects' the Cornovii, Dobunni and dominated Silures
- Anchored on legionary fortresses at Wroxeter and Usk
- Ten Forts at 29km average intervals
- Four forward 'Lines of Penetration'
  - ➢ Rhyn Park to extract Silver and Lead from Deceangli
  - ➢ Hindwell Farm to oversee the Ordovices
  - ➢ Clyro to supervise the Ordovices/Silures border
  - ➢ Abergavenny to dominate the hostile Silures
- Five of nine forts in system are Campaign Bases
  - ➢ Mixed Task Forces of legionaries and auxiliaries
- Naval base at Sea Mills other side of Bristol Channel
- Overwhelming force deployed of c25,000 men
  - ➢ Equivalent to 78 'Strength Factors'

Fig. 9.16. Typology diagram.

Antonine Occupation of the Lowlands Deployment of Strength

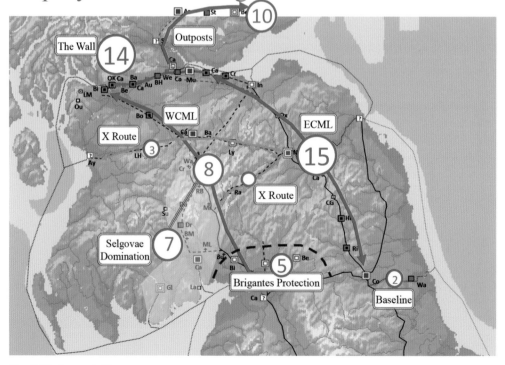

Fig. 9.17. Strength Factors.

Frontinus Completes the
Conquest of Wales –
the Control Phase
AD76 onwards

Summary of
Vital Statistics
of the
Lines of Control

	Number of Forts	Road Length	Nominal Garrison Manpower	Strength Factors	Ave Distance Forts
Baseline	8	251 kms	2,500	7.0	32 kms
South Coast LOC	1 leg + 7	255 kms	5,000 leg + 4,000	12.0 leg 10.0	32 kms
Silures LOC/ZON	11	346 kms	6,440	17.5	32 kms
Severn Valley LOC	1 leg + 5	239 kms	5,000 leg + 4,360	12.0 leg + 11.2	40 kms
Dee LOC	1 leg + 3	126 kms	5,000 leg + 3,500	12.0 leg + 9.5	32 kms
Central Wales LOC	7	227 kms	2,900	7.3	32 kms
West Coast LOC	10	269 kms	3,136	6.3	27 kms
North Coast LOC	5	150 kms	2,540	5.6	30 kms
Marches Cross Route	4	134 kms	1,000	4.5	33 kms
TOTALS	3 Leg +36 excluding duplicates	1,997 kms	15,000 leg + 30,376	114.9	32 kms

Fig. 9.18. Statistical summary.

Comparisons of Campaigns in Britain
Number of Fortresses/Forts and Manpower

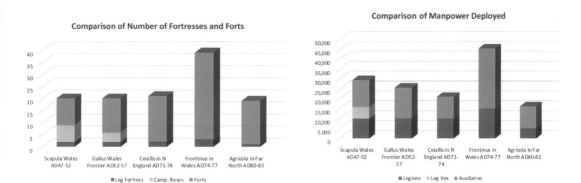

Fig. 9.19. Comparative graphs.

Diagrammatic Representation of
Forts Along Highland Line and Gask Frontier

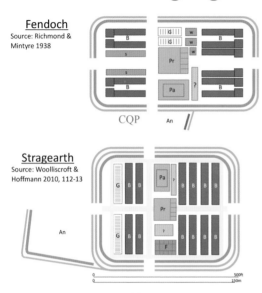

Fendoch
Source: Richmond &
Mintyre 1938

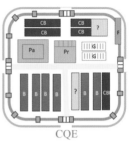

Elginhaugh
Source: Hodgson
Review of Hanson
Britannia XL 2008, 365-69

N

CQP   An

CQE

Stragearth
Source: Woolliscroft &
Hoffmann 2010, 112-13

An

CQP = 6 x 80 = 480
CMP = 10 x 80 = 800
CQE = 6 x 80 = 480 + 4 x 32 = 128
CME = 10 x 80 = 800 + X x 32 =
AQ = x 32 =
AM = x32 =

Fig. 9.20. Diagrams of forts.

Diagrammatic Representation of
Caractacus' Last Battle
(literal interpretation based on Tacitus' narrative)

Caractacus
and his
Comitatus

Scapula

Legionaries and
Auxiliaries
deployed
together

Source: Tacitus Annals xii.33-35

1. Caractacus chose ground where the 'entrances and exits were to our disadvantage but favourable to his troops'
   ➤ On one side there was a precipitously steep gradient
   ➤ Where there were a gentler approach routes he piled up stones to form a kind of embankment
   ➤ There was also a river of uncertain depth flowing past and here bands of fighters were stationed to provide defences
2. Caractacus and the tribal leaders encouraged their troops
3. Scapula alarmed by the river, the rampart, the mountains and numbers of defenders
4. Roman soldiers, prefects and tribunes demand battle
5. Survey of Britons' defences
6. Romans cross the river without difficulty
7. They suffer missile casualties at the barricade
8. Using testudo formation Romans tear down the wall of rocks
9. Engage at close quarters
10. Barbarians forced to retreat into the mountains
11. Romans follow up with both light armed auxiliaries with javelins and heavy armed legionaries
12. Massacred by swords and spears of the legionaries and the broadswords and lances of the auxiliaries
13. Wife and daughter of Caractacus captured and brothers surrendered, Caractacus escapes

Fig. 9.21. Diagrams of battles.

Campaign Scorecard 5:
The Antonine System in Scotland AD139-163

The Enemy: *Selgovae, Dumnonii, Novantae and Caledonii (*Allies*: Votadini and Venicones)*
Forces Deployed: 2 legions + 1 vexillation + c25 auxiliary units = c25,000 men = 64SFs

- ○ **Presumed Mission from Antoninus Pius to Urbicus in 139:** decommission the Wall the Army has just spent 17 years building, we are now expanding the Empire as in the days of Vespasian and Trajan: so re-occupy the lands that Agricola conquered in 79 and build my Wall on the model of Hadrian's but half the length across Forth/Clyde Isthmus
  - ▪ **Major Strategic Victory** with reoccupation of the Lowlands justifying a Triumph in Rome
  - ▪ Tactical Defeat of the Wall construction teams necessitating re-design
  - ▪ Eventual Strategic Victory with the Antonine Wall completed as the densest border line in the Empire

- ○ **Presumed Mission from Antoninus Pius in 157**: we have to abandon/mothball the new Wall because of the need for forces on the German Frontier and to put down revolts in our rear
- ○ **Presumed Mission from Antoninus Pius in 158:** we have defeated our enemies and we can re-occupy my forts in the North
  - ▪ 157 Strategic Defeat eventually averted in terms of re-activation of the whole Antonine system

- ○ **Presumed Mission from M. Aurelius to C Agricola in 163**: I and my brother Emperor have a war to fight in the East, we have trouble again on the German Frontier, we cannot afford the overhead of the Antonine system to hold down tribes who continue to resist – reactivate Hadrian's Wall
  - ▪ **Strategic Defeat** and pull back to Tyne/Solway in good order but a defeat nonetheless

- ○ **Overall Result** is a **Major Roman Strategic Defeat** with the Antonine Wall and all the forts forward in Stathearn and on the Tay and most in the Lowlands abandoned again.

Fig. 9.22. Campaign scorecard.

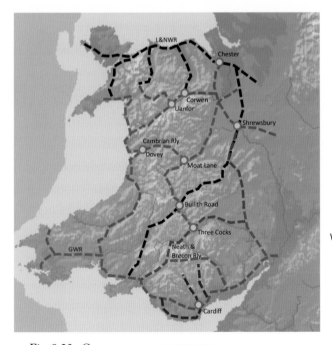

The Principal
Railways
of Wales
c1914

Nodal Forts		Railway Junctions	
Chester Leg Fortress	■	○	Chester
Penros	■	○	Corwen
Llanfor	■	○	Llanfor
Pennal	■	○	Dovey
Llwyn-y-brain	■	○	Moat Lane
Wroxeter Leg Fortress	■	○	Shrewsbury
Penmincae	■	○	Builith Road
Clyro	■	○	Three Cocks
Caerleon Leg Fortress	■	○	Cardiff

Fig. 9.23. Contemporary comparators.

Chapter 10

Conclusions

What can we conclude from the five case studies and the application of the D-LAM methods?

The challenge set at the start of this book was to test Edward Luttwak's thesis that the Roman Army had a grand strategy, that it analyzed military challenges, developed solutions and had the institutions to execute them. The test was whether we could see evidence for this thesis in the five case studies. We can draw out much evidence from the actions and behaviour of the Roman Army, and how it functioned under great stress, during the campaigns under the microscope here. The Roman Army in Britain was not the Roman Empire: there was much more to the empire than one of its armies deployed in a distant province. But it was nevertheless the embodiment of the Roman state in Britain and the principal determinant of how British tribes and people experienced the Roman Empire in the first century AD. Some of the elites were able to make choices and became client and allies, while others chose to fight – to become Caractacus and Calgacus, rather than Cogidubnus and Cartimandua. For most, however, the choice of being a friend of Rome or its enemy and victim was made for them by circumstances.

In first-century Britain, the Roman Army ruled the larger part of the territory: it was an enormous consumer of foodstuffs, animals, leather, clothing and building materials, and directly operated mines and probably imperial estates as well. It was not only the embodiment of the armed power of the Roman state, it also performed police, local government, customs and tax collection duties, as well as constructing roads and public buildings. It would have acquired booty from its campaigns wherever possible, killing and enslaving the populations with which it came into hostile contact. Conversely, it generally rewarded its allies well – Cartimandua was, for instance, rescued from her rivals – and probably (generally) paid for its supplies. Furthermore, a career in an auxiliary regiment on a distant frontier offered new worlds of opportunities for recruits, with the prospect of Roman citizenship upon retirement. The Roman Army also recycled its old barracks and bases into the basis of civilian towns, in support of the incorporation of Britain into the mainstream economy of the empire. Sometimes these towns were for alien implants of its own military veterans, as in the *coloniae* of Camulodunum or Gloucester, and sometimes for new tribal capitals or towns, like Wroxeter (where the legionary baths become the forum), Carlisle and Corbridge (Wacher, 1997).

The first chapter set out the extreme perspectives of the Roman Army and its campaigns as the acts of a greedy predator or a Pentagon-style planner. As the case studies show, the army was in many respects both. All personnel were no doubt enthusiastic about what waging war in Britain provided, given the opportunities it offered for the acquisition of moveable wealth and enslavable people. This does not preclude or exclude the Roman Army having the characteristics Luttwak set out. Indeed, as the case studies show, in Britain – particularly when the Roman Army came up against tribal societies in the North and West – it was operating against an effective and hard-to-pin-down opponent in a challenging landscape and climate that dramatically evened up the match. In these settings, much of the technological and doctrinal advantage of the Romans was negated. This demanded an effectively planned, continuously improving and efficiently executed response – and over time, the Roman Army learned how to respond. Roman Britain in the first and second centuries is therefore an excellent 'laboratory' to analyze and understand the true nature of the Roman Army.

There are three key insights to be drawn from the case studies:

- the Roman Army, whilst very effective tactically when it engineered a stand-up fight, failed strategically time after time in Britain;
- the reason for this failure was overstretch: the army was operating at or beyond its limits in a variety of respects;
- despite – or more likely as a direct result of – the pressured and sometimes precarious position the army found itself in, we can very clearly see it adapting to and learning from its successes, and even more from its failures.

Tactical success leading to strategic failure – the case study scorecards

That the Roman Army failed to achieve its strategic objectives in *Britannia* is somewhat at odds with both popular and, in some cases, academic perceptions of Roman military, technological and cultural superiority and invincibility in this period (Fischer, 2019).

What conclusions can be drawn from the case studies evaluating the actions of each of the governors against their presumed mission? We do not know what was in the letters of appointment they variously received from Emperors Claudius, Nero, Vespasian, Titus, Domitian and Antoninus. However, the contention here is that we can be reasonably confident that they received instructions, and we can make an educated guess as to what they were from the governors' actions.

The outcomes of the various campaigns are rated on a five-point scale:

- strategic Roman victory;
- tactical Roman victory;
- draw;
- tactical Roman defeat;
- strategic Roman defeat.

We also determine whether the victory or defeat could be described as major or minor.

This involves subjective judgements and is of course a massive oversimplification. Nevertheless, it can be instructive in pointing up just how challenging these campaigns were for the Roman Army and for the Roman state in *Britannia*. Strategic defeat often followed tactical victories. Our approach is designed to be deliberately judgemental and polarizing, for this is how the Romans themselves thought: in terms of either victory or defeat. They celebrated triumphs for victorious generals and named legions and new cities after victory – the XX Legion was honoured as *Valeria Victrix* after it had defeated Boudicca, and the city of Camulodunum had the formal name *Colonia Claudia Victricensis* as the site of Claudius' victory of 43 and his imperial cult.

A balance sheet for each of the five case studies is summarized in Figures 10.1 to 10.5. While recognizing that these are only a selection from among the Roman Army's British campaigns of the first and second centuries and form a small subset of the overall number of campaigns of the period across the empire, the record is clearly far from one of uniform victory.

There is actually only one unequivocal Roman strategic victory among the five campaigns, and this is Frontinus in Wales in 74–77, when he executed a textbook conquest and occupation. Gallus' policy of containment, although it did advance the border some way into the Wye and Usk valleys, has been assessed strategically as a draw. The other three case studies – Scapula's failed attempt around AD 50 to conquer Wales, the relinquishing of Agricola's gains in Scotland in 87 and the reversal of the forward Antonine policy in *c*.163 – are rated as major strategic defeats for the Romans. This verdict is despite each of these campaigns and systems having achieved some significant victories along the way: Scapula defeated Caractacus and the Ordovices and Silures in pitched battle, Agricola did the same to Calgacus and the Caledones, while Urbicus earned a triumph in Rome for his advance to the Forth/Clyde isthmus. Yet none of these successes resulted in lasting gains.

In two cases, the ultimate cause of failure was the requirement to redeploy troops to other parts of the empire – a problem outside the governors' control. *Britannia* and its tribes were not easy prey, and a key theme from the case studies is the continuing drain on resources caused by holding down tribes who were unwilling to acquiesce in their subjugation. It is clear that with four legions and their matching auxiliaries, a governor could expand the province, whereas with only three legions he could hold the south-west, Wales and Northern England – but apart from outposts in the Scottish Borders, that was all. With four legions in the province, the governor could endeavour, as Agricola did, to conquer the whole island. Only Syria had a garrison approaching this size, with four legions but not as many auxiliaries.

The strategic defeats in 87 and 163 were in a real sense self-inflicted harm since, after the army had defeated the enemy in battle and invested massive amounts in military infrastructure, empire-wide considerations dictated withdrawals, which were on both occasions achieved with admirable discipline. The conclusion here was not to start something that there was insufficient commitment, time and resources to complete. By contrast, in Wales the task of conquest was finished and in the 120s the work of occupation in bringing the tribes, at least those of South Wales, into the empire could begin, allowing garrison reductions and troop transfers out of the region.

This leaves us with Scapula's snatching of defeat from the jaws of victory in 52 when, having sent Caractacus to Rome for Claudius' triumph, his legions and auxiliaries tried to occupy the territory of the Silures. We hear about ambushes and the Romans suffering significant casualties, which may have forced them to brigade together in the large campaign bases visible in the archaeological record. In turn, however, this meant that, despite being able to deploy overwhelming force, Scapula's men were concentrated and therefore could not cover all the terrain effectively. If this was indeed the case, then the failure here was essentially one of doctrine. In the mid-first century, the Roman Army was still built around legionaries, although supplemented with auxiliaries. This configuration of forces, combined with a tactical doctrine based on concentration in campaign bases, was poorly adapted to manage the low-intensity hit-and-run guerrilla resistance offered by the Silures.

The Roman Army at overstretch in Britain

The Roman Army was operating in Britain at what was for Rome 'the ends of the Earth'. This sense of operating at the limits of capacity was true across several dimensions:

- the supply challenges would have been considerable, with legionary and auxiliary task forces of $c.30,000$ men operating in upland territory of Wales and the north of Scotland. Even if the army had wished to live off the land, it would have been unable to support itself through the campaigning season and the winter in garrison without steady streams of supplies from the south;

- there is evidence that lack of manpower availability became acute, so the lavish standards of fort spacings and landscape coverage under Frontinus clearly had to be limited to main lines under Agricola in the Lowlands. By the time of the Antonine Wall, with only three legions in the province, the wall line was densely held, but only with legionary cohorts pressed into use and with split units in smaller forts;
- the army was also operating at the limits of its military doctrine. The defeat of the Ordovices or Caledones in battle should have been decisive, but there were then no central places to occupy or elites to buy-off with luxury goods;
- the climate was a second enemy since the campaigning season was limited at this latitude. Winters in forts placed in strategic positions high in Snowdonia or at the mouths of the Highland glens would even wear down the morale of units from frontier regions with similar climates;
- and finally, the army was operating at the limits of its cultural experience: this was what was known as *ultima Thule*, the Caledonian forest situated in the farthest Ocean. With the exception of Vespasian and Hadrian, the ability of the emperor and his advisers in Rome to comprehend the experience of campaigning in northern or western Britain would be limited.

Thus, winning in Britain was harder, took longer and required more consistent and prolonged commitment than previous campaigns in Gaul, Illyricum and the Balkans. The combination of supply, manpower, doctrinal, climatic and mental stretch could easily tip over into overstretch when mistakes were made (Scapula) or imperial priorities intervened (Domitian and Marcus Aurelius). This helps to explain why, despite tactical successes often sustained over several years, and even after the much-sought 'decisive battle', the eventual outcome was still strategic failure.

Campaign Scorecard 1:
Scapula in Wales AD48-52

The Enemy: *Deceangli, Silures* and *Ordovices*
Forces Deployed: 2 legions + vexillations from 2 others + 20+ auxiliary units
= c30,000 men at the peak = 88SFs

Presumed Mission from Claudius in 48: Conquer the Welsh tribes and incorporate them into the Empire by whatever means necessary

- **48: Major Tactical Victory** in defeating and probably subjugation of the *Deceangli* and their valuable silver and lead resources
- **51: Major Tactical Victory** in pitched battle over Caractacus enabling Claudius' Triumph
- **52: Minor Tactical Defeats** reported by Tacitus when substantial legionary and auxiliary detachments are defeated and serious casualties sustained

Overall Result is a **Major Roman Strategic Defeat** given the inability to hold any of the territory of the major Welsh tribes, Scapula dies of exhaustion.

Fig 10.1. Scapula in Wales.

Campaign Scorecard 2:
Gallus in Wales AD52-57

The Enemy: *Silures* and *Ordovices*
Forces Deployed: 2 legions + 25 auxiliary units = 25,000 men = 78SFs

Presumed Mission from Claudius in 52: Complete Scapula's unfinished business and conquer the Welsh tribes?

- **55: Major Tactical Victory** establishing a forward Legionary Fortress at Usk
- **55: Minor Tactical Victories** in projecting force in a limited way into the interior along the River Valleys

o **Overall Result** is a *Strategic Draw* with Gallus's policy of Containment in place and the tribes effectively unconquered and independent

Fig 10.2. Gallus in Wales.

Campaign Scorecard 3:
Frontinus in Wales AD74-77

The Enemy: *Silures, Ordovices, Demetae and Deceangli*
Forces Deployed: 2 legions + c30 auxiliary units = 40,000 men = 115SFs

Presumed Mission from Vespasian in 74: As part of the overall Flavian Mission to complete the full conquest and integration of the island of Britain, defeat and absorb all the tribes of Wales into the military zone. You are building on Cerialis defeat of and absorption of the Brigantian Confederacy, and this campaign will lay the foundation for the conquest of the the far North.

- 74/75 **Major Strategic Victories** in defeating any direct opposition
- 75/76 **Major Tactical Victories** achieved in dominating the River Valleys leading into the interior of Wales
- 76/77 **Major Strategic Victory** over the Silures and Ordovices with the building of a tight interlocking network of forts and roads across the whole country

  o **Overall Result** is **Major Roman Strategic Victory** with a large garrison which was able to be reduced within three decades and two *Civitates* set up in the 120s.

Fig 10.3. Frontinus in Wales.

Campaign Scorecard 4:
Agricola in Scotland AD77-87

The Enemy: *Selgovae, Dumnonii, Novantae and Caledonii (Allies: Votadini and Venicones)*
Forces Deployed: 2 legions + 1 vexillation + 26 auxiliary units = c30,000 men = 78SFs

Presumed Mission from Vespasian in 77: As part of the next and final stage of the Flavian Mission to complete the conquest of Britain, defeat and occupy all the tribes of the North

- 77: Minor Tactical Victory over Ordovices who are testing resolve of the new Governor
- 77: **Major Tactical Victory** in the occupation of Anglesey and the defeat (and presumably extermination) of the Druids as a source of continuing cultural opposition
- 78: Minor Tactical Victories in completing the occupation and lock-down of Brigantian territory started by Cerialis
- 79: **Major Strategic Victory** with the occupation of the Lowlands of Scotland and their incorporation either as allies or subjects

Presumed Mission from Titus in 79: halt the campaign whilst the Empire wide strategy is reviewed
- 80 and 81: Major Tactical Victory in creation of the Frontier at the Forth/Clyde Isthmus and along the Gask Ridge

Presumed Mission from Domitian in 81: we are resuming the full conquest of Britain Strategy
- 82: **Draw** campaigning in Strathmore and Angus with near loss of IX Legion
- 83: **Major Strategic Victory** at Mons Graupius

Presumed Mission to Successor from Domitian in 83: complete the job building on defeat of the *Caledones*
- 84-86 Major Tactical Victory creation of secure forward base zone - new Inchtuthill legionary fortress at its core

Presumed Mission to Successor from Domitian in 87: send II Adiutrix and its auxiliaries to Danube Frontier
- Major Strategic Defeat as Roman Army pulls back to Lowland forts and eventually Stanegate on Tyne/Solway

  o **Overall Result** is a **Major Roman Strategic Defeat** with the effective limit of the Empire on the Tyne/Solway and the chance of total conquest given up.

Fig 10.4. Agricola and his successor in Scotland.

Campaign Scorecard 5:
The Antonine System in Scotland AD139-163

The Enemy: *Selgovae, Dumnonii, Novantae and Caledonii* (Allies: *Votadini and Venicones*)
Forces Deployed: 2 legions + 1 vexillation + c25 auxiliary units = c25,000 men = 64SFs

- o **Presumed Mission from Antoninus Pius to Urbicus in 139:** decommission the Wall the Army has just spent 17 years building, we are now expanding the Empire as in the days of Vespasian and Trajan: so re-occupy the lands that Agricola conquered in 79 and build my Wall on the model of Hadrian's but half the length across Forth/Clyde Isthmus
  - ▪ **Major Strategic Victory** with reoccupation of the Lowlands justifying a Triumph in Rome
  - ▪ Tactical Defeat of the Wall construction teams necessitating re-design
  - ▪ Eventual Strategic Victory with the Antonine Wall completed as the densest border line in the Empire

- o **Presumed Mission from Antoninus Pius in 157**: we have to abandon/mothball the new Wall because of the need for forces on the German Frontier and to put down revolts in our rear
- o Presumed Mission from Antoninus Pius in 158: we have defeated our enemies and we can re-occupy my forts in the North
  - ▪ 157 Strategic Defeat eventually averted in terms of re-activation of the whole Antonine system

- o **Presumed Mission from M. Aurelius to C Agricola in 163**: I and my brother Emperor have a war to fight in the East, we have trouble again on the German Frontier, we cannot afford the overhead of the Antonine system to hold down tribes who continue to resist – reactivate Hadrian's Wall
  - ▪ **Strategic Defeat** and pull back to Tyne/Solway in good order but a defeat nonetheless

- o **Overall Result** is a Major Roman Strategic Defeat with the Antonine Wall and all the forts forward in Stathearn and on the Tay and most in the Lowlands abandoned again.

Fig 10.5. The Antonine system.

Overall Campaign Scorecard
Five Campaigns

The Enemy: *Ordovices* and *Silures* in Wales *Selgovae, Dumnonii, Novantae* and *Caledonii* in North
Forces Deployed: 3 or 4 legions = 20,000 men plus 20,000 plus auxiliaries = 100SFs

- o **Presumed Mission from Claudius in 48** – complete the conquest of southern Britain
- o **Presumed Mission from Vespasian in 70** – complete the conquest of island of *Britannia*
- o **Presumed Mission from Antoninus Pius in 139** – decommission Hadrian's despised Wall and advance the frontier to the next Isthmus and build me my Wall

  - ▪ **Major Roman Strategic Defeat** = failure to occupy Silures in AD52 after Caractaus defeated in battle, Scapula dies

  - ▪ **Strategic Draw** = Gallus' policy of containment

  - ▪ **Major Roman Strategic Victory** = Frontinus' scientific occupation of the territory of the Welsh tribes

  - ▪ **Major Roman Strategic Defeat** = Romans' forced to give up north of Scotland after fourth legion withdrawn by Domitian for the Danube frontier

  - ▪ **Major Roman Strategic Defeat** = Antonine Wall give up after 20 years and pull back to the Tyne Solway.

- o **Overall Result** is a Major Roman Strategic Defeat for the Romans after a century of effort dug in on the Tyne/Solway and unable to hold the North – however the occupation of Wales has been successful at least in terms of being able to pull troops out

Fig 10.6. The overall campaign scorecard.

The Roman Army's response to waging war in Britain

Now we have made the mental shift from seeing the Roman Army in Britain as resuming its invincible progress, into understanding that the army was operating at the limits of its resources and doctrine, how did it respond as an organization to what was an extreme challenge?

What we see between campaigns is the Roman Army in Britain shifting its approach, testing and learning, and looking for new ways of conquering the tribes and holding their lands and people. This is exemplified over the three decades that it took to conquer the tribes of Wales:

- Scapula tried to conquer the *Silures* with large legion-based task forces and campaign bases but could not hold the territory;
- Gallus recognized that conquest was not practical given the state of the province and settled for a de facto frontier and a policy of containment;
- Paulinus tried for all-out conquest again but neglected the province at his back;
- Frontinus, supplied with a troop surge, worked out that the only way to conquer and hold the tribes of Wales was to lock down the conquered area hard, using a tight grid of forts linked by roads a day's march apart.

Frontinus' forts protected the troops from all but the most determined and large-scale attack, but also had sufficient density and inter-connectedness to effectively dominate the key river valleys where most settlement was to be found. The roads between forts could be patrolled on a daily basis to ensure that any resistance was spotted quickly, and action taken. This policy did not work overnight, requiring decades of commitment by the army, but after years of occupation Frontinus' policy could be seen to have succeeded and the garrisons began to be thinned out.

The roads and fort grid lockdown was the policy also deployed by Agricola in Northern England in AD 78 when he consolidated Cerialis' conquest and occupation of the Brigantes. However, in 80 in the Lowlands he could only cover the main north–south routes and the territory in between. Major areas like the Lake District and the Novantae of Galloway were left outside the grid system, as were the allied Votadini.

Agricola and his successor's approach to the conquest of the far north was to build a secure redoubt anchored on the new legionary fortress of Inchtuthil and the allied territory of the Venicones in Fife as the base for future operations in the region.

Moving forward to the Antonine episode, we can see similar evolutions and innovations in the approach of the Roman Army to challenging conditions. The original plan for Hadrian's Wall was modified from forts stationed behind the wall

(Plan A) to forts on the wall (Plan B), and was then completely abandoned by Antoninus, a rejection of everything that Hadrian had stood for. However, when Urbicus had apparently conquered the Lowlands easily and the army came to build his new northern wall, they first adopted the Hadrian's Wall Plan B design of forts at 15km intervals, an easy half-day's march.

When the opposition of the Dumnonii then got out of control, the army modified the plan to create the most densely garrisoned major frontier of the Roman Empire, well-integrated into the landscape with good sightlines to the north and effective intercommunication. This was done by pressing legionary cohorts into the front line, splitting units between forts and generally optimizing resources and deployments. The revised Antonine Wall was no theoretical exercise in military frontier creation – which arguably Hadrian's Wall Plan A had been – but a flexible and pragmatic response to a very real and immediate challenge.

Adapting and learning – resilience, flexibility and innovation

The remarkable consistency of approach of the Roman Army in the first and second centuries is what is normally stressed, whether in weapons, armour, tactics or fort layout. Many of these things were indeed consistent, but the Army's strategic flexibility, adaptation and innovation are underplayed: it had the ability to modify its operating model in the light of experience gained in the field and to test new options to find what would work against fresh challenges.

The Roman Army had an extraordinarily resilient operating model during this period which enabled it to survive setbacks and even outright defeats, and generally to emerge stronger from the experience.

To unpack this, some key factors we have seen in operation in the case studies are:

- **distinct culture**: the Army's esprit de corps and culture was very strong, and in this period the distinction between serving soldier and civilian was clear and instantly apparent. As in modern armies, legions and auxiliary units had their identities and symbols, which were stamped on buildings and tombstones (Fischer, 2019, p.xvii);
- **strong and inspiring leadership**: great emphasis on leadership and the qualities of a great leader can be seen in literature, inscriptions and the number of names of governors of Britain and other provinces and commanders of military units which we know (Tacitus, Josephus);
- **good networks and internal communications**: the Roman Empire was able to convey people and news very effectively when necessary. It took on average thirty days for an official to reach London from Rome (Bishop, 2014);

- **good career development**: Cerialis, Frontinus and Agricola had experienced careers in military and civil posts that had equipped them well to govern a province like Britain and to expand its frontiers (Hanson, 1987);
- **embedded ways of working**: we know from descriptions like those of Josephus and from remnants of surviving manuals how the Roman Army trained new recruits, developed specialisms and passed down its processes and skills to new generations, so that they instinctively knew what to do in a crisis or at a new camp. A training camp found in Xanten in *Germania* had practice ditches and corners of a type found in later periods in Wales (Vegetius; Fischer, 2019, p.241);
- **record keeping and intelligence**: an incoming governor could rapidly bring himself up to date by looking at the returns from all the units in his province. The governor's palace, often located in a legionary fortress, will have held extensive archives, as well as a substantial and sophisticated provincial staff which processed information and created intelligence appreciations (Austin & Rankov, 1995, p.244);
- **effective corporate memory**: the reoccupation of forts and roads, with minor improvements between campaigns, suggests that records of past campaigns were kept, so the Agricolan fort at Elginhaugh was replaced in the Antonine period by Inveresk, while other sites were exactly reoccupied (Hanson, 2007);
- **willingness to test and learn**: when solutions did not work, such as Scapula's strategy in Wales or the original designs of Hadrian's Wall or the Antonine Wall, the Roman Army changed it and tried something else.

The case studies – and general military studies – provide strong evidence that the Roman Army possessed all of these characteristics. A theme of this book has been the replicable model of operating, since the Army was strongly standardized in its way of working. Whether in Syria, Britain, Germany or Dacia, the new tribune in command could walk into his new fort and find his HQ (*principia*) and his house (*praetorium*) – see Figures 4.12, 4.21, 4.22, 5.15 and 5.16. Not only would he know where each room in the HQ was, and what it was for, but it would be populated by the same specialist troopers submitting the same returns to the provincial governor's HQ, with troops trained in the same manoeuvres and celebrating the emperor's birthday on the same day, exactly as he had done in his previous posting on the other side of the empire.

In the same way, when a new campaign was being planned, the Army would have checked the records compiled by the governor's *officium* and the surveys of earlier experiences of dealing with that enemy – finding what their strengths and weaknesses were, what had (and had not) worked before and what tactics should be used to counter them (Austin & Rankov, 1995, p.156).

The Roman Army put a great deal of effort into developing the careers of its most talented leaders through a succession of military and civilian posts across the empire, in frontier provinces and in peaceful ones. This tested individuals and at the same time developed them. This was a conscious central policy to grow effective leaders, create a high-performing and cohesive empire-wide team and refresh the leadership cadre on a continuous basis. It helped build links within the officer corps who would have built strong personal networks and reputations by the time they reached the top (PIR 1933–2015).

Provincial governors were members of the senatorial class who had progressed through the *cursus honorum*. They were members of the elite of the Roman Empire and specialists in what mattered: the art of ruling and the exercise of power, supported by an army and administration imbued with the imperial operating model:

> Strategy is more easily absorbed intuitively than consciously learned… Roman political culture of the Roman aristocracy was especially receptive to the lure of strategy. Its able bodied and able minded men were educated from a very young age in the realities of force, power and influence, and in the ruthless exercise of all three to advance themselves, their kin and their empire. (Luttwak, 2016, p.xiii)

To be an effective Governor of Britain, you had not only to be a top-rate general with the ability to command the largest provincial army in the empire – and one with a tendency to mutiny. You also had to administer justice in the non-military areas of the province and to co-operate with the client kings and queens allied to Rome. Furthermore, you had to work with the procurator in raising as much tax as possible to offset the cost of your army and administration without provoking a revolt by the subject peoples.

Having listed the characteristics of the Roman Army, I was struck by how similar they are to some of the characteristics of a successful modern global corporation. This comparison must not be pushed too far, and clearly the objectives and the cultural and ethical framework are totally different. However, the Roman Army did have a defined operating model, established business processes, effective communications and career development for its leaders.

In conclusion

The Roman Army lived up to its reputation as invincible on the field of battle and was largely victorious in defeating any opponents who foolishly took them on in open battle. It failed, however, to complete that full conquest of Britain which I believe was originally envisaged by Claudius and adopted as a renewed mission by Vespasian. The root cause was that the Roman Army was stretched – and at times overstretched – when operating in the Welsh or Scottish hills and mountains. It was operating at the limits of its supply, manpower, established doctrine, climatic zone and culture, against enemies who rejected what Rome was offering, were able to absorb a remarkable degree of punishment and resisted subjection for decades.

This led the Romans to deploy their best leaders and the largest provincial army in the empire, yet still they could not win decisively. The Roman Army in *Britannia* had to be at its very best to simply hold the province, let alone to expand it. This is therefore an excellent place to see the Roman Army in action at its peak and at full stretch. We witness leaders like Frontinus, Agricola and his successor and Urbicus and his successor making the most with their resources at their disposal, innovating and finding new solutions.

It turns out that *limes* was a very apt word for the Roman frontier in *Britannia*: here, at the ends of the Earth, the Roman Army was operating at its very limits.

Appendix 1

Visiting the Sites of the Campaigns

Where can you walk in the footsteps of Scapula, Gallus, Frontinus, Agricola and Urbicus?

One of the great pleasures of an interest in Roman history is marching in the footsteps of the Roman Army and its governors and visiting Roman sites across the empire. When my wife and I look at a field full of sheep on a Welsh hillside, we can see in our mind's eye a busy Roman auxiliary fort; when we view a row of terrace houses in a modern city, we can see the legionary fortress that lies beneath the suburban gardens and tarmacked roads. This is because we know what a Roman fort should look like from all the sites we have seen, whether those are physical reconstructions like the Saalburg or The Lunt, artistic interpretations such as the wonderful drawings and paintings by the late Victor Ambrus on *Time Team* or computerized reconstructions at Segedunum, Carvoran and many other sites. The visible remains, if any, and the situation in the landscape are a way of connecting with the Roman campaigns of the past.

When originally planned, this book was to include a gazetteer of Roman sites in Britain mentioned in the case studies, with illustrations and notes on what can be seen. Unfortunately, the pandemic prevented this from being developed as I would have liked; it has been very hard even to visit sites, and impossible to look at museum collections, except online. But such a gazetteer could be an interesting line of development for the virtual community outlined in Appendix 2.

Instead, I offer some short notes on the possible sites to visit for each case study, with references to the relevant pictures in the main text. Before that, however, I must flag up some indispensable books to illuminate your visits (and there are many more in the Bibliography).

For Wales, *Roman Frontiers in Wales and the Marches*, edited by Burnham and Davies, has a gazetteer of all relevant sites – forts, fortresses, roads and so forth. This will enable you to find any site you are interested in, accompanied by the latest excavation and thinking up to 2010.

For Scotland and the forts north of the Forth/Clyde, *Rome's First Frontier* by Woolliscroft and Hoffman will provide information on the key sites. For the Antonine Wall, there is *Rome's North West Frontier: the Antonine Wall* by Hanson and Maxwell from 1983, while the recent *The Antonine Wall Papers in honour of Professor Lawrence Keppie* (edited by Breeze and Hanson) will bring you up to date. For a general gazetteer on sites, there is *The Legacy of Rome: Scotland's Roman Remains* by Keppie.

Chapter 2: Scapula in Wales

A good place to start for Scapula is at the new base he founded at Gloucester Kingsholm, where the outline plan is known but not much else has been excavated. The 'eye of faith' is required, since there is nothing to see above ground except arguably a light rise marking the rampart of the fortress erected by *Legio XX* in AD 49. However, if you can obtain the ground plan (see Burnham & Davies), then a wander around the streets of Kingsholm may feed your imagination.

The site of the Roman victory over Caractacus has provoked much speculation but no certainty as to where it actually occurred. A lot of fun could be had in travelling to the various possible sites, since many hillforts in Wales and the Marches could fit Tacitus' description. One contender is Llanymynech, where the village itself straddles the border between England and Wales. Llanymynech Hill has a 57-hectare hill fort and there is a long history of mining and smelting of copper from the Bronze Age through to about AD 200. Apparently, there were mineshafts visible until landscaping for a golf course took place, and Offa's Dyke runs close by. Whether or not it is the site of Caractacus' last stand and Scapula's victory, it is well worth visiting.

To get some feel for what campaigning in the AD 40s and 50s may have been like, you could walk, cycle or drive along the Wye Valley. The key lines of penetration for the Roman Army were the river valleys that run deep into the interior. The Wye is a major river where it crosses into Wales at Hay-on-Wye, and the fertility of the valley between the hills is very apparent. The three successive campaign bases at Clifford/Clyro are worth exploring. The first was situated far too close to the river and is still a somewhat waterlogged field that now lies between the valley road and a closed railway (Picture 2.1). The second site, closer to Hay, is hard to locate, but the third is very well situated on a hill in the middle of the valley, with an excellent field of vision on all sides and still with easy access to the river (Picture 2.2) – a case of third time lucky for the Romans.

Chapter 3: Gallus' Strategy of Containment

The baseline for Gallus' campaign stretched from the legionary fortress at Wroxeter in the north, on the banks of the Severn, to the new legionary fortress constructed at Usk, on the River Usk, in the south. Both fortresses were initially constructed of wood and turf, and there are no visible remains of Gallus' work. They had very different fates, Wroxeter being partially rebuilt in stone and then seemingly mothballed in the 70s and 80s, before Hadrian used the buildings as the basis for the *civitas* capital of the Cornovii. The remains of that later town, with the foundations of markets and other civic buildings, are well displayed by Historic England, especially the 'Old Work' – an impressively large chunk of masonry that was part of the exercise hall of the baths. Whilst none of this relates to Gallus' era, you can get an excellent impression of the Roman Army's strategic understanding of the landscape and the importance of the Severn Valley. The area was a gathering ground for successive Roman task forces moving west against the Ordovices in the Welsh hills, and you can a good appreciation of this at Wroxeter.

Usk was given up as a fortress in the AD 60s, although part was probably held for auxiliaries. It is another site that requires you to use your imagination: however, if you go equipped with Burnham and Davies you can locate the position of the various parts of the legionary fortress of *Legio XX* under the very pleasant modern town. My ambition is to trace the length of Gallus' north–south road, stopping at the sites along the way, but I can only suggest this as a possibility, not having road-tested the route myself.

Chapter 4: Frontinus in Wales

The opportunities open out much more when we want to walk in the footsteps of Frontinus, if only because of the extent of his works across the whole of Wales.

One approach would be to split the visit into three sections, each based on one of the legionary commands. Starting at his new legionary base at Caerleon, where there are a wealth of Roman remains – including the baths and barracks – and an excellent museum that brilliantly displays the life and times of the *II Augusta*, you could then follow the Line of Penetration up the Usk Valley through Usk itself, where there was probably still a fort (although the fortress was dismantled). You could then go on to Abergavenny, where the fort site lies on the hill above the river: excavations are marked with paving stones, but the remains lie under the adjacent car park and town. Imagination is required at most stages of these itineraries.

The next fort up the valley is Pen y Gaer, which can be traced as earthworks around the current farm, which is then followed by Brecon Gaer. There are some gate remains displayed at Brecon Gaer, although these are from the later stone fort and not the Frontinan timber-and-turf fort. From here, an expedition could be mounted further west to look at sites leading to Llandovery and Carmarthen, where the later *civitas* capital overlies the Frontinan fort.

For the central command, it would be possible to start at Wroxeter and move up the Severn Valley, through Brompton and Caersws, and on to Pennal over the watershed.

In the north, the best base would be Chester, where there is another excellent museum and remains of the fortress to be seen. The highpoint of any visit to Roman Wales is the fort at Tomen y Mur. The site is on a high plateau in southern Snowdonia – you can easily imagine Roman soldiers looking out from there for their enemies. The walls of the fort and its gateways are clearly visible, and you can also trace features around the fort such as the parade ground and the site of the civilian settlement (*vicus*) and official guesthouse (*mansio*).

Chapter 5: Agricola in Scotland

The best place to start is Ardoch, which was originally founded by Agricola, although the multiple banks and ditches now visible come from later forts on the site (Picture 5.4). The defences are very well preserved and impressive. Although nothing is visible inside the fort, this is a very atmospheric site, a good place to appreciate the determination of the Roman Army campaigning in the far north and the logistical challenges they faced.

If you start to travel north, you can see the outlines of some of the many marching camps that lie on top of each other at Ardoch, some of which are signposted. You can follow the military road and examine the fortlet at Kaims Castle by requesting the key to the field from the farm.

It is quite hard to find the remains of the Gask Ridge line, but careful scrutiny of the map shows the road line and several of the tower sites are marked. Because the landscape has been partially forested in recent years, it is hard to appreciate quite how the line functioned. The site of the watchtower at Ardunie is now in a pleasant forested glade, but when constructed it would have had uninterrupted views off both sides of the ridge.

An interesting expedition would be to visit the sites of the forts at the mouths to the glens to determine for yourself whether they were glen-blocking or glen-penetrating. This trip could also take in the site of the legionary fortress at Inchtuthil on the Tay, visible only as earthworks.

Chapter 6: The Antonine Wall and System

Of our various case studies, the Antonine Wall offers by far the most to see. As befits a World Heritage Site as part of the frontier of the Roman world (thanks to Professor David Breeze), it has the best-explained sites. There is an excellent website, www.antoninewall.org, which lists all the sites and the top ten things to do if you are short of time. There is also a very good app for iPhone and Android to be downloaded that enhances your visits.

My own favourite sites are:

- Rough Castle and the fantastically well-preserved bank and ditch of the Antonine Wall along this stretch. The fort itself, which has its bank and ditch and an annex, is well displayed, with information boards that help bring the site to life.
- Bar Hill, where you need to be prepared for a fair climb, but it repays the effort with magnificent views from the fort towards the Campsie Fells to the north of the wall. Again, the fort is well displayed, and the hogsback fort site is impressive.
- Croy Hill, where there is a pleasant walk alongside the course of the wall to a well-displayed fort site, again with splendid views in all directions, including toward Bar Hill.
- Bearsden, where the bathhouse is displayed, although suffering from frost damage. This is less atmospheric than the other Antonine Wall sites, situated as it is amidst housing. Take care if parking on or crossing the busy road.
- Not on the line of the wall itself but definitely not to be missed is the Hunterian Museum at the University of Glasgow, with a superb dedicated display of Antonine Wall artefacts. These include most of the surviving distance slabs (Pictures 6.2, 6.3 and 6.4) and numerous altars recovered from the forts, together with artefacts including window glass and weapons, all beautifully lit and well explained.

Appendix 2:

Forts and Roman Strategy (FRoStrat) Using the Data-led Analytical Method (D-LAM)

How you can use the data and visualization techniques

As noted in the Introduction, one of my aims in writing this book has been to enthuse readers sufficiently that they will want to pick up and use the database analytical and visualization approaches demonstrated in the case studies.

I would love to see people use for themselves the tool sets and ideas set out in Chapters 7–9, which I have developed and evolved as I have worked on the case studies. They are designed to be easy to adopt and use, and only require basic IT skills in using the Microsoft Office suite, which has within it the ability to be used at a basic or quite sophisticated level.

To get going on building the database, all that is needed is a working knowledge of Excel. To then generate the graphics and visualizations simply requires the ability to transfer the data and present it in PowerPoint.

Those with greater IT skills and experience may wish to apply more advanced techniques, and I would encourage you to do this, both in terms of more advanced functionality for the database and sophistication of the graphical tools. One of my personal objectives for the future is to do exactly that.

All I would ask is that a reference is included to the original concept set out in this book, *Forts and Roman Strategy – a new Approach* (FRoStrat), and to the data-led analytical method (D-LAM) I have developed.

Another of my personal objectives is to build a very large open database of Roman military assets that could be populated by others to consistent standards. This will require some planning and thinking about governance of content and use. Again, I would be interested in other people's thoughts and approaches to this.

Building the Roman D-LAM community

If these ideas are to progress, it will be necessary to build the virtual D-LAM community to take this work forward. This could have, in ascending order of challenge, the following objectives:

- sharing thoughts and comments on the D-LAM approach and the case studies in this book;
- building and discussing new case studies from *Britannia* in the first and second centuries;
- testing the approach and techniques on other frontiers and provinces: Upper and Lower Germany, Raetia, Noricum Moesia and Dacia come immediately to mind, given the wealth of published excavation data and academic summaries and syntheses;
- pushing the technique even further and applying it to other Roman frontiers such as the desert frontiers, and other periods such as the third and fourth centuries.

In order to support the development of such a community, I have registered an online domain and set up Twitter accounts and a blog for interested people to share their ideas:

@FRoStrat1
@DataledAnalytic
frostrat.com

These can be accessed after the publication of this book. They will also provide an easy method for contacting the author, if so wished.

I propose to use frostrat.com and @FRoStrat1 to discuss Roman strategy and case studies, and @DataledAnalytic to develop the method and discuss topics such as database standards and development of graphical tools and techniques for Roman Army studies.

Bibliography

Frontinus, *Stratagemata. The Strategems and the Aqueducts of Rome*, trans. C. Bennett, Loeb Classical Library (Cambridge, MA: Harvard University Press, 1989).

Josephus, *The Jewish War, Books 1–2*, trans. H. Thackeray, Loeb Classical Library (Cambridge, MA: Harvard University Press, 1997).

Prosopographia Imperii Romani (PIR) Saec. I II and III (PIR) (Berlin: 1933–2015).

Suetonius, *Lives of the Caesars Vol. 2.*, trans. J. Rolfe, Loeb Classical Library (Cambridge, MA: Harvard University Press, 1914).

Tacitus, *I. Agricola. Germania. Dialogue on Oratory*, trans. M. Hutton & W. Peterson; revised by R. Ogilvie, E. Warmington & M. Winterbottom, Loeb Classical Library (Cambridge, MA: Harvard University Press, 1914).

Tacitus, *V. The Annals*, trans. J. Jackson, Loeb Classical Library (Cambridge, MA: Harvard University Press, 1937).

Vegetius, *Concerning Military Affairs* (Liverpool: Liverpool University Press, 1996).

Virgil, *Ecolgues. Georgics. Aeneid: Books 1–6*, trans. H. Fairclough; revised by C. Gold, Loeb Classical Library (Cambridge, MA: Harvard University Press, 1999).

Secondary Works

Abdale, J., *The Great Illyrian Revolt: Rome's Forgotten War in the Balkans AD 6–9* (Barnsley: Pen & Sword Books, 2019).

Austin, N. & Rankov, B., *Exploratio: Military and Political Intelligence in the Roman World from the Second Punic War to the Battle of Adrianople* (London: Routledge, 1995).

Bishop, M., *Handbook to Roman Legionary Fortresses* (Barnsley: Pen & Sword Books, 2012).

Bishop, M., *The Secret History of the Roman Roads of Britain and their Impact on Military History* (Barnsley: Pen & Sword, 2014).

Bishop, M., *Handbook to Roman Legionary Fortresses* (Barnsley: Pen & Sword, 2020).

Bowden, W., *Venta Icenorum: a Brief History of Caister Roman Town* (Coltishall: Norfolk Archaeological Trust, 2020).

Breeze, D., *The Northern Frontiers of Roman Britain* (Bath: Batsford, 1982).

Breeze, D., *Roman Scotland* (London: Batsford, 1996).

Breeze, D., *Roman Scotland: Frontier Country* (London: Batsford/Historic Scotland, 1996).

Breeze, D., *The Antonine Wall* (Edinburgh: John Donald, 2006).

Breeze, D., *Hadrian's Wall: a study in archaeological exploration and interpretation* (Oxford: Archaeopress, 2019).

Breeze, D., 'The army of the Antonine Wall: its strength and implications', in D. Breeze & W. Hanson (eds), *The Antonine Wall: Papers in honour of Professor Lawrence Keppie* (Oxford: Archaeopress, 2020).

Britannia, Volumes 1–51 (London: Society for the Promotion of Roman Studies).

Burnham, B. & Davies, J., *Roman Frontiers in Wales and the Marches* (Aberystwyth: RCAHMW, 2010).

Caruana, I., 'Carlisle: Excavation of a Section of the Annexe Ditch of the First Flavian Fort, 1990', in *Britannia* 23, pp.45–109 (London: Society for the Promotion of Roman Studies, 1992).

Coupar, S. & Bateson, D., *Hunterian Treasures: The Antonine Wall* (Glasgow: The Hunterian Museum, 2012).

Cunliffe, B., *Iron Age Communities in Britain* (4th ed.) (Abingdon: Routledge, 2005).

Current Archaeology, 'Roman marching camp revealed in Ayr', in *Current Archaeology*, July 2019, p. 353 (London).

Daniels, C., *Segedunum: Excavations by Charles Daniels in the Roman Fort at Wallsend (1975–1984)* (Oxford: Oxbow, 2016).

Davies, M., 'The Landscape at the Time of Construction of the Antonine Wall', in D. Breeze & W. Hanson (eds), *The Antonine Wall Papers in honour of Professor Lawrence Keppie*, pp.37–46 (Oxford: Archaeopress, 2020).

Davies, J. & Driver, T., 'Cefn-Brynich Farm: a New Claudio-Neronian Fort in the Usk, Powys, Wales', in *Britannia* 46, pp.267–73 (London: Society for the Promotion of Roman Studies, 2015).

Driver, T., Burnham, B. & Davies, J., 'Roman Wales: Aerial Discoveries and New Observations from the Drought of 2018', in *Britannia* 51, pp.117–45 (London: Society for the Promotion of Roman Studies, 2020).

Entwhistle, R., *Britannia Surveyed* (Pewsey: Armatura Press, 2019).

Fischer, T., *Army of the Roman Emperors: Archaeology and History*, trans. M. Bishop (Oxford: Oxbow, 2019).

Fraser, J., *The Roman Conquest of Scotland: The Battle of Mons Graupius* (Stroud: Tempus, 2006).

Frere, S., 'The Roman Fort at Colwyn Castle, Powys (Radnorshire)', in *Britannia* 25, pp.115–20 (London: Society for the Promotion of Roman Studies, 2004).

Frere, S. & St Joseph, J., *Roman Britain from the Air* (Cambridge: Cambridge University Press, 1986).

Gillam, J., 'Possible changes in plan in the course of the construction of the Wall', in *Scottish Archaeological Forum* 7 (Edinburgh: Edinburgh University Press, 1975).

Graafstal, E., 'Wing-walls and waterworks: on the planning and purpose of the Antonine Wall', in D. Breeze & W. Hanson (eds), *The Antonine Wall: Papers in honour of Professor Lawrence Keppie* (Oxford: Archaeopress, 2020).

Hanson, W., *Agricola and the Conquest of the North* (London: Batsford, 1987).

Hanson, W., *A Roman Frontier Fort in Scotland, Elginhaugh* (Stroud: Tempus, 2007).

Hanson, W. & Breeze, B., 'The Antonine Wall: the current state of knowledge', in D. Breeze & W. Hanson (eds), *The Antonine Wall: Papers in honour of Professor Lawrence Keppie* (Oxford: Archaeopress, 2020).

Hanson, W., Jones; R. & Jones; R., 'The Roman Military Presence at Dalswinton Dumfriesshire', in *Britannia* 50, pp.285–320 (London: Society for the Promotion of Roman Studies, 2019).

Hanson, W. & Maxwell, G., *Rome's North West Frontier: the Antonine Wall* (Edinburgh: Edinburgh University Press, 1984).

Hennig, M., *The Heirs of King Verica: Culture and Politics in Roman Britain* (Stroud: Tempus, 2002).

Hodgson, N., 'Were there two Antonine occupations of Scotland?', in *Britannia* 26, pp.29–49 (London: Society for the Promotion of Roman Studies, 1995).

Hodgson, N., 'Elginhaugh: the Most Complete Fort Plan in the Roman Empire', in *Britannia* 40, pp.365–68 (London: Society for the Promotion of Roman Studies, 2009).

Hodgson, N., 'Why was the Antonine Wall made of turf rather than stone?', in D. Breeze & W. Hanson (eds), *The Antonine Wall: Papers in honour of Professor Lawrence Keppie*, pp.300–12 (Oxford: Archaeopress, 2020).

Hoffmann, B., *The Roman Invasion of Britain: Archaeology versus History* (Barnsley: Pen and Sword, 2013).

Hogg, A., 'Pen-Llstyn: a Roman Fort and other Remains', in *The Journal of the Royal Archaeological Institute* 125 (London: Society of Antiquaries of London, 1968).

Isaac, B., *The Limits of Empire* (Oxford: Oxford University Press, 1992).

Jarrett, M. (ed.), *The Roman Frontier in Wales* (2nd ed.) (Cardiff: University of Wales Press, 1969).

Jarrett, M. (revised by P. Webster), 'Early Roman Campaigns in Wales', in R. Brewer (ed.), *The Second Augustan Legion and the Roman Military Regime*, pp.45–66 (Cardiff: National Museum and Galleries of Wales, 2002).

Jones, B., 'Searching for Caradog', in B. Burnham & J. Davies (eds), 'Conquest, Co-existence and Change: Recent Works in Roman Wales', *Trivium* 25, pp.57–63 (Lampeter: St David's University College, 1991).

Jones, B. & Mattingly, D., *An Atlas of Roman Britain* (Oxford: Oxbow, 2002).

Jones, R.H., *Roman Camps in Scotland* (Edinburgh: Society of Antiquaries of Scotland, 2011).

Jones, R.H., *Roman Camps in Britain* (Stroud: Amberley Publishing, 2012).

Jones, R.H., 'The curious incident of the structure at Bar Hill and its implications', in D. Breeze & W. Hanson (eds), *The Antonine Wall: Papers in honour of Professor Lawrence Keppie*, pp.86–95 (Oxford: Archaeopress, 2020).

Kamm, A., *The Last Frontier: the Roman Invasion of Scotland* (Glasgow: Neil Wilson Publishing, 2009).

Keillar, I., *The Romans in Moray* (Elgin: Moray New Horizons, 2005).

Kemkes, M. & Scholz, M., *Das Römerkastell Aalen, UNESCO-Welterbe* (Stuttgart: Theiss, 2012).

Keppie, L., *The Legacy of Rome: Scotland's Roman Remains* (Edinburgh: John Donald, 2004).

Laing, L., *The Archaeology of Celtic Britain and Ireland AD 400–1200* (Cambridge: Cambridge University Press, 2006).

Lugard, F., *The Dual Mandate in British Tropical Africa* (London: Routledge, 1922).

Luttwak, E., *The Grand Strategy of the Roman Empire; from the First Century AD to the Third* (London: Johns Hopkins University Press, 1976; revised 2016).

Mason, D., *Roman Britain and the Roman Navy* (Stroud: Tempus, 2003).

Matešić, S. & Sommer, C., *At the Edge of the Roman Empire: Tours along the Limes of Southern Germany* (Munich: Deutsche Limeskommission/Bayereisch Landsamt für Denkmalpflege, 2015).

Mattingly, D., *An Imperial Possession: Britain in the Roman Empire* (London: Allen Lane, 2006).

Mattingly, D., *Imperialism, Power and Identity: Experiencing the Roman Empire* (Princeton: Princeton University Press, 2011).

Nash-Williams, V., *The Roman Frontier in Wales* (Cardiff: University of Wales Press, 1954).

Pitts, L. & St Joseph, J., *Inchtuthil: the Roman Legionary Fortress. Excavations 1952–65*, Britannia Monograph Series 6 (London: Society for the Promotion of Roman Studies, 1985).

Pollard, N. & Berry, J., *The Complete Roman Legions* (London: Batsford, 2012).

Richmond, I., 'The Agricolan Fort at Fendoch', *Proceedings of the Society of Antiquaries of Scotland* 73, p.110 (Edinburgh: Society of Antiquaries of Scotland, 1940).

Roxan, M., *Roman Military Diplomas 1954–1977*, Occasional Publication 2 (London: Institute of Archaeology, 1978).

Roxan, M., *Roman Military Diplomas 1978–1984*, Occasional Publication 9 (London: Institute of Archaeology, 1985).

Roxan, M., *Roman Military Diplomas 1985–1993*, Occasional Publication 14 (London: Institute of Archaeology, 1994).

Russell, M. & Laycock, S., *UnRoman Britain: Exposing the Great Myth of Britannia* (Stroud: The History Press, 2010).

Shirley, E., 'The Building of the Legionary Fortress of Inchtuthil', in *Britannia* 27, pp.111–28 (London: Society for the Promotion of Roman Studies, 2011).

Shotter, D., The *Roman Frontier in Britain* (Preston: Carnegie Publishing, 1996).

Steidl, B., *Limes und Römerschatz: RömerMuseum Weißenburg* (München: Rupert Gebhard, 2019).

Trimontium Trust, *The Trimontium Story* (Melrose: The Trimontium Trust, 1994).

Viljoen, *My Reminiscences of the Anglo-Boer War* (AngloBoerWar.com).

Wacher, J., *The Towns of Roman Britain* (Abingdon: Routledge, 1997).

Webster, G., *Rome Against Caratacus: the Roman Campaigns in Britain AD 48–58* (London: Batsford, 1981).

Went, D. & Ainsworth, S., *Whitley Castle, Tynedale, Northumberland: an Archaeological Investigation of the Roman Fort and its Setting* (Portsmouth: English Heritage, 2009).

Wolfson, S., *Tacitus, Thule and Caledonia. The achievements of Agricola's navy in their true perspective*, British Archaeological Reports, British Series 459 (Oxford: BAR Publishing, 2008).

Woolliscroft, D. & Hoffmann, B., *Rome's First Frontier: The Flavian Occupation of Northern Scotland* (Stroud: The History Press, 2010).

Index

Africa:
  British in, during nineteenth and early-
    twentieth century, 84, 125
  Kenya, ix, 125
    Fort Hall (Murang'a) in, 125
    Kikuyu in, 125
  Nigeria, 15
  North Africa, 7
  Mauritanian expedition/war, 168–9, 177
    pottery from, found on Antonine Wall,
      168–9
    Victor, Moorish freedman, possibly from,
      169
  Morocco, 36
  Sokoto caliphate, 15
  Uganda, 15
Agricola, Julius, Governor, vi, viii, 4, 8, 10, 40,
    46, 52, 56, 58, 61, 63, 66, 86, 89
  assessment of final campaign in the North in
    AD 82–83, 130–2
  campaigns in Scotland by, 92–136
  defeat of Calgacus and Caledones by, 222
  finishing Frontinus' work in Wales, 131
  garrison size of, compared with other
    governors, 128, 130, 132
  methods adapted by, in Scotland, 92
  policy in Northern Britain, 228
  revolt under, 80–2
  Romanising mission of, 125, 177
Agricola's unknown successor, Governor, 93,
    123, 126–9
  assessment of work in AD 84–87 by, 131–4
  reduction in garrison under, 134
  relinquishment of Agricola's gains by, as
    strategic defeat, 222–3
Agriculture/farming:
  demand for foodstuffs, 53, 90, 220
  in Late Iron Age Scotland, 98–9
  mixed arable and pastoral, 100
  pastoral society, 36

Agrippina, 7, 38, 48
Antonine campaign:
  geographic area covered by, 137–8
  political and ideological background to,
    139–43
  strengths of, 177
  u-turns in policy and approach during, 178
Antonine Itinerary, 3, 9
'Antonine system', 159–65, 177
  abandonment of forts in Northern England,
    168
  deployment of units, 161–5, 168
  network of cross-routes in, 143–5, 163
  'the East Coast Mainline', 160
  'the West Coast Mainline', 160
Antonine Wall, 6, 93, 109, 119, 137–78
  assessment of, 175–8, 229
  debates on construction of, 146–57, 165–8
  debates on occupation periods, 169–72
  dismantling and burning of forts, 172
  distance slabs from, in Hunterian Museum,
    145, 150, 237
  evidence for rebuilding and maintenance,
    171–2
  final withdrawal from, as strategic defeat,
    172–4, 222–3
  garrison of, 157–65, 171–3, 176
  intervisibility between forts, 153–4
  scale of and labour required to build, 145
  superiority to Hadrian's Wall, 155
Antoninus Pius, Emperor, vi, 4, 6, 138–9, 170,
    172–3, 177
  acclaimed Imperator, 145
  death of, 172
  expansionist policy of, 139
    subsequent reversal of, 222
Arabian Desert, 1, 188
Armenia, 139
Auxiliaries, 192–4, 220
  civilian settlement (vicus) associated with, 84

parade ground, amphitheatre and *mansio* for, 84

  under Frontinus, 55–6, 63–4, 66, 70–1, 75–6, 80–1, 83–4, 86

  under Gallus, 38, 43–4, 46, 50, 52

  under Scapula, 24–5, 27, 29, 31, 33–5

Auxiliary cavalry wings (*alae*), 35, 52, 71, 162, 192–3

Auxiliary cohorts (*cohortes*), 32–3, 44, 162

  cohors equitata (cavalry unit), 193

    cohors quingenaria equitata (500-man cavalry unit), 112, 163

    turmae, 32

  cohors peditata, 192

    cohors milliaria peditata (1,000-man infantry unit), 83–4

  mixed infantry and cavalry, 143, 162

  quingenaria ('the five hundred'), 193

Atrebates, ix, 16, 62

Augustus, Emperor, 4, 8, 57

  garrison during conquest of Dalmatia and Pannonia by, 130

Balkans, campaigns in, 224

Balliol, John, 108

Belgae, 62

Belgica, 52, 130

Bolanus, Vettius, Governor, 10, 52–3, 121

Boresti, 134

Boudicca, 16, 19, 50, 53, 55, 58, 124–5

  aftermath of the rebellion, 51

  revolt by, 4, 19

Brigantes, 16, 20, 37, 58, 60, 67, 86, 89

  against Agricola, 124–5, 130, 133

  conquest and occupation of, by Cerialis, 228

  revolt by in *c.*AD 155, 169–70, 177

  tribal groups, 64

  under Antonine system, 140, 143–5, 161, 168, 173

Brigantian confederation, 23, 52, 131

Bristol Channel, 28, 44, 66, 71

Britannia:

  as drain on Roman resources, 222–3

  as source of glory and prestige, 51

  as the 'ends of the earth', 51, 223–4, 232

  possible abandonment of, 38

  possible strategy for final conquest of, 134–6

  warring tribes in, 100

British Army/forces, vi, 15

  Cardwell Reforms in, 84

  General Roy of the, 119

  in Afghan and Iraq wars, vi, 150

  in Anglo-Afghan wars, 138, 143, 150

  in Boer War, 111–12

  in India, 84

    on north-west frontier of, 36, 138, 143

  in late nineteenth century, 84

British Empire:

  in Africa, 84

  in India 36, 84, 138, 141

  in Kenya, ix

  in Nigeria, 15

  in Uganda, 15

'British Tribes', 37

  appearance of confederations, 168, 176

  discrepant identities and experiences of, 62, 91, 124, 138, 140–1, 168, 177, 220

Broch of Leckie, 138, 152

Caledones, 101, 107, 118–19, 127, 130, 133, 135, 168, 222, 224

Calgacus, 4, 19, 105, 135

  speech attributed to, 36

Caligula, 4

Calpurnius Agricola, Governor, 173, 177

Caracalla, Emperor, 177

Caractacus, 7, 13, 15, 18–21, 24–5, 28, 30, 32–6, 43, 46, 55, 135

  comitatus of, 15, 21

  family of, 20–1

  sent to Rome for Claudius' triumph, 223

Cartimandua, 'Queen' of the Brigantes, 16–17, 20–1, 36–7, 52, 55, 58, 220

Catuvellauni, 3, 10, 50, 124

Ceramics/pottery, 12, 168

  Samian ware, 173

Cerialis, Petilius, Governor, 4, 8, 10, 52, 56–8, 60, 63, 67, 86, 121, 125–6, 130, 132, 228

Civilis' Batavian revolt, 52, 57–8, 60, 67

Claudius, Emperor, 4, 7, 13, 15, 38, 48–9, 51, 55, 139, 222, 232

  Claudian crisis, 42

  expeditionary force to Britannia, 89

  triumph in Rome, 223

Client States, 1, 125

Cogidubnus, ix, 16, 36, 62

Colonialism:

British, ix, 140
Roman, ix
see also Imperialism
Conclusions from case studies and D-LAM, 220–4
   case study scorecards, 221–3
   five-point scale for campaign outcomes, 222
Constantius I, Emperor, 138
Construction materials, 90
Control Grid, 78, 82–4
Corbridge, 109, 127, 140, 143, 160, 165, 172
Corbulo, Roman general, in Armenia, 96
Corieltauvi, 23
Cornovii, 12, 23, 26, 30, 35, 39–40, 42, 47, 64
Cunobelinus, 15
Cursus honorum/career development, 3, 60–1, 140, 230–1
Cymry, 54

Dacia:
   campaigns in, viii, 8, 139
   government of, 2
Dacians, 4, 117, 134
Dacian War, 67
Dalmatia, 130
Danube, River:
   as frontier, 86, 108, 117, 134, 139, 168
   garrison on, in AD60s and 70s, 130
   Upper Danube, 130
Database, vii
Data-led Analytical Method (D-LAM), vii, 54, 72, 61, 198–203
   building the D-LAM community, 23839
   forts database, 198–203
   judgemental categories, 201
   purposes of forts, classification of, 201–202
   standardised database for, 198
   'strength factors' (SFs), 43–4, 72, 88, 157, 160–1, 201–203
   using D-LAM method independently, 238
Deceangli, 9, 16, 25, 27, 29–30, 35, 40, 43, 46–7, 62, 69, 83
Decianus Catus, 'procurator of the island', 50
Demetae, 10, 12, 62, 70, 77, 83, 130
Dio, 9, 50
Diplomas, 3, 56, 66, 84, 113
Dobunni, 11, 23, 26, 30, 35, 39, 47, 70, 80
Domitian, Emperor, 6, 60, 61, 86, 94, 117, 134–5, 176

Druids:
   as source of continuing resistance, 49
   as spiritual and religious leaders, 49
   attacked by Suetonius Paulinus, 49–50, 55, 81
   on Anglesey, 62, 71
   role in Late Iron Age society, 49
Duke of Cumberland, 98
Dumnonii, 23, 30, 130, 140, 142, 145, 152, 159, 168, 170, 229
Dumnonian peninsula, 66
Durotriges, 23, 30

East India Company, 138, 141
Eastern Desert Frontiers, viii
Eastern Kingdoms, 36
Eastern War, 172
Edward I, King of England, 97, 108
Egypt:
   military papyri from, 3, 87, 187
Elginhaugh debate, 121–2
   hoard as dating evidence, 126
Emperors, 1
   incomprehension of campaigning conditions by, 224
   power of, shown by conquest, 93
   setting of objectives for Governors by, 221

Failure:
   against Silures, 20–1, 35–6
   assessment of abandonment of the North, 134
   by Scapula, 46–7
   in *Britannia*, 178, 221, 224
   military, vi
   of Antonine campaign, 176
   of Antonine Wall, 169
   of conquest of *Britannia*, 57
   of Suetonius Paulinus' government, 50
   tactical defeats, 35
   strategic, in Scotland, 131–2, 137
Flavians, 1
   early period of rule, 80–1
   occupation of Scotland, 117
   regime of, 4, 86, 96, 177
Fort gates:
   Strathcathro type, 103, 104
   Tituli, 104
Forth-Clyde isthmus:
   during Antonine occupation 137, 143, 153, 161

during campaigns of Agricola, 93–4, 98, 104, 107, 109, 117–18, 122, 127
France (modern country):
the French in Morocco, 36
the French in Vietnam, 36
'Freedom fighters', 32
Frontiers, nature of, 45
de facto frontier of *Britannia*, 53
Frontinus, Julius, Governor, viii, 4, 7, 10, 46, 54–91, 121, 125
as author of *De Aquaeductu*, 60
as author of *Strategemata*, 60–1
campaigns in Wales by, 84–91
central task force of, 76
design of conquest by, 82–4, 228
garrison size during campaigns of, 66, 132
handover to Agricola, 72
northern task force of, 75
size and deployment of forces of, 84–9
southern task force of, 77
strategic victory by, in Wales, 222, 228
textbook campaign by, 89

Galba/Trajan Regime, 95
Gallus, Aulus Didius, Governor, vii, 8–9, 89
comparison with Scapula, 46–7, 53
fort building programme of, 37–42
legacy of, 53
policy of containment by, 42–3, 47–8
strategic 'draw' achieved by, in Wales, 222
strategy, assessment of, 47–9
success of, 46, 55, 58
Gangani, 10–11
Garrison size:
during Augustus' conquest of Dalmatia and Pannonia, 130
during campaigns of Frontinus, 66, 132
on Antonine Wall, 155, 157–65, 171–3, 176
on River Danube in AD 60s and 70s, 130
reduction in, under Agricola's unknown successor, 134–5
under Agricola, compared with other governors, 111–13, 116–17, 128, 130, 132
see also individual Governors
Gask Frontier, 106–107, 122, 127, 129, 169
as 'Rome's first frontier' 108
patrols along, 111–12, 159
signalling along, 111–12
spacing of forts on, 112

Gask Ridge, 108–109, 111, 113, 116–17, 119, 122
Gaul, 8, 13, 15, 19, 36, 57
Caesar's Gallic campaign in, 8
southern Gaul (*Gallia Narbonensis*), 60
Vercingetorix of, 19
warring tribes in, 100
Germania, 61, 172, 230
Danube frontier in, 4, 7, 13
Forest of, 61
Germania Inferior, 52, 140, 169
Germania Superior, 169
German *Limes*/frontier, viii, 45, 111, 173
Lower Rhine, 52
revolt on, 52, 57–8, 60, 67
Mainz, 140
Xanten, training camp in, 230
Germanicus, Roman general, in *Germania*, 96
Germany (modern state):
Prussian General staff in, 3
'Glen-blocking' forts, 113–14, 128, 132–3
Governors, 10, 13, 23, 53
as members of senatorial class, 231
of *Britannia*, 89
headquarters at Chester for, 134
palace of, including archives, 230
staff of (*officium*), 45, 55, 230
Grand strategy, 1–4, 178, 220–1
Greek Kingdoms, 36
Guerrilla warfare, 8, 18, 61, 67, 223

Hadrian, Emperor:
deification of, 139
drive for British *civitates* by, 177
reversal of Trajan's expansionist policy by, 139, 177
Hadrian's Wall, vi, ix, 1–2, 45, 139–40, 143, 170
debates concerning purpose of, 165
decision by Antoninus to abandon, 140, 148, 229
re-occupation(s) of, 172, 177
westward extension, 158, 165
serious break-in of northern tribes through, 174
'Hadrian's Wall system', 161
Hellenistic states, 13
'Highland Line', 108, 113, 116, 119, 123, 128, 130, 133, 188

Hillforts, 11–12, 26, 67, 72
  in Scotland, 98–9
Historia Augusta, 173
Human Resources (HR), 2

Iberia (*Hispania*), 130
Iceni, 16, 24, 50, 124
Illyricum, 57, 224
Illyrian revolt, 67, 130
Imperial estates, 220
Imperial household, 47
Imperialism:
  British, ix
Inchtuthil, 86, 87, 108, 113, 117, 123, 126–9,
  131, 133, 169, 172, 228
  effort required to build, 87
  possibly named *Victoria*, 97
Iraq and Afghanistan (modern states):
  Russians in, 36
  US-led coalition in Afghanistan, 36, 138
  wars in, 3, 150
Irish Sea, 23, 40, 64,137
Iron Age:
  continuity of, in Northern Britain, 94
Italy, 52, 75

Jerusalem, 1
  Jewish war of AD 132–35, 140
Julius Caesar, 8, 13, 15, 19, 51

Lancastrian Coast, 64
Land use in pre-Roman and Roman times:
  evolving knowledge of, 203
Leadership, viii, 4, 229
Legio II Adiutrix, 52, 55–7, 63–4, 72, 75, 86,
  104, 117, 133–5
  as amphibious warfare experts, 134
  dolphins and sea-goat as symbols of, 64
Legio II Augusta, 18, 23, 28–30, 33–4, 52, 66,
  77, 84, 140, 142, 145, 150, 161
  Charax, Claudius, commander of, 150
Legio VI Victrix, 2, 145, 161
Legio IX Hispana, 23, 30, 33–4, 52, 58, 104,
  118, 133
Legio X Gemina, 140
Legio XIV Gemina, 18, 23, 27–30, 32, 34, 38,
  42, 50–2, 55
Legio XX, 4, 18, 23, 27–34, 42–4

  as *Legio XXVV*, 52, 55, 64, 76, 86, 127–8,
    133–5, 145, 161, 222
  mutiny by Roscius Coelus, commander of
    XXVV, 52
Legio XXII Primigenia, 140
Legions, 24–5, 33, 46
  as part of task forces, 192
  cohorts (*cohortes*), 31, 71–2, 163
    standardisation in Augustan period, 191
  command structure of, 23–4, 113
  'forward containment', policy of, 46
  heavy infantry in, 35
  home bases of, 192
    amphitheatre at, 84, 176
    mansio associated with, *84*
  legionaries, 33, 46
    Manlius Valens, 37
  legionary fortress, 25, 39, 42, 72, 75, 191
    baths for, at Wroxeter, 221
    vicus associated with, 84
  number required to hold or expand the
    province, 55, 57, 222
  recruitment to, 33
  size and strength of, 32–4, 87, 191–2
  specialists in, 86, 97, 122, 14, 229
Limes, 154, 232
  primary purposes of, 155
Lines of Communication, 45, 71, 145, 160–1
Lines of Control (LoCs), 75–8, 80, 82–3, 88,
  90, 133
Lines of Penetration (LoPs), 22, 25, 27–8, 45,
  69, 70, 72, 75–6, 116, 127, 130, 133, 135,
  142–3, 160–1
Lingones, tribe, 60
Lucius Verus, Emperor, 169
Luxury goods, 36, 62, 224

Maeatae, 168, 176
Mainz, 117
Mapping of Roman forts:
  as tool for analysis, 203
  conventional methods, 181–2
  new digital and cartographical approach,
    181–97
    fort categories and standard codes, 183–6,
      196
    icons for forth size and unit type, 182
    standard diagrammatic notation, 183

topographic backgrounds, 182
        unit symbols on maps, 195
    Ordnance Survey conventions, 181
Maps, military, 97, 181–3
Marching camps, 31, 101, 104–105
Marcus Aurelius, Emperor, vi, 170, 172–3, 177
Mediterranean:
    World, 61
Mesopotamia, 117, 139
Metalworking/metals, 12, 17
    copper, 176
    gold, 13, 35, 78, 83, 176
    iron, 13
    lead, 13, 17, 35, 40, 62, 83, 176
        'lead pigs', 40
    refining, 13
    silver, 13, 17, 35, 40, 62, 83
Military bases:
    campaign bases, 42, 46, 67
    fortresses (aka vexillation fortresses), 25,
        27–8, 30, 33, 35, 192
    legionary fortresses, 25, 39, 42, 191–2
    lines of communication, 45
    marching camp, 31
    summer quarters/base (aestiva), 25
    winter quarters/base (hiberna), 25, 134, 224
Military ranks:
    Broad-stripe tribune (tribunus laticlavius), 23
    centurion, 24
    commander (legatus), 23
    narrow-stripe tribune (tribunus
        angusticlavius), 24
    praefectus castrorum, 23
    primus pilus, 24
Minerals:
    deposits of, 35
    extraction of, 81
    wealth from, 30, 48, 62
Mines/mining, 17, 35, 40, 43, 46
    operated by army, 220
    tribute, 46
Moesia:
    Inferior and Superior, 2
Money:
    Claudian coins, 42
    coinage, 10, 12, 26
    coin hoards, 169
    monetary economy, 36

money lenders, 42
    'taxation in kind', 36
    trade, 53, 62
Mons Graupius, battle of, 4, 36, 86, 101,
    105–108, 114, 118–19, 121, 127, 176

Navy/fleet (Classis Britannica), 44, 63–4, 67, 71,
    81, 106, 108, 135–6, 142, 158
    circumnavigation of Britannia by, 94,
        133–4
    marines, 63, 142
    naval base for, 69
    Ravenna Fleet as Flavian loyalists, 52, 63
    sea-borne supply, 98, 136
    sea transport by, 84
    surveying of coasts by, 134
Nero, Emperor, 4, 19, 38, 45, 47–8, 50–1, 55
    Burrus, praetorian prefect to, 49
    Decianus Catus, procurator to, 50
    imperial brand of, 51
    motives of, assessed by Suetonius, 50
    planned Parthian expedition by, 51, 55
    possible abandonment of Britannia by, 38, 50
    push westward by, 79
    Seneca, tutor to, 48, 50
Nerva, Emperor, 60
Nijmegen, 117
Noricum, 130
North Sea, 137
Notitia Dignitatum, 3, 190
Novantae, 99, 127, 140, 228

Octapitae, 10
Oppida, 7, 11, 36
Ordovices, 124–6, 130, 133, 135, 222, 224
    against Frontinus, 55, 58, 62–4, 69–70,
        80–1, 83
    against Gallus, 41–3, 46–7, 49–50, 53
    against Scapula, 9–10, 12, 15, 18–21, 23, 25,
        28, 32, 35–6
Otho, Emperor, 52

Pannonia, 130
    Vienna, 140
Parthia:
    Marcus Aurelius' war in, 177
    Nero's planned expedition in, 51, 55
    Trajan's wars in, 3, 139

Paulinus, Suetonius, Governor, 16, 48–50, 52–3, 55, 58, 79–80, 89
   attack on Druids by, 49–50, 125
Plautius, Aulus, Governor, 8–9, 15, 22, 66
   invasion by, in AD 43, 66
Pliny the Elder, 121
   Natural Histories (*Naturalis Historia)* of, 121, 125
Pollen analysis, 99
Population levels, estimates, 13, 55, 58
Prasutagas, 16, 36
Ptolemy's Geography (*Geographia*), 9, 97, 135
Publius Pertinax, Emperor, 1–2

Raetian *Limes*, viii, 173
Ravenna Cosmography, 9
Regni, 16, 62
River Rhine, 2, 7, 13, 57, 108, 130
   Rhine frontier, 168
Rivers (and their valleys) in *Britannia*:
   Clyde, 113, 129, 142, 171
      Clyde Valley, Upper and Lower, 140, 143
      Clyde Estuary, 143, 158
      Clydesdale, 130, 175
   Clywd Valley, 81–3
   Conwy Valley, 81–2, 90
   Dee, 17, 23, 27, 31, 40, 43, 67, 69, 75, 81
      Dee Estuary, 64
      Dee Valley, 29, 43, 64, 67, 75, 79, 83
   Dovey, 76
   Forth, 107, 119, 127, 129, 137, 141–3, 155, 159–60, 165
      Firth of Forth/Estuary, 98, 143, 159
   Loughor, 67
   Nithsdale, 127, 140, 143, 169, 175
   Rheidol, 76, 90
   River valleys in general, 71
   Rhymney Valley, 77
   Severn, 10, 16, 18, 28, 31, 43–4, 69, 76
      Severn Estuary, 28, 41, 44, 69
      Severn Valley, 26, 42, 64, 83
      Upper Severn, 38, 67, 70, 79
   Taff Valley, 77
   Tawe, 77
   Tay, 107, 109, 113, 118–19, 126, 129, 137
      Tay Estuary, 99, 143
      Upper Tay, 98
   Tewi, 70
   Trent, 16

Tweed, 172
   Tweedale/Valley, 140, 143, 160–1, 175
Tyne, 109, 126, 143
Usk, 28, 38, 41–2, 45, 53, 66–7, 69, 70
   Usk Valley, 41, 43–4, 47, 70, 77, 83
Vrynwy, 19, 28
   Vrynwy Valley, 38
Wye, 28, 39, 41, 53, 79
   Wye Valley, 28, 31, 41, 43–4, 70, 80, 82–3
Roman army in Britain (*Exercitus Britannia*), 57, 88–9
   allied cavalry of, 80
   as a learning organisation, 178, 221, 229–30
   as consumer of food and diverse materials, 220
   as embodiment of Roman State in Britain, 220
   as 'predator or planner', 1–4, 221
   barracks for, 71
   battlegroups from, 69
   booty or loot taken by, 2, 132, 139, 220–1
   centuries of, 71
   combined operations with Navy, 143
   comparison with modern corporations, 231
   culture and esprit de corps of, 229
   experience of hard campaigning by, 96
   flexibility, adaptation and innovation of, 229, 232
   overstretch experienced or risked by, 132, 135, 137, 170, 172, 178, 221, 223–4, 232
   patrol range by, 114
   record keeping by, 3, 141, 230
   responding to extreme challenge, 228–31
   scouts and agents for, 143
   sequence of conquest and occupation by, 119, 124, 133, 137, 142
   size and composition of, 57, 66, 132
   speed of movement, 165, 229
   strength factors (SFs), 43–4, 72, 88, 157, 160–1, 201–203
   supplies for, 84, 223
   surveying by, 97, 126, 135, 141, 150, 186
   theoretical manpower of, 98–105, 223–4
   use of 'shock and awe' tactics by, 90, 137
   veterans of, 80
Roman army in Europe, North African and the Middle East, evidence of, 137
Roman forts:
   chronologies of occupation, 181–2, 196

distance between, 88
fully excavated examples, 188
occupation periods, 196
purposes for, classification of, 202
standard layout/building plan for, 186–90,
    229–30
    barracks position crucial to, 187
    indicative of garrison of, 187–90
Roman High Command, 67, 134–5, 170,
    172–3, 177
    'Antonines' and 'Hadrianic school' within,
        170, 176–7
    grand strategy or strategies of, 178
Roman Roads in *Britannia:*
    Akeman Street, 23, 25
    Dere Street, 109, 121, 127, 129, 141–3,
        158–60, 163, 173–4
        as 'the East Coast Mainline', 160
    east-west road (from England into Wales), 39
    Fosse Way, 23, 25–6, 28–9
        'Fosse Way frontier', 23, 26
    north-south road (in Wales), 39–40, 43, 45
        north-south baseline road, 43, 46, 63, 70
    Watling Street, 22–3, 25–6, 28, 30, 34, 38

Salt/salt extraction, 27
Scapula, Ostorius, Governor, vi, vii, viii, 8–9,
    15–16, 21–5, 37, 43, 53, 55, 58, 62, 67, 69,
    89, 125
    assault on the Welsh tribes by, 15–22
    campaign statistics for, 32–5
    comparison with Gallus, 46–7
    failure and strategic defeat of, in Wales 21–2,
        35–6, 46–77, 222–3
    strategy in Wales of, 22–5, 46
    strategy of aggression by, 26–32
    tactical defeat of Caractacus, Ordovices and
        Silures, 222
Scotland (*Caledonia*), 19, 22, 58, 61, 66, 72, 84,
    88, 93, 117–18, 121
    as 'ends of the earth', 93, 96
    as 'Rome's north-west frontier', 137–78, 176
    Borders of, 22, 66
    Caledonian forest (*Caledonia Silva*) and
        mountains, 96, 121, 224
    Central Belt of, 122
    climate as 'enemy' of Roman army, 224
    contemporary perceptions of English
        invasion of, 94

distorted in Roman-era maps, 97
East Coast of, 22
eight tribes of, beyond the Great Glen, 135
fertile coastal lands of, 97–8
Flavian occupation of, 118–21
forests, clearance of, 99
Highlands/Highland Zone, 86, 97, 130
invasion route through the ages, 98, 128,
    130, 133
Iron Age structures in, 98–9
    settlement density in, 99
Lowlands, the, 12, 22, 46, 126–7, 130, 140,
    172–3, 175
    difficulty of 'Romanising', 175–6
    Lowland Dales, 127
        protectorate over some tribal areas of, 138
        reoccupation of, from AD 139, 137–8,
            143–5
native population, structures and settlements
    of, 99
physical environment of the North, 96–9
placenames in Ptolemy's Geography, 97
population levels in Late Iron Age, 100
repeated invasions of, 138
Romans' reasons for attempting conquest of,
    93
surviving Roman military remains in, 94
timescales of campaign in AD 82–86, 119,
    122–3
tribal society, nature of in Late Iron Age,
    100
undefended hut-settlements in, 99
unique challenges presented by, 96
Scottish National Museum:
    Roman-era finds in, 94
Sea-levels and coastlines, changes in, 98, 109,
    182, 203
Selgovae, 99, 130, 140, 142–5, 160–1, 168, 169,
    170, 175, 177
Senate and People of Rome (SPQR), 13
Senate, Roman, 2, 96, 123
    hostility of, towards Hadrian, 139
Seneca, 48, 50
Settlements:
    civitates, 38, 91, 177, 220–1
    coloniae, 33
    trading posts, 42
Severi, 1
'Severn and Trent Line', 35

Severus, Septimius, Emperor,
    in Scotland in AD 206–209, 66, 177
Silures, vi, viii, 4, 124, 130, 135
    against Frontinus, 55, 58, 60–1, 63, 66, 70,
        77–8, 80, 83, 88–9
    against Gallus 37, 40–1, 43, 45–7, 49, 53
    against Scapula, 9, 12, 15, 18, 21–5, 27, 30,
        32, 34–6
    civitas of, 38
    territory of, 28, 41
Sites in Britannia:
    books which illuminate, 233–4
    opportunities to visit, 233–7
Slaves/slavery, ix, 13, 132, 169
    enslavement, 36, 132, 220–1
Spain, 8, 13, 35–6, 57, 224
Stanegate Frontier/Line, the, 86, 131, 139
Statius, 52, 121
Stilicho, 138
'Strathmore Line', 108, 116, 119, 128, 132
Syria, 2, 222

Tacitus' Agricola, 7–8, 15–16, 24, 37, 48, 93–4,
    108–109, 118, 123, 125–6, 131, 176
    as biography, literary tour de force and
        political tract, 95–6
Taxation, 1, 119
Tool-set, graphical and cartographic, 204–19
    analytical tools (the 'tool-box') 22, 204–208
        context tools, 205
        overall campaign tools, 206
        tools for making comparisons, 207–208
        tools to analyse campaigns, 207
        tools to map campaigns, 206
    example of tool-set in use, with figures,
        208–19
        method applied to Agricola, 128
        Scottish Lowlands as 'laboratory', 137
    organisation theory and practice, vii, viii
    visualisation, vii, 54
Theodosius, Count, 138
Tiberius, Emperor, 57, 67, 139
Titus, Emperor, 1, 94, 108, 118–19, 127
Trade:
    in luxury items, 100
Trajan, Emperor:
    expansionist policy of, 177
        reversal of, by Hadrian, 139, 177
Trade, 53
    traders, 42

Trajan, Emperor, 4, 60, 67, 177
    commands in his era, 86
Trebellius Maximus, Governor, 10, 51–3, 55,
    89
Tree-cover, changes over time, 98, 111
Tribes, British:
    tribal interfaces, 80
    warriors, 101
Trinovantes, 50
Turpilianus, Petronius, Governor, 9, 50–1, 53,
    55
Tyne-Solway Line/isthmus, vi, 86, 127, 131,
    137, 143, 172

United States of America:
    'American Wild West', 53
    army/forces of, vi
    army in Vietnam, 24, 36
    Department of Defense, 3
    Empire of, 3
    native population, 62
    nineteenth-century trade goods, 62
    nineteenth-century US cavalry, 114
    US-led coalition in Afghanistan, 36
    westward expansion, 62
Urbicus, Lollius, Governor, 138–50, 168, 176
    advance to Forth/Clyde isthmus by, 222,
        229
    Berber origins of, 140
    cursus honorum by, 140
    occupation plan of, based on Agricola's, 143
    triumph in Rome earned by, 222

Vacomagi, 107, 133
Venicones, 100, 107, 119, 127, 142, 150, 159,
    161, 168, 228
Venutius of the Brigantes, 37, 130
    estranged husband of Cartimandua, 52
Veranius, Quintus, Governor, 9, 37, 48, 53, 55,
    89
Vergil's Aeneid, 96
    reference to Roman imperium in, 96
Verus, Julius, Governor, 170, 173, 177
Vespasian,
    as Emperor, 35, 52, 56, 60, 63, 67, 75, 94,
        108
    as legionary legate, 4
    Britannia policy and mission of, 56–60, 114,
        130, 134, 136, 232

Vexillations, 34, 52
Villa economies, 119
Vitellius, Emperor, 52
Votadini, 99, 130, 140, 142–5, 160, 168, 228

Water:
    for drinking and for irrigation, 60
    supply for Rome, 60
Wales, vii, 7–37, 46, 50, 53, 54–91
    as an area or territory, 55–91
    as 'Western front', 51
    campaign phase in, 62–9
    conquest phase in, 62, 69–72
    consolidation phase in 62
    control phase in, 62, 72
    failure to develop *civitates* in, 91

Flavian, 87
Four-stage process ('the four Cs') in, 62
Frontinian settlement in, 129
    mountainous zones of, 39–40, 83
Weapons, 62
Welsh Borders, 67, 79, 82
'Welsh Front' 32–3, 37, 52
Welsh tribes, 46, 128
Wine, 12
Writing tablets:
    found at Vindolanda, 3, 87, 141, 186–7,
        193–4

'Year of the Four Emperors', 52

Zone of occupation, 72

Placename Index

Places in England (modern country)
Alcester, 27
Aldborough (*Isurium Brigantium*), 124, 168, 176

Bagendon, 11
Berwick, 160, 175
Bewcastle, 161, 173
Brough-by-Bainbridge (*Virosidum*), 188
Brough-on-Noe, 172
Burlington, 22
Burgh-by-Sands, 169

Caister-by-Norwich (*Venta Icenorum*), 8
Carlisle, 58, 121, 125–7, 176, 221
Carvoran, 172
Catterick, 97
Cheviots, the, 109, 160
Cheshire/Cheshire Plain, 10, 38, 64
Chester (*Deva*), 23, 27, 31, 34, 38–40, 43, 64,
    66–7, 69, 75, 81, 84, 86, 127, 133–4, 163
Chesters (*Cilurnum*), 188
Chichester, 8, 62
Church Stretton, 19
Cirencester (*Corinium*), 8, 10–11, 26, 28
Colchester (*Camulodunum*), 17–18, 23–24, 36,
    55, 58, 221–2
    renamed as *Colonia Claudia Victricensis*, 222
Coventry, 27
Cirencester (*Corinium*), 8, 10–11, 26, 28

Corbridge, 142, 163, 221
Corbridge Red House, 121
Cumbrian Coast, 64

Dalswinton, 188
Droitwich (*Salinae*), 27

Exeter (*Isca*), 23, 30, 52, 66, 86

Fens, the, 16
Forest of Dean, 10, 91

Gloucester (*Glevum*), 23, 27–8, 33, 41, 43–4,
    52, 221
Gloucester Kingsholm, 18, 24, 27–8, 30–2, 35,
    38–9, 42, 44, 52, 64, 133
Gloucestershire, 10

Herefordshire, 10
High Cross, 23
High Rochester, 97, 174
Hindwell Farm, 39, 40
Holkham Camp, 16
Housesteads, 157

Jay Lane, 38–40

Kent, 23
Kinvaston 27–8

Lake District, 228
Lancaster, 97
Leighton, 28
Lincoln (*Lindum*), 52, 64
London (*Londinium*), 23, 50, 55

Mancetter, 28, 32, 38
Mendips, 35
Metchley, 27
Midlands, 28
  East Midlands, 23, 30
  North Midlands, 34
  West Midlands, 23, 26, 35
    'West Midlands triangle', 30, 33

Netherby, 161, 173
Newcastle, 169
Norfolk, 1
Northumberland, 97, 130, 175
North-west England, 66
North of England, the, 66, 88, 172

Pennines, the, 64

Ribchester, 172
Risingham (*Habitancum*), 174

Shap, 127
Shropshire, 11, 19, 26
Silchester (*Calleva*), 8, 36, 62
Solway, 126, 140, 143
South-east Britain, 36, 50
South-west England, 34
South Shields, 169
Stainmore, 58, 126
Stanwick, 17
Stonea Camp, 16
St Albans (*Verulamium*), 23, 36, 55, 124
Stretford Bridge, 39
Sudbrook, 12

The Lunt, 27, 33–4

Uffington, 22

Vindolanda, 3

Wall (*Letocetum*), 28
Wallsend (*Segedunum*), 188

Water Eaton, 27–8
Whitchurch, 38–9
Whitland, 77
Whitley Castle (*Epiacum*), 188
Whittington, 22
Winchester, 62
Wroxeter (*Viroconium*), vii, 22, 28–29, 31, 38–9,
  42–3, 52, 64, 67, 70, 76, 84, 86, 127, 221

York (*Eboracum*), 58, 86, 126, 133, 163, 168

Places in Scotland (modern country)
Aberdeenshire, 99, 105, 128, 133
Aberfoyle, 113
Angus, 107, 133
Annandale, 127, 140, 143, 163, 169, 175
Ardoch, 104–105, 109, 159
Argyll, 118
Auchendavy, 148, 158
Ayr, 127, 161, 175

Balmuidy, 148, 153, 157, 171
Bar Hill, 148, 152, 157, 158, 168–9, 173
Barochan, 107, 109, 113, 129
Bearsden, 151, 154, 157, 168
Bennachie, 99
Bertha, 107–109, 116, 159, 165
Berwickshire, 130
Birrens, 161, 169, 170, 171–3
Bochcastle, 113
Bothwellhaugh, 171
Buchan, 107

Cadder, 171, 173
Caithness, 136
Camelon, 107, 109, 121, 129, 159–60
Cappuck, 170–2
Cardean, 116, 121
Cargill, 116
Carriden, 148, 150, 157, 158, 158, 159
Carzield, 171
Castlecary, 148, 153, 157, 171, 173
Castledykes, 171
Castlehill, 152, 154, 155, 157, 158
Castlesteads, 143
Cramond, 158
Crawford, 143
Croy Hill, 152, 154, 158, 168, 171
Cultmalundie, 111

Dalginross, 113, 119
Dalriada, 100
Dalswinton, 126
Doune, 109
Drumquhassle, 113
Dumbarton, Rock of, 113
Duntocher, 152, 154, 168, 171
Durno, 107

Eildon Hill, 99, 143
Elginhaugh, 109, 121, 127, 141

Falkirk, 159
Fendoch, 113
Fife, 100, 119, 127, 130, 137–8, 142, 150, 161

Galloway, 127, 228
Glasgow, 138
Glenbank, 109
Glen Almond, 113
Great Glen, 99, 107, 108, 128, 133, 135

Highlands Fault Line (Highland Line), 97, 98,
   126

Innerpeffray, 105
Inveravon, 150
Inveresk, 141, 143, 158, 160
Inverness, 107, 133
Inverquharity, 116

Kaims Castle, 109
Kilpatrick, 155
Kintore, 105, 106
Kirkintilloch, 173

Logie Durno, 105
Loudon Hill, 161
Lowlands, 12, 22, 46, 86, 98, 165, 172

Malling, 113
Midgate, 109
Milton, 161
Mollins, 107, 109, 129
Moray, 105, 107–108, 133
Moray Firth, 99
Mounth, the, 98, 105–106, 133, 135
Mumrills, 148, 155, 157, 168, 171
Muiryfold, 105

Nairn, 99, 107, 128, 133
Newstead, 121, 143, 160–1, 163, 165, 169, 170,
   171–4, 176
Normandykes, 105

Old Kilpatrick, 148, 157, 158, 168, 171, 173
Outerwards, 171–2

Pictland, 100

Raeburnfoot, 143, 161
Raedykes, 105
Rough Castle, 171

Shetland Islands, 94, 136
   identified as *Thule*, 93, 96, 224
Sma'Glen 113
Solway Firth, 126, 140, 143
Stirling, 109, 119, 129, 159
Stonehaven, 97, 104–106, 133
Strageath, 105, 109, 121, 159, 171–2
Strathblane, 113
Strathcathro, 108
Strathearn, 98, 113, 159, 172
Strathmore, 98, 104, 106, 117, 123, 128
Straths, the, 100, 128
Strathspey, 108
Strathyre, 113

Traprain Law, 99

Ward Law, 99
Watling Lodge, 159
Western Isles, 136
Westerwood, 158

Ythan Wells, 105

Places in Wales (modern country)
Aber, 79
Abergavenny, 41–4, 46, 53, 70, 77
Anglesey, 48–50, 55, 77, 80–2, 90, 125

Bala Lake, 69, 75
Blackburn Farm, 70, 79
Brecon, 70
Brecon Gaer, 70, 77
Brithdir, 76, 78
'British Camp', 19

Brompton/Pentrehyling, 76
Bryn y Gefeiliau, 81
Buckton, 79

Caerau, 79
Caer Caradoc, 19
Caer Gaer, 76
Caer Gai, 75–6, 79
Caergwanaf, 77
Caerhun, 81
Caerleon, 163
Caerleon (*Isca*), 8, 28, 31, 42, 66–7, 69–70, 84,
    86, 127, 142
Caernarfon, 81
Caerphilly, 77
Caersws, 70, 76, 79
Caerwent (*Venta Silurum*), 42, 91, 124, 125
Canon Frome, 28, 31
Cardiff, 38–9, 42, 44, 46, 77
Cardiganshire, 11, 62, 130
Cardigan Bay, 76, 83, 90
Careg y Bwci, 78
Carmarthen (*Moridunum*), 8, 10, 77–9, 91, 176
Carmarthenshire, 70
Carrow Hill, 42
Castell Collen, 79
Castlefield Farm, 39
Cefn-Brynich, 41, 46
Cemlyn, 81
Chepstow, 28, 31, 41
Clifford I, 31, 33
Clifford II, 39, 41
Clyro, 41, 46, 53
Clywdian Range, 53, 91
Coast of, 25
Coed-y-Caerau, 42
Colbren, 77, 84
Collen Castle, 33
Colwyn Castle, 41, 79

Dinorben, 12
Dolgellau, 76
Dolaucothi, 56, 83, 91

Erglodd, 78

Ffestiniog, 81
Flintshire, 17
Forden Gaer, 76

Gelligaer, 77
Gower Peninsula, 83

Halkyn mountains, 17
Hindwell Farm, 43–4, 79
Hirfyndd, 77

Liety Canol, 78
Llandovery, 70, 77–8
Llanfair Caereinon, 79
Llanfor, 69, 71–2, 75, 86
Llandeilo, 70, 79
Llangefni, 81
Llanio, 78
Llanymynech hillfort, 19
Llwyn-y-brain, 81
Loughor, 77

Malvern Hills, 19
Marches, the, 8–14, 22, 29, 32, 35, 38, 46, 52–3
Menai Strait, 81, 82
Mid-Wales, 64
Monmouth, 39
Monmouthshire, 61

Neath, 71, 77
North-east Wales, 30
North-west Wales, 83
North Wales, 25, 27–8, 35, 53, 64, 81
North Wales Coast 71, 80

Offa's Dyke, 55

Pembrokeshire, 62, 83, 130
Penmincae, 79
Pennal, 76, 78
Pen-llwyn, 76, 78
Penrhos, 22
Pen-y-Gaer, 77
Pen-y-Darren, 77
Powys, 62
Pumsaint, 78

Rheola Forest, 77
Rhyn Park, 27, 29, 31, 34, 40, 43–4, 69, 75
Ruthin, 81

Snowdonia, 8, 71, 75, 81, 83, 224
South Coast of Wales, 67

South Wales, 23, 25, 30, 35, 40, 43, 82, 84
South-west Peninsula, 23
South-west Wales, 83

Three Cocks, 41
Tomen y Mur, 75, 78, 81, 83

Usk, vii, 28, 38–9, 41–2, 52, 61, 64, 70, 77
    see also Rivers

Vale of Glamorgan, 43, 47, 51, 66, 83

Waun-ddu, 78
Welsh Mountains, 39–40